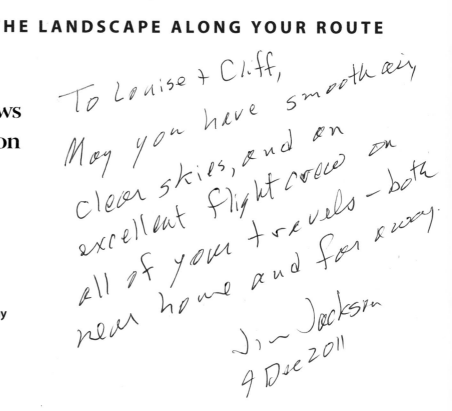

America from the Air

A GUIDE TO THE LANDSCAPE ALONG YOUR ROUTE

Daniel Mathews
James S. Jackson

Houghton Mifflin Company
BOSTON   NEW YORK
2007

To Louise + Cliff,
May you have smooth air,
clear skies, and an
excellent flight crew on
all of your travels — both
near home and far away.

Jim Jackson
4 Dec 2011

For Sabrina and Melinda

For information about permission to reproduce selections from this book, write
to Permissions, Houghton Mifflin Company, 215 Park Avenue South, New York,
New York 10003.

Visit our Web site: www.houghtonmifflinbooks.com.

Library of Congress Cataloging-in-Publication Data

Mathews, Daniel, date.
    America from the air : a guide to the landscape along your route / Daniel
Mathews, James Jackson.
      p. cm.
    Includes bibliographical references and index.
    ISBN-13: 978-0-618-70603-7
    ISBN-10: 0-618-70603-8
    1. United States—Aerial views. 2. United States—Pictorial works. 3.
Landscape—United States—Aerial views. 4. United States—Description and
travel. 5. Air travel—United States. I. Jackson, James. II. Title.
    E169.Z83M366 2007
    917.304—dc22   2007022546

Book design by Anne Chalmers

Printed in the United States of America
QWT 10 9 8 7 6 5 4 3 2 1

Acknowledgments

It is a pleasure to acknowledge the help, encouragement, and kindness given to us during the course of writing this book.

Jackson owes a particular debt of gratitude to Tom Benson and the late Len Palmer, two Portland State University geologists who first showed him how to see the Earth's geology from above. Their colleagues Scott Burns, Ken Cruikshank, and Dave Percy aided this project in various ways.

Our wives, sons, and daughters accepted us even at our most preoccupied and—dare we say it?—irritable.

Jeremy Bolesky and Craig Collins generously provided instruction in the ways of Photoshop. Martha Gannett and Craig Collins improved our cartography.

Allen Kenitzer, Scott Speer, and Troy Guinett of the Federal Aviation Administration and Miles Weber helped us to understand just where commercial aircraft fly across North America. Toni Hochard, U.S. Department of Transportation, helped us to understand which flights carry the most people.

Expert reviewers who critiqued parts of the manuscript tried to keep our facts separate from our interpretations: Ron Billings (Texas Forest Service), Rick Brown (Defenders of Wildlife, Oregon), Vickie Carson (Mammoth Cave National Park), Ann DalVera (San Juan National Forest), Jim Drahovzal (Kentucky Geological Survey), Nelson Eby (University of Massachusetts), Jay Harmon (Iowa State University), Al Hebb (Boston Harbor Islands National Recreation Area), Robb Jacobson (U.S. Geological Survey, Missouri), James Johnston (Forest Service Employees for Environmental Ethics, Oregon), Jack Hultquist (National Resources Conservation Service, New Brunswick), Chuck Kluth (Colorado School of Mines), Lou Maher (University of Wisconsin), JoAnne Nelson (BC Geologic Survey), and Joel Pederson (Utah State University).

Help with ground truth was given to our interpretations of aerial images by Lynette Babik (Michigan Proving Ground), John Brady (Missouri River Relief), Steve Brady (University of Georgia Cooperative Extension), Paul Corbit Brown (SouthWings, West Virginia), Marty Campbell (National Resources Conservation Service, North Dakota), Gilbert Francis (Tennessee Valley Authority), Gwen Hurewig (Chugach National Forest), Bob Leiby (Penn State Cooperative Extension), Jim Lowell, Mike Luken (Port of Sacramento), Steve Miller (Sunflower Electric Power Corporation), Nicole Norris (Delaware Division of Corporations), Jane Sattler, James A. Schmid, Chubby Starling (USDA Farm Service Agency, North Carolina), and Henry Sweets (Mark Twain Museum).

In acquiring imagery, we had kind help from Barbara Allen (Massachusetts Water Resources Authority), Frank LaFone (West Virginia University), Chas Law (Tennessee Valley Authority), Ray McDowell (California Resources Agency), Sharron McIff and David Davis (USDA Aerial Photography Field Office), Tavis Rogers (Phelps Dodge Corporation), and Jeff Smith (Grip Technology).

We also thank the NASA astronauts and technicians whose names we do not know for making their photos from space available to the public.

Our editor, Lisa White, and designer, Anne Chalmers, transformed our rough-and-tumble manuscript into the elegant guide you hold. We thank them and the field guide team at Houghton Mifflin, including Shelley Berg, Mimi Assad, Teresa Elsey, Evelyn Pyle, Jacinta Monniere, Taryn Roeder, Nancy Grant, and Katrina Kruse. Finally, we wish to thank our agent Russ Galen, who made the all-important connection between authors and publisher.

Contents

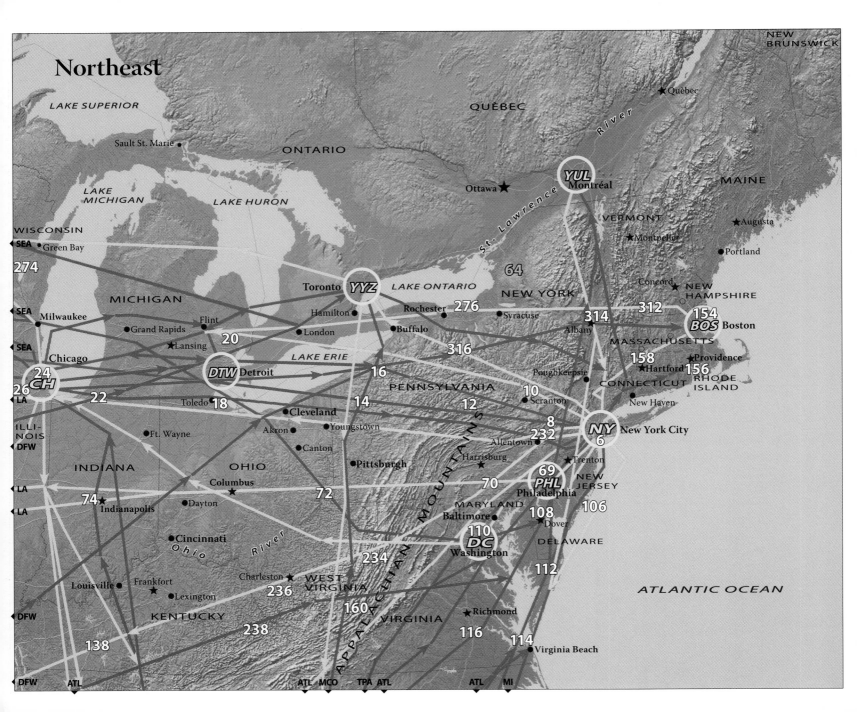

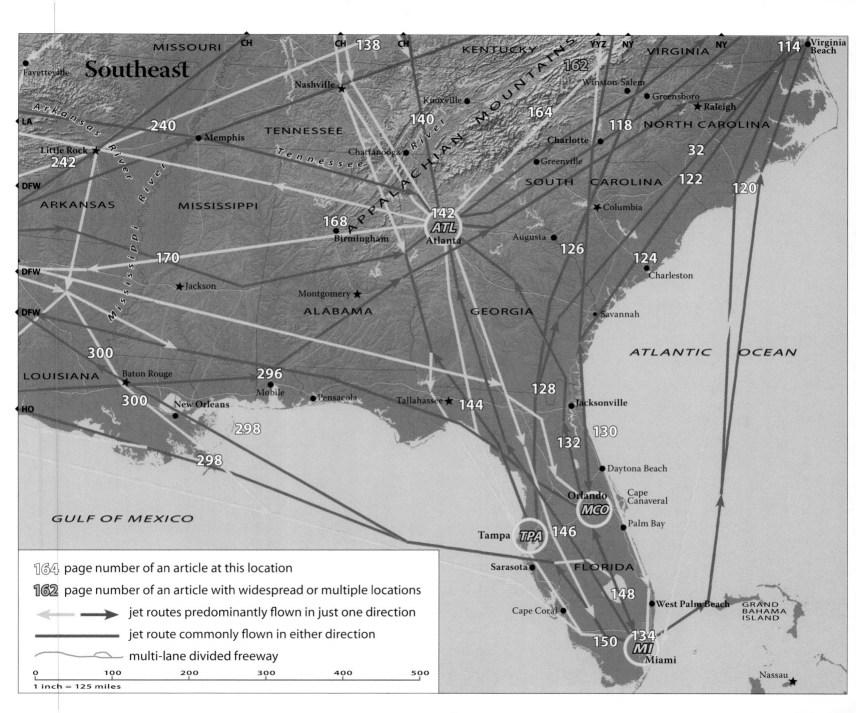

Southeast

MISSOURI

KENTUCKY

VIRGINIA

Fayetteville

CH   CH **138** CH

YYZ NY   NY   **114** Virginia
Beach

Nashville

Winston-Salem

Knoxville

162

LA

240

TENNESSEE

164

Greensboro

★ Raleigh

Memphis

Chattanooga

140

118 NORTH CAROLINA

Little Rock ★

Charlotte

Tennessee River

242

Arkansas River

32

Greenville

DFW

ARKANSAS

MISSISSIPPI

SOUTH   CAROLINA

122

168

★ Columbia

142

120

Birmingham

ATL

126

124

Atlanta

DFW

170

★ Jackson

Augusta

Charleston

Mississippi River

Montgomery ★

DFW

ALABAMA

GEORGIA

Savannah

300

ATLANTIC   OCEAN

LOUISIANA

Baton Rouge

296

300

Mobile

Pensacola

Tallahassee ★ **144**

128

HO

New Orleans

298

Jacksonville

132

130

298

Daytona Beach

GULF OF MEXICO

Orlando

Cape
Canaveral

MCO

Palm Bay

146

Tampa *TPA*

Sarasota

FLORIDA

Cape Coral

148

West Palm Beach

GRAND
BAHAMA
ISLAND

150

134
MI
Miami

Nassau ★

164 page number of an article at this location

162 page number of an article with widespread or multiple locations

⟵ ⟶ jet routes predominantly flown in just one direction

jet route commonly flown in either direction

multi-lane divided freeway

0   100   200   300   400   500

1 inch = 125 miles

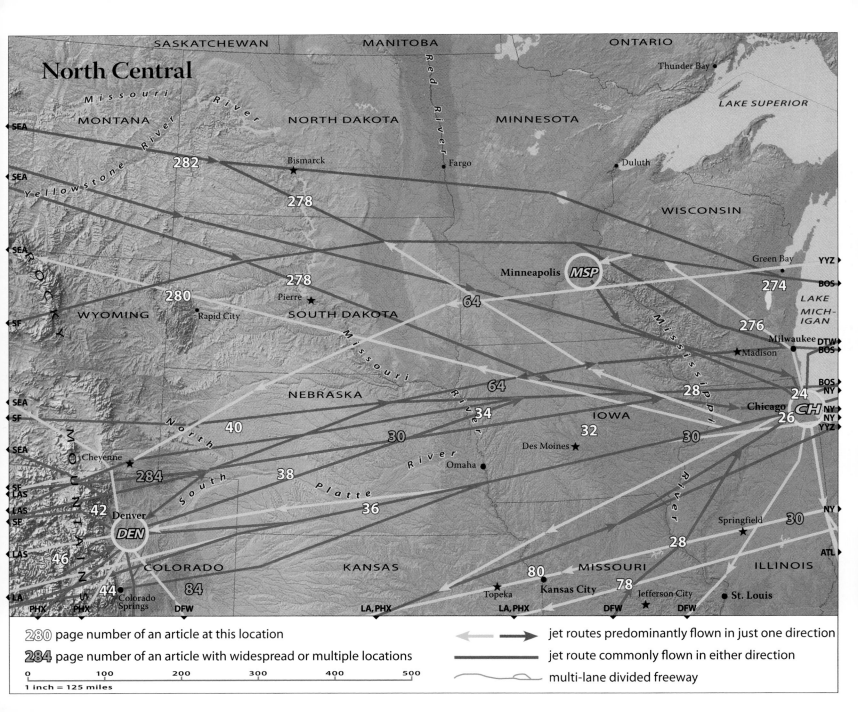

North Central

SASKATCHEWAN   MANITOBA   ONTARIO

Missouri River

MONTANA   NORTH DAKOTA   MINNESOTA

Thunder Bay •

LAKE SUPERIOR

282

Bismarck ★   Fargo •

Duluth •

278

Yellowstone River

WISCONSIN

SEA

SEA

SEA

278

280

Pierre ★

Green Bay •

Minneapolis *MSP*

YYZ

BOS

274

SF

WYOMING   Rapid City •

SOUTH DAKOTA

64

LAKE MICH-IGAN

276

Milwaukee • DTW

Mississippi

Madison ★ BOS

SEA

SF

NEBRASKA

64

28

BOS

NY

Chicago • 24 CH

North

40

Missouri River

34

IOWA

32

30

26 NY

NY

YYZ

SEA

SEA

Cheyenne ★

284

South

Platte River

30

Des Moines ★

Omaha •

38

SF

LAS

LAS

42 Denver •

DEN

36

River

30

Springfield ★

30 NY

SF

LAS

M O U N T A I N S

46

28

ATL

LA

PHX

44 Colorado Springs •

COLORADO

84

KANSAS

80

MISSOURI

ILLINOIS

St. Louis •

PHX

DFW

LA, PHX

Topeka ★

Kansas City

78 Jefferson City ★

DFW

LA, PHX

DFW

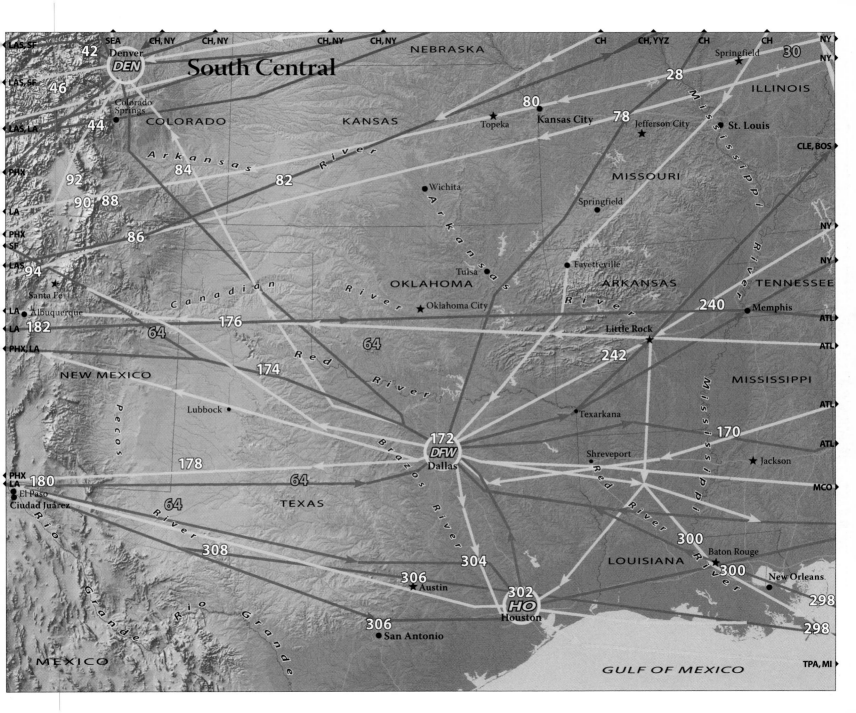

South Central

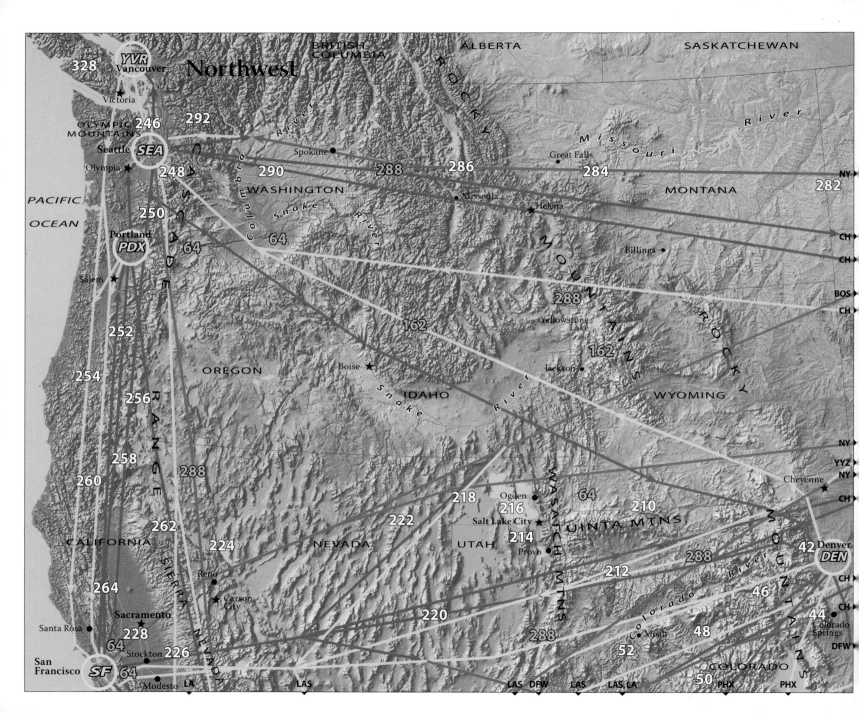

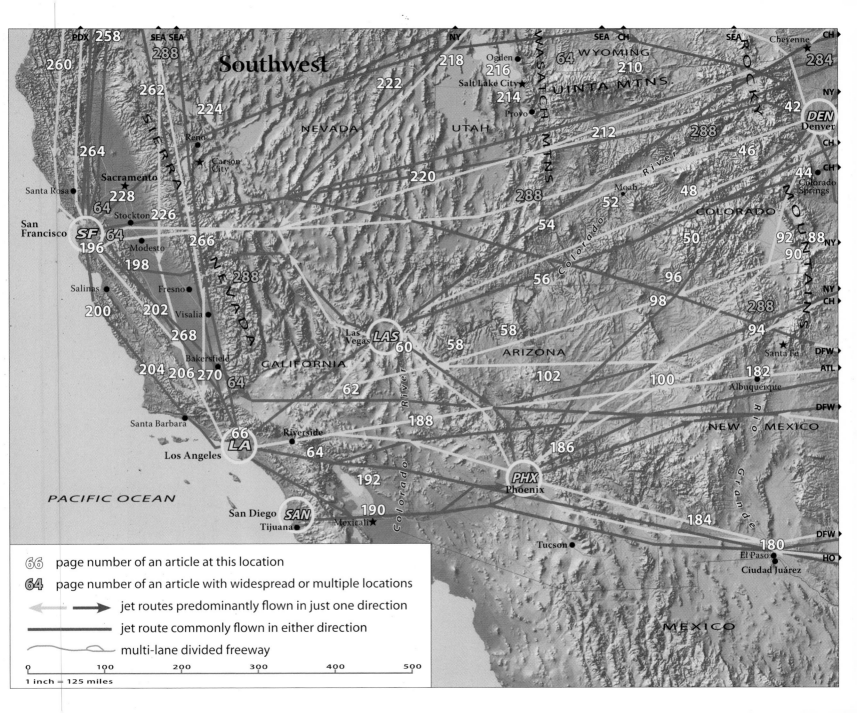

Southwest

PDX 258
260
SEA SEA
288
262
224
NEVADA
264
Reno •
★ Carson City
Sacramento ★
228
64
Stockton •
226
Santa Rosa •
SF 64
San Francisco
196
Modesto •
266
198
Salinas •
Fresno •
200
288
202
Visalia •
268
204 206 270
Bakersfield •
64
CALIFORNIA
62
Santa Barbara •
66
LA
Los Angeles
Riverside •
64
192
PACIFIC OCEAN
190
San Diego
SAN
Tijuana •
Mexicali ★

222
218
Ogden •
216
Salt Lake City ★
WASATCH MTNS.
214
Provo •
UTAH

64 **WYOMING**
210

UINTA MTNS.
212
288
54
288
52
Moab •
56
48
50

ROCKY
Cheyenne
★
284
42
DEN
Denver
46
44 Colorado Springs
COLORADO
92 88
90
288
94
182
Albuquerque •
Santa Fe ★

220
Las Vegas
LAS
60
58
58
ARIZONA
102
100
188
186
PHX
Phoenix
184
Tucson •
180
El Paso •
Ciudad Juárez

NEW MEXICO
Rio Grande

Colorado River

MEXICO

SIERRA
NEVADA

NY
SEA CH
SEA
CH
NY
CH
CH
NY
NY
CH
DFW
ATL
DFW
DFW
HO

66	page number of an article at this location
64	page number of an article with widespread or multiple locations
← →	jet routes predominantly flown in just one direction
——	jet route commonly flown in either direction
~~	multi-lane divided freeway

0   100   200   300   400   500

1 inch = 125 miles

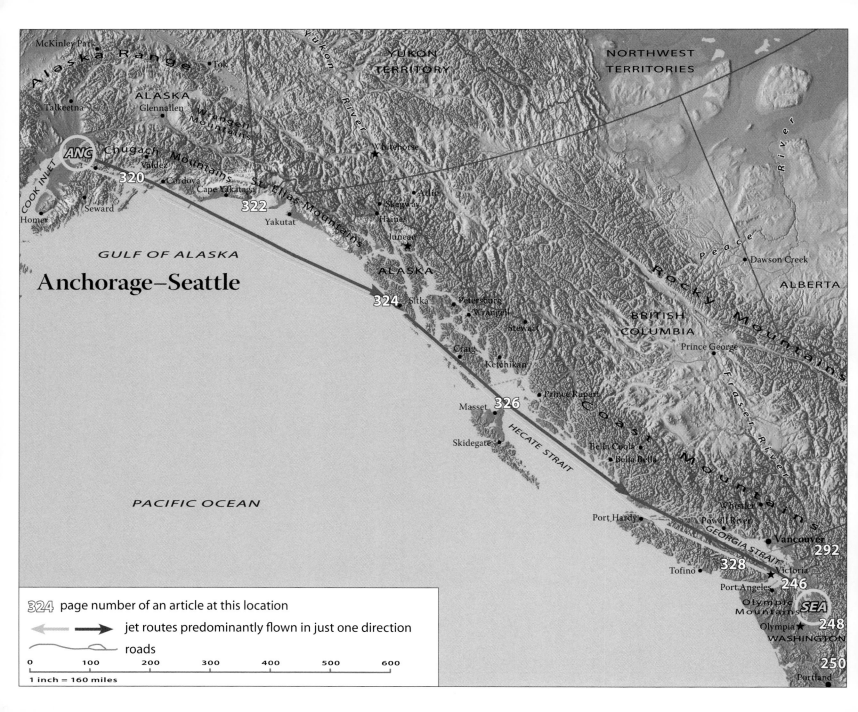

Anchorage–Seattle

GULF OF ALASKA

PACIFIC OCEAN

McKinley Park
Alaska Range
Talkeetna
Glennallen
Wrangell Mountains
ALASKA
Tok
Yukon River
YUKON TERRITORY
Whitehorse
NORTHWEST TERRITORIES
ANC
Chugach Mountains
Valdez
Cordova
Cape Yakataga
St. Elias Mountains
320
322
Yakutat
Atlin
Skagway
Haines
Juneau
Seward
Homer
COOK INLET
324
Sitka
ALASKA
Petersburg
Wrangell
Stewart
Craig
Ketchikan
Prince George
BRITISH COLUMBIA
Rocky Mountains
Peace River
Dawson Creek
ALBERTA
Fraser River
326
Masset
Prince Rupert
HECATE STRAIT
Skidegate
Bella Coola
Bella Bella
Coast Mountains
Port Hardy
Whistler
Powell River
GEORGIA STRAIT
Vancouver
292
328
Tofino
Victoria
Port Angeles
246
Olympic Mountains
SEA
Olympia
248
WASHINGTON
250
Portland

324 page number of an article at this location

⟵ ⟶ jet routes predominantly flown in just one direction

roads

0   100   200   300   400   500   600

1 inch = 160 miles

AMERICA FROM THE AIR

Introduction

We've written this guide for the many fliers like ourselves who se-cretly harbor a tingle of excitement as flight time approaches—so long as we fly in daylight, with auspicious weather and a window seat. Well, yes, it's also for you, you of little faith who gave up on window seats years ago, perhaps because the views had all merged hazily, their rivers unnameable, their mysteries intractable. Here we name places, unearth histories, and unravel landscape puzzles. Welcome aboard.

Paths Planes Fly

Articles in this guide are sorted into 14 corridors—assemblages of more or less overlapping flight paths. These flight paths embrace nearly all the 60 most heavily traveled city pairs in the United States.

If your flight is not on one of these corridors, look it up in the Index of Flights, page 343. You will find suggested sequences of articles for many trips that aren't so cluttered with contrails. But you'll have to skip around from corridor to corridor (of the guide, not of the plane).

Maps on the preceding pages of this guide largely reflect a re-cent edition of the Instrument Flight Rules (IFR) Preferred Routes published by the Federal Aviation Administration (FAA). Pilots frequently wish to depart from the preferred route to save fuel or to avoid bad weather and file a request to take a different specified path. The FAA grants the majority of these requests.

Preferred routes commonly, but not always, lump the airports within a metro area together, as this guide does. Different pre-ferred routes are sometimes given for different regional airports, for different times of day, or for different aircraft. Flights east from Oakland, California, for example, are more likely to take a north-erly option, whereas flights from San Francisco and especially San Jose more often take a southerly option. (We give more examples of such correlations in the corridor introductions.)

While the plane is near the departure and destination airports, pilots are directed in real time by local air traffic controllers.

For many city pairs, the FAA publishes no preferred routes. By tracking flights online, we were able to find customary routes, as well as to select among FAA preferred routes to find the ones most often followed. Our maps present the results of our investi-gations.

Each city pair typically has at least two flight paths—one for each direction—and they're often pretty far apart. Some city pairs, especially the longest and busiest routes, have four or more pre-ferred or customary paths. New York–Los Angeles is an extreme example, with paths wandering farther apart than the north-to-south extent of Colorado. (The most northerly New York–Los An-geles route that we have tracked repeatedly crosses a big corner of Wyoming; the most southerly one crosses a small corner of Okla-homa.) For that reason, we divide New York–Los Angeles into two corridors. If you take the northerly one, you are likely to fly over or very close to Chicago and Las Vegas, so it makes sense to include New York–Chicago, Chicago–Las Vegas, and other segments in the same corridor. If you take the southerly one, you are likely to fly near Philadelphia and Indianapolis, which join that corridor.

Why Planes Don't Fly Straight

For many decades, air navigation worked by triangulating be-tween radio beacons (Navigational Aids, or NAVAIDs) set up for this purpose by the FAA and the military. The easiest way to keep planes on precise routes and avoid midair collisions was to have the planes proceed directly from beacon to beacon. The FAA pre-ferred routes are expressed as sequences of NAVAIDs.

Today, it is possible for planes to navigate precisely using Glob-al Positioning System (GPS) satellites. But to meet safety require-ments for planes, GPS instruments must be far more sophisticated and expensive than those offered for cars and therefore won't be-come ubiquitous overnight. With the aid of these instruments, as well as the pressure of the increasing price of jet fuel, the FAA has undertaken a program that takes long-haul flights in uncongested parts of the country off NAVAIDs and puts them on more fuel-efficient paths, often straight lines, once the planes are out of their departure patterns. Flights in opposite directions can take almost the same straight line, as 1,000 feet of difference in altitude is accepted as a safety margin.

Back in the present, though: While preparing this guide, we tracked hundreds of flights on the Web; the majority flew from NAVAID to NAVAID. Since NAVAIDs are spots a lot of planes fly over, we include a lot of NAVAIDs in the locations we illustrate in this guide: Garden City, Kansas; Linden, California; Zuni and Albuquerque, New Mexico; Amarillo, Texas; North Platte, Nebraska; Bowling Green, Kentucky; Jamestown, New York; Carbondale and Williamsport, Pennsylvania; and Newport News, Virginia.

Three other reasons to fly crooked are to avoid rough weather, to avoid military airspace when the military requires it, and for greater fuel efficiency and speed when near the jet stream. We don't foresee those diminishing. It can be well worth going hundreds of miles out of the way to catch a ride on the jet stream eastbound or to avoid fighting it when westbound. Transcontinental flights in the northern third of the country are likeliest to make wide detours based on where the jet stream blows on flight day.

So, you're wondering which path your flight is going to take today? Sorry, we can't predict. A handheld GPS unit can often provide and record precise positions if held very close to the window for several minutes at a time. Some jetliners show you your progress on a digital map on a "personal TV" screen. If you aren't so lucky, try asking your flight attendant, during boarding, to pass along a request for the captain to announce an outline of the flight path soon after takeoff. If enough of us ask, we may find pilots making a habit of it before long.

If you have time, Internet access, and curiosity, you may enjoy tracking your itinerary daily for a few days before departure. The tracking Web sites we used are www.flytecomm.com, www.fboweb.com, and www.flightview.com. Other Web sites predict the weather and the position of the jet stream. If you see either severe storms or a contrary jet stream in your path, expect a substantial deviation.

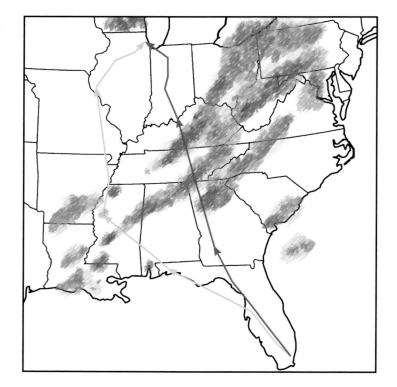

Here's a Severe Weather Avoidance Pattern (SWAP) taken by one Miami-to-Chicago flight in yellow, compared to the typical flight path in green. The blue to red colors show weather intensity.

Tips on Using This Guide

On many heavily traveled itineraries, you could read one of the corridor chapters from beginning to end. (That would be from end to beginning if you are flying south to north or west to east.) Pay attention to the cross-references to other chapters, at the lower right- and left-hand corner; these refer you to a subject that is visible from both your flight corridor and at least one other. Each article appears just once.

Most likely, some subjects in your corridor's chapter are far from your flight path because the common paths between any two cities diverge widely. You will have greater precision in turning to the right articles if you follow your flight on the map and pick your articles in sequence by their numbers on the map.

A few articles cover subjects so widespread that you could simply go ahead and browse them at any time, because you're likely to see these things by the time you've viewed any substantial stretch of the nation:

Center pivot irrigation (Great Plains to the Pacific), page 36
Forest fires (Rockies to the Pacific, and Southeast), page 288
Forests pests (Rockies and the Southeast), page 162
Interstate highway system (everywhere), page 76
Wind farms (scattered nationwide), page 65

On our maps and in our Index of Flights, major terminals are represented with either standard three-letter airport codes or non-standard two-letter codes. For cities with one major airport, we use the standard three-letter airport codes. For metro areas with multiple major airports, we treat all the airports as one destination or origin, and we give it a two-letter abbreviation so that we won't leave you scratching your head trying to think what airport those three letters stand for. Here are our two-letter abbreviations:

CH   Chicago (MDW, ORD)
DC   Washington, D.C., and Baltimore (BWI, DCA, IAD)
HO   Houston (HOU, IAH)
LA   Los Angeles (BUR, LAX, LGB, ONT, SNA)
MI   Miami (FLL, MIA, PBI)
NY   New York City (EWR, HPN, ISP, LGA, JFK, SWF)
SF   San Francisco Bay Area (OAK, SFO, SJC)

Remember that several airport codes are non-intuitive: MCI for Kansas City; MCO Orlando; MSY New Orleans; YUL Montreal; YVR Vancouver; YYC Calgary; YYZ Toronto. We have indexed the 30 busiest airports or metropolitan airport clusters in the United States, and the 3 busiest in Canada.

Before taking off, figure out which compass direction your window faces for the main portion of the flight. If you

fly west, right-side seats look north, left-side seats look south
fly southwest, right side looks northwest, left looks southeast
fly south, right side looks west, left looks east
fly southeast, right side looks southwest, left looks northeast
fly east, right side looks south, left looks north
fly northeast, right side looks southeast, left looks northwest
fly north, right side looks east, left looks west
fly northwest, right side looks northeast, left looks southwest

Then do your best to read the landscape, especially in the first 20 minutes of your flight. Refer to the map in this guide to see whether you are on one of the routes that we show.

The landscape in the image may seem upside down or sideways to you. Look in the image for distinctive shapes that would be easy to spot no matter which way they're turned. If the picture is oblique, the first caption on the image page tells which way the camera was facing. If the captions do not begin with "facing," the camera was shooting straight down, and the image bears a small North arrow. Those pictures were not taken from window seats.

Most photographs in this guide are of three types:

1. Snapshots from jetliner windows.
2. Astronaut photos. On most of these, you must adjust to a much broader scale. Try scanning the photo one-third at a time to spot something that looks like your view. Showing a broader area improves your odds of flying over it. We chose broad photos for locations where features we want to point out are spread over a large area.
3. Orthoquads, or photos shot straight down from about 20,000 feet up by joint state/federal programs and digitally corrected to remove perspective distortions. We selected scales roughly comparable to your jetliner view and printed them with north up. Most of these photos are mosaics of several tiles, leaving visible tile edges in places.

In addition, a few aerial photos were taken from small aircraft at low altitude.

CORRIDOR 1:

New York–Las Vegas or Los Angeles

Corridor 1A, the northern variants including Cleveland, Detroit, Chicago, and Denver, follows on page 6.

Corridor 1B, the southern variants including Philadelphia, Indianapolis, Kansas City, and Phoenix, begins on page 68.

Whether your flight takes Corridor 1A or Corridor 1B may depend on where the jet stream blows that day: Westbound flights avoid it, and eastbound flights seek it out. Near Los Angeles, most weekday flights are funneled either over Las Vegas or over a corridor encompassing Twentynine Palms and Palm Springs. Restricted military airspace, of which southeastern California has more than its share, affects these routes occasionally, but not predictably.

Given a window seat and a clear day, you will surely be struck by the enormity of the Great Plains and the Great American Desert.

To 19th-century explorer Stephen Long, the Great American Desert began on the western Great Plains and continued to San Diego, as aridity prevails in the basins between individual western mountain ranges. (That adds up to about half of your NY–LA flight time.) His mission was to assess the prospects for farming, and 20th-century irrigation was not yet envisioned. What you see in the West may be a desert, with sparse shrubs; a grassland; or a steppe, with both grasses and shrubs, predominantly sagebrush. Interspersed with the steppe are arid forests on the mountains, irrigated fields along some valleys, reservoirs above their dams, and the occasional startling apparition of golf courses and suburban sprawl, as well as areas of sand dunes or salty dry lakebeds. Power lines, dirt tracks, and wire fences intersect them all but require very sharp eyes to see from 37,000 feet up.

Geologists love arid regions because the rocks are in plain view. They're often drop-dead gorgeous, too. So don't be bored, dig in.

Mountains of the Rocky Mountain states were created by five main geologic processes, which we refer to often.

1. **The Laramide Orogeny** raised the Rocky Mountains proper, roughly 70 million to 40 million years ago, building on a related earlier phase that began 89 million years ago.
2. **Massive volcanic fields** erupted in many areas, including southwestern Colorado, between 46 million and 28 million years ago.
3. **The Rio Grande Rift** raised fault mountains in New Mexico and Colorado from 28 million years ago to the present; volcanism was initially huge, but has tapered off considerably.
4. **Basin and Range** extension raised fault block mountains and widely scattered volcanoes from western Utah to eastern California and in much of Arizona and New Mexico, mostly since 20 million years ago and ongoing.
5. **Present-day broad uplift** apparently centered in Colorado began 15 million to 5 million years ago, but this process remains mysterious and has no generally accepted name.

Between the front ranges of the Rockies and the Appalachians, precipitation gradually increases eastward. Ecologically speaking, the arid short-grass prairie gives way to the tall-grass prairie and in turn to the central and eastern hardwood forests, which then predominate all the way to New York. America's industrial heartland was carved out of these forests. The tall-grass prairie and a lot of former forest are now the Corn Belt, farmed with little or no irrigation. Parts of the short-grass prairie can be dry farmed for wheat, but most is either irrigated for wheat, corn, alfalfa, or other crops or grazed by cattle. Some is unused.

From Missouri and Illinois east to the foot of the Appalachians, there are more rolling hills than plains. Seen from seven miles up, the relief is subtle. Fairly flat-lying sedimentary beds underlie much of this heartland; the hills mainly reflect karst erosion rather than folding, faulting, or differential erosion. Limestone bluffs line many of the creek and river floodplains.

The Appalachians comprise four geologic sections, which you cross in sequence. From west to east, they are the

1. **Appalachian Plateau:** broad uplands dissected in dendritic patterns by valleys typically too narrow for farming.
2. **Valley and Ridge:** very long ridges and often broad valleys, dramatically parallel, with a northeast–southwest strike in this northern portion.
3. **Blue Ridge:** relatively inconspicuous under this corridor, though in places far to the south it achieves the greatest heights in the Appalachians.
4. **Piedmont:** low hills here and southward; it continues under other names into New England, where it becomes more mountainous.

Corridor 1A

NEW YORK—CLEVELAND—DETROIT—CHICAGO—DENVER—LAS VEGAS OR LOS ANGELES

❶ Hudson River ❷ Jersey City, NJ ❸ Ellis Island ❹ Liberty Island (Statue of Liberty) ❺ Governors Island ❻ Wall Street, near the southern tip of Manhattan ❼ Brooklyn and Manhattan bridges across the East River ❽ Williamsburg Bridge ❾ Brooklyn ❿ Queens

New York Harbor, New York

LOOK FOR bridges, tall buildings in Manhattan; the out-of-square lower-Manhattan street grid; docks in New Jersey.

An ample, well-protected harbor drew Europeans to settle here. The connection to Europe by sailing ship was paramount. The Dutch settled first at the south tip of Manhattan Island in 1626 ❻. Today, Wall Street marks the northern edge of their settlement, dividing the Manhattan street grid from the less orderly street patterns that began life as Nieuw Amsterdam.

In the 20th century, long piers extended from the Hudson River's east bank, providing berths for ocean liners. Freighters tied up in Queens, Brooklyn, and Staten Island and in New Jersey. That pattern changed late in the century with the advent of containerized shipping, facilitating transfer between ship, rail, and truck. Today, the main intermodal hub is on the west shore of the Hudson and along its New Jersey tributaries. Rail yards were originally built in New Jersey because land was cheap there, and neighbors who might object to the noise were few. Today these New Jersey yards are the hub of the modern New York port.

For New York's first two centuries, all interborough commerce and traffic was necessarily by boat. The Brooklyn Bridge ❼, designed by John Augustus Roebling, spanned the East River in 1883. Six later bridges reflect the amazing career of one man, Othmar Ammann, who supervised the design and construction of the Triborough, Bayonne, George Washington, Bronx-Whitestone, Throgs Neck, and Verrazano-Narrows bridges between 1926 and 1964. When first built, his two Hudson River bridges, the George Washington and Verrazano-Narrows, like their illustrious East River forebears the Brooklyn and Williamsburg ❽ bridges, were each the world's longest suspension bridge.

The Hudson here and for many miles upstream is as wide as such great rivers as the Ohio and Missouri. The flow of water in today's Hudson does not justify such grandiosity. Its bed was carved wide during the Ice Ages, when the Hudson was truly great, draining much of the meltwater of the continental ice sheet. That's because the ice sheet blocked the St. Lawrence River near Buffalo, diverting its entire flow down the Mohawk Valley to the Hudson.

At other times, when the ice sheet didn't reach quite so far south, it blocked the St. Lawrence near Montreal, diverting it into Lake Champlain—and from there down the Hudson. Later, the ice sheets melted completely, raising sea level to fill what had until then been the Hudson Valley, from SoHo to Hoboken, making the river look even wider. The Hudson is in fact a saltwater bay of the ocean, all the way up to Albany. All the rivers and many bays that we see around New York are post-glacially flooded river valleys.

The Laurentide Ice Sheet came south to Long Island twice, bringing enormous quantities of rocks from southern New England. These rocks remain on Long Island as two long east-west lines of hills, or moraines, marking the farthest the glacier advanced.

North of the George Washington Bridge, the Hudson River runs in a remarkably straight and narrow gorge whose western flank is the Palisades. The rocks of this cliff, of Jurassic age, have the same chemistry as basalt lava but are not basalt, because they solidified slowly underground. The Hudson River follows the contact between Newark Basin rocks, such as those cliffs, and the much older rocks of Manhattan and the Bronx.

When you fly west from New York, the first hills you see will likely be New Jersey's Watchung Mountains. Created by lava flows that erupted during the breakup of the supercontinent Gondwanaland, these hills were ancient valleys into which the lava flowed and froze. The solidified lava was harder than the older rock of the valley's sides, which therefore eroded first, leaving the resistant lava as hills. After the lava erupted, North America parted from Europe-Africa, opening the Atlantic Ocean.

New York's skyscrapers cluster at lower and midtown Manhattan, where metamorphic bedrock is close to the surface, providing sturdy footings. Although invented in Chicago, the steel-framed building, or skyscraper, first flourished in New York. The world's tallest buildings in succession included the Woolworth Building (1913), Chrysler Building (1930), Empire State Building (1931), and World Trade Center (1972).

Delaware Water Gap, Pennsylvania and New Jersey

LOOK FOR a river, with Interstate 80 on its north bank, turning to cut through a gap in long ridges; strata on opposite sides of the gap tilted at different angles.

Low altitude small plane view, facing southeast ❶ Mt. Minsi ❷ I-80 ❸ Delaware River in flood (June 2006), within Delaware Water Gap ❹ Mt. Tammany ❺ (in inset image, a broad scale satellite image) East Stroudsburg, PA ❻ Bushkill, PA

About 20 minutes west of New York City, the Delaware River, forming the border between New Jersey and Pennsylvania, cuts through a gap in Kittatinny Mountain. This ridge of Shawangunk quartzite rises between the northwest side of the Great Valley and the southeast margin of the Valley and Ridge Province. At the Delaware Water Gap, the Valley and Ridge is only 5 miles wide, with the Allegheny Plateau rising above it to the northwest. The Valley and Ridge extends southwest into Virginia, increasing to 45 miles in width.

Mt. Tammany ❹, a point on Kittatinny Mountain in New Jersey, faces Mt. Minsi ❶ across the gap in Pennsylvania. The fairly uniform crest of Kittatinny's ridge is slightly offset at the water gap: Mt. Tammany lines up 700 feet northwest of Mt. Minsi. Tammany and Minsi also show the same Shawangunk beds but tilted at different angles, indicating a fault at the water gap. The beds beneath Mt. Minsi dip 25 degrees northwest; those beneath Mt. Tammany dip 50 degrees northwest.

Upstream from Delaware Water Gap, the river runs southwest along the base of Kittatinny Mountain from a hairpin turn and another water gap at Bushkill, Pennsylvania ❺. East of Delaware Water Gap, the river flows southeast to Philadelphia. In addition to water gaps, which cut through Kittatinny Mountain at valley level and have the river in them, you may see "wind gaps" which notch the ridgelines only shallowly and have no streams through them.

During the last Ice Age, a glacier covered Kittatinny Mountain at Delaware Water Gap, advancing southwest a dozen miles to where it left a low terminal moraine.

Paleozoic rock layers with contrasting hardness underlie the Valley and Ridge Province. (See page 12.) Originally deposited as flat sheets, these layers were later compressed to create large-scale folds during the Allegheny Orogeny. Both stream and glacial erosion attacked the softer rock layers over the eons, forming long northeast-trending valleys. Harder rocks, such as sandstones and quartzites, resisted erosion to form the high ridges. Geologists see the easternmost valley of the province as the Great Valley. It has many local names: the Lebanon Valley here, the Cumberland, Shenandoah, and Coosa valleys at various points to the southwest.

All were carved in thick sequences of easily eroded claystones and limestones. All are bounded on the southeast by thrust faults carrying metamorphic rocks of the Blue Ridge Province.

William Morris Davis, the grandfather of American geomorphology, wrote an article called "The Rivers and Valleys of Pennsylvania" in 1889. Davis described a post-Paleozoic "Anthracite River" flowing northwest across Pennsylvania's folded ridges, eroding them to form a flat, or "mature," landscape. He inferred that the river system later reversed direction, flowing southeast to a growing Atlantic Ocean basin. Streams flowing across steeper slopes would capture streams flowing across gentle slopes until the Anthracite River drainage was dismembered. Further erosion and stream capture created the landscape we see today, according to Davis, with the wind gaps on the ridges representing small valleys carved by streams before the main streams carved out the present wider and deeper valleys. The water gaps cutting through the resistant rocks of the ridges represent the larger channels of the ancient river system.

"Superimposition" is Davis's concept that existing rivers are able to maintain their channels in a rising mountain range by eroding their beds as quickly as the mountains rise. The concept successfully accounts for some rivers that cut through Rocky Mountain ranges. Here in Pennsylvania, recent fieldwork shows a somewhat different story: faults and intense folds occur at many wind and water gaps, including Delaware Water Gap. Faults are linear features that fracture rocks, creating weakened zones where streams can incise rapidly. The Delaware Water Gap is no longer interpreted as a superimposed stream but rather as a location where water erosion selectively removed rocks that were weakened by faulting.

Davis's theory was created without the larger framework of plate tectonics, and he expressed misgivings about the flow reversal of a large-scale river system. Although his ideas about river and landscape evolution have been largely modified, his west-flowing Anthracite River is well established. Without plate tectonics, he could not hang his interpretation on the closure of the Iapetus Ocean to form the Appalachian chain with its west-flowing rivers, followed by the opening of the Atlantic and reversal of river systems.

WESTBOUND: Go to p. 232

Pennsylvania Anthracite Belt at Carbondale, Pennsylvania

LOOK FOR industrial sites served by rail lines or canals; open pit mines; reclaimed land.

❶ open-pit coal mines in varying stages of reclamation ❷ Delaware and Hudson Railroad line, now owned by Canadian Pacific Railway ❸ Lackawanna River ❹ Carbondale ❺ U.S. Hwy. 6 ❻ wind farm running along the top of a ridge parallel to the valley

EASTBOUND: Go to p. 232

Carbondale sits in the narrow valley of the Lackawanna River ❸, in the heart of Pennsylvania's anthracite coal district. Strip mines ❶ are common on the hills, and you may see surface signs of underground mines. This is the birthplace of the American coal industry and of two industries it spawned: canals and railroads.

Coal mining began during the War of 1812 when the British cut off their coal exports to the United States. William and Maurice Wurts were first to find anthracite at Carbondale. They sold shares in their new Delaware and Hudson Canal Company in 1825, the first U.S. company valued at over $1 million. Benjamin Wright, engineer of the Erie Canal, was hired to build a canal from nearby Honesdale to Kingston, New York. Mules pulled barges of coal on this canal to New York City until 1898, when the D&H became a railroad company. As the only canal company to make this transition, it became America's longest-operating transportation company.

Coal seams sometimes catch fire underground, and the fires are difficult to put out. In 1946, Carbondale's city dump flames spread to some abandoned underground workings. A 1950 attempt to drown the flames failed; a 1974 attempt to dig them out and extinguish them put an end to most fire symptoms, but a tendency for the snow to melt earlier from certain patches of ground looks suspicious.

The Lackawanna Valley is a northeastern arm of the Valley and Ridge Province. Local Pennsylvanian-age rocks include thick seams of anthracite coal. The rocks of the Lackawanna Valley form a broad syncline, or downwarp. Younger rocks crop out along the center of the valley floor, and older rocks crop out on the hills bordering the valley. Pottsville Formation sandstones resist erosion and, consequently, stand as the hills.

Lackawanna Valley coals are of the same age as coals in the Allegheny Plateau, farther west. The Lackawanna coals were buried deeper and folded more intensely, metamorphosing them to anthracite. The anthracite seams were once continuous across the area, but the seams that were raised up in anticlines were planed off by erosion and carried away; coals remain only in the synclines here.

From 345 million to 280 million years ago, swamps covered Pennsylvania and much of the Appalachian region south to Alabama. Dead vegetation accumulated in the swamps, eventually forming thick beds of peat. The swamps were periodically buried under sandstones and clays deposited by streams flowing west, away from a rising mountain range. At times, ocean waters flooded much of the region; later the sea would retreat again, and the system of swamps, streams, and rivers would resume its work. Burial beneath younger sediments would drive water out of the peat, converting it first to lignite, then to bituminous-rank coal. With further burial, heating, and compaction, the coal could be converted to anthracite, the highest coal rank, as it was in the Lackawanna Valley.

The deposition and subsequent deep burial of coals here resulted from a collision of the ancient North American tectonic plate with Gondwanaland; together they formed the supercontinent Pangaea. The collision created a mountain range above thickened continental crust immediately east of today's Valley and Ridge. The thickened crust subsided because of its own mass, creating a trough to its west where the Appalachian Mountains are today. Coal-bearing sediments of the Pennsylvanian and Mississippian periods filled this trough while the trough continued to sink, most of all at its eastern edge next to the mountains. Thus, the oldest sediments were buried deepest, and those closest to the collision zone were buried the deepest of all.

The Mississippian and Pennsylvanian periods are alternatively known as Carboniferous, or "coal-bearing," because that time, 360 million to 300 million years ago, was a time of extensive coal formation worldwide.

The final stage of the collision, the Allegheny Orogeny, gave a giant push to the basin full of sediments, which by then extended several hundred miles west. The sediments closest to the collision zone responded with intense folding and low-grade metamorphism. The Lackawanna Valley coals reached anthracite grade then and were folded in the syncline we see today. The zigzag ridges we see farther west in the Valley and Ridge Province (page 12) display their less intense folding owing to their greater distance from the collision zone. Farther still, and only gently shoved, the Appalachian Plateau was folded only minimally. The ancient sediments of the Midwest states were so distant that the collision's effects are all but imperceptible.

Valley and Ridge at Williamsport, Pennsylvania

LOOK FOR the boundary between a) a pattern of flat valleys between parallel linear ridges and b) forested uplands dissected by narrow, branching creek valleys.

Facing north ❶ Lycoming Creek ❷ Williamsport ❸ West Branch of the Susquehanna River ❹ South Williamsport ❺ Little League baseball complex ❻ Bald Eagle Mountain. Jetliner window photo under hazy conditions, which are all too typical.

Williamsport is on the north bank of the West Branch of the Susquehanna River ❸ where it is joined by Lycoming Creek ❶. On the south bank is South Williamsport, home of Little League Baseball. Look for five diamonds and the Little League complex on the east end of town ❺.

This valley is on the northwest edge of the Valley and Ridge Province. Bald Eagle Mountain ❻ rises above South Williamsport and extends 140 miles southwest past State College to Altoona. To the southeast, ridges and stream valleys make large-scale zigzags. Sandstones, resistant to erosion, hold up the ridges; easily eroded shales and limestones underlie the valleys. (See page 9.)

The Deep Valley section of the Allegheny Plateau rises north of Williamsport and continues west to the Ohio River Valley. Note the narrow valley cut by Lycoming Creek, typical of streams draining this section of the unglaciated plateau.

A branch of the Susquehanna Canal reached Williamsport in 1833. Trees logged in the old-growth forests upstream were sent here as log rafts. A seven-mile boom along the river caught them for the town's 29 lumber mills, the core of the Lumber Capital of the World. At its peak, Williamsport had more millionaires per capita than any other American city.

Towns along the West Branch perch on slender banks within a narrow valley. The river and its tributaries drain a large, rainy area, making this one of the most flood-prone regions in the United States. The main stem of the river floods roughly every 20 years, and flash floods occur on upstream branches most years. Flooding associated with Hurricane Agnes in 1972 inflicted $3.2 billion in damage, the most expensive U.S. natural disaster up to that time.

Sustained-yield logging was unknown in the 19th century. By 1920, Penn's Woods were scarcely wooded, and the timber industry had moved to West Virginia and the Great Lakes. Pine and hemlock dominated Pennsylvania's old-growth forest; the forest we see today consists largely of hardwood species.

Bald Eagle Mountain is held up by Tuscarora sandstone 445 million to 430 million years old. The rivers and tributaries incised their valleys in softer shales of several somewhat younger (but still Paleozoic) ages, leaving the older, resistant sandstones standing high as ridges. All of these sedimentary beds are tightly folded. The fold is also tilted, plunging into the earth about 10 miles east of Williamsport. The Susquehanna River stays within the shales, making a hairpin turn there around Bald Eagle Mountain.

Younger coals occur west and east of Williamsport, but none are found here. As these large-scale folds grew 300 million to 250 million years ago, erosion carried the local coals and their encasing shales and sandstones away to the northwest.

These Paleozoic sediments were deposited on the western margin of the Iapetus Ocean, which lay between ancestral North American and European continents. The Iapetus closed in three stages during the Paleozoic time. Partial closure during the Acadian Orogeny 415 million to 385 million years ago created a mountain range running along the present Piedmont. The shales overlying the Tuscarora sandstones were deposited in a delta shed from these mountains. Although they are not preserved here, it is possible that coals and coeval sands and claystones were deposited on top of the older shales in this region 320 million to 200 million years ago.

The Permian Allegheny Orogeny 260 million to 230 million years ago changed that and much more. This event represents the final closure of the Iapetus Ocean to create the supercontinent Pangaea. Central Pennsylvania was some distance west of the resulting mountain range but was caught between the collision zone to the east and the stable North American interior to the west. The sediments we see in the Valley and Ridge Province folded into the pattern we see today: large zigzags marching across the land. The younger sediments deposited before this event, including the coal-bearing strata, were removed by stream erosion and carried away to the west.

To the east, thrusting carried older rocks over the coal beds, burying them deeply enough to reach anthracite grade. To the west, the Appalachian Plateau was much less deformed, leading to larger, broader, and less spectacular folds.

Further uplift of the Appalachians occurred as the Atlantic Ocean opened during the Jurassic. Erosion then created much of the landscape we see today.

Allegheny River at Oil City, Pennsylvania

LOOK FOR narrow stream and river valleys, broad agricultural uplands.

The south-flowing Allegheny River ❺ cuts a narrow valley through the Allegheny Plateau in western Pennsylvania. The river and its tributaries form a dendritic drainage pattern characterized by narrow valleys separated by broad, flat uplands. This drainage pattern typifies rock strata lying in flat layers. Farther east, these same rock units are folded, and the streams and rivers erode the softer sediments to create a very different drainage pattern. (See page 160.)

Note farms in two settings here: the flat uplands ❶ and the river floodplain. Woodlands dominate the steeper ground above the river and streams.

You may spot small coal mine workings around Oil City ❻. Old oil rigs stand in some fields or around small industrial buildings. These modest operations represent the very beginning of oil production in the United States.

Rocks underlying this region include sands, claystones, and coals 360 million to 300 million years old. No glacial deposits are found here, as the great ice sheets stopped their advance some miles north in southern New York State. (See page 7.) The New York sector of the plateau holds no coal, and it is likely that coals once formed there were removed by the advancing glaciers. Rocks 385 million to 360 million years old underlie glacial drift there, and here rocks of the same age underlie the coal-bearing units.

Oil seeps are associated with the coal-bearing rock units. When "Colonel" Edwin Drake drilled the first commercial oil well near here, he was attempting to capture oil seeping into a nearby stream. At that time, oil was not used for heat or power; coal and wood performed that role. Rather, Drake sought to produce oil to replace whale oil in oil lamps. Whale oil was the principal source of lighting in many houses and streets, and the market for it was so robust that sperm whales were being hunted to near extinction.

Say what you will against the present oil industry, but at its beginning, it did much to save the whales.

Lake-effect precipitation drenches this region. Low elevations on either side of the Allegheny Plateau receive 40 to 45 inches of rain annually, and the highlands receive 45 to 48 inches. Much of the precipitation falls as snow in winter, when low-pressure systems moving across Lake Erie pick up moisture from the warm lake, then release it as rain or snow over the cold ridge tops of the plateau.

North America's largest stand of old growth hemlock-beech forest, with more than 4,000 acres preserved, stands 40 miles northeast of Oil City. Its admixture of large softwood trees contrasts with the uniformity of surrounding hardwood second growth, making it readily visible in all seasons. The natural area also includes about 1,000 acres where a 1985 storm blew down the ancient forest, and young hardwoods have replaced it.

Much of the Appalachian Plateau was clear-cut in the 19th century. In the west, hemlocks were cut for their bark for use in tanneries. Oaks and chestnuts were preferred species for charcoal, a common fuel before the adoption of coal, especially for use in the early iron foundries. The logs were covered in earth and burned to make charcoal. Small trees could be used, so a 25-year harvest cycle developed on plots near the early iron mines.

Mechanized logging developed at the end of the 19th century, leading to the Great Clearcut of Pennsylvania's woods between 1890 and 1930. Earlier logging had been confined to forests found along rivers. The tracts not accessible to the rivers were largely untouched well into the 19th century. Then rail lines were extended into the centers of uncut forest, permitting loggers access to still-virgin forest. The forest provided not only timber for lumber but also smaller trees as feedstock to distillation plants that produced acetate of lime, wood alcohol, wood tar, gases, and charcoal.

❶ Allegheny Plateau upland farms **❷** Oil Creek **❸** oil fields **❹** oil-field tank farm **❺** Allegheny River **❻** Oil City

Jamestown and Chautauqua Lake, New York

LOOK FOR a small city at the southeast end of a long, narrow lake.

Jamestown lies at the southeastern end of Chautauqua Lake ❶. At 1,308 feet elevation, this is one of the highest North American lakes that ever served as a primary path for freight. Town and lake share a valley originally cut by a river and later widened and deepened by a glacier. Look for drumlins ❻, low hills trending northwest to southeast. Their orientation reflects the direction of glacial flow across the Allegheny Plateau.

Jamestown sits on a recessional moraine that dams the valley to form both the lake and a waterfall on the Chadakoin River ❷. The river meanders through Jamestown before turning south to join the Allegheny. Note the streams and rivers here: Many are steep, suitable for mills. Few are navigable, rendering transport difficult.

Look for the railroad running along the river, through the city center, and westward along the south lakeshore ❹. Built as the Atlantic and Great Western Railroad, it later became part of the Erie Railroad. Other regional lines connected Jamestown to Pittsburgh and New York but not to the west. Limited transportation opportunities have been the norm throughout this area's history.

Timber and flowing water are the chief resources here. Water-driven mills converted the pine to lumber shipped in rafts to Pittsburgh during the 19th century. The city recruited woodworkers from New England to develop a furniture industry exploiting the hardwoods. By 1900, Jamestown's furniture industry was second only to that in Grand Rapids, Michigan.

The hardwoods also gave Jamestown a share in the potash industry of the 19th century. They were burned and their ashes boiled in iron pots, yielding potassium-rich salts. Ten acres of hardwood could yield a ton of pot ash used for tanning, dyeing, and household manufactures. Use of potash as plant fertilizer was minor at that time but is the principal use of potash today. It has been mined as potassium-bearing salts ever since 1861, when Germany opened the first potash mines. The United States rapidly grew dependent on cheaper imported potash, and the domestic timber-based industry folded. The United States did not develop its own potash mines until Germany embargoed potash exports during World War I.

This area is part of the Allegheny Plateau, which ends in a prominent escarpment above Lake Erie 15 miles west of Jamestown. A drainage divide along the escarpment's crest separates streams flowing to the Great Lakes and the St. Lawrence River from those flowing to the Allegheny River and ultimately the Gulf of Mexico.

Moist winds flowing off Lake Erie lift as they encounter the escarpment, condensing as orographic clouds. In the winter, these clouds drop significant lake-effect snow. In the summer, they commonly build into thunderstorms, which can generate intense rainfall and local flooding.

A native portage trail linked Lake Erie with Chautauqua Lake in the 17th century when the first French explorers visited the region. The portage, the lake, and its outlet to the Ohio River formed the shortest route between the eastern Great Lakes and the Mississippi River drainage. In 1749, the French explorer Pierre-Joseph Céloron de Blainville left a survey marker below Chautauqua Lake, and soon the French adopted the route as the principal link between French settlements at Quebec and New Orleans.

The French and Indian Wars were fought over the division of North American lands between France and England. A critical element of this conflict was control of the upper Ohio River, which linked the Allegheny River to the Mississippi.

❶ Chautauqua Lake ❷ Chadakoin River ❸ I-86 ❹ Atlantic and Great Western Railroad line ❺ Jamestown ❻ a drumlin

Toledo, Ohio

LOOK FOR a city straddling a sizable river mouth at the southwest corner of Lake Erie, with docks, rail yards, and an oil refinery on the east side of the mouth.

A large railroad switchyard between the mouth of the Maumee River ❷ and the BP oil refinery ❹ ends on a row of docks on Lake Erie ❸. This rail/ship interface is the reason an industrial city arose on this site. For cargoes of relatively low value per pound, such as coal, shipping cost is a huge factor in the delivered cost of the product, and even small savings in shipping cost are critical. Because ships move with very little friction and no rolling resistance, they are cheaper than rail on a weight/mile basis—so much cheaper that offloading rail cars full of coal in Toledo and taking the coal 688 miles by ship to Chicago via three Great Lakes is cheaper than simply keeping it on the rail cars for the 250 rail miles. Lakers sail the entire 688 miles without fighting much current or waiting in line for a lock, as Lakes Erie, Huron, and Michigan (unlike Lakes Superior and Ontario) are all at the same elevation.

Over the years, these docks have transferred enormous tonnages of black rocks bound for Chicago and other upstream ports. Back downstream come red rocks—iron ore from Lake Superior ports—along with grain and other cargoes. During some decades, Toledo handled more tonnage than any other Great Lake port. Even without the docks, Toledo would have been an important transfer point in the rail network, as rail lines to Michigan must round the west end of Lake Erie.

In recent decades, shipping volume is off. Coal mined in faraway Wyoming, with no access to water transport, overcomes its shipping-cost disadvantage with two cost advantages: Since it is mined from open pits, Wyoming coal is cheaper to extract than is Appalachian coal, and Wyoming coal has less sulfur, enabling aging midwestern power plants to meet current air pollution standards without installing expensive scrubbers.

A classic Rust Belt city, Toledo has fared better than some. The city and the county each had net population losses in the 1970s, 1980s, and 1990s. But if you define the metro area broadly enough, you can come up with slight gains from 1970 to 2000.

Toledo lost the Toledo Scale factory but held on to its other two signature factories: Libbey Glass ❺ and Jeep ❶. Toledo was once known as the world capital of glass and later as the birthplace of the Willys Jeep, which enjoyed a huge boom during World War II. In the 1980s, the Jeep partly inspired the SUV but then failed to keep pace when the fad bloomed. Then Chrysler turned things around and greatly expanded its Jeep plant. An equally large plant makes the transmissions for most GM trucks and SUVs.

Two Toledo oil refineries constitute 58 percent of Ohio's refining capacity. Oil refining concentrated here in 1887, a time when the world's top oil-producing region was, of all places, northwestern Ohio. In 1887, refineries mainly produced lamp fuel, and John D. Rockefeller was putting together a monopoly that by 1880 would control 90 to 95 percent of U.S. oil refining. Breaking his Standard Oil Company into seven regional companies was the first major action under the Sherman Antitrust Act, and it is still the most famous. Recent mergers brought six of the seven back together within three companies: BP Amoco, ExxonMobil, and Chevron-Texaco. Though right next to the docks, the BP refinery ❹ doesn't use them much. Crude oil arrives mainly by pipeline from the Gulf Coast states and Canada, and refined products leave by pipeline. The state still has producing wells, enough for 3 percent of its refineries' needs. Most of the wells are "strippers," pumping less than 10 barrels per day, the last trickle near the end of an oil field's life.

The Maumee River is the largest tributary that empties into any of the Great Lakes. The first Europeans called its lower valley the Black Swamp, a reputation that inhibited settlement here for the first few decades of the 19th century; once its swamps were drained, the valley excelled as farmland. The river served as the northernmost section of canals linking the lakes to both the Ohio and the Wabash rivers. The canals were an economic shot in the arm at first, but after a few decades, railroads took over freight hauling in the region, and canals were gradually abandoned.

❶ Jeep factory
❷ Maumee River
❸ Port of Toledo on Lake Erie
❹ BP oil refinery
❺ Downtown Toledo, OH
❻ Libbey Glass factory
❼ Sunoco oil refinery

Michigan Proving Ground, Romeo, Michigan

LOOK FOR test tracks and looping roads disconnected from the local road network.

❶ high-speed banked track ❷ precision steering and evaluation road ❸ east-west straightaway ❹ indoor test facilities ❺ durability road

Southern Michigan between Lake Erie and Lake Michigan is a grid of farms punctuated by small cities and towns. Detroit dominates the region's economy, sharing pieces of the motor industry with many outlying communities. Factories for car components and assembly are common, but their automotive nature may not be obvious from the air. Some facilities, however, are clearly associated with the motor industry.

Romeo, about 40 miles north of Detroit, is the oldest village in Michigan. You may not notice Romeo, but you will likely see the several looping roadways of the Michigan Proving Ground (MPG) just northwest of town. This test track is one of a dozen or so in North America used by the auto industry to test prototypes and products. When you read the estimated-mileage sticker on a new car, the numbers were certified at a test facility. When Detroit promotes a car for some performance capability, such as cornering or braking, the capability was first proven on a test track.

Among the many MPG facilities we see from the air are a 2.5-mile east-west straightaway ❸; a 5-mile high-speed track banked to 30 degrees ❶; a precision steering and evaluation road ❷; tracks surfaced with asphalt, concrete, or gravel; tracks over hills with grades ranging from 7 to 60 percent; and an undulating 7.5-mile durability road with various turns ❺. Smaller courses offer a full range of cobblestones, bumps, speed bumps, chuckholes, railroad crossings, and wet and muddy surfaces.

On indoor test facilities ❹, cars can accumulate miles 24 hours a day without a driver. Cars can be tested for electromagnetic compatibility with the environment: With their arsenal of electronic components, cars and trucks might be affected by external electric fields or might disturb those fields. Yes, there is also a gas station and a car wash.

Almost every city and town in the region surrounding the Motor City contains some auto industry presence. Henry Ford, born in Dearborn, Michigan, in 1863, may be partly responsible. Young Ford worked for a neighbor who owned a portable steam engine. Ford took the engine to nearby farms for threshing and other farm tasks. Ford moved to Detroit in 1891 to work in the Edison Illuminating Company power station. By this time, Karl Benz and Gottlieb Daimler had invented the first automobile, several companies were manufacturing cars in France, and the Duryea brothers (Charles Edgar and J. Frank) had built the first American automobile, in Massachusetts. Ford built his first car, the gasoline-powered Quadricycle, in 1896 and used it to attract investors for his short-lived first firm, the Detroit Automobile Company. Ford then founded the Henry Ford Company, only to resign when the investors brought in H. M. Leland to oversee production. That company subsequently became Cadillac, named after Antoine Laumet de La Mothe Cadillac, the founder of Detroit.

In 1903, at last, Ford helped found the Ford Motor Company. That winter, he drove a newly designed car to the land speed record. Soon the company was seeking publicity by entering cars in the new Indianapolis 500. He introduced the Model T in 1908, with a price tag of $825. Reducing the price in the following years, he sold 250,000 cars by 1914. That same year, he doubled, to $5 per day, the average wage in his factory. The key to low prices was his introduction of the moving assembly line. By 1918, half of the cars in the United States were Model Ts, and by the time they were discontinued in 1927, Ford had produced 15 million.

William Durant founded General Motors in 1908 in Flint, north of Detroit. Initially a holding company for Buick, it quickly absorbed Cadillac, Chevrolet, and Pontiac. Alfred P. Sloan Jr. joined GM in 1916, when Durant purchased Sloan's ball-bearing company. Sloan led GM past Ford in total sales in the 1930s.

Geographers ascribe the auto industry's concentration around Detroit largely to early advantage: In those first years, Ford, Durant, and Ransom Eli Olds independently developed cars and manufacturing techniques in this area. Detroit was also well placed to distribute its products around the rapidly growing Great Lakes and Midwest, as well as to eastern markets by rail.

In the 1970s, fuel-price shocks following the 1973 Arab oil embargo exacerbated losses of sales to foreign competition. Fuel-efficient European and Japanese fleets greatly eroded the Ford-GM empire in the United States. Thirty years later, fuel-price shocks returned, and Detroit was again undercut by fuel-efficient foreign-owned brands.

University of Notre Dame, South Bend, Indiana

LOOK FOR the campus just northeast of downtown South Bend, beside two small lakes, and the prominent football stadium toward the south side of campus.

❶ St. Joseph's Lake ❷ St. Mary's Lake ❸ Main or "God Quad" ❹ "Mod Quad" ❺ South Quad ❻ Notre Dame Stadium ❼ Joyce Center; the south dome houses basketball games, the north dome hockey and track and field events.

We often fly over college campuses, some within major cities and some well removed. Most campuses are designed similarly, starting with the broad lawns that are the literal *campus,* or field. Sidewalks crisscross the lawns, which usually align as north-south and east-west corridors, perhaps forming a cross or radiating from a crucial feature; buildings link together to form both open and closed courtyards; acres of parking border the campus, especially near the stadiums.

The American system of universities encompassing several colleges was modeled on Cambridge and Oxford universities in England. The General Court of the Massachusetts Bay Colony, a group of Cambridge-educated men, founded Harvard in the town of Cambridge in 1636. In Virginia, the College of William and Mary was founded in 1693 by Oxford alumni. Yale followed in 1701, then Princeton (1746), Columbia (1754), the University of Pennsylvania (1755), Brown (1764), Rutgers (1766), and Dartmouth (1769). Schools founded by Oxford graduates tend to have quads that are completely enclosed by buildings, whereas Cambridge graduates favored quads enclosed on only three sides.

These early American schools demonstrated the great importance the founders placed on education. At the respective times of their construction, Harvard's first building was the largest in New England, Princeton's Nassau Hall was the largest in North America, and the University of Virginia was deemed the largest construction project in the United States—perhaps in defiance of its designer's intentions.

Thomas Jefferson disliked the grand scale. Following his presidency, he designed the University of Virginia as an "academical village" and raised funds to found it. It opened in Charlottesville in 1825, the first U.S. school organized around its library rather than a church. Jefferson designed smaller structures on a human scale, linking them with covered walks and placing them around a lawn to encourage interaction, as on a village green. He left space for expansion, if needed later.

The University of Notre Dame was founded in 1842 on the site of an abandoned mission. Only six buildings were needed until 1879 ❸. Then an influx of donations from newly wealthy supporters, mainly from Chicago, funded a 20-year program that built the core of the central campus ❺ south of St. Joseph's Lake. A third period of construction, between 1920 and 1940, extended the campus south and west, including the football stadium. As at most U.S. universities, the 1960s saw a construction boom to accommodate the baby boom cohort. These buildings filled in the campus north of the stadium and east of the original core. Over the past decade, the new West Quad due west of the stadium accommodated the baby boomers' offspring.

The 1862 Morrill Land-Grant Act touched off a wave of public university construction after the Civil War. Within 20 years, 43 land-grant schools were founded, offering higher education to a much greater fraction of the population. Many of the new schools were placed in rural settings. Frederick Law Olmsted drew up campus plans for nine land-grant schools, including Cornell and the universities of Massachusetts, Maine, and California at Berkeley. He favored small single-use buildings rather than the multiple-use college buildings then in fashion. He replaced student barracks with more congenial dorms—though still humble by current standards. He considered open space an important element, and above all he integrated the campus with the adjoining community.

The City Beautiful movement, which began with the Chicago Columbian Exposition in 1893, gave campus planning another tweak. Daniel Burnham designed the Exposition grounds and later coined the term "City Beautiful." His Beaux-Arts plan incorporated symmetry about long axial paths and malls. Large buildings framed broad open spaces. This expansive sense of scale would dominate city planning until the Depression. Administrations of many new-building colleges and universities emulated it, viewing their institutions as small academic cities. Existing schools, such as the universities of Wisconsin and Texas, also incorporated Beaux-Arts principles as they rapidly expanded in this era.

Chicago, Illinois, and Its Waterways

LOOK FOR two very long, narrow, wiggly strips of green park running roughly parallel to the lakeshore, between O'Hare International Airport and Lake Michigan.

The entire Chicago metro area looks as flat from the air as it does from the ground. If you can pick out the rivers and creeks, a curious pattern emerges that explains why Chicago is here. Two long strips of park land ❶❸ follow small rivers. The one closer to the lake is a branch of the Chicago River ❸, running toward downtown ❸. The one closer to O'Hare ❼, the Des Plaines River ❶, rises in Wisconsin and runs for 50 miles south, parallel to the lakeshore and never farther from it than 12 miles, before bending sharply west and heading for the Gulf of Mexico. That's right: The "great divide" separating the two biggest river basins (St. Lawrence and Mississippi) in eastern North America is between those two parks—a ridge so low you can't even see it, called the Oak Park Divide. If you can find any other creeks, the odds are that they, too, will run mostly parallel to the lakeshore rather than right down to the lake.

What could have created a drainage pattern this strange? It was a lobe of the Laurentide Ice Sheet that scooped out Lake Michigan's bed during the Ice Ages. This lobe advanced many times, pushing broken rock in front of it like a humongous bulldozer. After each advance, it melted, leaving a thin outline of broken rock marking the limit of that advance. Those thin outlines, called moraines, are too low to see from your window, but they're a few feet higher than the St. Clair riverbed at the south tip of Lake Huron, so all of Lake Michigan drains via Lake Huron instead of crossing the moraines.

That low divide between the Chicago and Des Plaines rivers was the easiest place for the French voyageurs to portage between the Great Lakes and the Mississippi drainage. During especially rainy seasons, the divide became so swampy that they could paddle canoes across it. As early as 1673, the explorer Louis Joliet proposed replacing the portage with a canal between Lake Michigan and the Illinois River. Execution of his vision waited until 1848, making the Illinois and Michigan Canal the last major freight canal built in the United States and putting Chicago at the junction of trade between the Gulf of Mexico and the Atlantic basins. The time was ripe for this advance: In the first year the canal was open, Chicago's population grew sixfold.

A second role for canals here—and the reason why one canal was not enough—was to move sewage away from residential areas. The Sanitary and Ship Canal ❾ between the South Branch of the Chicago River ❿ and the Des Plaines River ❶ was completed in 1900, reversing the flow of a section of the South Branch so that ripe liquids could flow downhill to the Gulf of Mexico rather than collecting and putrefying along the lakeshore. You may see two canals running side by side for several miles. One is the S&S Canal; the other, the Des Plaines River where it was straightened and deepened as part of the old canal of 1848.

Canals linking the Mississippi to the Great Lakes provided the basis of Chicago's initial growth in the 1850s. After the Civil War, canals gave way to railroads. In 1862 and 1864, Congress passed two Pacific Railway acts authorizing five transcontinental railways with federal land grants. The five lines were completed by 1894 from the Missouri River to the Pacific; none ran all the way to the Atlantic. Chicago became the principal transfer point for freight and passengers between the East and the West. From the air, we see to this day, a plethora of train yards and tracks throughout Chicago.

More recently, Chicago became a hub for air travel as well; O'Hare ❼ ranked as the nation's busiest airport for several decades.

The Loop ❽, the collection of office towers defining Chicago's downtown business district, was the site of the first steel-framed tall building. The 10-story Home Insurance Company Building was completed in 1885 and raised to 12 stories before being demolished in 1931. At 1,450 feet, the Sears Tower is the tallest building in Chicago. The Aon Center (1,135 feet) and the John Hancock Center (1,130 feet) are nearby siblings, all built between 1969 and 1974.

❶ Des Plaines River ❷ Oak Park Divide ❸ Chicago River North Branch ❹ Evanston, IL ❺ Lake Michigan ❻ North Shore Channel (a canal) ❼ O'Hare International Airport ❽ The Loop; the long jutting pier is Navy Pier; the broad close-to-shore pier holds the Field Museum and Soldier Field ❾ Sanitary and Ship Canal ❿ Chicago River South Branch. Astronaut view, about 30 mi. across.

Fermilab and the Tevatron, Batavia, Illinois

LOOK FOR a giant figure 8 in a lake-studded park setting in the Chicago suburbs southwest of O'Hare or west-northwest of Midway.

Facing north ❶ Fox River ❷ DuPage Airport ❸ Main Injector ring ❹ Antiproton Source building ❺ Wilson Hall (main public building) ❻ buffalo (bison) farm ❼ Tevatron ring

Chicago approaches and takeoffs often distract fliers with this eye-catching geometric centerpiece of the Fermi National Accelerator Laboratory. The larger circle ❼, four miles around, is surface pavement overlying the Tevatron, the world's highest-energy particle accelerator. The name derives not from Teva-clad scientists trying to catch up with speeding particles but from being the first cyclotron designed to achieve 1 TeV, or tera-electron volt, of energy. Tevatron accelerates two beams in opposite directions, then redirects one so that the two collide with up to 2 TeV of energy.

Accelerators are the main tool physicists use to study subatomic particles. The first ring-shaped accelerator (or cyclotron), four inches in diameter, was built in 1929. Enrico Fermi was one of the first theorists of particles smaller than protons, neutrons, and electrons. In 1938, he seized the opportunity to emigrate from Fascist Italy when he went to Sweden with his wife to accept the Nobel Prize in Physics. His most famous experiment was the first controlled nuclear chain reaction, essentially a tiny prototype nuclear reactor. He built that in 1942, in a converted squash court at the University of Chicago, as part of an early phase of the Manhattan Project. The project's work developing the atom bomb continued at larger labs at Los Alamos, New Mexico, Hanford, Washington, and Oak Ridge, Tennessee, all still under construction in 1942. No weapons research was ever conducted at Fermilab, nor did Fermi work there. Named after him posthumously, it is devoted to "pure" research, that is, without direct practical applications.

After the war, Fermi and many coworkers formed a new University of Chicago institute to study peaceful applications of nuclear physics. Although Fermi died in 1954, his group's work there put Chicago at the top of the list of candidate sites for accelerators of ever-increasing size and power. The new facility, Fermilab, claimed the title of highest-energy accelerator in 1972 with its first cyclotron. It began running the Tevatron in 1983. The smaller, somewhat elliptical loop of the figure 8, called the Main Injector ❸, was added in the 1990s. It brings certain particles up to speed before injecting them into the higher-speed flow of the Tevatron.

An accelerator can be summarized as a copper tube designed to get subatomic particles traveling extremely fast. Once they're going fast enough, materials are inserted in their way, and then complex "detectors" make a record of particles flying off from the collisions. Particles can accelerate to greater speeds in circular designs—the bigger, the faster—as they fly lap after lap. The particles fly in a vacuum, passing through holes at the centers of a succession of copper rings that coax them along magnetically, in a perfectly timed sequence. Magnetic fields from stronger magnets encircling the tube shunt the particles back into a narrow beam down the center, so that they never run into anything until they are supposed to. The Tevatron's 1,000 electromagnets are superconducting, which requires them to be maintained, using liquid helium, at a chilly -450°F. That's barely 10°F above absolute zero. Refrigeration may have been the lab's greatest technical challenge.

The Tevatron, the Main Injector, and a smaller unit that produces antimatter ❹ are used together in experiments attempting to detect a trace of a Higgs boson. Theorists seem to agree that such a particle needs to exist in order for the "standard model" to work. (The standard model consists of six kinds of quarks, six leptons, and four force carriers, along with an antiparticle antithetical to each.) When Fermilab's protons and antiprotons collide, they demonstrate Einstein's famous conversion factor, $E = mc^2$: Extremely high speed (energy) enables two particles colliding to yield a much more massive particle. Borrowing words from Fermilab, "It's as if two tennis balls collided and a bowling ball flew out."

Proposals are afoot for a more powerful International Linear Collider. Three versions of its design were drafted, tailored to Japan, Geneva, and Fermilab. Being linear rather than circular, it would extend far north and south of the present loops.

Fermilab welcomes visitors. The top attraction is a herd of 40 to 75 bison ❺; for most tourists, bison are more charismatic than bosons and certainly easier to see. The lab's first directors saw their large new campus as an opportunity to preserve a good piece of native prairie, and it has served as a nature preserve ever since. Birdwatchers flock to it. The several hundred white-tailed deer, on the other hand, and the thousands of Canada geese that pass through seasonally, approach nuisance status.

Upper Mississippi River at Dubuque, Iowa, and Hannibal, Missouri

LOOK FOR long strings of barges; thin dams stretching across the Mississippi River, creating "lakes" without widening the river very much; floodplain margins.

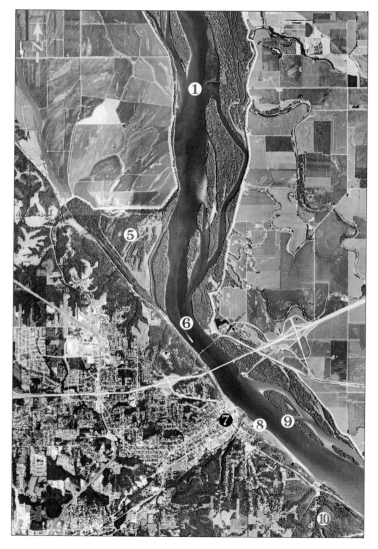

Facing north ❶ Mississippi River ❷ Lock and Dam No. 11 ❸ Dubuque ❹ Stumpf Island, Upper Mississippi River Fish and Wildlife Refuge ❺ lines of trees marking past riverbank ❻ tugboat pushing barges ❼ Hannibal ❽ Lovers Leap ❾ Shuck and Pearl islands ❿ Mark Twain Cave

Mississippi River dams and their locks are so numerous that they don't have names, only numbers: 1 through 27. Although recreational boaters enjoy the lakes, they exist primarily to keep the river deep enough for barges. The dams ❷ are not used for irrigation and only very modestly (by today's standards) for electricity generation or flood control: The reservoirs are kept nearly full at all times, leaving scant capacity to take on excess water at flood times. Some are designed to let floods flow right over the dam.

The Mississippi carries more shipping than any other inland waterway in the United States, if you exclude the seagoing ships on the Great Lakes. Steamboats arrived in New Orleans in 1811, shortly after they were invented, and immediately took over most commerce on the lower Mississippi and Ohio rivers. (The Ohio is the larger of the two where they meet. Navigable without dams, it carries more freight than the upper Mississippi, as does its tributary the Tennessee. It might have made sense to give the rivers one name from Pittsburgh to New Orleans, and another from Lake Itasca to St. Louis.) The Mississippi gets considerably smaller above St. Louis, and had rapids in two stretches: near Keokuk, Iowa, and at Rock Island, Illinois. In 1823, a brave captain of a small steamboat proved that the rapids could be ascended, fighting his way upstream after two days stuck on the rocks at Rock Island. Steamboat traffic grew exponentially thereafter.

Wrecks on the rapids were frequent; clamor for something to be done about them was incessant. A canal around Keokuk, and blasting and dredging at Rock Island, created a safe 4-foot depth, but industry standards for economical barging soon demanded 6 feet and then 9 feet, a demand that only dams could meet. The first upper Mississippi dam drowned the rapids at Keokuk to a depth of 6 feet in 1913 and briefly ranked as the world's most powerful electricity-generating plant. The full 9-foot system of 27 dams was completed in the 1940s. Three years later, Congress asked for feasibility studies on a 12-foot channel on the lower Mississippi.

In recent years, the debate on the upper river has been over replacing all the locks with ones twice as long. Fuel-efficient 1,200-foot barge trains are now the norm below the dams. To continue upriver, their operators must unhook and rehook barges, tediously taking them through each 600-foot lock in two batches. In recent years, barge traffic—carrying mainly corn, soybeans, and other farm products for export out of New Orleans—has been declining on the upper Mississippi. Barge boosters blame the decline on inefficient short locks; critics trace it to reduced farm exports and assert that economic arguments for rebuilding the locks only get weaker as traffic declines.

Piloting barges and steamboats on this straightened, deepened river is not the unpredictable, white-knuckle endeavor that Mark Twain wrote about. (Yes, there are still steamboats; they're in the leisure trade now.) Many flights between the Northeast and the Southwest pass over Twain's home town, Hannibal, Missouri. The cave Tom Sawyer and Huck Finn explored, now open to the public, is in a small side canyon just south of town ❿.

Stalactite-filled limestone caves are karst features (pages 139, 145), as are the side canyon and the limestone bluffs ❺ that typically enclose river floodplains within limestone regions. Most places where you could fly over the Mississippi or the Missouri in Iowa or Missouri show a crystal-clear contrast, as in this image, between the creek-incised river bluffs ❻ and the flat plain in between. Within a bend, the river cuts away at its banks on the outside of every curve and deposits sediment just downstream of the curve on its inside, thus creating endlessly shifting meanders. At one time or another, each square inch in the floodplain spent time as riverbed. However, today's dam- and levee-tamed rivers rarely shift course.

At 300 feet, the high point on the bluffs near Hannibal is Lovers Leap ❽, one of at least 50 lovers leaps scattered along the Mississippi, according to Twain. Jackson's Island, where Huck camped out, looms larger in his telling than the real-life islands on the Illinois side of the river, but locals think that Shuck and Pearl islands ❾ were likely joined in Mark Twain's day.

Hannibal was a transportation hub—the second-largest town in Missouri, briefly—during the steamboat heyday. After its railway bridge created an intersection of railway and river commerce, railway yards (now removed) were built on the flat floodplain at the foot of Lovers Leap. Most of the town itself is up on top of the bluff, safe from floods.

The Corn Belt

LOOK FOR seemingly endless rectilinear flat croplands; the contrasting darker green of woodland, in the swales, when present, shows where the land is slightly less flat than it appears.

❶ Eldridge, IA, just north of Davenport　**❷** U.S. Hwy. 61　**❸** Davenport Municipal Airport　**❹** I-80

Unless you fall asleep for an hour, it's hard to miss the Corn Belt, a gridded swath of cropland stretching from Ohio to eastern Nebraska. In 2006, Iowa, Illinois, Nebraska, and Minnesota planted 51 percent of U.S. corn acreage; the nation, in turn, produced about 40 percent of the world's corn. The same states plant almost as many acres in soybeans, accounting for the two-toned appearance of much of the cropland. Fields typically alternate between corn one year and soybeans the next, a classic crop rotation. Corn feeds heavily on nitrogen, and beans add nitrogen to the soil; one crop's pests diminish while the other crop is growing; corn is the cheap calories component in livestock feed, and soybeans are the cheap protein. The feed doesn't have far to travel, as Iowa leads the nation in pigs and eggs as well as in corn and soybeans.

The soils supporting Corn Belt agriculture are a legacy of postglacial processes. As Ice Age glaciers waned, meltwater rivers and streams delivered immeasurable masses of glacial debris. Prevailing winds lifted the finer-grained sediments and redeposited them across the landscape in great sheets of loess. Prairie grasses colonized the region, holding the loess in place and introducing a rich organic component. This 10,000-year process produced a great region with some of the world's richest and deepest soils.

Plows broke the sod in the 19th century, replacing the prairie with a diverse agriculture. Prior to World War II, farms in the Corn Belt practiced complex crop rotation, including wheat, hay, and oats to feed chickens, pigs, cattle, and workhorses. Federal agricultural programs altered these practices, so that today, much of the Corn Belt alternates soy and corn, with few other crops ever entering the mix. Recently, 61 percent of U.S. corn plantings and 89 percent of soybean plantings were genetically engineered seed.

If you're a bit thick around the middle, that may be a corn belt of another sort. No, we aren't saying that corn sweeteners cause weight gain (a speculative idea at this point) but simply that an astonishing percentage of the calories we eat are traceable to corn. Corn is the first-listed ingredient in the feed of American beef and dairy cattle, of both laying and broiling hens, and of pigs. High-fructose syrup manufactured from corn is almost the only calorific ingredient in most soft drinks and the first-listed one in many "fruit juices"; grain alcohol in liquor is largely corn alcohol; and corn starch, maltodextrins, citric acid, and a plethora of other clichés of ingredient lists also derive from the yellow grain. Many Americans eat more corn than do many traditional Mexicans whose staple food is tortillas. (If high-fructose corn syrup is a culprit in America's obesity epidemic, as some allege, the 1970s switch from cane to corn sugars may have been less influential than the changes in how it was retailed—portion size, pricing, unrelenting availability, and so on.)

How did corn take over America? It's a complex tale well told by several authors, notably Michael Pollan in *The Omnivore's Dilemma*. To begin with, corn is an efficient plant, yielding more calories per acre than any other grain. Long before it was ever subsidized, corn's naturally high yield led to problems: rampant alcoholism in George Washington's day and lethal vitamin deficiencies for European peasants when they subsisted on maize gruel.

All the same, U.S. corn is not inherently cheap enough to compete with sugar cane as a source of either sweeteners or ethanol. A sequence of political decisions with diverse motives made corn artificially cheap and sugar artificially expensive in the United States, and paid farmers to produce more corn. As cheap corn flooded forth from the heartland, industry looked for ways to use more corn and found them. Before long, corn was not only a lucrative industry but also a powerful constituency, successfully advocating government subsidy programs that became almost untouchable in Congress.

The latest twist is energy independence as a rationale for subsidies: Ethanol from corn is to substitute for imported gasoline. Growing corn, converting it to ethanol, and trucking the ethanol to gas stations (since it cannot run in pipelines) all use a great deal of fossil fuel, as much, under many circumstances, as the gasoline the ethanol replaces. Scientists debate whether corn ethanol either produces net energy at all or reduces the consumption of fossil fuels. Although the analyses may not be conclusive, they suggest that this is an example of industry manipulating farm policy for its own ends rather than a promising alternative energy source. Ethanol from sugar cane is energy-effective in the tropics, and cellulosic ethanol may some day become effective in the United States.

Hog Operations, Iowa and North Carolina

LOOK FOR rows of long, narrow, shiny-roofed warehouses; most in North Carolina are adjacent to a straight-sided lagoon. In Iowa, look also for rows of shorter, broader, arch-roofed rectangular structures.

❶ David and Elaine Struthers's Hog Farm, with hoop barns, Collins, IA ❷ Heart of Iowa Nature Trail, on the site of an old railway line
❸ four hog operations, Sampson County, NC, showing normal variation in lagoon color; the appropriate bacteria turn the lagoon pink when they flourish, and duckweed may cover it in bright green at other times

Forty percent of America's hogs live out their 165-day lives in a swath across Iowa and the adjacent corners of Illinois and Nebraska. Modern hogs live mostly indoors; what you see from the air are rows of long warehouses, each housing 800 to 4,000 hogs. The warehouses take up very little space compared to the surrounding cropland, much of which is devoted to feeding these pigs and, not so incidentally, recycling their waste into those same crops.

You may be able to see that a few of Iowa's parallel sets of barns are round-topped—silvery quonset hut shapes with caterpillar-like ribs. These "hoop barns"—reflective polyethylene tents, typically 32 feet wide and 70 feet long, stretched over tubular steel hoops—house the alternative method of raising hogs. Their lower capital costs, compared to the concrete-and-steel warehouses, suit them to niche markets, such as organic or higher-fat pork. The hoop barns also don't smell as bad and seem to offer the hogs, the farmers, and the whole neighborhood a more humane life.

In the conventional system, manure and urine fall through slots in the concrete floor. In Iowa, this glop remains under the hog house until it is taken out and injected into cornfields as fertilizer. In North Carolina, it gets pumped or sluiced out into a lagoon for anaerobic decomposition before being sprayed across crops. Pits and lagoons generate ammonia, hydrogen sulfide, and organic volatiles, which tend (putting it mildly) to displease the neighbors.

In the deep-bedded, or hoop, system, each new crop of weaners lives on a freshly installed bed of straw, cornstalks, or other organic material. The pigs socialize; they can burrow in their deep bedding. Their manure and urine soak into the bed and begin to compost. Bedding is added often enough to keep the pigs dry. The composting process generates heat that keeps the pigs warm even at -17°F in an uninsulated tent. In fact, too much heat can be a problem even with both ends of the barn open through summer; hoop barns are seen north of Iowa but not much to the south.

When each class graduates, its old straw bed is bulldozed out and usually left to compost some more before being used as fertilizer. Surprisingly, the compost method may not be better for the environment than the fresh-manure method. Composting releases greenhouse gases and nitrous oxide (an air pollutant), and any nitrogen released is fertilizer wasted.

Over eastern North Carolina, the number-two state for hogs after Iowa, you can easily spot rows of hog houses because they stand next to straight-sided lagoons. Hog farms lie almost jowl to jowl here, without enough cropland between barns either to grow most of the hogs' feed or to dispose of all the hogs' waste. Farmers must calculate exactly how much nitrogen and phosphorus their crop can utilize and limit the manure sprayed on it accordingly. Any excess is likely to end up in streams, where it causes algal blooms, oxygen shortages, and death of natural organisms—notably fish—that need waterborne oxygen.

Controversy boils perennially over how much lagoon water gets into North Carolina streams, causing fish kills and diseases and other ecological havoc. A 22-million-gallon spill in 1995 devastated the New River, and lagoon leakage is detectable in most streams; however, overall levels of nitrogen and phosphorus in the region's rivers did not increase during two decades of explosive growth in the hog industry. The odor problem remains undeniable. Undeterred, some in the industry do haul out measuring instruments and try to deny it. The resulting ill will has led to moratoriums on new hog farms in the state since 1997.

Opponents decry modern hog operations as "factories." In most people's eyes, eating grain all day in a sanitized warehouse isn't any life for a pig; wallowing in mud and slops in a barnyard is. However, issues of health, ecology, cost, and efficient conversion of plant crops into meat can be dealt with better in concrete-and-steel warehouses than in old-fashioned barnyards raising an equal amount of pork. Indeed, in old-fashioned barnyards, it would be next to impossible to raise the quantity of pork America eats.

In North Carolina, corporations own most hogs and contract them out to individual farmers. If a farm goes belly up, the farmer may walk away from it, leaving an unmaintained lagoon with no solvent party responsible. There are hundreds of abandoned lagoons. In 1999, Governor James Hunt set in motion a 10-year plan to phase out all lagoons and manure sprayfields. The ideal way to carry out the plan might involve digesters similar to those for sewage (see page 154) but whether these can be practical on a hog-farming scale remains to be seen.

Loess Hills, Iowa

LOOK FOR a small north-south belt of steep, eroded canyon terrain separating Iowa farmland from a river floodplain marked with traces of meanders.

❶ Loess Hills ❷ Monona Harrison Ditch, surrounded by traces of old meanders on the Missouri River floodplain ❸ Little Sioux River, straightened ❹ Preparation Canyon State Park ❺ Pisgah, IA ❻ Missouri River ❼ I-29 ❽ Little Sioux, IA ❾ Nebraska

Where the Missouri River separates Nebraska from Iowa, topography puts in a brief reappearance next to the floodplain. The change can be startling to eyes habituated to flat terrain.

It looks like miniature mountains with rugged slopes ❶, many steeper than 50 degrees. These peaks don't stand much taller than the flat fields a hundred miles east or west of here. They are the Loess Hills—heaps of windblown dust from the Ice Ages, eroded during the past 15,000 years.

Before the Ice Ages, the valley here was broader and gentler. During each of four Ice Ages, North America's biggest ice sheet flowed into the Midwest. As the earth warmed at the close of each glacial age, the Missouri filled with meltwater from a vast area of Canada, becoming a far bigger river than the one we see now. It carried a huge load of rubble and sediment ice-scoured from Canada, and looked like today's lower Yukon: a multitude of shifting fast-flowing braided channels and gravel bars. Several times, enormous lakes formed, collecting fine sediment. Soon the lake outlet channels eroded deeper, draining the lakes and exposing the drying lakebeds to winds stronger than today's winds. Dust flew skyward in great clouds. Dust settled everywhere downwind, thickest along the Missouri River, gradually tapering off for hundreds of miles eastward, as west winds were more frequent than east winds. The deposits are thicker on the Iowa side, exceeding 200 feet deep in places.

Loess (German for "loose") was first described in the Rhine Valley in the early 19th century. Its defining characteristic is layerless homogeneity, usually attributed to wind deposition. Particles are uniform in size because the wind sorts them. As the wind slows, the coarsest particles fall to Earth first; the finest clay particles are held aloft longest and carried farthest. Medium-sized silt particles predominate in Iowa, making an excellent soil, though the lack of clay keeps it from holding water well enough for some purposes. Iowa has some of the world's deepest topsoils, thanks to deep loess and to the sod-forming prairie grasses that held it in place for 15,000 years. Modern farming does not hold it in place as well.

Roadcuts through loess may look as though they were sliced with a knife. The interlocking silt grains can hold an 80-degree slope against gravity—but not against water, which erodes loess readily. Farmers in the area have to keep a sharp eye out for new gullies forming and stop them. The canyons you see incising the Loess Hills are gullies with a case of gigantism. They eroded episodically thousands of years ago; there is some new gully erosion locally, as we shall see.

Prior to white settlement, prairie grasses covered the Loess Hills (and most of Iowa) and prevented most gully erosion. Frequent grass fires killed off any tree seedlings that germinated, maintaining the dominance of perennial grasses that regrow from their roots after their aboveground parts burn. After white settlers took over, they suppressed fires, allowing a bur oak–dominated forest to spread over the Loess Hills.

At the foot of the Iowa hills, the straightened Little Sioux River ❸ contrasts dramatically with its former meander loops. The Missouri River ❻ looks only a little bigger—still undersized for its broad floodplain. Its old meander patterns, including many oxbow lakes, don't use the full width of the floodplain, as meanders do on the lower Missouri (page 80). The floodplain's width here was set by the river's braided Ice Age incarnation.

The Missouri has responded to dams upstream (page 278) by eroding its riverbed downstream from the dams. As the river cut its bed deeper, its surface dropped by the same amount. That lowered the water table under the entire floodplain and the water level of all the oxbow lakes on the floodplain. Many "ghost meanders" you see are oxbow lakes far along in the process of drying up. The lowered base level also restarted canyon erosion where several creeks emerge from the Loess Hills.

Why does the dammed river cut deeper? The faster water flows, the more sediment it can erode and then carry in suspension. The undammed Missouri earned its nickname, Big Muddy. Wherever the river slowed a bit, some sediment would settle to the bed; where the river sped up, some sediment would be picked up. These forces tended to balance out over the length of the river while it conveyed mountains of sediment from small headwater streams to Louisiana. Dams—big stop signs for sediment—release nearly clean water. Straightening and channelizing the river, the two main ways engineers improved it for barge traffic, make it flow faster. Cleaner, faster water is "hungry water" that eats the mud from its bed downstream from a dam, cutting the channel deeper.

Center Pivot Irrigation

LOOK FOR rows of big circles, each with a fine line along one radius.

❶ Soil in this area is sandy, and shows bare patches too sandy for crops; some may be "knob-knocked" spots: convexities leveled to facilitate irrigation. ❷ This pivot is in operation, and has soaked the sector from the 10:00 o'clock position to about 11:30. The line at 9:00 o'clock (like similar, sometimes doglegged lines at other angles on other circles) is the service road to the pivot mechanism. Its corners are a paler green, growing the same crop but without irrigation. ❸ Holstein, NE

You see them all over the West: circles made by a device called a center pivot irrigator, once described in *Scientific American* as "the most significant mechanical innovation in agriculture since the replacement of draft animals by the tractor." Invented in 1950, the device continues to round off more corners of fields every year.

Some farmers switch to it from dry (nonirrigated) farming, greatly improving their yields. Others apply it on land they could buy dirt-cheap because it was, before center pivots, too dry for any profitable use at all. Still others switch to it from "gravity irrigation," which conveys water in canals and then into the furrows between rows of plants. Advantages of pivot over gravity irrigation include more efficient use of water; saving the expense of building dams and canals; greater ability to tailor watering to the needs of particular fields; ability to apply liquid fertilizer in the water; and applicability to either flat or rolling terrain, and to soil too sandy to hold water in a furrow.

A typical irrigator is a quarter-mile-long pipe raised eight to fifteen feet above the ground on triangular metal braces on wheels. The wheels drive the entire structure slowly around the circle, like the hour hand around a clock. Water pressure drives the wheels on older models, but electric motors are increasingly used instead. A round field on a square plot leaves about 19 percent of the land dry. In very dry regions those are left unplanted and brown, but in most Nebraska fields in the photo they are growing corn "dry." Some center pivots have extension arms that irrigate most of the corners, making squares with round corners rather than circles.

Traditional models spray water all around, losing a lot to evaporation. About 65 percent reaches the root zone—more than with gravity irrigation but still wasteful. The new, improved center pivot is the low-pressure version, with vertical pipes down to a few inches above the crop. From there, the droplets don't have far to drop in the hot summer air and hit the rows of plants while avoiding the furrows. Better than 90 percent of the water reaches the root zone, rivaling more expensive buried drip line irrigation systems. Lower pressure requires less energy for pumping, as well as less water.

Pivot irrigators, together with abundant free water, have made U.S. farming some of the most economical in the world, at the same time affording many U.S. farmers a higher standard of living than most farmers elsewhere. Benefits are passed on to all of us in the form of supernaturally cheap food and in the export column in the U.S. balance of trade.

Water for pivot irrigation is pumped most often from wells drilled, right there on the farm, into aquifers—thick layers of porous sand or rock, with water filling the pores. Water in aquifers typically belongs to the surface property owners, whose use of it is not metered or charged for. Not surprisingly, aquifers in the West are suffering serious depletion.

Aquifers are like subterranean rivers flowing ceaselessly, albeit at near-glacial rates, to the sea. Some heavily used western ones flow especially slowly. In many, wells suck water out at several times the aquifer's recharge rate. Some "fossil" aquifers are glacial in a different sense. The granddaddy of them all, the Ogallala aquifer—the source for most wells in western Nebraska, Kansas, Oklahoma, the Texas Panhandle, and eastern Colorado—is largely Ice Age water. Its inflows became meager at the end of the last Ice Age, when summers in the Rockies turned hot and dry, and glaciers disappeared from Colorado.

Within a few areas, the Ogallala has already declined to levels that make further pumping uneconomic. Larger areas in Kansas and Texas may have a few decades' worth at present rates of use. Nebraska pumps the greatest volume from it, but also has the deepest reserves—many decades' worth. When it is gone, farms will probably have to return to ranching or dry farming, and High Plains crop yields will decline. If global warming were to bring 1930s-scale drought, many desiccated crop circles might revert to desert or sand dunes.

Center pivots are far from the worst culprit in aquifer depletion. They look great in terms of water efficiency and cost/benefit ratio compared to most big water projects or compared to hog factories, a newer consumer of Ogallala water. Still, for the Ogallala farming region to remain highly productive will require increased restraint in accepting the aquifer's gift of sweet 12,000-year-old ice water.

Bailey Yard, North Platte, Nebraska

LOOK FOR a large rail yard just west of a midsize city within the broad Platte River valley.

❶ North Platte River ❷ North Platte Canal ❸ Union Pacific Railroad right of way ❹ Bailey Yard ❺ engine repair shop
❻ South Platte River ❼ town of North Platte

The Union Pacific Railroad and Interstate 80 follow the irrigated valley of the Platte River across Nebraska. Towns along the rail line all seem the same from the air, save for one: North Platte, Nebraska, hosts the world's largest rail yard ❹, seemingly a maze of tracks stretching west of town. Every day, 10,000 freight cars pass through this yard. Two classification yards sort a third of these into trains: westbound on the north side and eastbound on the south side of the main line. You will see many coal trains from Wyoming's Powder River basin stopped in the yard for inspection en route to eastern and southern power plants. Empty coal cars returning from the east are stored in sidings on the northwest side of the yard. On the south side of the yard, the huge engine repair shop ❺ can repair 750 locomotives each month.

Coal trains account for 40 percent of the Union Pacific's traffic and 20 percent of its revenue. They frequently occupy all three main line tracks where they emerge at either end of the Bailey Yard. The 1970 Clean Air Act created a demand for the low-sulfur coal of the Powder River basin and greatly reduced demand for the high-sulfur coal from the Illinois basin and parts of the Allegheny Plateau. The Union Pacific was among the last railroads to relinquish its steam engines for diesels; it owned coal mines along its right of way in Wyoming and operated them mainly to fuel its own engines, as they were so far from markets. The Clean Air Act resulted in new mines, new diesel engines, new track on the Union Pacific's main line, and the longest new-built rail line since the Depression. It made the main line east of North Platte the busiest freight line in the world.

Most rail yards are found near big cities. The Bailey Yard is halfway between Omaha and Denver and halfway between Chicago and Salt Lake City. North Platte was laid out by Grenville Dodge, chief engineer of the Union Pacific during construction of the yard in 1866. From here, the line divided: A northern leg went to northeast Wyoming and the Black Hills, and a western leg went to Cheyenne and then to Utah for a rendezvous with the eastward-building Central Pacific and the famous golden spike. (See page 216.)

The Platte River valley has been a major east-west thoroughfare for more than 175 years. The Oregon Trail followed the North Platte River ❶ into Wyoming, where it traced the Sweetwater River to South Pass on the Continental Divide. The same route was used by pioneers on the Mormon Trail and by Forty-Niners.

The Pony Express, a relay of ponies and riders operated privately with a U.S. government mail franchise, followed the Platte in 1860 and 1861, delivering mail between St. Joseph, Missouri, and Sacramento, California, in 10 days. The Pony Express could not compete with the telegraph after it was completed in 1861, and the company went into bankruptcy. Four years later, the company and its mail franchise were sold to Wells Fargo Company for $2 million.

The Union Pacific, seeking a lower pass suited to year-round travel, followed the South Platte River ❻ to Julesburg, Colorado. From there, it gained elevation while crossing the plains on the "Cheyenne Gangplank," a wedge of debris eroded from the Rocky Mountains and deposited on the plains.

The Platte River, said to be an inch deep and a mile wide, is a classic example of a braided river: a network of small channels and bars that may change with every flood. Braided rivers develop where (1) stream banks are easily eroded, (2) there is a large supply of sediment, and (3) stream volume changes both rapidly and frequently. Such conditions typically occur within mountain ranges. They were present on the Platte River into the mid-19th century, including spring floods and intermittent summer droughts that caused frequent changes in the channels and kept the islands free of vegetation.

Flying over the Platte today, we see a river very different from the one the pioneers knew. Stream diversion and water-storage projects introduced in the late 1880s greatly reduced water flow fluctuations. Lateral channel migration declined, and thick vegetation colonized the islands between the braided channels. The Platte River Recovery Program agreement, signed in 2006, plans to restore high spring and summer water flows on the Platte in an effort to restore lost habitat for threatened and endangered species, including the whooping crane. If your view of the Platte shows less vegetation within the Platte valley than our image, you will know that this plan is having an effect.

Sand Hills, Nebraska

LOOK FOR a rippled pattern stretching as far as the eye can see; it is a vast field of large dunes stabilized by a thin veneer of grasses.

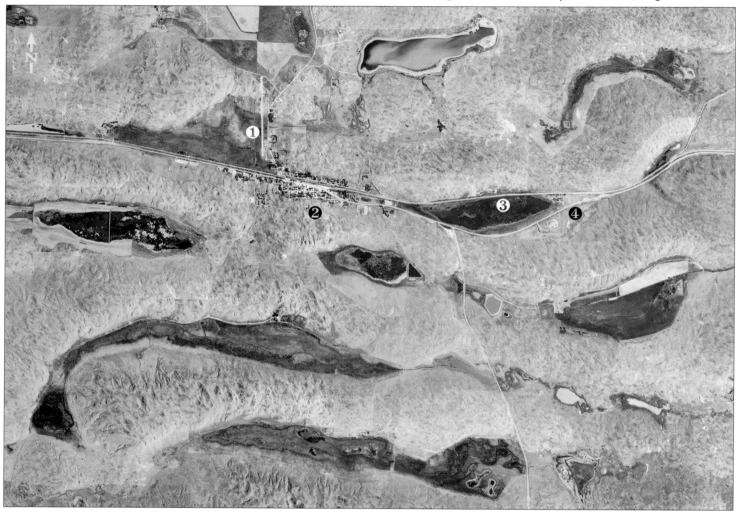

These sand hills stand 200 to 280 ft. above the intervening meadows, lakes, and fens.

❶ Grant County Airport ❷ Hyannis, Nebraska ❸ Burlington Northern Santa Fe Railroad ❹ NE Hwy. 2

Nebraska's Sand Hills are by far the largest dune field in North America and may be the largest stabilized dune field in the world. At most times of year, you'll see a striking difference between the dry hills themselves and the valleys in between, which cradle a mix of lush pastures, ponds, and marshy fens. You might infer that the valleys expose some hardpan subsurface that can hold moisture near the surface. In fact, the water does rest on an impervious layer, but that's 400 to 500 feet down. Everything above that is a deep aquifer: coarse sandy rock material full of water.

Where the water table (the top of the aquifer) is about two feet below the surface, lush tall grasses tap into it. Where the water table reaches the surface, a fen develops. Where the land surface drops a little below the water table, a pond results. Where the water table is down three feet or more, the valley is dry and no greener than the adjacent dunes.

The ponds and fens are waterfowl heaven. The lush meadows are heaven for cattle, and the hills themselves come close. The first cattlemen to reach the Sand Hills were stunned by their good fortune. The bison and the Plains Indians, when they roamed freely a few decades earlier, were doubtless equally pleased.

A hundred years ago, many settlers, hoping to turn more of their acreage into lush tall meadow, dug ditches to drain the fens. The settlers soon learned, to their chagrin, how subtly and broadly unified the water table is and how difficult it is to do as good a job of regulating it as nature does. They might convert their fen happily, only to find within a few years that they had also dried up their pond and the lush pasture they started out with.

In the 1970s, government subsidies and center pivot irrigation technology led to another round of attempts to cultivate the sands. This phase has not entirely ended, but it is faltering, and it is doing damage. Row crops expose more sand to wind erosion, which damages young crops or buries nearby pastures. Chemical runoff contaminates wells. Local drawdowns of the aquifer for irrigation demonstrate the risk of drying up the valleys and losing their whole ecosystem. Most ranchers and government agencies now agree that the Sand Hills are excellent for beef ranching and ill suited for other agriculture. Although ranching here seems sustainable as long as overgrazing is avoided, ranches, as in the rest of the plains, are growing in size by buying each other out. People are trickling away.

After 150 years of grazing by cattle, the grasses grow thicker on the hills than they did before cattle arrived, because the ranchers stop prairie fires from sweeping through. The Sand Hills are by far the biggest area dominated by native prairie grasses on the plains in the United States.

The sand blew in during and soon after the last Ice Age. As far as we can tell, it has been stable for several thousand years, with a few brief interruptions. The last widespread active dunes were probably about 900 years ago. Early-19th-century explorers reported finding active dunes, but it is unclear whether they saw an entire landscape of active sand or only bits here and there. Most fens and pastures have a layer of peat thick enough to show that those valleys were in place and fertile for thousands of years.

In the 1930s drought, much of the vegetation appeared to die, yet the hills stayed put. We can thank the prairie sod's massive tangles of roots, which would take several years to decompose. Some of the grass species maintain a bit of life in their roots even during multiyear droughts that apparently kill their aboveground parts; these roots spring back to life when rains return.

If some combination of climate change and inappropriate agriculture were truly to kill off the grasses, these dunes unleashed could do a lot of damage to America's breadbasket. Scientists are studying what it would take to unleash them. Feedback loops are hypothesized that could go in either direction: desertification or revegetation. It's difficult not to be impressed by the record of apparently rapid restabilization after past episodes of active blowing dunes. (That record isn't written, of course; it's inferred from evidence in the sands and peats.)

Some climate models predict that climate change itself may work in mysterious ways in Nebraska. A recent high-resolution run of a global circulation model concluded that global warming's strongest effect on Nebraska summers (not the other seasons) within the next 50 years may be to make them cloudier and therefore a little wetter and not significantly hotter.

WESTBOUND: Go to p. 284

Front Range, Dakota Hogback, and Denver Basin, Colorado

LOOK FOR a very thin, tawny ridge running along the plains/foothills boundary; once you're over the Front Range, look for areas of gentle, rolling topography near summit elevations.

Facing northwest ❶ Longs Peak; all the snowy peaks in the image are the Front Range, and the ones to the right of Longs are in Rocky Mountain National Park. ❷ North Table Mountain ❸ Dakota Hogback ❹ South Platte River ❺ downtown Denver

EASTBOUND: Go to p. 284

A great array of high mountains with broad foothills, the Front Range, can be seen from all flight paths entering, leaving, or overflying Denver. Below the foothills, the long, skinny, low ridge of the Dakota Hogback ❸ marks where the Rockies meet the Great Plains. The prize for peak spotters will be 14,255-foot Longs Peak ❶, located 50 miles northwest of downtown Denver in Rocky Mountain National Park. On its east side, facing the plains, Longs has the Diamond, a 2,000-foot gorgeously sheer vertical face beloved by big-wall climbers. The Colorado state quarter features Longs Peak. From a south window you will see Pikes Peak (next page).

The Rocky Mountains are a continent-scale system of many distinct mountain ranges, many mountain fronts, but only this one has Front Range as its proper name. In both Montana and Alberta, people use the term Rocky Mountain Front or speak of front ranges in a lower-case sense.

Look for expanses of gentle rolling topography along the crest of the mountain range. These subsummit flats are seen in many Colorado and Wyoming ranges and contrast with more consistently pointy mountaintops in Glacier National Park, the Wasatch Range, the North Cascades, or the Tetons. The highest paved mountain crossing in the United States cruises the subsummit flats for several miles north of Longs Peak.

The Rockies rose between 80 and 45 million years ago, then wore down considerably by 35 million years ago. One long-standing view of subsummit flats is as remnants of a low plain. More recently, geologists have identified processes that can produce flat surfaces high in the mountains, and propose various views on just how low the region was 35 million years ago. Most geologists accept that it has been rising for at least 8 million years, producing total uplift of thousands of feet.

The Front Range is the biggest of the Laramide thrust-fault blocks that created most of the U.S. Rockies. These faults go unusually deep—most of the way through the earth's crust, possibly into the mantle in some cases. "Basement rocks" crop out abundantly in these ranges. Sediments and sedimentary rocks around the earth are a thin veneer, like the paint on a house, with the house's exterior walls representing the earth's crust. Underneath the thin veneer lies the "basement" of dense crystalline rock, such as gneiss and granite, mostly over a billion years old. Laramide basement outcrops range between 1.1 billion and 1.8 billion years old.

The Dakota Hogback stretches, with a few gaps, nearly from Wyoming to New Mexico. At Fort Collins, 60 miles north of Denver, it has a twin hogback running in parallel. Throughout its long range, it remains the same thing: an upturned edge of erosion-resistant Dakota Group sandstone. This tawny layer, which underlies much of Colorado, is warped up and exposed as a hogback around the margins of the Laramide uplifts, where basement rocks rose on thrust faults and pushed the overlying sedimentary layers aside. Those layers right next to the uplift are tilted at varying angles. The softer sedimentary layers eroded away, forming strike valleys, while the resistant rocks became hogbacks. Dinosaur bones are common in the Dakota Group and the underlying Morrison Formation. One stretch of the Dakota Hogback, near Golden, Colorado, displays many dinosaur footprints and is called Dinosaur Ridge. The first Apatosaurus (AKA Brontosaurus) fossils were collected nearby in the 1870s.

Denver lies in the middle of the Cretaceous Denver Basin, an area that subsided by 10,000 feet starting around when the modern Rockies first rose. As it subsided, it filled with sediments from the rapidly eroding mountains. Organic material was buried and heated, leading to oil and natural gas deposits that are exploited today. From your window you can see many well pads and refineries.

Although Denver sits in a topographic basin a few hundred feet deep, residents like to think of it as a mile-high place, not a low place. They are right, of course. This small basin is at the center of an enormous domal uplift; the east-tilted Great Plains are just one flank of it. Vast, subtle upwarps like this are difficult to explain as a conventional plate tectonic effect. Although they have yet to establish a consensual name for either this particular one or the phenomenon in general, few geologists deny that it is real.

Pikes Peak and Environs, Colorado

LOOK FOR a broad, high mountain somewhat east of any others of comparable height, with a road to its summit and an open-pit mine to its southwest.

Pikes Peak stands front and center as you view the Colorado Rockies from the plains. Its prominence is striking from some flights, especially when snow differentiates it from lesser peaks, but it was all the more so in the days when transcontinental travel was low and slow: Pikes Peak appeared a day earlier than anything else, after weeks or months of vacant horizons. It offers a bigger view from the top than the other Rockies, if sheer acreage or humanity's impact are what you want to see. Both a highway and a cog railway offer access to that view, attesting to the mountain's gentle slopes. Colorado Springs ❷ and the U.S. Air Force Academy lie at its eastern foot, and Denver is just 63 miles to the north.

With the summit thus domesticated, Zebulon Pike, the lieutenant whose name it commemorates, is often ridiculed for writing, on the day he gave up trying to reach it: "No human being could have ascended to its pinical." The mockery is unfair. He didn't say that no one would ever climb it, only that no one could have done so under the circumstances he faced: "with the condition of my soldiers who had only light overalls on, and no stockings" at -4°F, in snow-covered terrain, in November 1806, with no food except what game they might hope to shoot and no sign of any such game since leaving distant river bottoms.

Old mine dumps from the 1890s Cripple Creek gold rush pock hills southwest of the mountain. Today, a large, active, open-pit gold mine ❹ there uses the cyanide heap leach method. Cripple Creek's gold deposits derive from volcanism that broke through the billion-year-old host rock about 32 million years ago, probably associated with the opening of the Rio Grande Rift.

Pikes Peak's prominence is hard to explain. In general, Colorado mountains rose too far from plate boundaries to be readily explained by plate tectonic theory, which developed first as an explanation of ocean plates. Geologists don't have a comparable breakthrough theory to explain ups and downs of the earth's crust in continental interiors. It appears that the Earth's mantle forces the crust up and down in places, but explaining why is little more than guesswork. It's very difficult to study the mantle, as it's too deeply buried to study directly; seismic recordings of earthquakes form the principal data.

Pikes Peak is part of the Front Range uplift, one of the longest of the great Laramide fault block uplifts that form most major ranges in Colorado and Wyoming. The northern half of this uplift remains a nearly continuous series of impressive peaks, many over 14,000 feet. The southern half of the uplift, with the grand exception of the Pikes Peak massif, is lower in elevation. Pikes Peak's pink granite, which makes up much of the southern half, dates to about 1.1 billion years old, younger than many of the widespread granites in the Rockies (but still not young, by a long stretch). A 26-mile-long block within the Pikes Peak granite has been rising on local faults over the past 20 million years or so, and that uplift raised Pikes Peak to prominence. It might be related to the Rio Grande Rift, and thence to plate tectonics, or it might be driven by mantle forces.

"Flatirons" of richly colored resistant sandstones crop out as the Garden of the Gods at the western edge of Colorado Springs. Parts of the same Fountain Formation reappear in Golden, just west of Denver, under the name Red Rocks, and again, much taller, in Boulder, where they are officially named the Flatirons. All three cities view their orange outcrops as unique objects of civic pride. Because they are older (or lower) than Dakota sandstones, Fountain sandstones lie between the Dakota Hogback and the mountains. (See previous page.)

Facing east-northeast. Pikes Peak, with Pikes Peak Highway switchbacks just below the summit, and continuing just below the ridge-top to the left ❶ High Plains ❷ Northern outskirts of Colorado Springs, CO ❸ Cripple Creek, CO ❹ Cresson Project gold mine ❺ Victor, CO

Climax at the Apex of Colorado

LOOK FOR a large open-pit mine and nearby tailings pond in a north-facing cirque by a high pass crossed by a railroad line.

The U.S. Rocky Mountains culminate in the Sawatch Range, which holds Colorado's three highest peaks ❻❼. Fifteen of its peaks are higher than 14,000 feet—more "fourteeners" than any entire state aside from Alaska. These gentle-sloped giants are the north end of the raised western flank of the Rio Grande Rift, and also may lie at the center of a vast domal uplift. (See page 182.)

The Elk Range ❷❸, immediately to the west, is steeper and more photogenic. Contiguous in part, the two ranges divide northwestward, opening a valley that nestles the fabled resort of Aspen ❹. The valley north of the Sawatches holds Vail, and Breckenridge lies over another pass along the freeway east of Vail. So look for ski trails everywhere, and look for signs of mining in the upper Arkansas River valley, between the Sawatch and Mosquito ❾ ranges.

Leadville ❽ (population 2,688, elevation 10,152 feet) is in that valley on a small mountain creek, the Arkansas River at its headwaters. Leadville distinguishes itself as the nation's highest county seat, and home of the National Mining Hall of Fame. This valley is the heart of Colorado mining, the crux of Colorado's history and economy. No other state has been a major player in all the main mining sectors: oil and gas, coal, hard-rock mining, and uranium.

The town began in 1859 as a gold rush town named Oro City. Within two years, more than 5,000 miners lived here, but the gold placers quickly played out. Miners departed, leaving Leadville a small hamlet. One who stayed was Alvinius B. Wood, trained in the science of metals and ores. Seeking the source of the placer gold in 1875, he found streams carrying the mineral cerussite, or lead carbonate, a relatively uncommon lead ore that miners called "horn silver." This particular cerussite is associated with silver. A second boom ensued. In 1893, when Leadville claimed 60,000 inhabitants, the United States changed its currency from the silver standard to the gold standard, precipitating the collapse of silver prices, the closure of mines, and the rapid depopulation of Leadville. A lesser gold boom followed the Silver Panic after new gold deposits were found east of town. Throughout its late-19th-century booms and busts, Leadville continued to produce the base metals lead and zinc. Most tailings piles and ponds around Leadville date from that period.

Railroadmen who hauled ores from Leadville gave the name Climax to the high point (11,318 feet) on Fremont Pass, at the head of the Arkansas River Valley. The Climax Mine ❶ fills about three miles of north-facing cirque just north of the pass.

Miners first identified a gray, veined ore at Climax as galena, or lead sulfide. Later, they identified it as graphite. Finally, an assay at the Colorado School of Mines identified it correctly as molybdenite, a sulfide of molybdenum, a metal of no known use. The claims languished until World War I, when the Germans used molybdenum in "Big Bertha," a cannon that fired shells into Paris from 100 miles away. The Climax Molybdenum Company formed and produced moly for use in alloys, toughening steel for wartime use as armor plating and shell casings. Today, 70 percent of world molybdenum production goes into steel alloys like chrome-moly, providing great hardness and corrosion resistance. The remainder goes into lubricants, orange pigments, and oil refining.

Over many of its 65 years, Climax accounted for at least half of world molybdenum production. Operations ceased in 1981, rendering Leadville a bust town once again, as the lead and zinc mines had shut down previously. The mine owners kept a skeleton crew in place, thinking to resume mining when molybdenum prices warranted it. In 2006, Phelps Dodge announced a plan to rebuild the mine to meet modern standards and to reopen it in 2009.

Mines around Leadville produce 3 percent lead-zinc ores and 0.3 percent molybdenum ores. The remaining 97 or 99.7 percent of the mined rock was traditionally disposed of as tailings piles in nearby valleys. Over most of the district's history, there was little or no concern for pollution, and there has been contamination on a mammoth scale.

Facing east (low-altitude small plane image)
❶ Climax Mine complex, with Tenmile Range

Facing west (Astronaut's very broad view of Colorado's apex)
❷ Capitol Peak, 14,130 ft., and Snowmass Mountain, 14,092 ft., Elk Range
❸ Maroon Peak, 14,156 ft., Elk Range
❹ Aspen, CO
❺ La Plata Peak, 14,336 ft., Sawatch Range
❻ Mt. Elbert, 14,433 ft. (highest in CO), Sawatch Range
❼ Mt. Massive, 14,421 ft. (second highest in CO), Sawatch Range
❽ Leadville, CO, just below snow-covered Turquoise Lake, at head of Arkansas River valley
❾ Mt. Lincoln, 14,286 ft., Mosquito Range
❿ South Park, headwaters valley of the South Platte River
(snow conditions of April 9, 2006)

Black Canyon of the Gunnison, Colorado

LOOK FOR a deep, crooked gash running all the way across a broad, gentle, domal upwarp.

Facing north ❶ Gunnison Uplift ❷ Black Canyon of the Gunnison (too deep for the river to show) ❸ igneous veins

Many deep canyons and many wide canyons crease the American West, but none can equal the Black Canyon of the Gunnison simply as a stunning crack in the ground, a narrow slot ❷ cutting through the middle of a plateau ❶. The canyon averages 2,000 feet deep and at the Narrows it is only 1,300 feet across.

From a plane, we are struck by the way the canyon cuts across a visible upwarp of the surface. It suggests the same idea that John Wesley Powell developed when he first rafted down the Grand Canyon: Since a river cannot possibly have flowed up onto the plateau in order to cut the canyon, the river must have been there first, on a flat plain, then kept cutting downward to keep pace as the plain warped upward to become a plateau. An excellent concept, the "antecedent stream" explains many canyons across uplifts in the West and held sway for decades as an explanation for both the Black Canyon and the Grand Canyon, but no longer.

Black Canyon's near-vertical dark gray walls are decorated with contrasting pale veins ❸ that may be visible if sunlit and if you are close. These are ancient Precambrian metamorphic and igneous rocks. Unlike many southwestern canyons, this one has layered rocks only up on top, a thin veneer of Jurassic and Cretaceous sedimentary rocks on the plateau that thicken toward the surrounding valleys. Patches of 28-million-year-old volcanic tuff overlie those sediments in places. The plateau is a Laramide uplift, but unlike the others, it retains no rocks deposited during the Paleozoic. The Laramide uplifts—a distinctive feature of the Rocky Mountains of Colorado, Wyoming, and parts of three neighboring states—raised very old basement rocks between 70 million and 45 million years ago. The basement of metamorphic and granitic rocks provides the cores of the major ranges of this region, though it took further uplift events much later to produce the landscapes we see today.

The rocks tell several interesting stories, of which cutting the Black Canyon is only the most recent. The dark gray metamorphic rocks record an ocean setting prior to their metamorphic alteration 1.7 billion years ago in a subduction zone. The pale igneous veins in the canyon walls date from that episode.

A thick interval of sediments overlies the metamorphic basement across much of the West—in the Grand Canyon, for example. Equivalent strata are missing on the Gunnison Uplift. They were likely eroded away during the uplift of the ancestral Rocky Mountains 300 million to 320 million years ago, concurrent with the Allegheny Orogeny in the Appalachians. The ancestral Rockies were a highland sufficient to fill adjoining basins (like Utah's Paradox Basin, page 53) with impressive quantities of sediment.

East of the Black Canyon, the Gunnison cuts a valley in volcanic rocks erupted from the San Juan and West Elk mountains about 28 million years ago. Volcanoes covered the landscape with lava and ash, shoving the stream drainages around to create a river system emptying westward into a large lake whose lake bed deposits include the Green River oil shales. Although the volcanic surface layer was ephemeral by geologic standards, it temporarily made the Gunnison Uplift a low area, a basin for a new main river channel, which eroded a valley in the volcanic layer. That confined it within its present course before it encountered the underlying sediments and metamorphic rocks.

The Gunnison River began cutting the Black Canyon about 2.5 million years ago when the river's base level dropped dramatically. Base level is the elevation of the basin where the river empties and thus the theoretical lowest elevation to which it can erode. The Gunnison flows into the Colorado today, but between 5 million and 2.5 million years ago, it flowed into a lake (a later one than the Green River Formation lake). The Colorado River captured this lake when one of its tributaries eroded headward into the lake basin, quickly emptying it. The Colorado's base level, which was sea level, became the Gunnison's base level, empowering the Gunnison to erode its present gorge.

The Gunnison Uplift slopes southwestward to the broad valley of the Uncompahgre River. The high San Juans to that river's south and the Uncompahgre Plateau to its west are, respectively, younger and much older than the Laramide uplifts and form a transition between the Rockies and the Colorado Plateau.

San Juan Mountains, Colorado

LOOK FOR a broad area of high mountains, 40 to 60 miles across in any direction, broken only by narrow, diversely oriented valleys.

Facing north-northwest ❶ Telluride, CO ❷ Ouray, CO ❸ upper Animas River valley ❹ Elk Range ❺ Continental Divide
❻ U.S. Hwy. 550 ❼ Animas River canyon ❽ Silverton, CO ❾ headwaters of the Rio Grande ❿ Vallecito Creek
A Mt. Sneffels, 14,150 ft. **B** Wetterhorn Pk., 14,015 ft. **C** Uncompahgre Pk., 14,309 ft. **D** Handies Pk., 14,048 ft.
E Vestal Pk., 13,864 ft. **F** Storm King Pk., 13,752 ft. **G** Pigeon Pk., 13,792 ft. **H** Turret Pk., 13,835 ft. **I** Animas Mtn., 13,786 ft.
J Sunlight Pk., 14,059 ft. **K** Windom Pk., 14,082 ft. **L** Jagged Mtn., 13,824 ft. **M** Mt. Eolus, 14,083 ft. **N** Jupiter Mtn., 13,840 ft.

The San Juans are unusual among Colorado mountain ranges: they are not a Laramide fault block and do not look at all linear from the air. Recreationists find more solitude, remoteness, and challenging peaks here than elsewhere in the Colorado Rockies. Thirteen of the state's 54 peaks exceeding 14,000 feet are here. Six of those peaks are outside the frame of the photo, giving some idea of the San Juans' extent. The ski resort town of Telluride (inset photo and ❶) is also famously off the beaten track.

The San Juans comprise several volcanic centers active from perhaps 40 million to 5 million years ago. In the latter part of that span, enormous ash flows erupted from 18 caldera centers. When it was all done, a volcanic plateau covered most of the southern Rocky Mountains. The 18 calderas in the area required careful field mapping, as erosion has obscured their original outlines. The caldera-forming eruptions were on a scale far exceeding any volcanism within the tiny geologic snapshot we call historic time. The La Garita caldera in the eastern San Juans is the largest "supervolcano" yet identified in the geologic record.

Not one of today's peaks is a volcano. These are erosional mountains; some of them are eroded in volcanic material. Some of the steepest peaks are granitic and metamorphic rocks exposed by deep glacial erosion. Mt. Sneffels **A** and Mt. Eolus **M** are granitic intrusions; the Grenadier Range **E** is quartzite and slate with foliations steeply tilted; and the Needle Mountains (**G** through **K**, in the foreground) are an outcrop of Precambrian gneiss about 1.7 billion years old, likely representing the southwestern edge of the North American precursor continent at that time.

The volcanoes formed a swath from the San Juans northeast to the Front Range near Denver. Gold, silver, copper, zinc, and lead were emplaced together with rising magma along this line, the Colorado Mineral Belt. Mining is largely played out now within the belt. The notorious Summitville gold mine in the eastern San Juans declared bankruptcy and ceased maintaining its cyanide heap leach pond after the pond leaked, sterilizing 17 miles of the Alamosa River in 1990. More than $100 million have been spent on it as a Superfund site, yet it still releases heavy metals and acid mine drainage.

The Animas River canyon ❼ has a narrow-gauge railroad built in 1881 to serve the mines around Silverton ❽. Several movies featured action on its cliffside rails. Converted for tourism in 1948, the train has grown to operate year-round, running four different trains pulled by 1920s-vintage coal-fired steam engines. The modern highway stays out of the canyon, reaching Silverton by crossing plateaus west of the river ❻. Its continuation to Ouray ❷, originally blazed as a toll road and an unfinished rail line for miners, was nicknamed the Million Dollar Highway after low-grade gold ore was spotted in the roadbed.

The photo looks north-northwest from a path taken by many flights between the Bay Area and the Southeast. Flying on Corridor 1, you are more likely to see the San Juans' north side: the town of Ouray nestled at the foot of a mountain front featuring broad Uncompahgre Peak and dramatic Mt. Sneffels. The latter ought to be "Snaefell" ("snow mountain") after either of two real mountains, salient points on Iceland and the Isle of Man. It caught nomenclatural sniffles from a Jules Verne character who says "Sneffels" for a fictional Snaefell offering a route to the center of the earth. A pathetic tag for a noble peak.

Facing north: ski trails above Telluride

Canyonlands National Park and Upheaval Dome, Utah

LOOK FOR a Y-shaped confluence of two winding rivers in red-canyon country; a concentric double-ring crater between the two rivers.

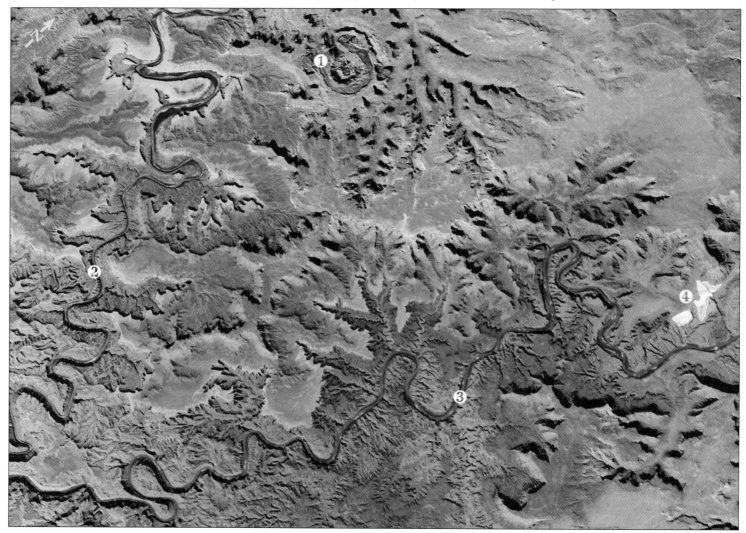

❶ Upheaval Dome ❷ Green River ❸ Colorado River ❹ potash mines. Broad astronaut view about 24 mi. wide

Canyonlands National Park lies where the Green and Colorado ("red") rivers meet ❷❸. As spectacular eroded red-rock semidesert surrounds it in all directions, you won't be able to pick out any particular area as national park–level scenery.

The canyons are only modestly deep by Colorado Plateau standards. Cataract Canyon, the 14-mile run of whitewater below the confluence, is a mecca for adrenaline addicts. Boulders tumbling from the canyon walls and debris flows coming down side canyons created rapids here. Both rivers are placid above the confluence, and the Colorado was placid for 100 miles downstream even before Lake Powell drowned it. Rivers undergo periods of both deposition and erosion. During an earlier period of erosion, the Colorado carved a deep gorge: at one point in Cataract Canyon, the bedrock lies 260 feet below the present river surface. Then the river deposited, or at least failed to remove, 250 feet of debris and sediment.

The sedimentary rock formations seen here continue across much of red-rock Utah and Arizona. Up close, the formations display great variety. Some are solidified sand dunes, some are stream deposits, and some are shallow sea deposits. Although rusty reds predominate, the palette ranges to green. Look for Canyonlands cliffs rimmed with white sandstones that lack iron oxides.

White sandstones accent the center of a concentric double-ring "crater" about three miles in diameter, called Upheaval Dome ❶. How can it be both a dome and a crater? Some force deformed the generally horizontal rock strata into an abrupt dome here, and then stream erosion (flowing out through the one broken side) removed the softer rock to leave the crater rims.

Terrestrial and extraterrestrial hypotheses to account for the dome have competed since the 1930s, and the controversy flourishes unabated today. The extraterrestrial theory starts with a meteor impact long ago. Upheaval Dome is not a meteor crater; the theory views it as the structure deep in the earth beneath a meteor crater, revealed after millions of years of erosion removed the overlying rock. After the impact blasted a circular mass of earth into the sky to form a crater, the earth below the hole domed up in a gravitational adjustment. Such isostatic adjustments are well established in geology, and this subcrater version of it is supported by studies of small splashes made by heavy objects dropping into a fluid. There are no meteorite particles here (they could have all been carried off by erosion) and many other features seen in other impact sites are lacking.

The terrestrial theory involves salt. A vast salt deposit underlies the region, and it is well known that salt deposits can flow. They're not as zippy as a glacier, but they could outrun a tectonic plate. Salts are less dense than most other rocks and consequently may rise isostatically, pushing rock strata above them into domes. However, seismic reflection data show no salt dome under Upheaval Dome. Since salt can rise forcefully enough to rupture and pass through overlying strata, a refined hypothesis calls Upheaval Dome the "pinched-off tail" under a salt body that, like the crater in the extraterrestrial theory, was removed by erosion. The rising salt blob could have left the strata upturned around the hole it passed through. Canyonlands has several salt domes, but no other pinched-off tails have been identified. Impact proponents argue that those other domes show what a salt dome looks like around here.

In any case, salt flow certainly shaped this landscape. Buried salt deposits exceed 5,000 feet thick east of the park. Movement along faults in and near the park apparently deflected the salt upward, creating domes and drawing salt from the east. When salt rising along a fault line reached groundwater, it dissolved and was carried off, leaving a linear cavity that overlying rocks collapsed into, creating a straight salt valley. Several local salt valleys have rivers crossing them rather than running downvalley; one such oddity inspired the name Paradox Valley and thence Paradox Formation for this geologic unit. Slippery salt layers are also blamed for the mobility of canyon wall blocks, the cause of Cataract Canyon's cataracts.

Paradox salt is about 85 percent halite (common salt) along with some gypsum and potash salts. Potash is mined ❹ just east of the park. The Paradox Basin also holds oil fields. Uranium ores (geologically unrelated) were economically important here for a few decades, leaving a tailings pile Superfund site just north of Moab.

Waterpocket Fold, Utah

LOOK FOR a landscape of parallel bands of cliffs, hogbacks, mesas, and zones of rugged badland, all in contrasting cream and red colors.

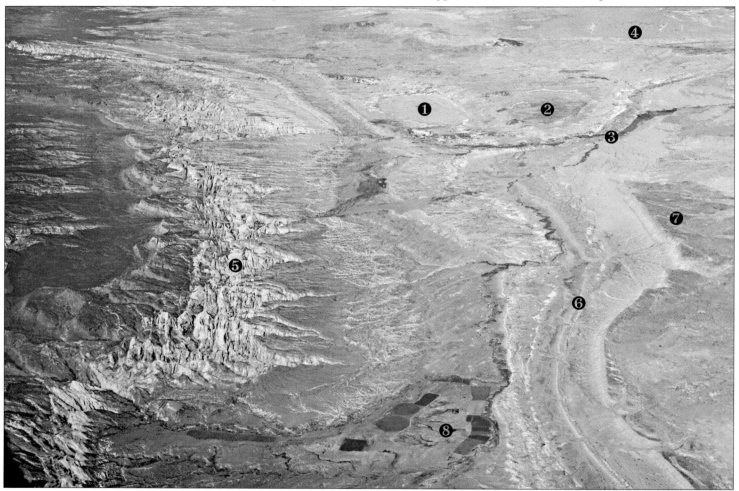

Facing north ❶ Blue Flats ❷ Red Desert ❸ Caineville, UT, and Fremont River. UT Rte. 24 crosses Capitol Reef National Park from the left, within the pale canyon, then continues east down the Fremont. ❹ Caineville badlands ❺ Navajo Sandstone ❻ hogback ❼ South Caineville Mesa ❽ Sandy Ranch, one of the remotest ranches you'll ever see; two center pivot irrigation circles

This 100-mile Utah ridge may be the closest thing to a geological fireworks display that air passengers will see in the United States until one of the Cascade volcanoes surprises us again. If you fly east at this latitude, the ridge offers a dazzling introduction to red rock.

The fold is a monocline covering a Laramide thrust fault. Imagine a block rising on a fault while covered with a dozen thick blankets; the blankets would fold into a softened step shape. On the Waterpocket Fold, more than a dozen sedimentary formations are the blankets covering a Laramide subsurface fault. As it stripped most of these layers from the raised plateau, erosion left an upturned edge of each rock unit exposed on the steep eastern flank of the monocline, from the oldest on the west to the youngest on the east. (Some geologists prefer to call this monocline an anticline, as the strata that turn upward here slope downward again far to the west, very gently.)

The right-hand 40 percent of the area shown is underlain by the youngest formation, the Mancos Group, deposited in shallow Cretaceous seas. The S-curved buff cliffs and skinny hogbacks ❻ paralleling them are erosion-resistant sandstones; the bluish gray flats are crumbly shales, which continue northeastward as heavily gullied, nearly barren badlands ❹. Plants have a difficult time growing in dry southern Utah, and high selenium content in Mancos shales commonly makes it even more difficult.

Strata near the center of the photo include the late Jurassic Morrison Formation, famous for dinosaur fossils. The prominent jagged cream-colored band ❺ is the Navajo Sandstone and other Jurassic sandstones. Darker red Kayenta and Wingate sandstones crop out west of the Navajo. Desert-varnished Wingate Sandstone cliffs also crop out in the Escalante and Glen canyons, where they are well-known calendar photo subjects. The dark green pine forest on the left edge shows that the ridge is high enough to increase precipitation and reduce evaporation rates.

The red and orange pigments are iron oxides. The Navajo Sandstone was laid down as windblown sand dunes. Geologists extrapolate that these broad and deep dunes were an active "erg," a dune field on the scale of the Sahara's. The principal mineral in these sands, quartz grains, originally eroded from somewhere in the Appalachian Mountain system. West-flowing rivers carried the sands across the United States 190 million years ago.

At the Waterpocket, Navajo Sandstones erode into steep domes that seem to reflect their original dune shapes. One of the most perfect of these was named Capitol Dome, and then the whole fold was named Capitol Reef, in a vernacular usage of "reef" to mean a long cliff. When the area became a national monument in 1937, the name Capitol Reef won out over "Wayne Wonderland," a name heavily promoted by Wayne County residents. Geologists, reserving the term "reef" for formations that originated as ocean reefs, prefer the older name. "Waterpockets" are small basins eroded in the sandstone, holding water after thunderstorms or, in a few cases, year-round. Waterpockets figured heavily in early accounts, since desert explorers needed to know where to find water.

Capitol Reef National Monument was graced for its first two decades with a single volunteer custodian. He was eventually promoted to paid superintendent, but still given no staff. The acreage was sextupled in 1969 and promoted to a national park in 1971.

The Waterpocket Fold is the longest of many long folds on the Colorado Plateau. The Henry Mountains just east of here, and other ranges farther east, are "laccoliths" raised by magma that rose into sedimentary strata, bulging some of the uppermost layers upward without piercing them. Later erosion exposes part of the intrusion in some laccoliths. Mountains west of Waterpocket Fold are the easternmost Basin and Range mountains, part of a line of normal-fault-block ranges bisecting the length of Utah. Volcanic rocks overlie them in places.

If the cliffs and hogbacks ❻ and ❼ faced a mirror-image set of cliffs across a valley, they would represent an anticline—an arch, or raised fold—that perversely became a valley thanks to differential erosion. Anticline valleys are common. Equally paradoxical is the appearance that water erosion is especially potent in the desert. The bulk of water erosion occurs not during normal rainfall but during rare floods, including flash floods on small streams. The Southwest has plenty of those, and the lack of plant cover also leaves it highly vulnerable to erosion.

Lake Powell, Utah

LOOK FOR a long reservoir with intricate side canyons in brilliant red-rock country; pay attention to the width of pale—or green—margins around the lakeshore.

Facing southwest ❶ Navajo Canyon and Tower Butte ❷ The Narrows, the downstream continuation of the lake leading to Glen Canyon Dam and Page, AZ ❸ Boundary and Dominguez buttes ❹ Padre Bay, the largest single expanse of open water in Lake Powell ❺ Gooseneck Point ❻ Last Chance Bay ❼ upstream continuation of Lake Powell ❽ Billie Flat Top ❾ Rock Creek Bay

Lake Powell is the most spectacular and largest reservoir in the Southwest, or at least it was designed to be. The lake was 97 percent full as recently as September 1997 but has been shrinking since then. The Colorado River hasn't been delivering the volume of water allotted to downstream users, who have priority over a full lake. If you fly over it repeatedly over the years, keep track of how big it looks or how wide its banks look.

The colorful Navajo Sandstone surrounding the lake was deposited 175 million years ago as sand dunes, part of a sand sea the size of several western states. Its rusty color lies in a thin coating of iron oxide that helps to cement the sand grains together.

Lake Powell began to fill in 1963 with the completion of Glen Canyon Dam, whose primary purpose is to even out big year-to-year fluctuations in water supply: Water stored in Lake Powell is released during dry years so that Colorado and Utah need not resort to extreme conservation measures in order to deliver 7.5 million acre-feet to Arizona, Nevada, and California. The 1922 Colorado River Compact allocates 7.5 million acre-feet every year to the states above Glen Canyon and 7.5 million acre-feet to those below. After several dry years when there was zero water left for Mexico, additional acre-feet were allotted to Mexico.

Prior to 1922, the river flowed over 16 million acre-feet annually, so allocation of 15 million acre-feet seemed reasonable. We're now learning that the whole century before 1990 was anomalously wet in the Southwest. Tree-ring studies suggest that over the past 400 years, the river averaged more like 13.5 million acre-feet. Ancient pollen deposits show that the Southwest has had long wet/dry cycles ever since the end of the last Ice Age. In short, prehistory offers scant assurance that the current drought will be reversed in our lifetimes or that we can count on 15 million acre-foot flows on the Colorado River.

Lake Powell exacerbates the shortage as much as it alleviates it. Almost a million acre-feet of water vanish from Lake Powell every year through a combination of evaporation and infiltration into the permeable sandstone.

After the dam cut off the river's flood cycles, beaches and sandbars in the Grand Canyon, downstream from Lake Powell, began to disappear. They normally tend to wash away while the river is at low to average levels and then to be replenished during floods. But the discomfort and scenic loss their disappearance inflicts on whitewater customers are nothing compared to what it does to full-time residents of the river and its banks. The river's ecology within Grand Canyon National Park has been severely altered.

Only trivial volumes of water are taken out of Lake Powell for use nearby. Electricity generation is an incidental purpose of the dam. For comparison, the newer coal-fired plant, next to the dam in Page, Arizona, generates twice as much electricity. During the present drought, electricity generation at Glen Canyon Dam is 25 percent below the dam's design output.

Considering water issues, ecological effects, and power generation and looking at the downward trend, Glen Canyon Dam may already be near the end of its economically defensible life. At some point, any reservoir will fill with sand and silt—stuff the river would carry out to sea if it had no dams. This inevitable event may take 20 years or 500, but well before that point, it would fail to generate electricity or to store worthwhile amounts of water. The lake's future owners can't simply wait for it to turn into a mud plateau and then walk away.

Beautiful as Lake Powell is, the flowing river and canyon were more so. It was a stretch of the Colorado unique in its gentle current: Novice rafters could float serenely. If roads had reached it before dam builders did, Glen Canyon might have become just as popular for float trips as it is today, in drowned form, for powered cruising. Glen Canyon Dam is the one that Edward Abbey's fictional Monkey Wrench Gang wanted to blow up. Today, real-life enviros campaign merely to have the lake drained, the dam left in place as a sad relic.

As lake levels recede, they expose not the old Glen Canyon but its mud-coated evil twin. So far, this seems not as bad as many had feared. The mud retains moisture, supporting more plant and animal life than ever. From the air, you may spot green fringes on the lakeshore. Even up close, vegetation may camouflage the soiled banks during the transition until the mud washes away again. Flash floods on mud-lined tributaries have shown that they can remove a 40-year accumulation in just a few years.

The Grand Canyon, Arizona

LOOK FOR the canyon, of course, as well as the orientation of its side canyons and the slopes and colors of its walls.

Facing north-northeast ❶ Kaibab Limestone ❷ Redwall Limestone ❸ Great Unconformity separating billion-year-old metamorphic rocks from overlying 550-year-old sediments ❹ Colorado River and the inner canyon, here called Lower Granite Gorge ❺ Separation Canyon, an eroded fault line bearing a north- and a south-flowing creek on opposite sides of the Colorado. The entire image shows the western Grand Canyon, to the west of the canyon's best-known sites. Foreground is Hualapai Indian Reservation, background is national forest, and middle ground, from the river roughly to the canyon rim, is in Grand Canyon National Park.

It's hard to miss: a canyon 1 mile deep, more than 200 miles long, and up to 18 miles across, with walls of reddish rocks in contrast to the grays and greens of the surrounding plateau country. Its side canyons would be state parks in many of the United States; the isolated buttes would be tourist attractions. Here, these lesser features can be lost to the scale of the Grand Canyon.

The Grand Canyon begins where the Little Colorado River (in a narrower deep canyon east of the main canyon) joins the Colorado River. Above (and north of) this junction, the Colorado flows south within Marble Canyon. The Grand Canyon ends at the Grand Wash, a fault-related cliff east of Lake Mead.

Faults cross the canyon, many of them marked by side canyons from either north or south. If you see a straight tributary stream in its own canyon ❺ trending either northwest or northeast, it is almost certainly on a fault. The northeast-trending Bright Angel fault is the most prominent.

If we can move past our sense of awe, there are many smaller features to observe. The Kaibab Limestone forms the uppermost cliff at the top of the canyon ❶ and underlies the surrounding tree-covered Kaibab Plateau. A slope leads down to the next cliff, the light gray Coconino Sandstone. Below, another slope leads to the wide bench of the Esplanade, supported by the underlying Supai Group sandstones. The Redwall Limestone, which is often light gray rather than red, forms the prominent cliff face about halfway down ❷. Below more slopes, the bright cliffs of Tapeats Sandstone stand just above the narrow inner gorge holding the Colorado, which may appear as no more than a thin strand ❹.

The inner gorge itself is eroded in Precambrian granitic and metamorphic rocks 1,750 million to 800 million years old. Everything above it is Paleozoic, 245 million to 544 million years old. The Paleozoic ages contain a gap, or unconformity, of 100 million years unrepresented by any rocks present today. Those 100 million years are dwarfed by the "Great Unconformity" at the top of the Inner Gorge, where more than 250 million years are missing. You won't see the "small" unconformity, but you will, perhaps unknowingly, see the Great Unconformity ❸.

The youngest rocks within the canyon occur in the west. Look on the north side for dark gray basalts extending from the rim to the river. If you trace the dark gray lava flow outcrop from the river to the plateau, you will see cinder cones and lavas of the 600-square-mile Uinkaret volcanic field. Most of the flows are less than 1.2 million years old, the last erupting around AD 1200. At least 150 lava flows descended to the canyon floor, damming the Colorado to form a lake at least thirteen times. Eventually, the river overtopped each lava dam, creating waterfalls up to 2,000 feet high. The largest lakes reached Utah, dwarfing today's Lake Powell.

John Wesley Powell led the first scientific expedition through the canyon in 1869, and formulated the first of many explanations for its origin. Current hypotheses are based on a well established big picture that Powell could not have foreseen: Colorado Plateau uplift followed by Basin and Range collapse on the plateau's western border. From near sea level 65 million years ago, the Colorado Plateau attained some, if not all, of its present elevation during the Laramide Orogeny. At that time it included much of the present southern Basin and Range Province. Its western margin collapsed as the Basin and Range opened about 9 million years ago.

These topographic changes inevitably caused sweeping changes in the courses taken by rivers. Between 12 million and 5.5 million years ago, the upper Colorado River drainage emptied into a huge lake east of today's canyon, but there was no canyon to drain the lake west to the Grand Wash area. The water apparently did drain from the lake to the Grand Wash, but its course is speculative.

Remarkably, this grand cross-section of almost 2 billion years of geologic time is only a few million years old. Most likely, as the Gulf of California opened in late Miocene time, a lower Colorado River flowing into the gulf advanced northward by headward erosion. Eventually, a Kaibab Plateau tributary of this river captured the upper Colorado to begin draining the ancient lake. The newly enlarged Colorado River then began carving the Grand Canyon 6 million years ago, well before the Uinkaret lavas first erupted and flowed into the canyon 1.2 million years ago.

Today, the Colorado continues to erode its channel but gently, without the powerful floods that sometimes descended the river before Glen Canyon Dam was built.

Hoover Dam and Lake Mead

LOOK FOR a tall south-facing dam wedged in a narrow canyon; a small-town street grid with vestiges of buildings on the reservoir's west bank near its north end.

Facing northeast ❶ Sentinel Island in Lake Mead ❷ Fortification Hill, in Arizona ❸ Paint Pots ❹ Painters Cove ❺ Hemenway Wall, in California ❻ Hoover Dam ❼ Colorado River in Black Canyon

When Hoover Dam was built, no other dam came close in size. To this day, it remains the archetype of a high dam, as the Golden Gate is an archetype of suspension bridges. Awe for its beauty and size inspired at least two generations of dam builders. Excavation began in 1931, and construction was finished in 1936—stunningly fast, considering the leap in ambition and technique that it required. The Depression had hit hard, and it was easy to find men willing to work for four dollars a day in 110-degree heat on the deadliest construction project in U.S. history. Men at the top fared much better: Warren Bechtel and Henry Kaiser joined the project as small local construction bosses, emerging five years later as captains of industry.

Getting the dam built was a priority of President Herbert Hoover, both before and during his administration. The Democrats took over in 1933 and promptly changed the dam's name from Hoover to Boulder. The original name was restored in 1947.

It was the first structure to exceed the Pyramid of Cheops in total volume of masonry. Once the world's tallest dam, it now ranks 18th. Once the world's most powerful electricity-generation facility, it relinquished that title, as well as "most massive," to Grand Coulee Dam just a few years later.

Its reservoir, Lake Mead, remains the largest artificial lake in the United States when it's full, but from 2003 through 2007 it stayed at least 75 feet drawn down. At 100 feet below full pool, it yields about 65 percent of the surface area you see on a map. The biggest exposed lakebed area is at its north end, above the confluence of the Muddy and Virgin rivers. Just northwest of the confluence, 500 residents evacuated the town of St. Thomas before rising lake water flooded it in 1938. At 54 percent full in 2007, the lake exposes the old St. Thomas street grid, a sort of wet ghost town. You may spot it on flights between Las Vegas and Colorado.

The lake's changing shape demands other relocations from time to time, such as towing entire marinas full of boats to new locations.

Whether the lake level will rise or fall in the future is a perennial topic of conversation in the area. The answer hangs on both natural and political forces. Nature's cycles of drought across the Southwest are poorly understood. We can be almost certain, though, that the overall supply will be lower than what the politicians expected when they originally allocated water among the seven states that share the Colorado Basin with Mexico. When the states renegotiated the allotments in 2006, the three states below Glen Canyon Dam agreed to take less water during dry years in return for more during wet years. The object was to reduce drawdowns of both Lake Mead and Lake Powell. But Lake Mead lost the priority it enjoyed over Lake Powell, so it's difficult to say how much improvement Lake Mead will see.

Las Vegas, the fastest-growing U.S. metro area, gets its water from Lake Mead. Between its golf courses, its casino waterworks, and its dry air, Las Vegas probably evaporates more water per resident than any other major city. It is already taking close to its full allotment from the Colorado. Nevada holds water rights to 105,000 acre-feet per year from the Virgin River, but only if Nevada draws the water from the Virgin; upon reaching Lake Mead, it becomes shared Colorado River water. An impoundment and pipeline to divert it first would cost a billion dollars, as opposed to no cost for letting gravity take it to Lake Mead, where the existing waterworks can pump it out. Las Vegas took its threat to build the billion-dollar pipe to the negotiating table for the 2006 Colorado River Compact.

Las Vegas Wash enters Lake Mead at its northwest corner, where Las Vegas now sprawls down to the shore. It used to be a dry wash except during occasional rainstorms. Its fairly steady flow today comes largely from the Las Vegas sewage treatment plants. This water was pumped up from Lake Mead, to which it is now returning as treated sewage plant effluent. The water, after chlorination, is certified sterile enough to drink.

Mojave Desert, California

LOOK FOR a cluster of black blobs with small reddish peaks and lava flows like west-tapering tails; sand dunes.

Inland southern California holds the hottest and most desolate-looking broad desert and near-desert area in the country, the Mojave (mo-HAH-veh). In between the freeways, only a few forms of human endeavor make inroads: mining, military exercises, ranching to a lesser degree, and, more recently, off-road vehicle recreation. The land is extremely slow to recover from any of these uses. Tank tracks made in 1942 and in 1965 look equally fresh.

As seen from the air, vegetation ranges from stippled to absent. Drought-tolerant shrubs such as creosote bush and bur-sage provide the remarkably even stippling. (Certain creosote bushes are in the running for "world's oldest living thing"; the winner depends on what rules you set.) A bush that covers a 3-foot diameter might require all the moisture available within a 15-foot-diameter circle, so bushes that size would all be about 15 feet apart. During a wetter-than-average winter (winter being the wet season, such as it is), seeds lying dormant spring into action, blooming into a short-lived sward of annual plants in between the shrubs. Those annuals are about all that the Mojave Desert has to offer sheep or cattle. Areas with no visible plant life include basalt flows, white-crusted lake beds, sand dunes, and the Devils Playground **❺**.

More than 50 small volcanic centers punctuate the Mojave. The Cima volcanic field **❷** holds a dozen small cinder cones with tongue-like basalt lava flows. Cima eruptions changed in chemical composition over the past 7 million years. The younger ones resemble Hawaiian lava: They absorbed little material from the earth's crust as they rose out of the mantle. Older ones are typical of continental basalts. The change is evidence of the Basin and Range crust stretching and thinning over time, since very thin crust would allow rising magma to pass through quickly, with little alteration.

Rock material eroding from the mountains moves into the valleys during storms or the rare earthquake and then stays put for want of sufficient streamflow to carry it farther. Much of the scant rain that does fall here runs quickly off of the mountains and then sinks just as quickly into the coarse valley fill material, where it

charges underlying aquifers. Without vegetation to suck it up or soil to hold it at the surface, not much is lost to evaporation. As a result, some water is available to those optimistic enough to drill for it and pump it; you will see the occasional cluster of center pivot irrigation circles. Some appear abandoned.

The lowest, flattest part of the desert was a large lake for several thousand years during at least two Ice Ages. Just a small remnant of this Lake Mojave, called Soda Lake and displaying a whitish soda crust **❹**, becomes a lake briefly during the wettest winters. The evaporite crusts of different eastern California dry lakes consist of several minerals, most of them useful enough to warrant mining. Borax was the most valuable for many decades in the late 19th to early 20th centuries, when "20-mule teams" hauled it to market. Trona is another mined evaporite, as are common salt and calcium chloride, the products of the Cadiz Lake evaporator ponds 70 miles south of Cima. (Photo on page 189.)

Gold and silver were also mined in the Mojave. A cyanide heap leach gold mine was active in the 1990s, when environmentalists campaigned to create a Mojave National Park. Although the military raised little objection to a park, the mining, ranching, and off-road vehicle interests opposed it effectively. Compromise produced the Mojave National Preserve, a new breed of national park–like chimera. The preserve contains two national natural landmarks, historic preservation areas (ghost towns and abandoned mines), several mines and claims (but no new claims will be accepted), cattle-grazing allotments (to be retired if and when owners sell willingly), a lot of designated wilderness, a grand train station in the middle of nowhere, and a place named Zzyzx (rhymes with Isaac's). The latter has a long history, first with the Indians, later a stagecoach stop and railway stop named Soda Springs, then renamed Zzyzx—"the last word"—as a Christian health spa built by Curtis Howe "Doc" Springer, a health scam artist. Now it is the California State University Desert Studies Center, run by the state university system **❸**. The freeway exit sign still reads Zzyzx.

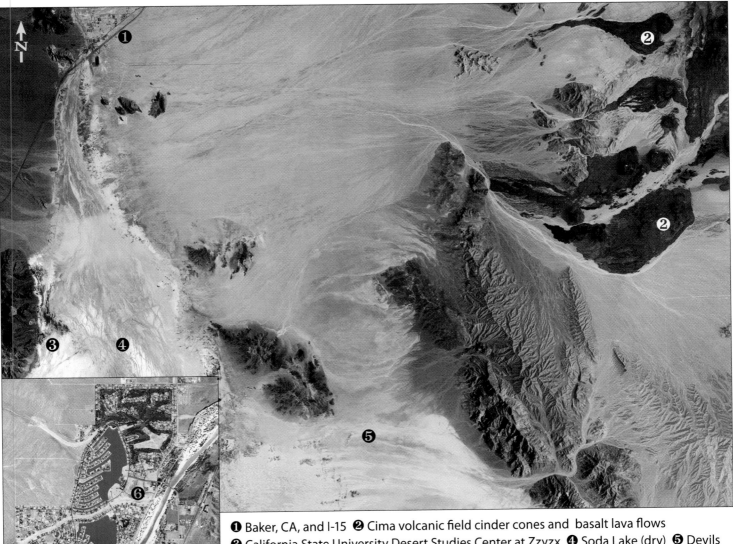

❶ Baker, CA, and I-15 ❷ Cima volcanic field cinder cones and basalt lava flows
❸ California State University Desert Studies Center at Zzyzx ❹ Soda Lake (dry) ❺ Devils
Playground ❻ new community of Silver Lakes, at Helendale, a few minutes southwest of
area above (see discussion on p. 188)

Wind Farms at San Gorgonio Pass, California

LOOK FOR rows or grids of slender white towers and turbine blades. Turbines may require binoculars to see them well from cruising altitude, but these are usually overflown during descent or ascent.

Wind farms line both sides of Interstate 10 between San Bernardino and Palm Springs. This cluster and Tehachapi Pass are the most productive wind resource areas in the United States. However, Texas has overtaken California as the state with the most wind megawatt capacity. Topography determines the best places for wind power, either by funneling prevailing westerlies through an east-west valley or by making them rise over a long north-south ridge. San Gorgonio Pass does both: A long east-west valley rises gradually from Los Angeles to 2,600 feet here, with mountains closing in on both sides. (Granted, in parts of the Great Plains, lack of topography seems to do the trick equally well.)

The largest turbines currently on land use 150-foot blades on 300-foot towers; such blades sweep a circle larger than a football field. The turbines are rated at 1.5 or 1.8 megawatts—enough to power 430 to 515 average American households if running at full capacity day in and day out. In reality, fluctuating wind speeds reduce output to a small percentage of capacity. At 29 percent, San Gorgonio's output is among the highest: a 1.5-megawatt turbine at San Gorgonio can power 125 average households. Efficiency increases with size, so turbines trend ever larger as engineering hurdles are overcome. Offshore turbines can be larger because boats can bring and set up bigger pieces than trucks can. Current designs limit offshore farms to water depths of 100 feet or less. We're unlikely to see farms off the West Coast, which drops off too steeply, but there are many promising sites off the Atlantic Coast.

If you see spinning rotors alternating with still ones, it may be because the power grid can't use the full output right now or because winds are high. Every second turbine may be set to shut down automatically during high winds, when spinning turbines affect each other's airflow, potentially inflicting stress damage. Controls shut a turbine off by "feathering" its blades into an ineffective position, leaving them free to rotate idly in either direction.

Wind energy's environmentally benign reputation is besmirched by reports of wind farms littered with carcasses of birds struck by rotors. The worst case is Altamont Pass, California, the first large wind farm complex built in the United States. It kills more than a thousand birds of prey per year because it was sited in an area that is both excellent raptor habitat and a migration corridor, and its 5,600 turbines are (by current standards) small, numerous, fast-spinning, and low. It seems that spinning blades become a blur to birds at much lower speeds than they do to humans. For certain slow-reproducing species, a hundred deaths a year can be a threat, at least locally. Nevertheless, golden eagle populations around Altamont seem to be holding steady, and they are the worst known case. West Virginia ridge crests, a newer focus of controversy because of their importance to migrating songbirds, may prove unsuited to turbines.

Overall, the number of birds killed by rotors is infinitesimal in comparison to the big-time bird killers: pesticides, TV broadcast towers, power lines, oil spills, cars, plate glass windows, and house cats. We are not joking. One Wisconsin TV tower probably killed 30,000 birds in one bad night, more than most large wind farms will kill in 30 years. Bird safety should be a concern in designing and siting wind farms, but it is no excuse for not building any. Design improvements include tubular towers that birds can't perch on; buried power lines; ultraviolet-reflective paint on the blades for better avian visibility; and bigger rotors moving at slower speeds. Most of these improvements are already the norm.

To some people, wind turbines are eyesores. Others find them beautiful. We look forward to seeing this aesthetic controversy play out. We wonder whether the local opposition to wind farms is considering the alternatives—such things as the Grand Canyon browned out by smog, the Appalachians cloaked in dead fir trees, mountains with their tops removed, salmon disappearing, vast mudflats on the sites of former scenic reservoirs, millions of asthma sufferers, premature human deaths. Or, we could try living without electricity. Our guess is that people will learn to love the sight of wind turbines.

Facing south ❶ foot of San Jacinto Mountains ❷ rows of wind power turbines in the San Gorgonio Pass wind resource area, just east of Cabazon, CA ❸ I-10

A Dozen of the Largest U.S. Wind Farm Areas

Tehachapi Pass, CA. By the freeway crossing the range of mountains dividing the Central Valley from the Mojave Desert. Under southerly variant paths from SF to PHX, DFW, and the East.

San Gorgonio Pass, CA.

Altamont Pass, CA. By I-580 in coastal hills. Flights east of SFO, OAK.

Solano County, CA. On low hills just north of the broad Sacramento River estuary. Flights east or north of SFO, OAK.

Stateline, OR/WA. Twelve miles east of a huge bend in the Columbia River. SEA-DEN, PDX-MSP, PDX-CH.

Maple Ridge, NY. 25 miles east of the east end of Lake Ontario. MSP-BOS.

Buffalo Ridge, MN. A very long, but subtle north-south ridge in the SW corner of Minnesota. SEA-NY, SEA-CH.

Storm Lake, IA. Turbines are widespread in northwestern Iowa, notably near this town on the north shore of a small rounded lake. CHI-SEA.

New Mexico Wind Energy Center. The largest of 3 large sites on the NM plains near the NM/TX line. LA-DFW, PHX-DFW, SFO-DFW, LA-ATL.

King Mountain, TX. On a mesa east of the Pecos River. LA-HO.

Blue Canyon, OK. Near Lake Lawtonka, a squarish reservoir northwest of DFW. LA-ATL, DEN-MSY, PDX-HO.

Evanston, WY. Hills near I-80, 60 mi. east of Great Salt Lake. SFO-NY.

Los Angeles, California

LOOK FOR the lines of steep mountain fronts and lower hills intersecting the vast urban area, and the subtler slopes of alluvial fans spreading onto the valley floors.

❶ Santa Monica Mountains ❷ Santa Monica, CA
❸ Inglewood oil field ❹ Los Angeles International Airport
❺ Hollywood Park Racetrack

❻ Signal Hill oil field ❼ Long Beach, CA ❽ Long Beach Harbor
❾ HMS *Queen Mary* ❿ oil-field production islands

The City of Angels and its extended household occupy four alluvial plains bounded by the Pacific Ocean and three mountain ranges. The Los Angeles Basin holds Los Angeles International Airport (LAX) ❹ and much of the city. To the north, the Santa Monica Mountains ❶ separate it from the San Fernando Valley. The San Gabriel Valley extends east of Los Angeles, bounded on the north by the San Gabriel Mountains. The Santa Ana Mountains with its northern outliers, the Chino and San Jose hills, separate the Inland Valley from the Los Angeles Basin. The Palos Verdes Peninsula interrupts the coast's general southeast to northwest trend.

Faults cut through the basin, many of them active. Look for linear breaks in the topography, especially along mountain fronts: Major faults bound all the ranges. A series of active faults underlies a northwest trend of hills stretching from Seal Beach to Beverly Hills. Most of Los Angeles's 60 oil fields occur along this trend.

Flights out of LAX typically take off westward into the prevailing wind, then turn north or south over the Pacific. Flights to southern U.S. cities often circle the peninsula and pass over Long Beach. The Long Beach ❸ and Los Angeles Terminal Island container terminals jointly form the world's third-busiest container port. (See page 300 for different meanings of "busiest port.")

The Spanish founded Los Angeles in 1781 as a "pueblo," a farming center meant to supply food and horses to the presidios at Santa Barbara and San Diego. These military posts defended the missions, which asserted Spain's claim to California. The Spanish did not intend Los Angeles to be a center of the empire.

For most of a century, Los Angeles played second fiddle to San Francisco, which enjoyed the benefits of the gold rush and the first transcontinental railroad. San Diego, with its fine harbor, was the southern rival. After the Gadsden Purchase, Los Angeles's leaders lobbied the Southern Pacific to bring its line from the East to their city rather than San Diego. The rails, completed in 1883, linked Los Angeles's mediocre San Pedro harbor to the Bay Area as well.

Los Angeles remained a minor city for another 50 years, failing to either develop a major central city or spawn bedroom communities. That began to change in the 1940s, when Pacific Electric Railway, a system of passenger lines, was built by Henry E. Huntington and his partners to promote their residential subdivisions all across the Los Angeles Basin. The lines did not need to make a profit as long as the houses sold well. Developers initiated a basin-wide grid; every tenth street was later widened to accommodate the growing fleet of cars and trucks.

Oil was first discovered here in 1892, near Dodger Stadium. The discovery was near one of the many oil seeps in the basin. The great Signal Hill field, tested in 1921, proved to be one of the largest in the United States. Covering barely 1,100 acres, it produced 500,000 barrels of oil per acre. No other field on Earth approaches this measure.

The rugged topography evident throughout greater Los Angeles results from the collision of a major ocean spreading center, the East Pacific Rise, with North America 1,000 miles south of Los Angeles. A new ocean basin opened, forming the Gulf of California between Baja California and North America. North of the gulf, a transform fault separated the Pacific Plate from the North American Plate. As this fault moved, the Los Angeles Basin was transferred to the Pacific Plate and began to move northwest with it.

Mountains around Los Angeles rise on many faults tied to the San Andreas Fault. The Los Angeles Basin lies between the east-west-trending Transverse Ranges, which include the San Gabriels, Santa Monicas, and others farther west, and the northwest-trending Peninsular Ranges, which start with the Santa Anas and continue south. Between 18 million and 12 million years ago, a crustal block that would later form the Transverse Ranges lay west of the Santa Ana Mountains. The block rotated clockwise for 6 million years, opening several basins. Six million years ago, a fault along the western margin of the San Gabriels began to move as a segment of the San Andreas fault system, bringing the western Transverse Ranges close to their present positions. The ranges collided with each other along thrust faults, creating the mountains north of Los Angeles.

On these sparsely vegetated mountains, winter rains frequently cause flooding and debris flows in the canyons and out onto the plains. After 6 million years of seasonal deposition, the resulting alluvial plains slope gently away from the mountain fronts.

Corridor 1B

NEW YORK—PHILADELPHIA—INDIANAPOLIS—KANSAS CITY—PHOENIX—LAS VEGAS OR LOS ANGELES

❶ Penn's three original squares ❷ Penn Square ❸ Delaware River ❹ Benjamin Franklin Bridge ❺ Camden, NJ ❻ Schuylkill River
❼ Philadelphia International Airport ❽ Fort Mifflin ❾ home games of the Phillies, Sixers, and Eagles ❿ Walt Whitman Bridge

EASTBOUND: Go to pp. 232, 6

Philadelphia, Pennsylvania

LOOK FOR the narrow streets subdividing the blocks bounded by wider streets within the city center; note the flat topography to the east and the rolling topography to the west.

Philadelphia is a fall line city, located where rapids limit navigation on the Delaware River. William Penn founded the city on high ground between the Delaware ❸ and the Schuylkill ❻ rivers in 1681. He used an orthogonal grid to lay out a street plan. Boston, New York, and other colonial towns at that time consisted of disorganized networks of roads and tracks that in many cases grew from farm or woodland paths. Penn designed wide streets to limit the spread of fires. He envisioned a city of very large lots—a small farm, essentially, for each residence. He gave his new city four parks, now known as Rittenhouse Square, Franklin Square, Washington Square ❶, and Logan Circle.

Penn's grid proved a boon to real estate speculators: They knew in advance where the city would develop. The grid concept was soon adopted throughout the United States, to the delight of developers everywhere. Within Philadelphia, land became too expensive to sustain Penn's bucolic vision, so new streets were built dividing the original blocks to create the tight grid seen today.

Swedes had settled Delaware Bay before Penn's arrival. Sweden lacked the surplus population that thriving colonies require, so Penn advertised for immigrants in several countries. Members of minority Christian sects were drawn to the "city of brotherly love" planned by a devout Quaker who guaranteed religious freedom to all. Newcomers made Philadelphia the largest city in the American colonies by 1776. Germans settled the farmlands west of Philadelphia, creating the "Pennsylvania Dutch" region, a corruption of the German word "Deutsch." Few, if any, Dutch people settled there. Better farmland than any found near other colonial cities, the "Dutch Country" nourished Philadelphia's growth. Penn himself never quite immigrated: He spent his last years in England.

Geographers see an enduring divide between northern and southern strains in midwestern cultural norms, perhaps traceable to Penn. British settlers first immigrated to Boston or New York and then moved west along the Mohawk River valley to the southern Great Lakes area. As Pennsylvania filled with immigrants, German and central European settlers moved into the Ohio River valley or via the Great Valley into the Appalachians.

Flights in and out of PHL ❼ offer a close-up view of a significant Revolutionary War battleground, Fort Mifflin ❽. British troops took Philadelphia early in the war, then besieged and bombarded this small fort. The handful of patriots inside held out long enough to allow Washington and his troops to escape to Valley Forge.

The Delaware Valley iron industry, based on charcoal and local iron deposits, was an early core of manufacturing in Philadelphia. The steel industry developed on this base, using local coal and importing iron ore from Canada and South America. Steel mills and many factories that use steel can be seen along the Delaware between Philadelphia and Trenton, New Jersey, 28 miles upstream.

Ferries provided the only transportation across the Delaware until the Benjamin Franklin Bridge ❹ opened in 1926. It was the world's longest suspension bridge for five years. Today, the longest suspension bridge in Philadelphia is the Walt Whitman Bridge ❿.

Metamorphic rocks of the Piedmont Province underlie the city. Across the Delaware River, sandstones and shales of the Coastal Plain lie on the Piedmont, covered in turn by a thin veneer of younger sands and gravels, especially along streams and rivers. Philadelphia's skyscrapers, like Manhattan's, are built on metamorphic rocks so strong that no deep pilings are needed.

In recent years, parts of north Philadelphia subsided unexpectedly. Engineers first supposed that either of the most common causes of subsidence was at work: collapse of limestone caves or liquefaction owing to earthquakes. Limestones are known around Philadelphia but not where subsidence is a problem. In the past century, a few earthquakes rattled the Northeast, none large enough to liquefy soil. Geologists found that all subsidence occurred in areas of dirt fill. By studying topographic maps published in 1899, they found a system of streams filled to create level building sites.

WESTBOUND: Start with pp. 6, 232

Gettysburg, Pennsylvania

LOOK FOR passes in South Mountain, specifically Cashtown Gap occupied by the main highway leading west; the town of Gettysburg and the park to its south.

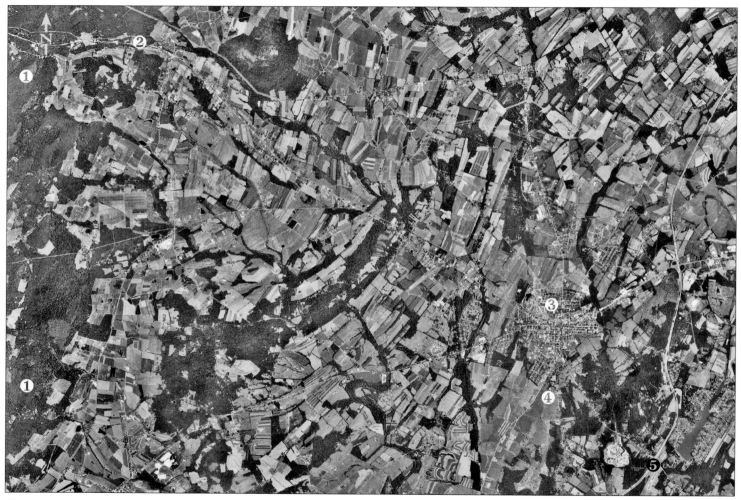

❶ South Mountain ❷ U.S. Hwy. 30 at Cashtown Gap ❸ Gettysburg ❹ Cemetery Hill in Gettysburg National Battlefield
❺ U.S. Hwy. 15

South Mountain rises west of the Gettysburg Basin, a broad valley of red soil with a small college town at its center. U.S. Highway 30 runs over Cashtown Gap ❷ on South Mountain. The Great Valley, extending from northeast Pennsylvania into Alabama, lies on South Mountain's west side. Piedmont uplands form the basin's east flank. From its headwaters here, the Monocacy River flows south through Maryland to the Potomac. These topographic elements greatly influenced the Civil War battle of Gettysburg.

South Mountain is the north end of a very long feature, the Blue Ridge Province. If you follow South Mountain southward, it peters out just past the Potomac in Virginia but not before a similar elongated mountain rises parallel to it, just to its west. That ridge, the Blue Ridge, continues to Georgia. Metamorphic rocks carried to the surface on thrust faults underlie both of them and characterize the Blue Ridge geologic province. Immediately to its west lies the Valley and Ridge Province, starting with the Great Valley.

Before rail or modern roads, topography and bedrock determined ease of travel and therefore several centuries of history. Travel was problematic in both the Piedmont uplands and the high ridges to the west, whereas the Great Valley and the Triassic Gettysburg and Culpeper basins provided paths for migration, commerce, and armies.

The Union and Confederate armies spent the winter of 1862–63 on opposite sides of the Rappahannock River west of Fredericksburg, Virginia. Igneous and metamorphic Piedmont rocks underlie this area of narrow valleys, steep ridges, and poor roads. In the spring, both armies moved to the Triassic basins, where the land is less challenging and roads were better. In May, General Robert E. Lee won a major victory at Chancellorsville, 12 miles up the Rappahannock from Fredericksburg. He decided to invade Pennsylvania and take its capital, Harrisburg, in order to threaten major Union cities and cut the rail line supplying the Union Army. He hoped that a successful northern campaign would bring a European nation into the war on the Confederacy's side.

On June 3, Lee marched his troops in groups that crossed the Blue Ridge into the Great Valley by way of three wind gaps south of the Potomac, then turned north up the Great Valley to mass at Chambersburg. From there, Lee could either send troops northeast to Harrisburg or rapidly move them through Cashtown Gap to Gettysburg. He sent some troops to York and Carlisle, to threaten Harrisburg.

Meanwhile, the Union army moved north on the other side of the Blue Ridge through the Culpeper Basin. The opposing generals were only partially aware of each other's moves. Lee did not learn that the Union Army was north of the Potomac at Frederick, Maryland, until June 28. In response, he pulled his troops back from York and Carlisle while ordering the bulk of his army to move east through Cashtown Gap.

The Union army under George Meade moved toward Gettysburg, taking up defensive positions along the Pipe Creek line, at the Piedmont edge above Gettysburg. Only a small Union detachment was in Gettysburg when the first Confederate soldiers arrived. The outnumbered Union forces retreated to Cemetery Hill ❹, a ridgeline south of town. A basalt dike underlies the ridge, making it next to impossible to dig defensive trenches there, yet in the end, the defenses held. The Confederates failed to pursue the Union detachment, so Meade reinforced it by night. The next day, Lee sent his troops against both Union flanks without success. On July 3, he sent George Edward Pickett's brigade in one more assault on the center of Cemetery Ridge. The high-water mark of the Confederacy is said to be the highest point reached by Pickett's men in this final failed assault.

Lee withdrew the next day. His supply trains used Cashtown Gap while the main army took Fairfield Gap, the next pass to the south. The two armies moved back into Virginia via the Great Valley and soon were camped in nearly the same places where they had spent the previous winter. Three factors may account for this seemingly inconclusive battle's reputation as the keystone battle in the war: the grotesque number of casualties, Lincoln's address at the battlefield, and the fact that it remained the northernmost incursion by the army of the South.

WESTBOUND: Go to p. 14

Wheeling and Moundsville, West Virginia

LOOK FOR either Wheeling, a city centered on a lozenge-shaped island in the Ohio River, or Moundsville, a town facing a sharp bend in the Ohio, with a tall smokestack on the west bank, in the crook of the bend.

❶ Martins Ferry, OH ❷ Bridgeport, OH ❸ historic Wheeling, WV, on Wheeling Island ❹ Fort Henry Bridge, I-70
❺ mainland part of Wheeling ❻ Wheeling Creek

❼ Dilles Bottom power plant with large heap of coal; dark diagonal bar is shadow of smokestack ❽ Moundsville, WV
❾ Grave Creek Mound ❿ West Virginia State Penitentiary

EASTBOUND: Go to p. 14

The Ohio is the large river you cross after the Mississippi, eastbound, or after the Susquehanna, westbound. An easily navigable river through the heart of a resource-rich region, the Ohio was the most valuable river in the U.S. economy for well over a century. In recent decades, economic trends converged to throw the upper Ohio region into decline. Some call Wheeling "the buckle on the Rust Belt."

Wheeling ❸❻ and Moundsville ❽ lie 11 miles apart on the West Virginia bank. Moundsville has two nationally registered historic places bigger than a city block, so you have a chance of spotting the structures, if not their many ghosts. The first is the Grave Creek Mound, ❾ built 2,200 years ago during the Adena culture period. In contrast to later Mound Builder cultures that built long mounds and serpent-shaped mounds, the Adena built conical mounds. This is the largest one that has been found. When first measured, it was 69 feet tall and 295 feet in diameter. That would have required well over a million basketfuls of dirt dug from the surrounding plain. The mound was surrounded by a wide, dry moat, 5 feet deep, interpreted as a "sacred circle," since the Adena also built circular moats without mounds. The Adena cremated their high-ranking dead in mortuary houses and piled dirt on the ashes to make a precise conical mound. The Adena repeated the process, on top of the existing mound, with subsequent dignitaries. Large mounds like this one held several layers of stacked mortuary remains.

Across the street from the Grave Creek Mound is the West Virginia State Penitentiary ❿. The main perimeter is a castellated stone wall 823 feet long and 24 feet high. West Virginia's second-oldest state building, it was built with convict labor shortly after West Virginia's 1863 secession from Virginia. Its location was chosen for its proximity to Wheeling, the original state capital. The prison was used for more than a century, until the state supreme court determined that its 5-by-7-foot cells, each triple-bunked during the 1920s, constituted cruel and unusual punishment. The prison spent many of its 129 active years on a list of 10 most violent prisons. Today, it is used to train prison guards in riot control, for TV show sets, for guided tours, and for overnight "ghost hunts" at $50 a head. The guides enjoy a reputation for ghoulish humor.

Just across the river from Moundsville lies Dilles Bottom, Ohio, barely perceptible as a town but bearing an enormous buff chimney inside a sharp river bend—part of a coal-fired power plant ❼ built to demonstrate innovative technologies to reduce nitrogen oxides and sulfur dioxide, the two main causes of acid rain.

The upper Ohio valley first became an industrial powerhouse in the early 19th century because of the confluence of coal, iron ore, lumber, and water transport. In the 1850s, iron mining moved to upper Michigan, but the Ohio River hung on to a good share of iron and steel smelting. Local coal was still burned for heat, while coke made from Pennsylvania coal replaced charcoal as the carbon source used to convert iron to steel.

A double whammy hit the region's economy in the 1970s. First, America's steel industry nearly collapsed, primarily because of insufficient investment in new technology in the postwar years, while foreign competitors built more efficient mills. Second, the Clean Air Act sent power plants looking for low-sulfur coal, which is not found in Ohio or northern West Virginia. Midwestern and northern Appalachian coal will be consumed eventually, and technologies to burn it without emitting much sulfur dioxide already exist, as the Dilles Bottom plant shows. But power companies have largely postponed installing those technologies in a context of ever-changing regulations. The high-sulfur coal has to wait.

As for steel, a restructured and retooled industry now competes effectively with foreign producers. Its modern, competitive steel mills, however, efficiently produce steel with a small fraction of the labor force that their predecessors employed. Their success has not brought many jobs to lift local economies. Wheeling once had huge blast furnaces roaring and sparking away through the night; now it has none. What it has instead is the white-collar headquarters of Wheeling-Pittsburgh Steel Corporation, which went through two bankruptcies before reemerging as an exemplar of the new, efficient, small steel producer. The town now parlays its old Victorian houses and green, mountainous setting into tourist attractions.

WESTBOUND: Go to pp. 28, 30, 32

Indianapolis Motor Speedway, Indiana

LOOK FOR a squared-off oval racetrack just inside the squarish freeway ring around the city, northwest of the city center and a few miles northeast of Indianapolis International Airport.

❶ Indianapolis Motor Speedway ❷ Wabash River ❸ radial streets aligned with Monument Circle, the geometric center of the city ❹ Indiana State Capitol building ❺ RCA Dome, home of the Indianapolis Colts, likely to be demolished in 2008 ❻ I-70, from Indianapolis International Airport

EASTBOUND: Go to pp. 32, 30, 28

The first thing you'll notice about Indianapolis is a symmetry unbroken by any hill, lake, seashore, or major river. Superimposed on its rectilinear grid are several diagonal spokes and a circumscribing freeway. The diagonals ❸ radiate from Monument Circle, a small circle at the center of a square exactly one mile square. Within its bounding North, South, East, and West streets, this square mile contains the city's essentials: the state Capitol ❹ and the homes of the Colts and the Pacers.

Such things do not happen by accident. During a century in which most new states chose small towns as their capitals, hoping to limit the influence of big-city politics, the Indiana General Assembly took the opposite tack. The assembly picked a nearly uninhabited swampy area in the center of the state; hired the architect Alexander Ralston, who had apprenticed with L'Enfant, the architect of Washington, D.C.; and planned its capitopolis to cover only the one square mile.

Once it had grown to become the state's largest city, it never relinquished that rank. It's the second-largest state capital in the United States. Although it is not an unusually wealthy city, it is the only big city in or near the Rust Belt to match the nation's population growth rate over recent decades. Its largest corporation, Eli Lilly, is in a rust-free industry that thrived when the Rust Belt declined in the late-20th century.

It almost didn't work out that way. A hundred years ago, automobiles were the new thing, and Indianapolis, with a slew of fledgling car manufacturers, vied to become the Motor City. Carl Fisher, after making his fortune providing the Prest-o-Lite acetylene gas that fired early headlamps, felt that what the local industry needed was a test track: It was difficult for car designers to find a road smooth enough and vacant enough for speeds greater than 20 miles per hour. (See page 130 for more on Fisher.) He bought 238 acres and built what may be the second thing you notice about Indianapolis: the fabled Speedway ❶. Look for it a few miles northeast of the airport. On its east flank is a golf course; on its west flank, a residential subdivision for people who simply can't get enough of the roar of internal combustion engines. (One must wonder: Can these marriages be saved?)

The first race, in 1909, was an effort to get more people interested in cars. It was supposed to go two laps (a full five miles!) but was canceled halfway through on account of mayhem. The pavement, consisting of tarred gravel, had broken up, cars had burned, and two drivers, two mechanics, and two spectators lay dead or mortally injured. To improve safety before the next event, the owner had the entire track paved with more than 3 million bricks; hence the Speedway's nickname, "the Brickyard." The bricks are still there, covered by asphalt now except for a bare brick finish line three feet wide: a literal brick yard.

The small races held the following year didn't generate enough interest, so Fisher shot for the moon, raising the bar in 1911 from two laps to two hundred. An Indianapolis-built car called a Marmon won the first Indy 500. The oldest annual car race in the world, it remains the most popular. In recent years, it has expanded to embrace its two main rival formats: NASCAR, which races modified mass-production cars on the oval; and Formula 1, which sets parameters for building race cars from scratch, as Indy does, but races them on an erratically winding track. You can see the Formula 1 track's wiggly line crossing the center of the oval. Only those three races are held at the Speedway.

Capable of holding 400,000 spectators, the Speedway is the most capacious spectator sport facility in history, breaking a record set 18 centuries earlier when Emperor Trajan enlarged the Circus Maximus to hold about 300,000 chariot-racing fans. *Plus ça change . . .*

The Speedway is technically not *in* Indianapolis but in the town of Speedway, entirely surrounded by Indianapolis. A nearby car racetrack, O'Reilly Raceway Park, is so much smaller that it may be difficult to pick out unless you are taking off or landing at Indianapolis Airport. The Raceway lies due west of the Speedway and north-northwest of the airport. A relatively delicate oval about half the Speedway's length, it has a tiny pond in the infield, several longer loops around it, and a 4,400-foot straight-line track next to it. It holds far more races each year—including drag races on the straight track, truck races, and stock car races—before far fewer spectators.

Interstate Highway System

LOOK FOR various on- and off-ramp geometries on the freeways.

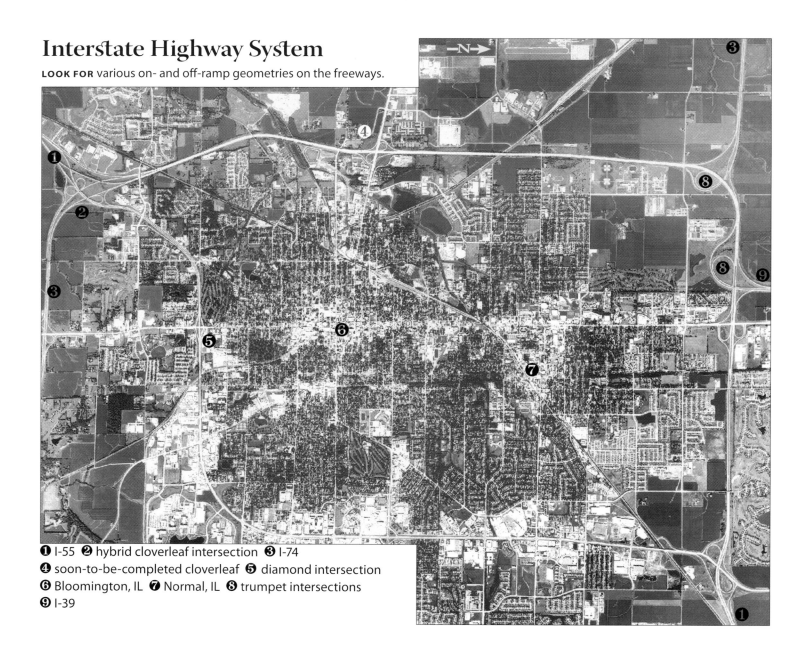

❶ I-55 ❷ hybrid cloverleaf intersection ❸ I-74
❹ soon-to-be-completed cloverleaf ❺ diamond intersection
❻ Bloomington, IL ❼ Normal, IL ❽ trumpet intersections
❾ I-39

If there's anything truly inescapable while scanning America from the air, it's the interstate highways. Few of us can recall the time when they were not there, cutting through cities, feeding suburbs, and marking the open countryside.

The interstates are built to a standard design: at least four lanes 12 feet wide, shoulders 10 feet wide, limited access. From the air, their most interesting feature is the geometric variety of interchanges. The cloverleaf may be the most pleasing, the diamond ❺ the most abundant, and the proliferating hybrid ❷ designs the most interesting. In urban settings, where land is expensive, adding lanes to existing highways can produce intersections with three, four, or five ramps and lanes placed one above the other in stacks. To our knowledge, the High Five stack in north Dallas is the tallest intersection at the time of this writing. No doubt taller stacks are envisioned. The cloverleaf requires more land than some alternatives, but its safety record is good except where traffic is really heavy.

The interstate system culminates 100 years of highway development in the United States. During the 19th century, railroads expanded across the continent, creating a web of freight and passenger carriers and clearing the roads of most horse-drawn wagon freight. Pierre and Ernest Michaux began serious production of bicycles in France in 1867; within a few years, thousands of bicyclists were using America's dirt wagon roads for business and pleasure. Cyclists banded together to lobby their state legislatures for improved roads. (Only in recent years have dirt and mud had a positive association for some cyclists.)

Communities lacking rail service did not sit idle in their isolation. The Grange movement, lobbying for rural mail delivery, found a common cause with the bicycle community. Within a decade of the Rural Free Delivery (RFD) Act of 1893, more than 8,000 postmen were delivering mail to farms across the country. It was only a short time before Congress saw the need to improve rural roads.

The automobile, invented in Germany and soon popular across Europe, was still a novelty on this side of the Atlantic in 1900. That was soon to change. By 1904, 34,000 cars had been sold in America, and the American Automobile Association was booming. In 1914, the United States had more than 500,000 cars but only a few thousand miles of paved road. The AAA and state road departments lobbied for a major federal role in road building; with passage of the Federal Aid Road Act of 1916, they got it. This act authorized $25 million in federal matching funds per year for roads. Over 40 years, this system would build 200,000 miles of roadway.

The Road Act created a fine network of highways, but with an incalculable—and apparently inexcusable—number of stop signs and lights. A solution was presented by the Pennsylvania Turnpike, America's first long-distance, limited-access superhighway. A failed railroad venture had partially dug tunnels through the Allegheny Mountains before exhausting its capital; the turnpike took over its route. Upon opening in 1940, this toll highway cut travel time across the state in half.

Possibly seeking public works to spur the economy, possibly seeking to bring highway travel up to the standards he had seen in Hitler's Germany, President Eisenhower in 1952 proposed spending $50 billion to build 40,000 miles of superhighways. Four years later, Congress established the Highway Trust Fund, enabling construction of the present 46,564-mile system.

The routes were first drawn in 1938 by the Bureau of Public Roads. The Department of Defense was not asked to identify its highway needs until 1960, when more than 2,200 freeway bridges were already in place. Many of the bridges do not meet DOD specs: A trailer carrying an Atlas missile will not pass beneath them. Nevertheless, "defense needs" were used to sell the project to the American people, who responded over the years by generating urban myths of the interstates as "defense" roads—to move people and matériel or to provide ubiquitous emergency-landing strips.

A more likely defense objective was to move civilians to the suburbs and to Arizona. This surprising but more realistic and certainly more "successful" defense-related motive was brought to light in 2006 in the book *Wildfire and Americans* by Roger G. Kennedy, a veteran of Eisenhower's and later administrations. By 1950, Edward Teller was pushing population dispersal as a way to reduce bomb casualties in future wars. Popularly known as the "father of the hydrogen bomb," Teller, of course, did at least as much as anyone to multiply potential bomb casualties, but he wanted to mitigate them at least on our side. He wanted sprawl. We got sprawl.

WESTBOUND: Go to pp. 28, 30, 32

Missouri Floodplain at Rocheport, Missouri

LOOK FOR an east-west freeway crossing a big mud-colored river, with a village just west of the bridge; signs of past flooding.

❶ Katy Trail on former rail right of way, at the foot of the river bluffs ❷ Moniteau Creek ❸ Rocheport, MI ❹ tugboat pushing two barges on Missouri River ❺ Overton Chute, dug by Army Corps of Engineers as habitat restoration ❻ water-filled deep scours excavated by 1993 flood ❼ sand left by 1993 flood ❽ I-70 ❾ fields in crop production on floodplain

EASTBOUND: Go to pp. 28, 30, 32

brackfast at the Mouth of a large Creek on the S.S. of 30 yds wide called big Monetou ❷ . . . Several Courious Paintings and Carveings in the projecting rock of Limestone inlade with white red and blue flint, of a verry good quality . . . We landed at this Inscription and found it a Den of rattle Snakes

—Journal of Capt. William Clark, June 7, 1804

Typical midwestern river topography starts with a flat floodplain six to ten times wider than the river, bounded by bluffs in two fairly smooth parallel curves. Steep, branching creek valleys cut through the bluffs, creating a wormy pattern of contrasts between forested valley slopes and cleared farms on the rolling upland. In mid-Missouri, the uplands (a karst region) rest on fossil-rich Mississippian limestones, exposed on the river bluffs.

Just 15 years after Lewis and Clark's breakfast, ferry service across the river was offered at Moniteau Creek; Rocheport ❸ was founded in 1825. By the 1830s, Rocheport was a principal port for busy steamboat traffic, but the town's growth turned negative after 1850. In 2000, population was 208, many of whom live in hundred-year-old houses restored to historic verisimilitude. Several offer bed and "brackfast" accommodations to touring bicyclists.

In Lewis and Clark's day, a typical stretch of floodplain included a lot of slow, shallow water in the form of sloughs, side channels, and backwaters whose configuration shifted after each flood, as the main channel itself might shift. It was a distinctive wetland ecosystem, less than 5 percent of which is left today.

White people went to work changing all that as soon as they started settling. Moving the river into a single, narrower, deeper channel, and keeping it there, was obviously good for both riverboats and farmers. With federal funding and bigger machines, these channelization efforts accelerated enormously after 1930. They were often sold as "flood control," among other purposes, though some hydrologists have calculated that they actually increase flood heights. They didn't do anything about flood weather, and they redefined flooded floodplains from "natural safety-valve mechanism at work" to "natural-disaster site."

The great flood of 1993 ranks third among Missouri River floods in terms of flow rate; the 1844 and 1951 floods were bigger, yet 1993 surpassed their river levels while racking up the greatest dollar figure for damage from any U.S. river flood. What made it both higher and more costly was development on the floodplains, in a context of river-control engineering that could not deliver as much control as people expected.

During the flood, Rocheport was a favorite site for network news reports of townspeople heroically stacking sandbags. Seven or eight thousand sandbags were stacked, and after nine weeks above flood stage, the town was spared from destruction. But the most impressive part is what the region did after the river slipped back into its bed: It turned a major corner in floodplain management.

After 1993, farmers voluntarily sold substantial acreages and easements to government agencies for conversion into conservation lands. For the farms that remain on floodplains, the Department of Agriculture is working on developing flood-tolerant varieties of soybeans and corn. Managers, trying to learn from scratch how to reconstruct pieces of floodplain habitat, bulldozed gaps in levees to invite water back onto the plain. (The standing water you see in the photo may approximate the acreage swamped at similar river stages 200 years ago.) They dug the Overton Chute ❺, designing it to be a backwater most of the time, connected to the river only at its lower end, but expecting the river to activate it and redesign it during high-water stages. Over time, Mighty Mo may leave it high and dry, or it may move right in and adopt it for a main channel. No one really knows; nor does anyone know how much wet floodplain habitat it would take to save the endangered species that use it.

Lewis and Clark named the creek Monetou (an Algonquian word from far to the east, popularized by French traders) after the "spirits" painted and inlaid on the limestone bluffs. Those pictographs were apparently blasted to bits during construction of the Missouri-Kansas-Texas Railroad (M-K-T, or Katy for short). Abandoned after a 1986 flood washed out tracks, the Missouri River line became Katy Trail State Park ❶, at 225 miles the longest trail in the rails-to-trails movement. Most of its nearly level miles adjoin bluffs or river or both. It's perfect for multiday bike trips, which have become a mainstay of Rocheport's economy.

Kansas City, Missouri and Kansas

LOOK FOR bridges crossing the Missouri in the city, the valley of the Kansas River.

❶ Missouri River ❷ General Motors Fairfax assembly plant blocking the runway of the former Fairfax Airport, which launched most of the B-25 bombers for World War II; the aviation factory was adjacent ❸ Kansas River. The state line is a straight line from the confluence south; northward, it follows the Missouri River. Kansas City, KS, is on the left. ❹ Kansas City Downtown Airport, until 1972 the site of hair-raising jetliner takeoffs and landings over buildings and river bluffs ❺ Broadway Bridge ❻ I-70.

After meandering south for many miles, the Missouri River makes a hairpin bend where it meets the Kansas River ❸ and flows on to the east. Rail lines, stockyards, grain elevators, and refineries along the river display the city's commercial history. Away from the river lie its boulevards, residential developments, and parks.

Bluffs above the rivers are held up by flat layers of limestone deposited in shallow seas 318 million to 300 million years ago. The limestones are interlayered with softer shales, which do not persist as bluffs. The Independence glacial advance 610,000 to 780,000 years ago produced much of the topography we see. Two ice lobes extended south from the main glacier at that time: One crossed Nebraska to enter Kansas from the northwest, and the other crossed Iowa to enter northwest Missouri. At their maximum, they met in the Kansas City area. The glacier blocked preglacial river valleys. As the glaciers melted, a blocked valley filled with a lake extending across northeast Kansas. Eventually, this Lake Atchison overflowed in a massive flood, eroding spillways and outflow channels to form the valleys of the Big Blue River and the Missouri River below Leavenworth, Kansas. Union Station and the railroad right of way between the Missouri River valley and the West Bottoms of the Kansas River lie in one of these partially filled glacial spillways.

Missouri was admitted to the Union in 1821, the same year that François Chouteau established a trading post on the Missouri below the hairpin bend. Following a flood in 1826, Chouteau moved his establishment off the floodplain. This was not the last flood here. In 1844, a flood destroyed the river landing at rival city Independence, Missouri. Flooding on the Missouri and its local tributaries has been a fact of Kansas City life up to the present day.

In 1833, John McCoy platted Westport 4 miles to the south on the Santa Fe Trail. McCoy also established on the Missouri a riverboat landing to lure travelers going west on the trail. By 1848, Westport replaced Independence as the principal point of debarkation to the Santa Fe Trail. It became a trade center supplying parties bound for California and Oregon as well.

Missouri incorporated the City of Kansas, named for a plural form of the local Kansa tribe, in 1853. (Draw your own conclusions about how "Kansas" should be pronounced.) Eleven years later, the Union army defeated the Confederate army here in the Battle of Westport, ending Confederate influence in Missouri.

Railroads played a critical role in the growth of the city. The Kansas Pacific began construction to Lawrence, Kansas, in 1863 and was completed to Salina, Kansas, in 1867. The Pacific began service in 1864, following delivery of a steam engine, four flatcars, and rails by boat. This enabled westward rail service to begin in 1864, a year before rails connected Kansas City to St. Louis and points east.

The most important post–Civil War event may have been congressional funding for the first Missouri River bridge. Located beside the present Broadway Bridge ❺, Hannibal Bridge was completed in 1869, opening the territory of Kansas to the railroads. Within a decade, rails linked Kansas City to Santa Fe, Denver, and Texas, creating two markets in Kansas City: in cattle and in wheat.

The meat-packing industry began with pork in 1856, adding beef in 1868, when the railroad companies built the first stockyards. By the end of the century, the four largest meat packers in the United States formed a core element in the local economy, and Armour was the largest employer in the city.

The first gristmill near Kansas City was built in 1852 by Mathias Splitlog, a Wyandotte Indian. The first grain elevator was built in 1871. The introduction of Turkey Red winter wheat in 1874 eventually led to new milling techniques requiring capital investments beyond the means of small millers. The combination of expanded elevator storage capacity and larger mills led to the concentration of the milling industry in Kansas City at the expense of smaller operations across Kansas by the end of the century.

In the early 20th century, William Rockhill Nelson used the editorial pages of his *Kansas City Star* to promote a "city beautiful" program with many parks and boulevards. J. C. Nichols began to build a shopping complex and housing development south of downtown in 1922: The Country Club Plaza was the first shopping center in the United States, and the Country Club development was the country's largest residential development by a single builder. Kansas City claims more fountains than any city other than Rome and more boulevards than any city other than Paris.

Cattle Feedlots at Garden City, Kansas

LOOK FOR rectilinear industrial facilities, with truck traffic but without large buildings; if you miss this particular town, which has three of them, there are others on the Great Plains.

❶ feedlots ❷ Atchison, Topeka, and Santa Fe Railway (now Burlington Northern Santa Fe) ❸ Arkansas River

Garden City, Kansas, appears as a grid of streets on a plain covered by both rectangular and circular irrigated fields. The streets were first laid out along the Atchison, Topeka, and Santa Fe railroad tracks ❷. The Arkansas (pronounced ar-KAN-zas) River ❸ in Kansas bounds Garden City on its south.

A power plant, with coal yard, smokestack, and ponds, lies southwest of town. The plant can burn either Wyoming coal or natural gas from fields beneath Garden City.

Three enormous feedlots lie within a few miles northwest ❶, northeast, and southeast of town. Although surrounded by fields of grain, the feedlots operate on a scale far beyond that of the local growers. The largest feedlot uses 360 million tons of corn per year; Finney County produces about 2 million tons. The rest comes from the Corn Belt by rail and then by truck for the distance from town to feedlot. Each truck holds just 100,000 pounds, so you'll likely see a truck making a delivery. Pipes shoot the grain into the many pens, each holding around 100 head of cattle. A steer consumes about 32 pounds of feed per day, retaining about 4 pounds as meat and bone. The remainder finds its way into either the atmosphere or the manure lagoon alongside the feedlot.

The cattle arrive at 6 months of age and depart for one of four nearby meat-packing houses at 14 months. Four meat-packing companies slaughter and market 80 percent of U.S.-born cattle.

Finney County farms grow winter wheat, corn, sorghum, hay, soybeans, and sunflowers. Introduced to Kansas in 1839 at the Shawnee Mission, wheat remains the Wheat State's leading crop. Early wheat varieties suffered during Kansas winters and yielded poorly. German Mennonites emigrating from the Ukraine in 1874 brought Turkey Red winter wheat, which proved well suited. The first U.S. crop survey, in 1919, found Turkey Red planted in 82 percent of Kansas wheat acreage.

Major Stephen H. Long, who explored in 1820, called the western Kansas prairies part of the "Great American Desert." Major Long had been taught to look for trees as the sole indicator of lands suited for farming. In western Kansas, trees grew only on the floodplains of creeks and rivers, of which the Arkansas was the largest. Largely because of his indictment, the Great Plains were among the last places settled in the lower 48.

The native grasses grow one to four feet tall if you spoil them but often stood more like one to four *inches* tall when they were heavily grazed by buffalo. Several of the grasses may have co-evolved with buffalo here, and surprisingly, the inches-tall condition is optimal for them. They evolved to endure trampling better than competitors did and to recycle the animal waste back into protein. They respond to cycles of heavy grazing with strong root growth, building up belowground reserves that nourish later re-growth. The bottom line is that the combination of buffalo grass and buffalo yielded remarkably high biological productivity for such arid soils.

Before 1870, North America had possibly 70 million bison. By 1900, the population was below 1,000. They were killed off in the 1870s in order to starve the warring Plains Indians into submission. Cattle soon took their place on the High Plains. Ranchers faced little competition from farmers at first, but the economics of Manifest Destiny set mechanisms in motion that would soon replace ranchers with farmers near Garden City, while leaving feedlots that served the railroad.

The Santa Fe began rail service through southwest Kansas in 1872. As an incentive, the United States gave the railroad 10 square miles of land for every mile of railroad it built. Finding itself in the land development trade, the Santa Fe built up business by offering free shipping of household goods to settlers staking homesteads along the line.

Garden City was settled and its rail station built in 1879. Pens—ancestors of today's feedlots—were built to hold cattle awaiting shipment to slaughterhouses in Kansas City. But within a few years, the government's and the railroad's inducements produced a land rush, as intended, and the local ranchers faded westward before the onslaught of wheat and irrigation.

The large feedlots in Garden City date to 1951, when Earl Brookover opened the first commercial feedlot in western Kansas. His successful marriage of grain and young cattle led to the dozens of industrial-scale lots now found across the plains. The rail line had already attracted feedlots to the area, and these stayed while open-range grazing moved west to the short-grass prairies.

WESTBOUND: Go to p. 36

Short-Grass Prairie at Las Animas, Colorado

LOOK FOR northeast-flowing Purgatoire River joining the east-flowing Arkansas River; ranch buildings with small feedlots; areas of irrigated fields.

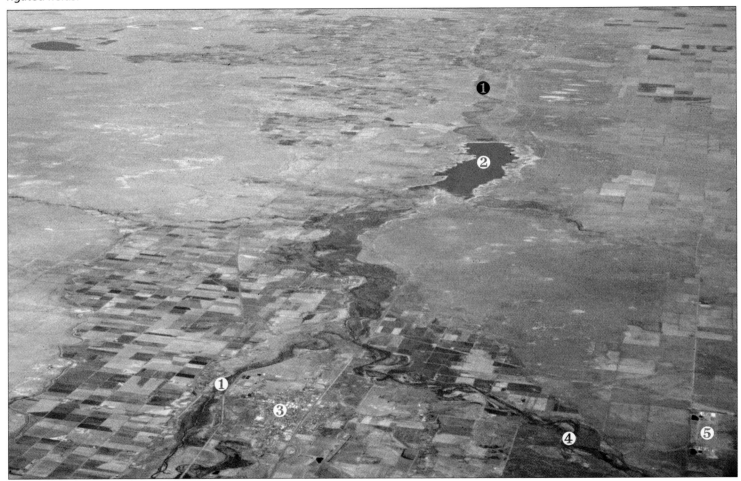

Facing east-northeast ❶ Arkansas River ❷ John Martin Reservoir ❸ Las Animas ❹ Purgatoire River ❺ background pens

EASTBOUND: Go to p. 36

Sooner or later, your transcontinental flight will cross the short-grass prairie, that north-south zone between the eastern margin of the Rocky Mountains and the slightly wetter prairies farther east on the High Plains. The short-grass prairie will appear green in the spring and early summer and, possibly, in the late summer as well. Riverbanks and floodplains host brush that remains green through summer, often in strong contrast to the brown-gray of the broad intervening uplands. Scattered at distances measured in miles and tens of miles are small feedlots, disclosing the one economic activity that occurs throughout the zone: cattle ranching.

The Mountain (or Main) Route of the Santa Fe Trail followed the Arkansas River ❶ across western Kansas to La Junta, Colorado, where it turned south skirting the Purgatoire River ❹ to Raton, New Mexico. The trail was established in 1821 for international trade between Missouri, in the United States, and Santa Fe, then in northern Mexico. After the 1846–48 Mexican-American War, when the U.S. Army used the trail, it became the chief commercial route into the newly acquired territories of the Southwest.

Cattle came to southeastern Colorado in the 19th century, following the expansion of the railroads and the growth of eastern cities. A mild and wet winter in 1881–82, allowing a rapid increase in cattle, was followed by the drought of 1883 and the death of hundreds of thousands of cattle—but not before severe overgrazing damaged the prairie. Many cattlemen in the following century continued to overgraze the short-grass prairie, which in many areas remains severely damaged today.

In the old days, cattle were left to graze until they reached market weight. After World War II, calf/cow operations became the norm here. The ranches run large, as each calf requires 10 acres. After six months, calves are placed in "background pens," the small feed pens seen in this region ❺. The calves remain in background pens for two months, eating from a trough in the close company of other cattle, before moving to large industrial-style feedlots where they spend their final year (see page 82).

Domestic cattle derive from a European "proto ox," the aurochs. The last known aurochs was killed in 1627 in Poland. Columbus and later Iberian immigrants introduced longhorn cattle to the New World in the 15th century. In 1690, 200 head were driven to a Spanish mission on the Sabine River in Texas. As buffalo were extinguished from the prairies in the mid-19th century, Texas longhorns took their place. Longhorns were replaced in turn, as the open range was fenced, by cattle that reach market weight faster.

The short-grass prairie occupies the western part of the High Plains, an arid region extending from the Texas Panhandle north through eastern Montana and into Manitoba. Precipitation averages about 10 inches per year, much of it falling during the summer. Unlike the mixed- and tall-grasses prairies to the east, the soil of the short-grass prairie dries completely in most years following the summer rains. Both cold- and warm-weather grasses grow during the rainy season, going dormant when the rains end. Prickly pear cactus grows among the grasses, doing especially well during the dry years. The sparse vegetation of this zone results in less organic material forming in the soil and also renders fire a less important element than for the prairies developed farther east.

The Colorado Piedmont is a plateau covering much of southeast Colorado. Marine sediments deposited before the uplift of the Rocky Mountains underlie the Piedmont. Once the Rockies had risen, rivers delivered a thick covering of sediment onto the Piedmont. During the last 10 million years, the Rockies rose while the High Plains tilted eastward. The young sediment covering eroded from the Colorado Piedmont and the Arkansas River and its tributaries carried it away. The succeeding Ice Ages imposed a desert climate here, and strong winds reworked the remaining stream deposits into dunes. As the Ice Age waned, winds carried dust and silt from deglaciated regions to the High Plains, leaving a top layer of loess which, if irrigated, supports farming, including melons, onions, alfalfa, and grains. Without irrigation, the soils support only grazing in average rain years and verge on renewed dune activity in drought years.

Eagle Tail Mesa and Capulin Mountain, New Mexico

LOOK FOR flat-topped low mountains east of the Rockies, rimmed with cliffs on all sides, their outlines ranging from scalloped to rococo; cinder cones and larger volcanoes.

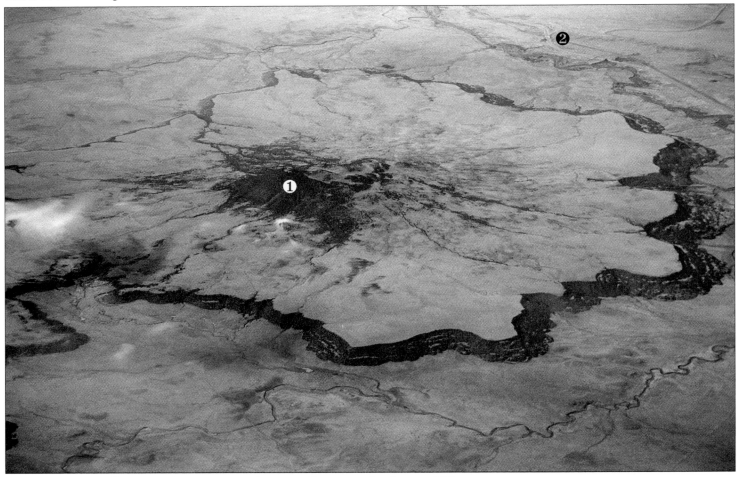

Facing southwest ❶ Eagle Tail Mountain cinder cone ❷ I-25, south of Raton, NM

on opposite page, facing north ❸ Capulin Mountain

Mesas occur where a flat, strong, erosion-resistant layer lies on top of a region of softer material that is deeply scoured by stream erosion. In southeast Utah, a mesa's cap rock layer may be a sandstone; in central Colorado, it may be volcanic welded tuff.

On Eagle Tail Mesa, a prominent central cinder cone is your clue that the cap rock here is basalt lava. Eagle Tail's cliffs stand 400 feet tall above their surrounding plains; the cinder cone ❶ adds another 1,300 feet. Eagle Tail is within the Raton-Clayton volcanic field, a region of volcanoes and mesas stretching 100 miles across the Colorado–New Mexico borderlands and just into Oklahoma, providing that state's highest point.

North of Eagle Tail, the largest mesa, Raton Mesa, reaches a 9,627-foot promontory at Fisher Peak, towering 3,700 feet over the Purgatoire River at Trinidad, Colorado. Stacking many lava flows on top of each other, Raton's basalt sheet reaches 500 feet thick in places. (See page 335 for an aerial view of Fisher Peak.) The Santa Fe Trail crossed Raton Mesa at Raton Pass, a 3,000-foot ordeal to ox or mule teamsters who may have thought they would get off easy by staying east of the Rockies. Interstate 25 crosses the pass today.

Well to the east rises the field's biggest volcano, the 8,720-foot Sierra Grande composite cone. Just northwest of that, the cinder cone of Capulin Mountain ❸ stands a thousand feet above the plain. A paved road winds to its summit. Capulin has some of the youngest lavas in the field, probably less than 10,000 years old.

Many of the mesas originated from highly fluid basalts that flowed southeastward down broad, gentle valleys. Subsequent erosion lowered the adjacent land surface while the young lava flows remained intact; in this process, called topographic inversion, a southeast-trending ridgeline took the place of a southeast-trending valley. Subsequent lava flows filled new valleys in between the old flows, so the oldest lavas cap the highest mesas, and younger lavas cap lower mesas. Right up through the most recent lavas, the process continues: Lava fills existing stream valleys, displacing the streams, which then carve new channels somewhere else.

The 3,700 feet of relief at Fisher Peak show the sheer volume of material eroded from the western Great Plains in just a few million years. Between 11 million and 4 million years ago, sediment from the Rockies spread across almost the entire western plains, forming the thick Ogallala Formation. The plains were even flatter than they are now, a gentle slope from the Rockies to the Mississippi.

The Raton-Clayton volcanoes began erupting 9 million years ago, as the whole region was gradually tilting to the east. Broad uplift centered in Colorado raised the western plains, converting them from a region where rivers distributed sediments to a region where rivers stripped sediments away. Although the 3,700 feet excavated from Trinidad after the basalt flow ceased may be an extreme case, the rest of eastern Colorado was also deeply eroded. The tilting is still going on.

Nebraska, Kansas, Oklahoma, and the western Texas Panhandle were scarcely touched by this erosion. The High Plains surface, a western belt across those states, has remained little changed for 4 million years. Wherever you see big cliffs on the High Plains, they likely have the Ogallala surface at the top; the height of the cliff thus equals the post-tilt erosion. That includes Scotts Bluff in Nebraska, the Mescalero Escarpment in New Mexico, the Caprock Escarpment in Texas (page 174), and the sub-lava surface on these mesas in southeast Colorado and northeast New Mexico.

South of Eagle Tail Mesa, erosion has stripped down to a plain on top of a lower erosion-resistant layer, the Dakota Sandstone. That plain drops off in turn at a south-facing line of cliffs, the Canadian Escarpment. Beyond the Canadian River lie the Pecos Valley and the Llano Estacado.

Spanish Peaks and the Stonewall, Colorado

LOOK FOR a pair of high mountains resembling volcanoes, alone at the east front of the Rockies; dozens of straight, sharp, skinny ridges in their vicinity.

Facing southwest ❶ La Veta, CO ❷ dikes (sharp ridgelines) ❸ West Spanish Peak

Facing northwest ❹ the Stonewall, not a dike, but a hogback ❺ Middle Fork Purgatoire River, here a small creek ❻ CO Hwy. 12 ❼ Stonewall, CO

❽ (on facing page) gas well pads in foothills

The first things most air passengers notice about the Spanish Peaks are their solitude, standing apart from any linear chain, and their long slopes to the surrounding lowland. Look for sharp narrow ridges ❷ radiating from the base of the taller one, 13,626-foot West Spanish Peak ❸. These ridges are dikes that solidified from rising magma, along with the solidified magma cores of West and East Spanish peaks. Keep looking: the area has more than 500 dikes; many run west-southwest to east-northeast, unconnected to the two peaks. The dikes range up to 14 miles long and 100 feet high; some form clean vertical walls. The dike swarm extends east just past the north-south freeway, Interstate 25.

This all may appear volcanic, but no volcanic rocks have been found. Look closely at the higher peak: if it isn't snow-covered, you may see horizontal sedimentary layers. Possibly, volcanoes erupted here, up above all the rocks we see now, and later erosion left no trace of them. Or, all the magma solidified without reaching the surface. Either way, differential erosion left two peaks standing majestically alone, masquerading as volcanoes. Erosion removed the soft sedimentary rocks, sparing not only the granitic column at the center of each peak but also the west peak's sedimentary layers. Softies no more, those are now metamorphic rocks, toughened by spending time close to hot magma. "Contact metamorphism" involves heat but little pressure, leaving the layers undeformed.

The magma came up between 27 million and 21 million years ago, apparently part of the Rio Grande Rift's grand-opening festivities. Over that 6-million-year span, a range of magmas produced both light and dark intrusive rocks.

Rio Grande rifting occurred after the main (Laramide) mountain-building events in the Rockies were over. During those events, plate tectonic forces compressed the western United States horizontally, forming plateaus and mountain uplifts. Afterward, the plate tectonic regime changed, stretching the entire area in an east-west direction. In the broad Basin and Range Province (far west and southwest of here), stretching was expressed primarily as countless normal faults. In contrast, along a line through the center of New Mexico and into Colorado, extension was expressed as rifting, with several long blocks dropping along deep normal faults. Some rifts, like this one, have volcanoes, and others don't.

What may look like the biggest dike near the Spanish Peaks is the Stonewall, ❹ a tall, vertical stretch of the Dakota Hogback. Cretaceous Dakota Group sandstones once lay flat across a wide area between today's many Dakota Hogbacks—at the Black Hills, South Dakota; the Waterpocket Fold, Utah; here; and along the Colorado Front Range. (See page 42.) Each instance is an edge of an erosion-resistant sandstone layer, standing out among less resistant sedimentary layers where Rocky Mountain uplifts warped them upward. The hogback characteristically draws a line between mountains and plains, as it does here between the Sangre de Cristo Mountains—originally a Laramide uplift—and the plains. Spanish Peaks magma pierced, rather than warped, the flat sedimentary layers underlying the plains.

Colorado Highway 12 ❻ runs north-south in the strike valley right behind the Stonewall, then follows the Purgatoire River ❺ where it has cut Stonewall Gap near the village of Stonewall ❼. The highway descends the Purgatoire into a coal-mining area with towns named Cokedale and Boncarbo. The Sangre de Cristos have iron ore as well; the ore and the coal once fed a smelter 60 miles northeast of here in Pueblo. The mines shut down in the mid-1990s, but there is still coal to be mined when prices warrant. The foothills have many curling roads that end in clearings resembling crude parking lots—a rougher pattern than the cul-de-sacs in ranchette developments (next page). The cul-de-sacs here are drilling pads ❽ for methane gas generated by deep coal beds.

Spanish Peaks beers are brewed in Bozeman, Montana, watched over by a different set of Spanish Peaks.

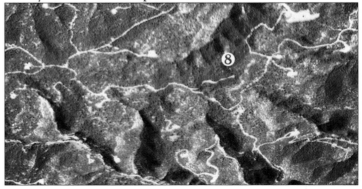

Sangre de Cristo Mountains and Ranches, Colorado

LOOK FOR a very long, narrow linear mountain range; in its foothills, look for a network of curving residential streets and cul-de-sacs with few visible residences.

Facing southwest ❶ roads of the Sangre de Cristo Ranches development ❷ Trinchera Creek ❸ Mountain Home Reservoir ❹ pivot-irrigated crops on the San Luis Valley floor ❺ Sangre de Cristo Creek ❻ U.S. Hwy. 160 just east of Fort Garland, CO

The Sangre de Cristo Mountains wall in the San Luis Valley on its east. This linear chain is so very long that from the air, it looks like three mountain ranges. Colorado's fourth highest peak, 14,345-foot Blanca Peak, is in a central cluster distinct from the more linear northern and southern sections. All three sections include 14,000-footers. The range was originally raised by the Laramide mountain-building events and then raised again much later on Rio Grande Rift faults that are still active today.

South of Blanca Peak, suburban-style arcuate roads and bulbous cul-de-sacs cut through the sagebrush and pinyon pine ❶. Ranchette development sprawls here not only because of spectacular views of the Sangre de Cristos but also because of land-use history. The San Luis Valley ❹ was the first part of Colorado to be settled by Euro-Americans, beginning in 1849. The town of San Luis is Colorado's oldest and remains 88 percent Spanish-surnamed.

Elsewhere in the West, land that looked attractive in the 19th century was claimed in relatively small parcels by homesteaders or miners; forested mountains became national forest. A different pattern prevailed under the Spanish system in New Mexico and southern Colorado: The Mexican governor in Santa Fe handed out enormous land grants to men who convinced him (which was apparently not difficult to do) that they were capable of utilizing them and defending them from Indians and from the United States. Grants that he made were reaffirmed in the 1848 Treaty of Guadalupe Hidalgo that turned these territories over to the United States after the Mexican-American War. However, U.S. property law was ill prepared for the Spanish system, which gave but did not spell out rights to the common settlers, not only to the titular grantees. Descendants of original settlers were still pressing claims in court more than a century later.

Beginning in 1969, publishing magnate Malcolm Forbes bought the old Trinchera Grant and divided it into four huge developments. One development was subdivided into ranch lots, each with 40-plus acres; one was split into more than 3,000 wooded 1- to 3-acre lots interlaced with big common meadows; and a third, the one in the photo, averages 5-acre lots with big views.

The fourth, the "jewel," is Trinchera Ranch, a lodge on 171,400 acres embracing the Trinchera Creek ❷ watershed. In 2004, the Forbes heirs donated extensive development rights on the ranch to a land trust for preservation as wildlife habitat but held on to rights to operate the lodge and to build 17 residences up to 10,000 square feet each. These palatial homes in the middle of a nature park may be built for 17 buyers of shares in the ranch. (Members of the legendary Trinchera elk herd all receive free passes.) Although this plan certainly takes advantage of tax laws, the indirect subsidy for preservation is modest compared to the ones that prevail in the West for mining, ranching, and irrigated farming. The idea of donating (or selling) development rights to conservation groups sworn never to exercise them is gathering steam in the Rockies.

Some see a threat that if ranching economics get any tougher than they already are, ranchers throughout the Rockies will fail and sell out to developers. A few studies suggest that big cattle ranches commonly offer better wildlife habitat than five-acre development tracts. That would depend, though, on how much the native vegetation is altered, how massive the ranchette construction is, how many months the homes are occupied, and so on. One might question whether the residential demand for marginal rangeland will ever approach the West's supply of it, yet the size of the Forbes developments as seen from a window seat would give one pause.

The San Luis Valley has a long history of large subdivisions of small lots often sold sight unseen and sometimes abandoned once they were seen. Abandoned lots can be bought for back taxes or in foreclosure, attracting more speculators. The Forbes developments have much less of that kind of history than do some others nearby on the valley floor, and they contain more finished homes than are obvious from the air. These are thoroughly rural home sites, typically entailing digging a well and a septic tank and using snowmobiles if year-round access is desired. A few main roads have power lines, but many buyers away from those lines stay off the grid, installing solar or wind power.

Great Sand Dunes, Colorado

LOOK FOR an area of sand dunes nestled in a crook in the west flank of a long, high, linear mountain range, the Sangre de Cristos; the dunes are on the east edge of a broad, flat valley with many center pivot circles.

Facing northeast ❶ Rito Alto Peak, 13,794 ft. ❷ Crestone Peak 14,294 ft., highest point in the northern section of the Sangre de Cristo Mountains ❸ Wet Mountains ❹ Pikes Peak, 14,110 ft. (p. 44) ❺ Sand Creek ❻ Great Sand Dunes ❼ Medano Creek ❽ northern slope of middle section of the Sangre de Cristo Mountains ❾ San Luis Lake, on floor of San Luis Valley ❿ Dry Lakes

Colorado's Great Sand Dunes are higher and more stable than most of the world's dunes. The highest dune stands more than 700 feet above its surroundings and has been at the same place for more than 100 years. A unique topographic setting makes this possible. The dunes are at the downwind corner of a large, flat, windy, arid valley with scant vegetation to hold soil or sand in place. The two most frequent wind directions are west and south-southwest. As the prevailing winds reach the mountain toe, they are met by cold air drainage coming off the mountains; the cold air slips underneath the warmer air, lifting the prevailing airflow. The sand-size particles, too heavy to rise, are left behind in front of the mountain.

Two creeks maintain the outline of the dune area ❻ by endlessly cycling the sand. After they descend from the Sangre de Cristo Mountains, Medano Creek ❼ flows south along the east side of the dune field, then turns west. Sand Creek ❺ flows west along the north side of the dunes, then turns southwest. Creeks normally sink into sand, disappearing from the surface and entering the aquifer. But these creeks encounter a hard pan of calcium carbonate about 20 feet down. During winter, the creeks are dry at the surface, but in late spring and early summer, the season for both snowmelt and thunderstorms, the creeks flow visibly on top of 20 feet of saturated sand. At these times, the creeks quickly pick up any sand that encroached on their bed over the winter, carry it around to the south and west sides of the dunes, and then drop it on the basin floor, where they spread out in an ephemeral, shallow lake. After the lake dries out in summer, the sand is lifted by the prevailing winds and redeposited on the upwind side of the dunes.

These dunes are darker than many because the sands include gray basalt grains mixed in with quartz. When granitic rocks weather, they yield grains of quartz, feldspar, and mica, minerals that make granite speckly. Further weathering in the presence of water alters the feldspars and micas to very fine grains of clay minerals. Grains of quartz, which resist alteration, remain sand-sized in large numbers. As all these particles wash downstream, clay grains come to rest in lakes and floodplains, whereas the coarser quartz grains settle in different locations as pale sand.

In this valley, much sediment derives from the volcanic San Juan Mountains. Basalt sediment typically weathers to fine particles, given plenty of time, but in this case, it travels only a short distance to the dunes, so some of it is still sand-sized grains. Other grains, nearly black with magnetite, collect in pockets that appear as shadowing on the dunes.

The San Luis Valley is the largest and southernmost of four broad valleys that collectively bisect Colorado. It and at least one of the others are expressions of the Rio Grande Rift. (See page 182.) The Rio Grande rises in the San Juans on the valley's west side, flows into the valley, and drains its southern half. The valley's northern half is a closed basin not drained by any surface stream; nevertheless, much of its water may still enter the Rio Grande, via the basin's aquifer. Although it holds no large playa lake, the basin has small playas ❾❿ whose varying salt content supports various algae, giving the ponds varying Necco-deco hues. The area around many of the ponds looks desolate, almost like mine spoils, but these are natural ponds, with natural tints.

The human activity that harms the playas is off-site: Agricultural water use has lowered the valley's water table, lowering water levels in the ponds and drying up many small ones, including several within the dune field as well. Irrigated crops hold more of the valley's soils and sands in place than nature did, leading to concerns that irrigation may gradually starve the dunes of their supply of sand. Alternatively, the cropland soil that does blow onto the dunes at this point is laced with herbicides and pesticides that potentially threaten the rare flora on the dunes.

The dunes were upgraded to a national park, Great Sand Dunes National Park and Preserve, in 2000. Preservation of the watershed above the dunes as far as the Sangre de Cristo crest was legislated in the same act, but it seems that preserving a natural wonder made of blowing sand may also require preserving the "sand shed" upwind of the dunes, as well as the water table under them. The more we learn about the web of life, the more we see that preserving national parks and monuments is a monumental task.

WESTBOUND: Go to p. 50

Valles Caldera and Jemez Mountains, New Mexico

LOOK FOR a broad, roughly circular mountain valley with four hills in its center; the mountain slopes west of the Rio Grande Valley with many deep, parallel gullies and the town of Los Alamos above them.

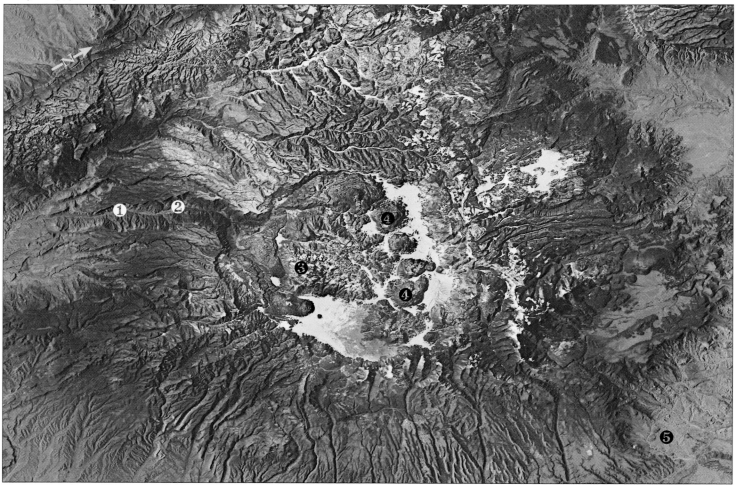

❶ San Diego Canyon ❷ Jemez Hot Springs ❸ Redondo Peak, within Valles Caldera ❹ rhyolite lava domes ❺ Los Alamos, NM
Broad scale astronaut view about 50 mi. wide

Until you are directly over Valles Caldera, the Jemez Mountains rising west of the Rio Grande may appear shapeless. With a close view, you will see a circular rim of cliffs encompassing a broad, round valley. (Your view will be less all-encompassing than this astronaut photo.) Four rounded peaks rise from the valley floor ❹. Streams, cutting narrow canyons, descend the mountain's flanks. San Diego Canyon ❶ is a deep gorge conspicuous on the southwest flank, with white travertines near its midpoint.

Many ranges overlooking the Rio Grande are fault blocks, perhaps with a few cinder cones. The Jemez Mountains, in contrast, are a large volcanic pile enclosing the resurgent Valles Caldera. Their southern lower flanks expose dark lava flows that erupted about 10 million years ago; their northern lower flanks expose lavas 6 million to 2.8 million years old. The two eruptive episodes produced 340 cubic miles of rock to form the base of the Jemez. Then the style of eruption changed.

About 1.4 million years ago, 12 cubic miles of pumice and volcanic ash erupted from a system of deep fractures arranged in a giant circle around the Jemez summit. Some fine-grained volcanic material was propelled to perhaps 70,000 feet above the vent, where the jet stream picked it up and carried it across North America. Much of the pumice and ash, however, rose in the volcanic cloud to lesser elevations before falling back to cover the landscape nearby. The rapid evacuation of this material left a great void in the magma chamber beneath the mountain. The remaining surface rocks collapsed into the emptied magma chamber, leaving a broad, round valley known to the geologists as the Toledo Caldera. To this point, Valles Caldera has a story similar to Oregon's Crater Lake caldera.

Three hundred thousand years later, a second explosive eruption of ash and pumice almost obliterated the Toledo Caldera. Again volcanic material ascended high above the Jemez from a ring of fractures around the summit, and again a circular valley formed where the summit collapsed into an emptied magma chamber. This second eruption obscured the Toledo Caldera and created the Valles Caldera valley we see today. To this point, the formation of the Valles Caldera is similar to that of many multi-stage calderas, some of them found in the San Juan Mountains. As with many other large calderas, its valley was internally drained and was in time filled by a large lake. But this volcano still had serious life in it.

One hundred thousand years later, new magma rose, pushing part of the caldera 3,000 feet up to form Redondo Peak ❸. This last stage makes Valles Caldera a "resurgent caldera," more like California's Long Valley Caldera. Raising its bed drained the lake via a breach in the southwest crater wall, quickly eroding San Diego Canyon in the soft tuff deposits on the mountain's flank. (Tuff is made of fine airborne volcanic ash particles consolidated into rock where they fell to the earth.) Finally, eruptions of rhyolite lava built smaller peaks on the caldera floor. Rhyolite lava is typically too viscous to produce lava flows, instead piling up around the vent as a dome, as on Mt. St. Helens. Rhyolite eruptions often explode pumice and ash into the air, and Valles Caldera's last eruptive phase, which sputtered along intermittently until 100,000 years ago, was no exception.

Hot springs rise on the caldera's western side and along a line above the Jemez fault, which San Diego Canyon follows. Jemez Hot Springs ❷ flow up through the fault's fractured rocks within the canyon. Over the years they have left visible deposits of white travertine, a strongly patterned, often perforated form of limestone formed where hot springs water cools. Travertine was the preeminent building stone of ancient Rome.

You will see little development within the caldera, thanks to the Dunigan family. Their 89,000-acre Baca Ranch was long known for ecologically sensitive timber management and ranching and for New Mexico's second largest elk herd. In 2000, the federal government bought the ranch for $101 million to create the Valles Caldera National Preserve, which will allow limited public access.

Mesa Verde, Colorado

LOOK FOR a mesa topped with a patchwork of green woodland and reddish burns, incised on its south side into long parallel valleys and ridges.

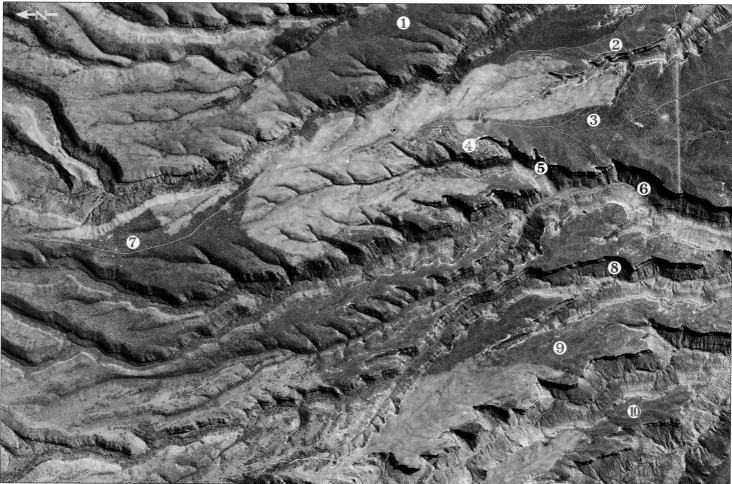

❶ Park Mesa ❷ Cliff Canyon and Cliff Palace ❸ Chapin Mesa, with many ruins of mesa-top habitations ❹ Mesa Verde NP headquarters ❺ Spruce Canyon ❻ Navajo Canyon ❼ park road ❽ Long Canyon ❾ Wetherill Mesa ❿ Wildhorse Mesa. Each mesa is a branch of Mesa Verde, and several of the canyons hold cliff dwellings. Spring would show somewhat more green than this fall view.

EASTBOUND: Go to p. 50

Many mesas with distinctive outlines can be seen from flights near the Colorado/New Mexico line. The most famous one—the one that is Mesa Verde National Park—can be recognized by a long, scalloped arc of cliffs on its north side, contrasting with a south side of fingerlike north-south ridges divided by narrow canyons, the ridges tapering gradually down to the Mancos River. Alcoves in the canyon walls hold Mesa Verde's cliff dwellings. (They are inconspicuous from 35,000 feet up.) These long, shallow alcoves were made by freeze-and-thaw cycles crumbling a water-permeable layer of limey sandstone. This happens where a thin layer of impermeable shale causes the sandstone cliff immediately above it to seep groundwater, concentrating the freeze-and-thaw activity at the seeping level.

The mesa is conspicuously *verde* (green) in contrast to the surrounding lower-elevation sagebrush/grassland. A fair amount of green remains even after the park saw 56 percent of its surface scorched by intense fires within a seven-year period, 1996 to 2003. The biggest fire, in 2000, burned almost half of the mesa. Burns can be seen in various stages of regrowth. It's difficult to predict what color the mesa top will be in any one of the next few years.

Fires here are not mishaps. They're the nature of the region—and especially of the pinyon-juniper woodlands that make Mesa Verde *verde*. Over most of the Rockies, the Colorado Plateau, and the Great Basin, summer brings many lightning storms with little or no rain. All common native plants have an ecological fire strategy. Pinyon pine and juniper trees are fire avoiders, which is more or less a euphemism for defenseless. They respond to fire by going up in smoke; they reseed into the burn a few years later and compete effectively until the next fire. In the natural scheme of things, 60-year-old pinyon-juniper stands were found wherever sheer luck had kept fire out for 70 years. Such stands were not extensive, and pinyon-juniper stands 150 years or older were uncommon, occurring mainly on rimrock—areas with such thin soil over the bedrock that plants could not grow close enough together to carry a fire.

A century ago, without an accurate conception of the consequences, the mission of the fledgling Forest and Park Services was to put out forest fires. Seventy years later, Mesa Verde was cloaked with more pinyon pine and juniper trees than it had ever seen. Dry fallen needles and twigs carpeted the ground surface. Under those conditions, any lightning strike during a dry month is likely to set the tree canopy ablaze and burn every tree in sight. Pinyon/juniper may be the extreme example of a western forest type for which decades of putting fires out have made the fire prognosis more severe, and no less inevitable, than it would have been naturally.

You might think that it would be fiendishly difficult to figure out what to do about fire in this park, but in fact, few alternatives exist; budgets will not foreseeably provide for thinning the entire forest to a density that would keep fires from spreading. The only realistic option is to create fire-safe thinned zones around valuable structures and vulnerable sites, then let the rest burn. Burned areas can be reseeded, if necessary, then maintained (using prescribed fire) as a naturelike mosaic of more and less flammable vegetation types.

Pinyon pine's way of ensuring reseeding after a burn is to produce large, oily, protein-rich, tasty seeds that birds and rodents will seek out. The seeds are a bit smaller than commercial pine nuts (from close pine relatives) and just as good. The critters will eat a lot, cache a lot to feed themselves through winter, and, inevitably, forget a few of the cached seeds. The forgotten seeds stand a decent chance of growing into trees.

Cliff-dwelling Indians also relied on these rich nuts as a winter staple. The Indians who built Mesa Verde's cliff dwellings were part of a group that thrived and grew in the area for at least 700 years but built and occupied cliff dwellings for only the final century or less, before moving away in the 13th century. The Southwest entered a period of chronic drought that may have made it difficult to grow enough food. One hypothesis holds that violent raids to obtain food became common, forcing people to build defensible villages like these cliff dwellings; when drought and famine persisted, most people abandoned the Four Corners area in search of more productive fields. Mesa Verde's people grew maize, beans, and squash on top of the mesa, in soil derived from loess that has enough clay in it to retain moisture ❸. It was a good location during normal rainfall years but too high above the creek in dry years.

Ship Rock, New Mexico

LOOK for a spiky crag in the middle of flat desert, with three prominent rays emanating from it to the south, west, and east-northeast; power plants marked by groups of tall smokestacks.

Facing northwest ❶ Red Wash; the slopes beyond it rise to the Carrizo Mountains ❷ San Juan River; town of Shiprock, NM, is on the river out of the frame to the right ❸ west dike ❹ Ship Rock ❺ satellite necks ❻ east dike, lowest of the three and inconspicuous at this angle ❼ south dike, 6 mi. long, 300 ft. high ❽ San Juan Generating Station, east of Shiprock (on facing page)

The Navajo called it the Winged Rock. When Ship Rock ❹ appeared on the horizon, 19th-century travelers may have thought that it looked like a mirage ship. It could be seen from Mesa Verde on clear days, but those are rare today, thanks to smog from nearby coal-fired power plants and sometimes smoke from forest fires.

Seen from seven miles up, Ship Rock and its radiating dikes ❸❻❼ can cut through a lot of haze, like a banner headline screaming "Earth Forces at Work!" The dikes originated as molten rock squeezed into cracks in the earth as rising magma domed the earth upward. Ship Rock itself is a volcanic neck, a stub of the main mass of magma frozen within a volcanic vent. A few little black thumbs near its base are stubs of satellite supply pipes ❺.

The land surface was roughly 3,500 feet higher than now, almost twice as high as the 1,700-foot rock; the dikes we see today were magma that froze short of reaching the surface. Over time, any erupted volcanic rock eroded away, and rivers carried it off along with 3,500 feet of shale and sandstone. The volcanic breccia in the volcanic conduits is a stronger rock, and it resisted erosion.

Geologists puzzle over whether rising magma forcibly splits the earth to create a dike or flows into preexisting cracks. At Ship Rock, we might infer that pressure from rising magma at the center created the radiating cracks. However, close study shows that the magma flowed into those cracks first and later created the main pipe. The dike locations were controlled by preexisting cracks in the basement rock, 5,000 feet below, and their strong appearance of radiating from the rock is illusory, as it is not perfectly centered.

Ship Rock is part of the Navajo volcanic field. Similar but smaller volcanic necks and a few maars can be seen south and west of Ship Rock. Geologists speculate that around 30 million years ago, the Ship Rock vent fed a maar, a shallow crater left where hot magma approaching the surface encounters groundwater and flashes it into steam. The magma explodes in fine particles through the explosion crater, and a ring of debris falls around the vent.

The plain here is part of the San Juan Basin, named for the San Juan River, which passes through Shiprock, New Mexico, carrying the melted snows of the San Juan Mountains. Coal, oil, and natural gas from basin strata have been exploited for more than a century, leaving signs of industry scattered across the land.

The four biggest coal-fired power plants ❽ in Arizona and New Mexico are on or near the Navajo Reservation; a fifth large plant is planned near Ship Rock. The plants were located far from the Arizona and California metro areas they serve, because there was coal ready to be mined here, and electricity is cheaper to transport long distances than coal is. The biggest power plant, near Glen Canyon Dam (page 57), receives coal by slurry lines from mines on Black Mesa, Arizona. The second and third biggest are east of the town of Shiprock, in the heart of San Juan Basin coal mining.

Two other reasons the plants are here are poverty and clean air. The Navajo Nation Council has generally treated jobs and royalties as offers they can't refuse, regardless of the serious health and environmental costs. The Southwest's formerly clean air offered a lot of headroom before the plants would start impinging on Environmental Protection Agency (EPA) air standards.

As the plants went on line, southwestern spectacles, including the Grand Canyon, got more difficult to see. Congress responded to the growing issue by amending the Clean Air Act in 1990 to raise air quality standards for national parks. Coal-derived pollution is a fairly small part of the problem at Grand Canyon but a major part of it at Mesa Verde. Although the region's coal is relatively low in sulfur, the plants are dirty in terms of mercury, carbon dioxide, and especially nitrous oxide: The Four Corners Power Plant near Shiprock emitted more nitrous oxide than any other U.S. power plant in 2005, while ranking 17th in power generation from coal.

Zuni Mountains, New Mexico

LOOK FOR a large, elliptical, forested northwest-to-southeast-trending mountain range framed by a single or double hogback ridge.

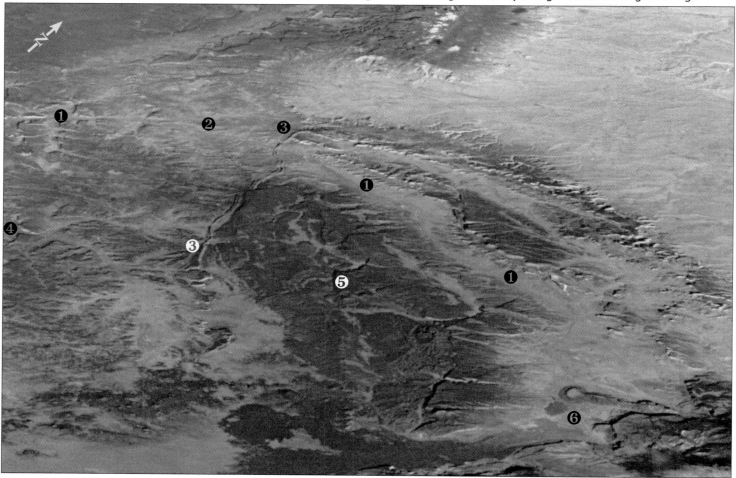

❶ strike valley followed by I-40 and U.S. Hwy. 66 ❷ Gallup, NM ❸ hogback ❹ Zuni, NM. Many flights pass over either Gallup or Zuni, as each has a NAVAID beacon. ❺ Zuni Mountains. In the Southwest, verdure is a good clue to higher elevation where the topography is not dramatic. ❻ Grants, NM, below club-shaped Black Mesa. Broad astronaut view about 70 mi. wide

If you pass this way on a flight from the Northeast, your crossing of the western mountains shows them in a sequence of different types and histories (described elsewhere in this corridor):

- First and highest, the Sangre de Cristo range, a strikingly linear range that originated as a typical Rocky Mountain uplift but was later uplifted anew as the eastern fault block of the Rio Grande Rift
- Just west of the Rio Grande valley, the Valles Caldera, a broad (but no longer especially high) rift-related volcanic complex
- Mt. Taylor, a relatively young 11,301-foot composite volcano with many small lava cones nearby
- The Zuni Mountains, the southwesternmost of the granite-cored (Laramide) Rocky Mountain ranges
- West of a broad desert plain, San Francisco Mountain, a 12,633-foot composite volcano with many small lava cones nearby

The Zuni Mountains ❺ are not among the highest or showiest Rocky Mountain ranges, but we like the visual aid they offer for picturing a bulge of ancient granite rising up through the vast plain of Cretaceous sediments. Hogback ridges ❸ arc around them; each features a cliff facing inward and an outer slope dipping steeply away from the mountain range.

Interstate 40 and remnants of U.S. Route 66 follow a broad valley ❶ around the north side of the Zuni Mountains. The Atlantic and Pacific Railroad (precursor of the Sante Fe) took that route around the Zunis because of coal deposits near Gallup, ❷ a stop on the main stagecoach route. State Highway 53 follows a much older route through a smaller valley around the south side, connecting the villages of San Rafael, 10 miles south of Grants ❻; Ramah, just south of a small lake dammed within a narrow valley; and Zuni ❹, the largest community, with a paved airstrip.

Precambrian granite more than 1 billion years old provides the Zuni Mountains' core. The surrounding hogback consists of sedimentary rocks 300 million to 70 million years old, leaving a gap of more than 700 million years between formation of the granite and deposition of the oldest sediments. Less than 70 million years ago, the Zuni Mountains rose, bending the overlying rock layers. Erosion stripped the sediments from over the crest of the uplift, exposing the granite core and leaving hogback cliffs and strike valleys. Similar hogbacks line Laramide uplifts throughout the Rocky Mountains.

The village of Zuni is the oldest inhabited site near the Zuni Mountains. Álvar Núñez Cabeza de Vaca was first to report large cities north of Mexico when he and four companions returned after nine years on an ill-fated expedition that began in Florida and reached Mexico City. The Viceroy of New Spain then sent Cabeza de Vaca's slave, Estéban, to guide the priest Marcos de Niza in search of the wealthy cities. Estéban reached Zuni, where he was captured and killed. On hearing of his death, Fray Marcos viewed one Zuni village from a distance and took possession of the entire region in the name of New Spain. Back in Mexico City in 1539, Marcos reported "Seven Golden Cities of Cíbola."

The following year, Marcos returned to Zuni with an expedition of 200 armored cavalry, 200 infantry, 2 small cannons, 300 recruited Indians, 1,000 horses, and many oxen, cows, and sheep, all under the command of Francisco Vásquez de Coronado. Approaching Zuni with 100 soldiers, Coronado was repulsed by a barrage of arrows and stones. He then laid siege, using the cannons, and soon accepted the Zunis' surrender. His joy in victory must have been short-lived when he found that Cíbola held neither gold nor silver nor copper nor knowledge of metalworking. The name lives on as the Cibola National Forest, partly on the Zuni Mountains, and the Cibola National Grasslands farther east. Coronado carried on as far as Kansas before returning to Mexico in 1542.

The Zuni and neighboring tribes drove the Spanish from New Mexico in 1680, only to be reconquered 12 years later. By 1890, they were raising sheep and cattle and making jewelry from silver and turquoise—all industries introduced by the Spanish. The main Spanish New Mexico settlements were in the Rio Grande valley, far from the Zuni.

The Americans established Fort Wingate at San Rafael in 1862. It served as Kit Carson's base when he starved the Navajo out of Canyon de Chelly in a scorched-earth campaign, killing cattle herds, burning fields, chopping down thousands of peach trees, and smashing thousands of pots to prevent the Navajo from taking food with them as they fled the valleys.

San Francisco Mountain and the Meteor Crater, Arizona

LOOK FOR a horseshoe-shaped cluster of high (often snowy) peaks just north of a midsize city (Flagstaff, AZ); a crater amid a flat plain just south of Interstate 40, 34 miles east of Flagstaff.

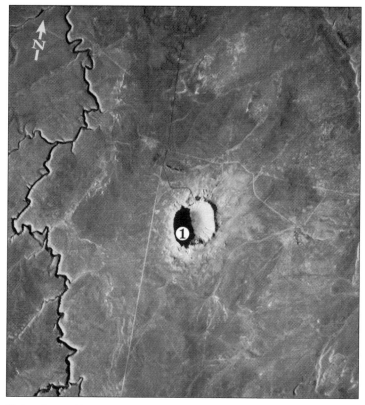

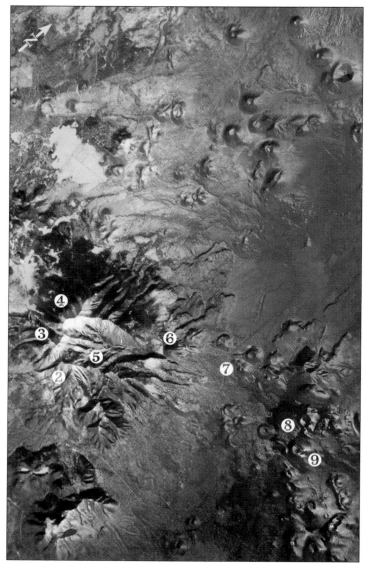

❶ Barringer Meteorite Crater. Astronaut view about 5 mi. wide. Peaks of San Francisco Mountain: ❷ Fremont Pk. ❸ Agassiz Pk. ❹ Humphreys Pk. ❺ the San Francisco Mountain caldera ❻ Sugarloaf ❼ U.S. Hwy. 89 ❽ Bonito Lava Flow ❾ Sunset Crater. Astronaut view about 13 mi. wide.

San Francisco Mountain rises above Flagstaff to an elevation of 12,633 feet, Arizona's highest. It rests on the Colorado Plateau at an average elevation of 7,500 feet, leaving it with an appearance of somewhat modest relief as seen from your window. Cinder cones are thick on the ground to the north and east; the tallest is Sunset Crater, ❾ about 10 miles east of the summit. These 600-plus volcanic vents scattered over 2,000 square miles make up the San Francisco Volcanic Field.

San Francisco Mountain is a composite volcano, one formed by dozens or hundreds of eruptions of lava flows and pyroclastic debris. Today, it appears as a horseshoe-shaped group, the six San Francisco Peaks, because its former summit collapsed, leaving a caldera ❺ that was later breached. Small glacial cirque basins are carved into the caldera. Small lava domes occur around the summit, on the lower slopes, and around the foot of the mountain.

The volcanic field commenced activity 7 million years ago. Domes of dacite and rhyolite erupted 3 million to 2 million years ago, only to be buried under an andesite stratovolcano, the predecessor to San Francisco Mountain. After lava sequences built the cone to 6,900 feet above its base, creating Agassiz Peak ❸, an explosive Plinian eruption interrupted, but did not terminate, construction of the composite cone. At its maximum height, San Francisco Mountain was likely a symmetrical cone, similar, perhaps, to Japan's Mt. Fuji. But then the upper slopes of the mountain collapsed, depositing debris fans on its slopes. The last eruption, 20,000 years ago, emplaced the Sugarloaf rhyolite dome ❻.

Sunset Crater, the youngest of many basalt volcanic vents surrounding San Francisco Mountain, began erupting in the winter of 1064–65 and continued intermittently for perhaps 150 years. (Tree ring chronology enabled scientists to pinpoint the year.) Just south of Sunset Crater, smaller cones extend southeastward in a line probably above a fracture or fault line. Around Sunset's base, several older cones are partly buried by Sunset's scoria.

Sunset Crater rises 1,000 feet above a one-mile-diameter base— a little higher on the east side, suggesting a westerly wind during its eruption. Its reds, pinks, and yellows inspired John Wesley Powell to name it for the sunset. The colors probably result from fumaroles in the vent following eruption of the scoria debris.

Many cinder cones first erupt a pile of gas-charged scoria to build a symmetric cone. (Strictly speaking, cinders are simply scoria pieces smaller than fist size.) Much of the gas in the rising magma escapes in that phase, leading to a quieter phase of basalt lava flows from the base. The Kana-A Lava Flow to the northeast has a long, narrow shape, indicating that it filled a narrow wash or dry stream channel; such a lava flow that finds and follows a stream is called an intracanyon flow. The northwestward Bonito Lava Flow ❽, on the other hand, has a broad pancake shape, filling a small basin between the margin of Sunset Crater and several older, nearby cones.

Like other Arizona volcanoes, the San Francisco Volcanic Field is near the transition between the Colorado Plateau and the Basin and Range. Some geologists relate the volcanism to crustal thinning in the Basin and Range; others infer that it may result from a mantle hot spot beneath the Colorado Plateau.

The Barringer Meteorite Crater ❶, popularly known as Meteor Crater, was the first feature on Earth to be recognized as a meteor impact crater. A young feature little disturbed by erosion, it is about 1,300 yards in diameter and 600 feet deep, rising 100 to 200 feet above the surrounding desert. The crater rim is mantled by fragments of both the local rocks and the meteorite; this material ranges in size from a micron to 100 feet. The underlying sedimentary rock strata lie flat a few hundred yards from the crater but turn upward at the crater's edge. The crater has an almost square shape rather than the circle we might expect from observing the moon. Widely spaced, northwest-trending faults with small displacements break the rocks surrounding the impact site, and may account for the crater's shape. Study of the structure suggests that 50,000 years ago, a meteorite 130 feet in diameter struck Earth obliquely at a speed of about 8 miles per second. Its impact was equivalent to a 15-megaton nuclear explosion—about 150 times the force of the bombs used at Hiroshima and Nagasaki.

WESTBOUND: Go to pp. 58, 60, 188, 62, 64, 66

GEORGIA

Charleston

Savannah

CORRIDOR 2:
New York–Philadelphia–Washington, D.C.–Florida

ATLANTIC

128

Tallahassee ★ 144

Jacksonville

130

132

Daytona Beach

Orlando
MCO

Cape
Canaveral

Palm Bay

Tampa TPA 146

The lure of a subtropical climate in winter helps make this the nation's most densely flown corridor. If your Florida airport is in the Miami or Orlando areas, someone will be deciding whether you take a land or water route between there and North Carolina. The water routes save time and jet fuel and may offer glimpses of Grand Bahama island, but as window-seat passengers, we would cross our fingers for the land option. Weather sometimes affects the decision; more often, it may be made by NASA or the Navy. NASA needs jetliners out of the way when it contemplates a launch from Cape Canaveral. The Navy often trains or maneuvers in the area off its Atlantic seaboard bases. The Navy seems not to mind heavy traffic directly over Norfolk, Virginia, which is typically overflown on both the land and water variants, both northbound and southbound.

The option by land, in or out of Orlando or the three Miami-area airports, tends to hug the coastline attractively near the fine old coastal cities of St. Augustine, Florida, Savannah, Georgia, and sometimes Charleston, South Carolina. Preferred land routes involving Boston or JFK fly over Charleston, whereas those involving La Guardia, Newark, Philadelphia, or Washington, D.C., diverge inland to Richmond, Virginia, or Raleigh, North Carolina. To or from Tampa, the routes are a little farther inland over Georgia and South Carolina, but combine with the east Florida routes between North Carolina and the Northeast.

Preferred routes northbound to Boston fly right over JFK airport. Boston departures for east Florida fly offshore, crossing Block Island, Rhode Island, and the eastern tip of Long Island before coming ashore again over the Delmarva Peninsula. The Boston to Tampa preferred route flies over Washington, D.C.; Greensboro, North Carolina; and Columbia, South Carolina.

On any route, you are likely to fly over at least one display of the interplay of sand, sediment, waves, wind, ocean currents, and rivers. Barrier islands are a landform especially well developed all along this coast. Inland from barrier islands lie estuaries with phantasmagoric swirls of shifting mud and vegetation. Science still has much to learn about how, and how quickly, barrier islands form. It's clear, though, that many jetties, sea walls, and other efforts to preserve coastal features that suit us were built in ignorance of beach and island processes. In many instances, they have already proved counterproductive and inordinately expensive to sustain. Watch for flow patterns of sediment around jetties.

A little-known, often subtle pattern to watch for is the parallel ovals of Carolina bays. (See page 122.) Look for them on land, not the seacoast, as they're misleadingly named. Although most abundant and visible around Bladen County, North Carolina (numeral 122 on the map), they are widespread on the coastal plain from Virginia to Georgia.

SOUTHBOUND: Start with pp. 6, 72

Atlantic City, New Jersey

LOOK FOR the Boardwalk, barrier islands, and estuaries.

The Atlantic City Boardwalk can be seen running along the western edge of the beach. It was built in 1890, following a hurricane that destroyed the previous boardwalk. The original was built in 1870 as an east-west boardwalk. Its original purpose was to allow tourists to shed beach sand while moving from the beach to the Atlantic City hotels.

Tourists aren't the only force of nature moving Atlantic City's sand. Atlantic City ❽ is at the northeast end of Absecon Island, a barrier island separating the Atlantic Ocean from two estuaries: Absecon ❼ and Lakes bays. Like all barrier islands on the Atlantic seaboard, Absecon is a dynamic feature responding to both longshore drift and the post–Ice Age rise in sea level. Its response to rising sea level entails shifting northwestward; the island will continue to move into the estuaries. This is a slow process, one that will not be completed during our lifetimes unless its pace picks up considerably. The response to longshore drift, on the other hand, is fast enough to observe over the course of a few years or decades. It looks as though you can even see it happening in the photo—a broad pale sheet of sand angling beneath the blue marine water ❿.

Atlantic City was originally built on a dune field just west of the beach. Storms occasionally flooded the beach, dune field, and city, moving lots of dune sand into the estuaries. Storm currents also moved beach sand offshore, where longshore currents carried it away. Storms from the northeast tend to move sand southward, whereas hurricanes or tropical storms from the southeast move it northward. The net effect here has been southward movement and loss of sand from the Atlantic City beach front. To slow the movement, engineers build angled jetties called groins. But after more than 75 years of these efforts, it's clear that groins provide only temporary relief, at best. Recently, the Army Corps of Engineers and local governments here upped the ante, bringing in 3.2 million cubic yards of sand. They plan to add sand every three years.

North of Atlantic City, the Mullica River enters Great Bay ❾ behind more barrier islands. Its mouth is a flooded valley typical of river mouths along the Atlantic seaboard from the New York Bight to South Carolina. When the most recent Ice Age was at its maximum, the river carried lots of glacial sediment and deposited it as a delta on a shoreline that, because of the lower sea level, lay several miles east of the present coast. What was once a river valley is, now that it's flooded, a bay that widens as it approaches the barrier islands. The river meanders formed after sea level rose, slowing the river's current. As the ice sheets melted, returning their water to the sea and raising sea level, delta sands were reworked into beaches, dunes, and barrier islands and continually pushed westward. Barrier islands are a fluid, ephemeral feature in the context of rising sea level.

The forest on the mainland is part of the New Jersey Pine Barrens ❹. The pitch pine, dominant here, likes the sandy, acid soils. In colonial days, pitch was a valuable commodity used to caulk wooden ship hulls. The pines themselves were too small to use as wood for shipbuilding. Seeing little other value in the sandy terrain and its stunted trees, colonists called them Pine Barrens. Some ecologists prefer the more sensible term New Jersey Pinelands and take considerable interest in them as a region where many plant species reach either their northern or their southern range limit.

NORTHBOUND: Go to p. 6

❶ Great Egg Harbor River ❷ Atlantic City Airport ❸ Mullica River ❹ New Jersey Pine Barrens ❺ Great Egg Harbor Bay ❻ Ocean City ❼ Absecon Bay ❽ Atlantic City on Absecon Island ❾ Great Bay ❿ sediment streams in the Atlantic Ocean

Dover and Delaware Bay, Delaware

LOOK FOR a small city set back from the bay, bookended by a NASCAR race track and a large Air Force base.

❶ Dover International Speedway ❷ Dover ❸ Delaware Legislative Hall ❹ St. Jones River ❺ Dover Air Force Base

A mosaic of farms cut by wooded streams typifies Delaware as seen from the air. The streams begin abruptly as sizable streams, form a dendritic drainage pattern, and drain into Delaware Bay without finding a major river first.

Delaware is one of the least-populated states, with 400 people per square mile, so the state capital at Dover makes a greater impression than one would expect for a city of 32,000 people.

The St. Jones River ❹ meanders through Dover, widening into Silver Lake and several small lakes in town before flowing past Dover Air Force Base into Delaware Bay. Follow the river downstream from Silver Lake to the third bridge, where a "wishbone" road wraps around the state house. The Green, a formal square surrounded by colonial buildings, is just west of the state house.

Delaware's intensive agriculture takes advantage of well-drained, nutrient-rich sandy soils. The sands around Dover were deposited by an ancestral Hudson River that collected water and sediment from ancestral versions of the Delaware, Raritan, and Schuylkill rivers. The ancestral Hudson left a deposit of sands stretching from northern Delaware through eastern New Jersey to Raritan Bay.

The sandy soils overlie marine clays deposited during a Pleistocene interglacial stage when North America's glaciers had melted away and those in Greenland and Antarctica were a fraction of their present size. The additional water in the world's oceans raised sea level enough to drown much of the mid-Atlantic coastal plain.

The drainage pattern was established during the last Ice Age, when the bay was dry land. These streams joined an ancient Delaware River that flowed through a broad valley to the Atlantic shore well east of the present coastline. The stream pattern we see from the air thus shows the imprint of two different worlds: one dominated by a Hudson River continuing southwest from its present course and one dominated by the Atlantic Ocean flooding inland west of its present beaches.

European explorers visited the bay long before Samuel Argall named it for his patron, Baron De La Warr, in 1610. Dutch settlers first colonized the Dover area in 1631 but were soon killed by Lenape natives. Swedish colonists settled at Wilmington in 1638. Peter Stuyvesant took possession of the colony for the Dutch in 1655. William Penn received his Pennsylvania land grant from King Charles II in 1681, and Delaware was added to it the following year. Lord Baltimore, of the Maryland colony, disputed Penn's claim to Delaware, and the dispute continued until 1776, when Delaware declared its independence both from the English crown and from Pennsylvania. Delaware ratified the U.S. Constitution in Dover in 1787 before any other colony, earning its nickname "The First State."

Penn founded Dover in 1683. The town center was laid out in 1717. The state house was built in 1722 as the county seat and became the state's capitol building in 1777, when the capital was moved from New Castle to Dover to provide a more secure location during the Revolutionary War.

Since that time, Dover became Delaware's second city as Wilmington grew into the state's commercial center. Dover does have its attractions, though. The Dover International Speedway is the large racing oval on the north side of Dover. When the NASCAR track ❶ holds its main annual events, the 100,000 spectators make Dover the (temporarily) largest city in Delaware.

Dover Air Force Base ❺ is home to the 436th Airlift Wing, the third-largest "industry" in Delaware. The airfield was among the Civil Aviation Administration's 1940 municipal airports built for coastal air defense. The city of Dover purchased a 587-acre site for $35,000, and the CAA paid for construction. Initially, the airport serviced antisubmarine forces. Today, it hosts a fleet of C-5 Galaxy aircraft, accounting for 25 percent of Air Force airlift capacity.

Dover holds one invisible attraction: Businesses seeking Delaware registration file their papers here. More than 500,000 U.S. companies are registered in Delaware, including more than half of those on the New York Stock Exchange. One reason for this is that Delaware imposes no taxes on companies registered within the state but whose activities occur outside the state. There are no residence or banking requirements. One person can hold all the corporation's offices. The state's corporate law framework has been in place for more than 200 years. The net effect is a low-cost, stable paper environment for a business's nominal location.

Washington, D.C.

If you want to **LOOK FOR** these things, study up on them in advance, locating them on the image; once they come into view, time will be short.

- The confluence of the Potomac River ❼, the smaller Anacostia River ❻, and the short Washington Channel ❺
- The Washington Mall, running east to the Capitol from the Lincoln Memorial on the Potomac
- The White House facing the Ellipse, a large park next to the mall
- Pennsylvania Avenue, the most conspicuous of several diagonal boulevards, connecting the White House to the Capitol
- The Washington Monument, central to the mall, south of the White House
- The Jefferson Memorial ❺, south of the Washington Monument across the Tidal Basin
- Reagan National Airport ❽ across the Potomac
- Robert F. Kennedy Memorial Stadium ❷ on the bank of the Anacostia, up East Capitol Street from the Capitol
- The Supreme Court is the discrete white marble building east of the Capitol. The Library of Congress is a block to its south. Union Station faces the Capitol building across a large park.

The District of Columbia's height limit for buildings of 160 feet confers prominence upon the Capitol and a few ecclesiastical steeples. Largest and most visible are the neo-Gothic Episcopal Washington National Cathedral ❾, with three square towers; and the neo-Romanesque Catholic Basilica ❶, with a dome and a narrow steeple. Both were built over the course of the 20th century. Arlington, Virginia, directly across the Potomac, has no height limit, making its tall office towers look like "downtown." They rise immediately north of the Arlington National Cemetery.

Washington, D.C., is a fall line city: It lies at the upstream limit of navigation on the Potomac. Just above the mall, the Potomac emerges from a gorge cut through hills of the Piedmont Province, which underlies the city's hilly northwest. Two other Piedmont valleys are parks. The larger one, Rock Creek Park, swings in loops through northwest Washington to meet the Potomac at the point where the Chesapeake and Ohio Canal begins ❿. The canal, built between 1828 and 1850, pierces the fall line navigation limit, then hugs the Potomac shore westward for 184 miles. The Coastal Plain underlies the city center and continues southeast.

Congress enacted the District of Columbia as the U.S. capital city in 1791. Virginia and Maryland offered a diamond-shaped parcel straddling the Potomac and embracing two colonial towns: Alexandria and Georgetown. In 1846, Congress returned the west-bank sector to Virginia. Pierre L'Enfant initiated the district's design, placing the Capitol ❸ prominently on top of Jenkins Hill. He designed a north-south, east-west grid of streets cut by broad diagonal avenues to focus on two seats of power: the White House ❹ and the Capitol. L'Enfant was applying a principle of Baroque city design established in 18th-century Europe: Impress the power of the state upon the citizenry.

A French engineer who worked with George Washington during the Revolutionary War, L'Enfant ardently sought this commission. His plan included 15 large open spaces where diagonals intersect major streets. He did not want the open spaces sold to developers. In fact, he so wanted to slow the city's development that he refused to publish his design, so Washington relieved him of his position. His successor, Andrew Ellicott, was able to reconstruct most of the plan from memory, as he had previously served as the site's surveyor.

Today, L'Enfant's plan is well preserved, thanks in part to the work of the 1901–02 McMillan Commission, formed to commemorate the District's centenary. The commission drew up a plan to preserve L'Enfant's design in future development, specifying the current height limitation. The plan extended the mall west and south of the Washington Monument, created the "federal triangle" of government offices between the mall and Pennsylvania Avenue, unified the rail terminals at Union Station, and specified the parks we see along the Potomac today.

❶ Basilica ❷ Robert F. Kennedy Stadium ❸ Capitol and Supreme Court, with Union Station to their left ❹ White House
❺ Jefferson Memorial facing the Tidal Basin, the head of the Washington Channel; Washington Monument, on the mall, stands midway between White House and Jefferson Memorial ❻ Anacostia River ❼ Potomac River ❽ Reagan National Airport
❾ Washington National Cathedral ❿ Chesapeake and Ohio Canal terminus at Rock Creek, just downstream from the fall line

Delmarva Peninsula

LOOK FOR small farm plots with long, narrow buildings; barrier islands on the Atlantic coast; flooded valleys on the Chesapeake Bay coast.

This thin sliver of farmland separates Chesapeake Bay from the Atlantic Ocean. Flights between New York and Florida traverse it on the Atlantic side southbound and on the bay side northbound. The Maryland-Virginia state line runs almost east-west where the peninsula abruptly doubles its width.

The Virginia National Wildlife Refuge includes the southern end of the peninsula, Cape Charles. Even from 40,000 feet, you should be able to see the variety of habitats there, though you may not be able to distinguish maritime hardwood forest from myrtle thickets or grasslands or whether a pond holds fresh or brackish water. In the fall, migratory birds follow the peninsula south to the refuge, where they settle in the millions until suitable winds arise to carry them over Chesapeake Bay.

A series of barrier islands runs parallel to the coast from there to Delaware Bay. The southerly ones are relatively undeveloped. Their ends typically thin and curve away from the ocean in response to both tidal and storm currents. Dunes develop slightly curved shapes in response to prevailing winds. Vegetation colonizes and stabilizes the dunes. The dune ridges at the ends of the islands show the growth of the barrier island in response to longshore drift.

Tidal flats ❸ develop behind the barrier islands. Grasses take root in the flats, helping to trap muds and silts brought in by high tides and storm surges. A filigree of channels drains the resulting salt marshes during low tides.

Salt marshes and lagoons on the bay side of the peninsula developed in response to rising and falling sea levels during the Ice Ages. At present, we are in the rising phase of the cycle as the ice caps in Greenland and Antarctica continue to melt.

The peninsula is an upland of the Atlantic coastal plain; the bays are flooded river valleys. During the Ice Age, when sea level was as much as 390 feet lower and the Atlantic coastline about 50 miles east of here, the Susquehanna River flowed through the present Chesapeake Bay. Many of the Susquehanna's Ice Age tributaries are now minor estuaries. Lower-peninsula towns occupy highlands and must tap groundwater for drinking, as surface streams are almost nonexistent.

The slender southern arm of the peninsula is nowhere more than 35 feet above sea level. Its sandy soils support truck farms that feed Washington, D.C., Baltimore, and much of northern Virginia. Chickens are the other big Delmarva product. The first factory chicken farm was built on Maryland's eastern shore in the 1930s. The poultry industry began growing to its present scale in 1968 when Perdue Farms opened its first chicken-processing factory at Salisbury, Maryland. There are perhaps 5,100 chicken houses on Delmarva today. Look for long, narrow buildings, often with metal roofs, and for grain silos, enough of them to store feed for 600 million birds. Local farms produce some grain, but the bulk of the feed arrives by rail from the Midwest Corn Belt.

The birds' waste fertilizes nearby farms, but there is more of it than can be used locally. Runoff from the farms carries large volumes of nitrogen and phosphate compounds into the streams, into the groundwater, and ultimately into Chesapeake Bay, where they feed massive algal blooms; when the algae die, their decay consumes oxygen, leaving dead zones in the bay. The bay waters we see today do not have the clarity known in past years.

The Delmarva Peninsula is about 10 miles wide in its southernmost Virginia section. It becomes much wider at the Virginia-Maryland border. Delaware claims its northern and western portions, where it separates the Chesapeake and Delaware bays. The late-19th-century version of the peninsula's name was Delmarvia, taking an equal number of letters from each state. Such evenhandedness scarcely seems fair, as the peninsula encompasses Delaware *in toto* and only modest portions of Maryland and Virginia.

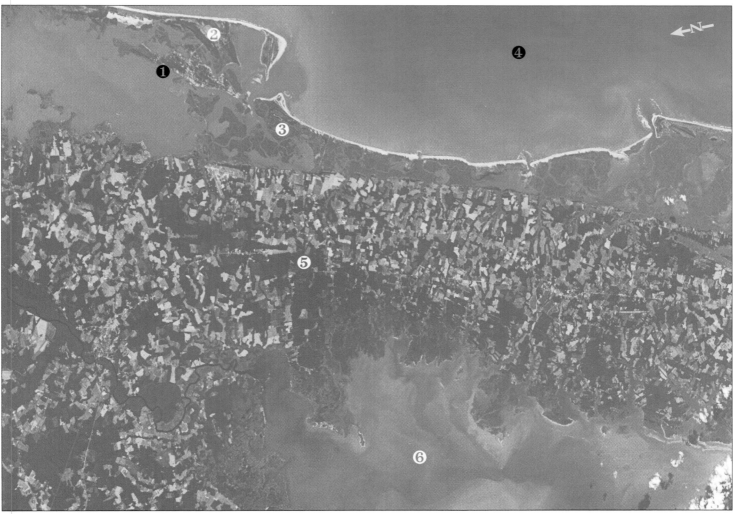

❶ Chincoteague Bay and Island ❷ Assateague Island, a barrier island ❸ tidal flats on Wallops Island ❹ Atlantic Ocean
❺ Delmarva Peninsula ❻ Chesapeake Bay, a flooded river valley

Chesapeake Bay and Newport News, Virginia

LOOK FOR the double, long, thin, broken strand of the bridge-and-tunnel crossing Chesapeake Bay; port and shipyard facilities in the cities clustered west of the structure's south end.

❶ James River Bridge ❷ Newport News ❸ Hampton ❹ Monitor Merrimac Memorial Bridge-Tunnel ❺ Hampton Roads
❻ Hampton Roads Bridge-Tunnel; these two bridge-tunnels are much shorter than the Chesapeake Bay Bridge-Tunnel (out of the frame to the right) ❼ Dismal Swamp ❽ Portsmouth ❾ Norfolk ❿ Corridor 2 contrails over Chesapeake Bay, in astronaut view

In its lower reaches, the James River is a wide saltwater estuary. After running southeast for many miles, the river turns abruptly northeast for about 12 miles before entering Chesapeake Bay ⓾ through a pass 2 miles wide, 20 miles west of the open Atlantic. The northeast-trending segment is Hampton Roads ❺. ("Roads" is an old term for an anchorage less sheltered than a true harbor.)

Several Virginia cities crowd the shores of Hampton Roads: Newport News ❷ and Hampton ❸ on the north shore; Portsmouth ❽ and Norfolk ❾, with their large Navy shipyard and naval base, respectively, on the south shore. Growth has fused them to Virginia Beach, founded on the Atlantic shore a few miles east and now home to the jet fighter base, Naval Air Station Oceana.

The Chesapeake Bay Bridge-Tunnel carries U.S. Route 13 between Norfolk and the Delmarva Peninsula. The bridge-tunnel looks like a very long causeway with a gap in the center where it descends into its tunnel section to allow ships in and out of the bay.

Chesapeake Bay is the largest embayment on the U.S. Atlantic coast. Buried beneath it is one of the six largest impact craters known on Earth. Although you can't exactly see this vast crater— even geologists were unaware of it until quite recently—you can see some of its effects on the shoreline. Hampton, Newport News, and Virginia Beach all sit above the crater's southeast rim. The James is just one of three large estuaries in a row that bend northward before entering the bay: The York turns as sharply as the James; the Rappahannock, more gently. The row of bends in these rivers marks the location of the crater rim. The crater's north end underlies a narrow segment of the Delmarva Peninsula at Belle Haven, and its eastern margin lies beneath the Atlantic, 20 miles offshore. The crater lies under 550 yards of sediment and water.

The Chesapeake Bay impact crater resulted when an extraterrestrial object struck the earth 36 million years ago. Geologists cannot say what it was, so they call it a "bolide": an unknown extraterrestrial object up to six miles in diameter that strikes the earth explosively, leaving a crater.

A crater 4,200 feet deep was first outlined in 1993, based on seismic data acquired for oil and gas exploration. Later, the U.S. Geological Survey took a more direct look by drilling seven bore-holes around the crater. These suggest that the bolide hit a marine shelf, killing everything on it and creating a lifeless environment for at least a thousand years. Sediments absorbed much of the impact, leaving a "small" crater 50 miles in diameter. If it had struck land, the bolide would have created a much larger crater and likely greater devastation.

Captain Christopher Newport commanded the lead ship that carried the Jamestown colonists to Virginia in 1607. The colonists abandoned their first settlement but soon met up with Newport and learned that reinforcements were coming—the good news the town was named for, according to one version. Other versions invoke an Irish founder named Sir William Newce.

Collis Huntington developed the deepwater port for his Chesapeake and Ohio Railroad in 1869. Huntington had previously cofounded both the Central and Southern Pacific railroads with Mark Hopkins, Charles Crocker, and Leland Stanford. In 1886, Huntington chartered the Newport News Shipbuilding and Dry Dock. Warships were built here during both world wars, when the port was a major embarkation point for Europe. After World War II, the shipyard built the first nuclear-powered carrier and submarines. Merging with Northrop Grumman in 2001, it became a pillar of the military-industrial complex.

Navy-dominated Norfolk is doubtless one of the best-defended coastal communities on the Atlantic. Its defenses were not so strong on January 1, 1776: When the British Navy attacked, the Virginians burned their own town to the ground. Norfolk has the distinction of being the only U.S. city completely destroyed in war and later reconstructed. The first Continental Navy Yard was built here in 1801. Sixty years later, the USS *Merrimack* sailed for Norfolk to save the yard from becoming a Confederate facility. It failed and was scuttled. The Confederates raised it and clad it in iron as the CSS *Virginia,* which fought the ironclad USS *Monitor* inconclusively in Hampton Roads in 1862. Today, Norfolk hosts the Navy's Second Fleet.

The first Chesapeake Bay Bridge-Tunnel opened in 1964 and was called one of the Seven Engineering Wonders of the Modern World. The 17.6-mile structure saves 95 miles between Norfolk and Wilmington, Delaware. A second, parallel span opened in 1999.

The Fall Line at Petersburg, Virginia

LOOK FOR a small city midway along a 15-mile stretch of a small river between where it is dammed to make a narrow reservoir and where it enters a widened estuary with bulbous curves.

Petersburg is a small city south of Richmond, Virginia's capital. The two cities ❶❼ are on the fall line at the Appomattox and the James rivers, respectively.

East of Petersburg's city center, yet surrounded by development, lies an area of forest with some small fields: Petersburg National Battlefield Park ❷. It preserves the site of Fort Lee, where General Grant held General Lee under siege from March 31, 1864, to April 1, 1865—the longest siege in U.S. history. After Petersburg fell, Richmond was evacuated and burned. Lee surrendered to Grant on April 10, 1865, at Appomattox, 70 miles west of Petersburg.

The fall line is an imaginary line connecting the highest navigable points on the rivers and streams draining the Appalachian Mountains. It occurs where Coastal Plain Province sediments thin out westward and give way to the older metamorphosed rocks of the Piedmont. (You'll see that rivers on the rolling Piedmont terrain cut narrow valleys with broad bends. Downstream, on the flat Coastal Plain, they meander.) The fall line became known as a line of cities founded in the colonial era. They sprang up where goods had to be either portaged or transferred from water to land modes of transport. Later, the cities grew when mills were built exploiting the drop in the river to power machinery.

Beneath the Coastal Plain, sediments of Cretaceous to present-day age form a wedge that thickens eastward beneath the Atlantic Ocean. The sediments were deposited as the Atlantic Ocean widened between North America and Africa. They eroded from the Appalachian Mountains, which likely formed an imposing massif at one time. Data from offshore oil-exploration wells indicate that deposition (and erosion of the mountains) was rapid during two episodes between 160 million and 65 million years ago. Oddly, deposition was slow between those periods and slow again after them,

60 million to about 5 million years ago. One of two things might explain this: The ocean was suddenly deeper or the mountains suddenly higher during each accelerated-erosion period. During the past 5 million years or so, sedimentation increased to rates not seen for 60 million years. The recent increase may be caused by Ice Age glaciation in the north and concurrent increased rainfall in the south. During this last episode, some uplift of the Piedmont (and the rest of the Appalachians) seems likely, as we see that erosion has resumed along and west of the fall line.

The fall line in Virginia served as a border for competing native groups prior to European contact. The Powhatans, an Algonquian-speaking group, occupied Virginia east of the fall line. They exploited the rich resources of Chesapeake Bay for their diet and did not venture far inland. The Siouan-speaking Monacans and the Mannahoacs occupied the Piedmont, with limited access to the bay. Early European writers report areas of savanna and grassland on the Virginia Piedmont, in contrast to the forested Coastal Plain. This suggests that native people substantially influenced the vegetation here, as they did in many parts of North America.

English colonists altered both Piedmont and coastal Virginia, replacing native forests and grasslands with grains and the evil weed, tobacco—a Virginia plant already in high demand in Europe. Today, abandoned Piedmont farms not covered by development tend to grow Virginia pine and tulip poplars. The Coastal Plain here supports a mix of southern species at the northern limit of their range—longleaf pine, scrub oak, and bald cypress—together with more northerly species, including white cedar and pond pine. Were these species typical of the region prior to European contact? Farming, abandonment, renewed farming, and renewed abandonment make this question difficult to answer.

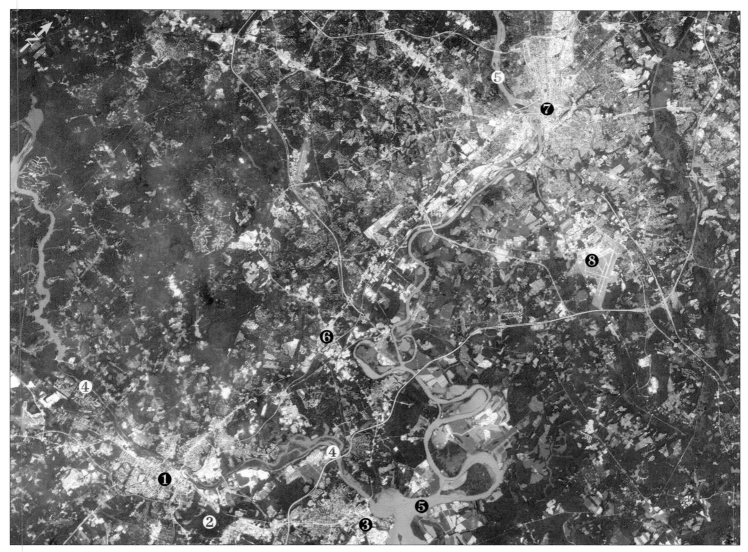

❶ Petersburg ❷ Petersburg National Battlefield Park ❸ Hopewell ❹ Appomattox River ❺ James River ❻ I-95 ❼ Richmond ❽ Richmond International Airport (Byrd Field)

The Carolina Slate Belt at Albemarle, North Carolina

LOOK FOR the rectilinear, almost gridlike, drainage pattern of a series of reservoirs, their lake arms, and their tributary creeks.

A series of hydroelectric dams ❸❼❽ impounds the Yadkin River ❺ as it flows across the Carolina slate belt. The river flows freely for only a few hundred yards below High Rock Dam before entering Badin Lake, the oldest of the Yadkin's lakes. The small arms of both lakes, as well as their tributary creeks, make right-angle turns, as though the underlying streams etched a grid pattern in the bedrock. Three miles below Badin Dam, the Yadkin's name changes abruptly to Pee Dee River at its confluence with the Uwharrie River.

The uplands here are almost evenly divided between small farms and woodland. Cotton and row crops are typical. Salisbury and Lexington developed along the first rail line through the region; rails reached Albemarle 40 years later, in 1891. Towns away from the rail line are few and small, reflecting a region that had neither navigable streams nor a good road system. Cotton farming supported most of these settlements as recently as the 1980s.

Metals played a greater role in the region's development. Prior to the 1848 California gold rush, gold mining was significant. The Reed Gold Mine, 15 miles west-southwest of Albemarle, became the nation's first, in 1799, and others followed nearby. Beginning in 1913, L'Aluminium Française, a French metal refiner, built the town of Badin ❻, the dam, and one of the first aluminum smelters. The French company sold it to ALCOA (Aluminum Company of America) at the beginning of World War I.

The Piedmont, a region of old metamorphosed rocks, runs northeast from Georgia to Pennsylvania. The Carolina slate belt is a large section of the Piedmont in both Carolinas, southern Virginia, and Georgia. In the Yadkin River area, it comprises a variety of volcanic rocks. The oldest include tuffs and rhyolite flows 700 million to 600 million years old. Tuffs erupt violently as ash columns that may ascend 10 miles into the air and be dispersed across thousands of square miles. Rhyolite makes the most viscous of lava flows, rarely moving more than a few miles from their vents. The oldest volcanic rocks probably originated locally as a composite volcanic cone similar to those of the Cascade Range. The slate belt is thought to hold the remains of several such volcanoes from late Precambrian to Cambrian time.

These ancient volcanoes erupted on the floor of a large ocean. Their deposits were covered, over time, with marine sediments, later metamorphosed to argillites, the "slates" of the slate belt. Chemical analysis of the lavas suggests that there may have been two very different volcanic settings. The older volcanics erupted far away during continental rifting that separated and removed a small fragment from an ancestral South America. This fragment rode on an ancient ocean plate and eventually became linked to a volcanic island arc. This ocean basin continued to close by subduction until the continental fragment and its island arc collided with North America about 470 million years ago, in the Taconic Orogeny. All these rocks were metamorphosed during that event.

The rectilinear valleys and low ridges seen from the air are due to folding and fracturing of these ancient volcanic piles. The streams and rivers erode the softer rocks and the fractures to form the trellis drainage pattern.

❶ Albemarle ❷ Pee Dee River ❸ Norwood Dam ❹ Lake Tillery ❺ Yadkin River ❻ Badin ❼ Badin Dam and Lake, with rectilinear arm on the right ❽ Tuckertown Dam and Reservoir; High Rock Dam and Lake are just out of the frame at top right

SOUTHBOUND: Go to p. 32

The Carolina Slate Belt at Albemarle, North Carolina   **119**

Barrier Islands at Cape Fear and Onslow Bay, North Carolina

LOOK FOR narrow barrier islands, inlets, ovals, and military facilities.

❶ several similarly oriented ovals in this area are Carolina Bays (see p. 122)
❷ Intracoastal Waterway ❸ Oak Island ❹ Cape Fear River, with Sunny Point military facilities on both sides ❺ Carolina Beach ❻ Cape Fear on Smith Island ❼ tip of Bogue Banks, and Bogue Inlet ❽ Onslow Beach
❾ New River ❿ Camp Lejeune (including most of the green area in photo)

NORTHBOUND: Go to p. 32

Capes, shoals, barrier islands, and inlets form the Carolina coastline. The Atlantic routes (over water) between Florida and northeastern airports pass between the land and the sea either at Cape Fear ❻ or at the New River ❾ inlet, both in North Carolina. The New River is in the middle of a long bight of coastline, Onslow Bay. Flights that instead take the land routes see similar coastal features—for considerably longer—in Florida, Georgia, and South Carolina.

On clear days, Cape Fear should be visible either under the plane or, if you take a New River route, about 20 miles west of the flight path when it is out over the ocean. The New River is a typical Atlantic Coast flooded river valley that forms an estuary reaching more than 10 miles inland. About 30 miles to the northeast, you may see Cape Lookout and the Outer Banks, at the far end of Onslow Bay.

Few streams reach the ocean in this section of coast. Geologists suggest that this area may receive less sediment than any other portion of the Atlantic shelf. Nonetheless, we see sandy beaches on barrier islands just offshore. These residual beaches derive their sand from erosion of local bedrock. Elsewhere along the Atlantic coast, rivers deliver sand to the continental shelf, from where it is distributed to the beaches.

The New River lies just south of a boundary between stable beaches to the north, with impressive barrier islands and bays, and shrinking barrier islands, only minimally separated from the mainland, to the south.

More than 25 miles long, Bogue Banks is the largest barrier island on Onslow Bay. The sizable dunes just behind the beach and the forest behind the dunes demonstrate the long-term stability of this island. Its eastern tip and the western tip of the next island, Shackleford Banks, are growing toward each other, shrinking the intervening inlet. Nearby dredging may be responsible.

Bogue Inlet, at the west tip of Bogue Banks ❼, lies above the ancient valley of the White Oak River. Browns and Bear islands, between Bogue and Bear inlets, support little vegetation. Photos from the 1930s show that their sand dunes have expanded into the lagoon.

Onslow Beach ❽ endures heavier use than its barrier island neighbors. Across its narrow lagoon is the Marine Corps' Camp Lejeune ❿, founded in September 1941 for amphibious training, taking advantage of its 11-mile beach. Although beach erosion and dune migration during storms are the norm on barrier islands, the Marines' landing operations here entirely overwhelm natural beach processes. Geologists report that current erosion rates exceed 15 feet per year.

Topsail Island continues the series of barrier islands westward from the New River. Dredging maintains a deep channel through the inlet and may contribute to changes on both adjoining islands. The Onslow Beach shoulder is eroding; the Topsail Island shoulder is growing.

Seventy-five miles northeast of Cape Lookout is Cape Hatteras. On very clear nights, the beam from its lighthouse may be seen at considerable distance. This lighthouse was erected to help passing ships avoid the shoals known as the "Graveyard of the Atlantic." More than 600 ships have sunk there. Rising sea level and the erosion of the Outer Banks by hurricanes and lesser storms have brought the shore much closer than it was when the lighthouse was built. Hurricanes occasionally drive storm surge waves over most barrier islands in the Southeast.

Sea level has been rising about six inches per century as a result of global warming. The long-term effect of both storms and rising sea level is to move barrier islands toward the land. Sand from the islands builds up in the lagoons as tidal deltas that appear as flat, marshy estuaries broadly patterned with diverging streams. Over time, the tidal deltas may become thickly vegetated salt marshes. Since no major river feeds sand to the Outer Banks, sand moved to the lagoons is not replaced on the beach side of the islands. The lighthouses may eventually need to be either moved or abandoned.

Carolina Bays

LOOK FOR ovals, all similarly oriented northwest to southeast, on the coastal plain. About 80 oriented ovals are in the image.

❶ Tatum Millpond Bay ❷ Reedy Branch Bay ❸ hog operation with pink lagoon (see p. 32) ❹ Cape Fear River ❺ White Lake, lined with boat docks ❻ Black Creek Bay ❼ Bay Tree Lake ❽ Horsepen Bay. This image of Bladen County, NC, is about 11 mi. wide.

A **fascinating and mystifying** little-known geologic feature is on view for air passengers over the coastal plains of the Carolinas and Georgia. Despite centuries of recorded comments on a troublesome type of wetland known locally as a "Carolina bay," broad awareness of a geologic phenomenon here goes back only to 1933. In that year, aerial photos of the bays were published, and a large pattern jumped out: neat ovals oriented in parallel. Barely perceptible from ground level, the ovals were an overnight sensation as an aerial image. Most journalism attributed them to a meteor shower—remarkable at a time when only one crater on Earth was generally accepted as meteor-caused, and the idea of a meteor impact wiping out the dinosaurs was far in the future.

The easiest bays to see are lakes ❺❼❽, of which the largest, Lake Waccamaw, is seven miles long. Although a few are naturally well drained, the majority were seasonal swamps called "pocosins," a nuisance to farmers, who drained and plowed them. After conversion to farmland, some remain accentuated as perfect oval fields with white outlines consisting of sandy rims a few feet high, highest at the southeast end. You may also see some as deeper green ovals on a paler background, since they are more moist than their surroundings.

Bays occur from Florida to Delaware or perhaps New Jersey, concentrating near the North/South Carolina border. Estimates of their original number range from 10,000 to 2.5 million. They harbor unique, interesting, and in many cases threatened flora and fauna. Wetlands-protection laws should save many of those that remain. The Savannah River Site (see page 126) holds the best collection of bays preserved with close to their original ecology—300 of them.

The term "Carolina bay" has murky origins, apparently referring not to water but to the several kinds of broadleaf evergreen bay trees often found in these swamps. The origin of the bays is cloudier still. Hypotheses divide into terrestrial and extraterrestrial camps, with most of the geologists lined up on the terrestrial side. Strong prevailing winds are said to have shaped the bays and built up their sandy rims at a time when they were all lakes. The lakes could have originated as the outlets of underground streams flowing through, and dissolving, limey bedrock.

Extraterrestrialists ask, "Where else on Earth are such lakes found?" In response, geologists point to plains full of north-south-oriented lakes near the Arctic Ocean in Alaska and Canada; they calculate that prevailing winds, sometimes from the east and sometimes from the west, set up wave currents that elongate those lakes north and south. A paper on the Carolina bays postulated analogous winds paralleling the coastline in both directions, elongating the lakes at their northwest and southwest ends.

However, those tundra lakes are emphatically not neat ellipses; they are irregular. And you have to have lakes first in order for wind to elongate them. Plains densely clustered with lakes are found in areas that were formerly covered with ice sheets or are currently permafrost. Neither of those conditions prevailed on the Carolina coast when the bays formed, during the Ice Ages. In more temperate settings, karst dissolution can produce a plethora of ponds, as we see in Florida (see page 144), but nowhere on earth do karst lakes compare to Carolina bays in size or areal density. It also isn't clear that all Carolina bays were ever lakes: a 2007 study of 30-foot-deep sediment cores in one purported bay found no peat or aquatic fossils that would indicate a former lake floor, but did find extraterrestrial particles at the bottom, beneath wind-blown bay sediments and above regionally typical material. This looks like potent evidence supporting the impact hypothesis, and it calls for cores to be taken in other bays for further confirmation.

Finally, in many instances, two or more elliptical bays at the same elevation overlap, with an intact elliptical rim on one of them. That is difficult to explain with lakeshore erosion.

So the extraterrestrialists have not given up. Meteorites as impactors are unlikely here: The bays are shallow, and lack characteristic meteor impact stress features. What they may resemble is found at Tunguska, Siberia, the site of a powerful 1908 explosion generally agreed to have been caused by a small comet core. This streaking lump of "dirty ice" vaporized before hitting the ground, leaving no crater and only traces of comet dust, but knocking trees down radially for miles, and excavating neat oval bogs. Could a larger comet have shattered on entering the atmosphere, breaking into millions of bits that each exploded near the ground surface?

Charleston, South Carolina

LOOK FOR a city filling a small peninsula amid a welter of lazy rivers; a gleaming white two-towered bridge crossing northeastward from the peninsula.

❶ Stono River ❷ Intracoastal Waterway ❸ Ashley River ❹ Charleston ❺ Cooper River Bridge ❻ Cooper River ❼ Wando River
❽ Fort Sumter ❾ site where the *H. L. Hunley* attacked the *Housatonic* and was raised again in 2000

In this venerable southern port and cultural center, stately rows of pre–Revolutionary War houses line the waterfront, having withstood the worst recorded earthquake east of the Mississippi, as well as one of the worst hurricanes. A tavern built around 1712 still stands, on a street still paved with cobbles.

Charleston was founded in 1670 by a friend of Charles II, the British king whose reign commenced the Restoration. This founder, Anthony Ashley-Cooper, gave his monarch's name to the town sandwiched between the Ashley and Cooper rivers ❸❻. By the time of the American Revolution, Charleston was the largest town in the South, and wealthy Bostonians were buying winter homes here.

In 1860, South Carolina was the first state to secede from the United States; Charleston saw the first shots fired in the Civil War, as well as the first major action, the bombardment and capture of Fort Sumter, a small Union outpost at the harbor mouth ❽. Blockading all Confederate ports was a crucial Union strategy, and Charleston became a hotbed of blockade-running sailors. It chalked up another first in 1864: the first use of a submarine to sink a ship. The 34-foot sub *H. L. Hunley* held a crew of eight to drive the hand-crank propeller, plus one to steer and pull the rope that detonated a torpedo on the end of a spar. All nine died when the torpedo sank the sub along with the target, USS *Housatonic*, which lost five Union crewmen. The Pyrrhic ratio was in fact worse than 9:5, as the *Hunley* had previously sunk twice during test dives, the first time drowning five of its crew members and the second drowning all of the eight crewmen, including promoter H. L. Hunley himself. Granted, it led the way to bigger things.

Today, the U.S. Navy is Charleston's leading employer. The title of busiest Atlantic port south of Baltimore usually belongs to Savannah, Georgia; Norfolk, Virginia; or Charleston, depending on year and definition. Yet Charleston has not ranked among the South's largest cities in the past century.

A magnitude 7.6 earthquake struck just northwest of Charleston in 1886. Most pre-1886 houses still standing in Charleston were damaged and now display the "Charleston lean." It was the most powerful U.S. earthquake east of the Mississippi in historic times. (The three 1811–12 New Madrid quakes *on* the Mississippi were bigger.) Charleston's quake puzzled geologists long before plate tectonics theory was developed, and it puzzles them still. Regions this far from tectonic plate boundaries rarely suffer big quakes, but field work in coastal sediments reveals a long history of earthquakes here. This gives geologists and geophysicists good problems to attack: What causes this stress pattern? And when could it produce another major earthquake?

The eight-lane Arthur Ravenel Jr. Cooper River Bridge ❺ opened in 2005. In the astronaut photo, two ghost bridges shadow it. They are predecessor Cooper River bridges that were torn down in 2006, a few months after the photo was taken. The older two-lane bridge was thrillingly high, steep, and narrow when it opened in 1929, an engineering marvel for its day. An adjacent three-lane bridge augmented it in 1966. Tens of thousands of runners used to cross both bridges every year as part of a 10-kilometer race. Now they sweat a little harder racing up the new one, which was built much higher to let today's bigger ships into the port.

The new bridge looks much like a suspension bridge, but if you fly into Charleston, you'll get a close enough look to see the difference: Its cables are all straight, fanning out from the diamond-shaped towers, as opposed to a suspension bridge's vertical cables hanging from two main cables that sag in an arc. This is a cable-stayed bridge, a structure popular in Europe and East Asia in the past 20 years but less so in America. Suspension bridges are preferred for most spans longer than 2,500 feet, but engineers increasingly look to cable-stayed bridges as option A for spans in the 1,000- to 2,500-foot range and as option B for longer spans on sites where suspension cables would be difficult to anchor. At 1,546 feet, Cooper River's is the second-longest cable-stayed span in North America. The fourth and fifth longest, with H-shaped white towers, are also on the southeast coast, in Jacksonville, Florida, and Brunswick, Georgia. As Brunswick and Charleston both host NAVAIDS, some flights may provide views of all three. The world's longest, in Japan, is 2,920 feet, and China is building a considerably longer one.

Savannah River Site, South Carolina

LOOK FOR a largely forested tract with a few industrial-scale buildings on the northeast bank of the Savannah River.

The Savannah River Site (SRS) is hard to miss from the air. Its 310 square miles of forests contrast dramatically with the surrounding patchwork of small cotton and soybean fields on the upper Coastal Plain. The hardwood forests on the bottomlands obscure dozens of small, oval Carolina bays which are more intact ecologically than those elsewhere. (See page 122.) The percent of forested land on the site grew from 48 percent to 80 percent between 1951 and 1988, through the largest mechanized tree-planting program in U.S. history.

Note the dark color of streams originating on the Coastal Plain, in contrast to the red water of the Savannah River and other streams draining the Piedmont, about 25 miles to the northwest. Blackwater streams drain pinelands and wetlands, and carry acidic products of plant decay, especially tannic and humic acids. Red streams from the Piedmont carry less organic matter and more inorganic silt as well as more oxygen, and are able to support more diverse aquatic life.

A network of roads connects large industrial structures within this forest. There is nothing that resembles housing, nothing that even resembles a barracks. The SRS is a federal facility built to manufacture tritium and plutonium-239 for nuclear weapons. The five largest buildings are nuclear reactors ❷. Others are for processing the reactors' products ❶. The Savannah River and the many artificial lakes ❸ meet the site's heavy demands for fresh water.

SRS's tale is a small history of the cold war. DuPont and Company designed, built, and operated the original facility beginning in 1951. In the same year, the Savannah River Ecology Laboratory opened to monitor the site's impact on the local flora and fauna. Three reactors were operating by 1955, when the site first shipped plutonium to a weapons fabrication plant. As the cold war began to wind down, SRS became the first designated National Environmental Research Park. In 1981, environmental cleanup began. SRS continued producing nuclear materials for weapons until 1991, when the cold war ended. Five years later, the on-site Defense Waste Processing Facility began incorporating radioactive waste into glass material for long-term storage. SRS began shipping glassified radioactive waste to the New Mexico Waste Isolation Pilot Project in 2001.

Given enough time, it may be inevitable that fluids stored in underground tanks and unlined pits will leak and enter the groundwater. The Coastal Plain sediments beneath the site are gravels, sands, clays, and small amounts of limestone. Metamorphic rocks of the Piedmont lie beneath them. Both Piedmont and Coastal Plain rocks contain aquifers, layers of permeable rock through which water can move. Both also contain impermeable layers that prevent water from moving deeper.

Contaminants sinking into the ground often dissolve in the first, or highest, groundwater aquifer they encounter. Monitor wells over a 50-year period show tritium, nitrates, heavy metals, and radionuclides in the shallow aquifer, which flows slowly toward local streams and the Savannah River. Fortunately, an impermeable layer separates these aquifers from the deeper aquifers that supply the local drinking water.

Although not originally designed as an experiment in groundwater flow or contaminant remediation, these are now the important activities at SRS. An experimental treatment for contaminated groundwater, devised there in 1983, is now operating at an industrial scale. A treatment column processes 500 gallons per minute. At this rate, cleanup will still take many years.

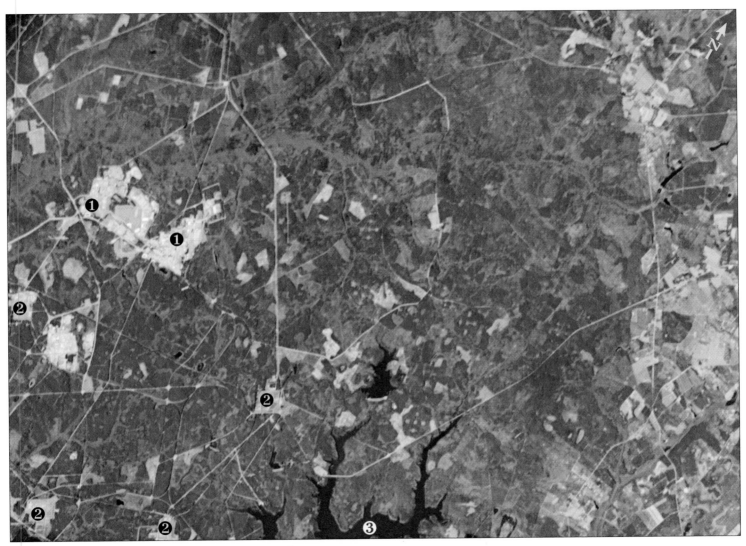

❶ waste processing facilities ❷ nuclear reactors ❸ Par Pond

Okefenokee Swamp, Georgia and Florida

LOOK FOR brown water stippled with many islands, in a large undeveloped area, either green or extensively blackened from fires.

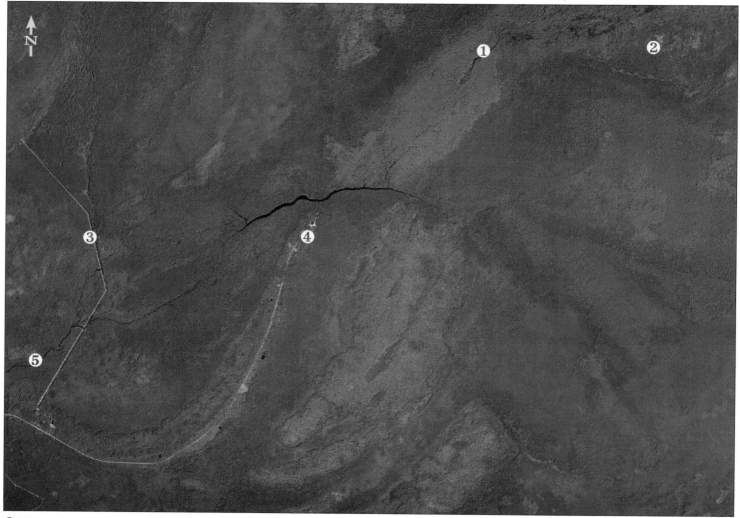

❶ Middle Fork Suwannee River ❷ Floyds Island ❸ Suwannee River Sill ❹ road end at Stephen Foster State Park
❺ Suwannee River

A **body of fresh water** so large, encircled by so much swamp, and so filled with both solid islands and floating islands, you know when you fly over it that this must be the home of Pogo Possum: the Okefenokee Swamp. With good sunlight, you may observe the brown color of the swamp water. Decaying organic matter adds tannic acid to the water, rendering it the color of tea.

Many commercial flights fly above the western margin, where the Suwannee River ❶❺ drains the swamp and flows to the Gulf of Mexico. You may be able to spot the levee ❸ and small dam built on the west side in 1960 to raise the water level a few feet, and the few rail lines, canals, and roads that have been built along the margins of the swamp.

Fewer flights pass over the southeastern margin, where the smaller St. Marys River drains the swamp and flows to the Atlantic Ocean. Trail Ridge, composed of Aeolian sand dunes deposited during the Ice Ages, bounds the east side of the swamp and extends south to Lake Okeechobee in central Florida.

The 70 "fixed" islands may be covered with longleaf pine or hardwood trees. Elsewhere, pinelands, hardwood hammocks, and cypress swampland are interspersed throughout the Okefenokee. The soil is nutrient-poor and acidic. Carnivorous plants, including large pitcher plants, sundews, and butterworts, flourish because they can supplement the soil's scant nutrients with those they collect from hapless insects.

The "floating islands" are mats of peat detached from the lake bottom and are moving about the swamp driven by wind or water currents. These tend not to move far, for the swamp's depth averages two feet. Okefenokee is a Seminole term for "land of the trembling earth," referring to the movement of shrubs and trees when a person stamps on the nearby soil enthusiastically.

Within and around the swamp are 60,000 acres of prairie, formed during prolonged droughts when fires burned both the vegetation and the underlying peat.

Native groups inhabited the Okefenokee when the Spanish built missions on its borders in the 17th century. Between the First and Second Seminole wars, many Seminoles took refuge in the swamp; they had abandoned their village on Floyds Island ❷

before General C. R. Floyd managed to find it in 1838. Few Euro-Americans sought to exploit the swamp until railroads reached its northern margin in 1861. By 1898, rail lines surrounded the swamp, enabling logging and turpentine distillation to penetrate it.

The Okefenokee's old-growth cypress was especially inspiring to loggers. Eleven miles of canal were dug on the east side in 1891 by the Suwannee Canal Company, which intended to log the old growth before draining the swamp and converting it to farms. A recession ended the company but not the dream. Loggers removed more than 431 million board feet of old growth before the timber supply was exhausted in 1927.

The Okefenokee National Wildlife Refuge was created with 430,000 acres in 1936. Cattle ranching was still allowed, but became problematic with bear and wildcat hunting no longer permitted. Ranching ceased by 1958. In 1974, Congress created the Okefenokee National Wilderness Area with 353,000 acres taken from within the wildlife refuge.

Drought in 1954 and 1955 reduced the water level, resulting in a series of forest and peat fires. The Suwanee River Sill ❸, a levee, was then built to raise the water level and reduce the fire hazard during extended drought. It proved ineffective and was partially breached in an effort to restore the natural hydrology. You are likely to see blackened areas, if not actual smoke plumes, when you fly over the swamp. April and May of 2007 brought record fires: One that invaded the swamp from the north was declared the largest wildfire in Georgia history, only to be stripped of that title a few days later by a fast-growing new fire in the south part of the swamp. The second fire blew on into Florida to become that state's record wildfire as well. The combined fire swept most of the swamp area.

As for Pogo Possum, Albert Alligator, Howland Owl, and the other critters: The comic strip set in the Okefenokee was drawn by Walt Kelly and first appeared as *Bumbazine and Albert the Alligator* in 1943. *Pogo* debuted in 1948 through the pages of the New York *Star*, where Kelly was the art director. By the late 1950s, *Pogo* was syndicated in 600 papers. A cartoon for Earth Day 1971 bore the caption, "We have met the enemy and he is us."

St. Augustine, Florida

LOOK FOR a small city on a peninsula adjoining a large tidal inlet. Look for the small fortification.

As you fly above Florida's northeast coast, you may not notice St. Augustine. Although it is the oldest settlement continuously inhabited by Euro-Americans in the New World, it is not the largest. The city sits on a small peninsula between a minor slough and a larger tidal inlet. A wide barrier beach separates it from the Atlantic. A four-pointed star fortification marks the site of the colonial Spanish Castillo de San Marcos ❺. You'll find this where the tidal inlet turns south after crossing the large, sandy barrier islands. The narrow grid of streets to the west and south of the fort retains the Spanish colonial settlement's pattern. Across the inlet, the modern beach communities are built with larger blocks. Here, the streets curve in concentric patterns typical of leisure communities. West of the old town and across a tidal marsh, modern residential housing tracts display a modern rectangular pattern of larger blocks and wider streets.

Two features key to the development of Florida in the 20th century are also visible: the railroad and U.S. Highway 1. You will find the railroad by looking west of the Castillo, where a narrow right of way cuts straight across the marshland and then turns west to cross a bridge over the small slough. Next to the railroad bridge, the broad, white highway bridge carries U.S. 1 over the slough and then turns south.

Looking farther west, undeveloped land is marked by a number of large rectangular, water-filled pits, among which you should be able to find a few active open pits. Some of these pits were coquina quarries; others were sand and gravel pits. Coquina is a shell-rich limestone used as a building stone during the early development of St. Augustine.

St. Augustine was settled by the Spanish under Don Pedro Menéndez de Avilés on St. Augustine's Day, August 28, 1565. The Timucuan native village of Seloy preceded this settlement, as did the French settlement at Fort Carolina north of here on the St. Johns River in 1564. Fort Carolina motivated Spain's King Philip II to dispatch Menéndez to Florida with orders to remove the French.

The English founded colonies in Georgia and the Carolinas and ventured into Florida with attacks on St. Augustine in 1586, 1668, 1702, and 1740. Spain ceded Florida to the British in 1763 in exchange for Havana. The Treaty of Paris in 1783 returned Florida to Spain, which ruled the colony until 1821, when Spain sold Florida to the United States.

In 1885, Henry Flagler, a cofounder of Standard Oil, began development of St. Augustine as a winter resort. He built the Alcazar and the Ponce de Leon hotels for wealthy northeastern clients. To bring them south, Flagler organized the Florida East Coast Railway between New York and St. Augustine and later extended the railroad to Palm Beach and Miami.

In addition to providing northerners with easy access to Florida, the railroad provided transport for Florida produce, especially citrus fruits, to northern cities. Orchards of oranges, grapefruit, and tangerines thrived on the well-drained sandy soils found along the eastern side of the Florida peninsula. These soils were poor in nutrients, stimulating the development of Florida's phosphate fertilizer industry. Citrus growing in northern Florida was abandoned after a series of severe freezes in the early 20th century. Today, the industry is concentrated in the southern counties of the state, where it remains focused on the east side's sandy soils.

U.S. Highway 1 ❷ is a product of the Good Roads Movement, which arose in 1910. Carl Fisher was an Indiana developer who built the Indianapolis Motor Speedway and then began investing in Miami property. He was a proponent of the first transcontinental interstate road, the Lincoln Highway, from New York to San Francisco. He followed this in 1914 with his Dixie Highway proposal to link the Midwest with Miami. The resulting hard surface road was built as U.S. 1 along the east coast of Florida. When it reached Miami, Fisher was there to receive the tourists, just as Flagler had been when his railroad reached Miami years before.

❶ Tolomato River and Intracoastal Waterway ❷ U.S. Hwy. 1 ❸ borrow pit ❹ railroad right of way ❺ Castillo de San Marcos ❻ St. Augustine ❼ Davis Shores ❽ Matanzas River and Intracoastal Waterway ❾ Vilano Beach ❿ Conch Island

Trail Ridge Heavy Mineral Mines, North Florida

LOOK FOR white rectangular pits, some with lakes and some with green vegetation.

West of Jacksonville, a linear series of mines appears as white rectangular pits. These are mines for heavy minerals including rutile and zircon. You will see water-filled lakes where mining is ongoing, large rectangles of light brown to white soil where mining has occurred, and other rectangles with a hint of green color where older pits have been restored.

These mines exploit placer deposits, loose sedimentary grains laid down by wind or water. The placers are young by geological standards, and the sands are not cemented together. This makes placer deposits suitable for dredging, the least expensive of mining techniques. Ponds are dug on the mine site. Dredges then move a mixture of heavy mineral grains, sand, clay, and water to a wet mill, where centrifuges separate the heavy grains from the lighter material. Ores make up only 5 percent of the rock mass here. After centrifuging, the concentrated ore consists of 80 percent heavy minerals, and it is ready to go to a refinery for further processing. The clay and sand tailings are dumped in the pond behind the dredge. Eventually, the pond is reclaimed with topsoil and vegetation.

Rutile is a primary ore for titanium, used principally as white pigment in paint. When you look at a white wall, a white sign, or a white sheet of paper, you are looking at titanium oxide. Titanium is also used in place of steel: It is similar in strength and melting temperature but lower in density, making it ideal for aviation. Titanium may make up as much as 30 percent of the weight of the aircraft you ride. Zircon is the primary ore for zirconium, a staple of the jewelry trade and cable television sales.

Placer mining of heavy minerals began in the Jacksonville region during World War I. Ilmenite, another primary ore for titanium, was initially mined south of Jacksonville Beach at Ponte Vedra Beach. These deposits were exhausted in 1929, and now the old mine site is part of a luxury resort. Placer mining resumed in the 1940s, when the first pits opened atop Trail Ridge.

The ridge itself extends all the way from the eastern margin of Georgia's Okefenokee Swamp to Orlando. It once carried the Alachua Trail, a thoroughfare for native people traveling parallel to the coast before the arrival of Europeans. The ridge consists of sand dunes deposited during the Ice Age, when sea level was 300 feet lower than it is today. Originating by erosion of the southern Appalachians, the sand was transported to the Atlantic by streams and then south by longshore drift, adding to the beach deposits of the Ice Age Atlantic shore. Prevailing winds drove the sands to their current position and piled them up into dunes. The ridge averages 150 feet elevation, which is not trivial in low-elevation, low-relief Florida. Trail Ridge is the largest of several north-south-trending ridges in central Florida, all of them resulting from similar beach processes.

On the east flank of Trail Ridge, near Starke, is Kingsley Lake, the highest lake in northeast Florida. The lake is more than 90 feet deep and is thought to be located on a giant sinkhole, a reminder that beneath the sands lie the limestones of the Florida Platform.

❶ restored heavy mineral mine sites ❷ active heavy mineral mine ❸ U.S. Hwy. 301 ❹ Hugh, FL

SOUTHBOUND: Go to pp. 144, 146, 148, 150
Trail Ridge Heavy Mineral Mines, North Florida   **133**

Miami Beach, Florida

LOOK FOR patterns of deeper and shallower water; locations of fishing boats; barrier islands, sea walls, and jetties.

❶ Hialeah Park racetrack ❷ Miami International Airport ❸ Orange Bowl stadium ❹ Biscayne Bay ❺ Virginia Key ❻ jetties maintaining the boat channel ❼ Miami Beach ❽ shallow water ❾ deep water (Atlantic Ocean)

NORTHBOUND: Go to pp. 150, 148, 146, 144

This happens quickly: Flights departing Miami and West Palm Beach typically start out eastward, turn, and cross the cities within minutes. Arriving flights also offer brief views of the urban centers. Much on view is a built environment: the beach, the roads, the parks, the islands, the Miami port with its cruise ships, the many palm trees, and, of course, the buildings. Nature survives just offshore, where you may see small craft anchored over shoals formed by reefs, favored by both divers and fishermen, or larger vessels anchored between the reefs, possibly dredging the sea floor.

Miami Beach and other beach cities sit on barrier islands separated from the mainland by tidal bays. The Intracoastal Waterway runs through the bays, connecting them with canals. In the barrier island system, gaps, some natural and some not, allow access to the Atlantic for boats, barges, and ships. Jetties ❻ flank the inlets to prevent longshore currents from blocking them with sand.

Above the beaches rise seawalls. During storms, they rebuff the waves with some success, but the retreating ocean water sweeps much of the beach sand offshore. Some waves surmount the walls, and flooding occurs whenever major storms come ashore.

The beaches separating the urban landscape from the ocean are no longer natural beaches. The seawalls and jetties exemplify "hard" beach stabilization. These efforts to keep beach sand in place sometimes prove effective, but in most cases they simply transfer beach-erosion problems to a nearby beach, in a vicious circle of sand one-upmanship. In the past 30 years, "soft" beach stabilization has been preferred; for example, in "beach nourishment," sand is pumped to the beach from offshore or trucked in from onshore sandpits.

Most Atlantic beach sands, including the broad Daytona Beach, are derived from the Appalachian Mountains, transported by rivers to coastal deltas and then moved long distances along the coast by longshore currents. Although Cape Canaveral is more than 200 miles from the Appalachians and far from any river draining them, the cape is nonetheless covered by sand eroded from them. These sands are made of quartz, a relatively hard but light mineral.

If you walk on the beaches near Miami, you may find that the sand feels softer than on beaches north of Palm Beach. Sands along the southeast Florida coast include a portion of limestone, made of calcium carbonate, which is much softer than quartz. Beaches near Miami no longer have as much quartz sand as they used to. Hard beach stabilization resulted in the loss of much of the original sand during hurricanes and northeasters. In the past 20 years, sand was piped ashore from troughs on the shelf between reefs; that sand derives largely from limestone torn off the reefs.

The continental shelf here goes out only a couple of miles before descending steeply into the South Atlantic Bight. Warm tropical waters flow out of the Caribbean through the Florida Strait between Cuba and Florida, then turn northeast, joining the Gulf Stream. With few rivers entering the Atlantic in southeast Florida, the ocean water is clean, warm, and conducive to growing tropical reefs. Until 2,000 years ago, reefs actively grew just off Palm Beach. A slight drop in sea temperature, probably caused by a shift in currents, ended reef growth there.

The remains of past reefs constitute a carbonate shelf extending from Miami to the Bahamas—and inland across south Florida. Within the past 5,000 years, the sea was probably five feet higher in south Florida, growing coral where there is land today.

Miami and the other cities of southeast Florida grew up along Henry Flagler's Florida East Coast Railway. Flagler developed these towns as winter holiday destinations for northeasterners. In 1894, he extended his rail line from Jacksonville to West Palm Beach, and in 1896, to the village of Miami. In each town, Flagler built a large resort hotel. By 1912, his trains reached Key West on tracks placed over pilings. The 1935 Labor Day Hurricane destroyed the Key West rail line and much of the Keys. The state purchased the right of way and rebuilt it as a highway in 1938. At the time of his death in 1913, Flagler had invested more than $50 million, one-third of all the capital invested in Florida development at the time.

Nashville ★

Knoxville ●

140

TENNESSEE

River

Tennessee

APPALACHIAN MOU

Chattanooga ●

142
ATL
Atlanta

168
● Birmingham

PI

CORRIDOR 3:
Chicago–Atlanta–Florida

Circumventing storms is the most frequent reason for pilots to deviate from the small number of preferred routes in this central corridor. Those severe weather avoidance paths can be drastic, as shown on page 2.

Agriculture is diverse here. The flat farms of central to northern Illinois and Indiana are part of the Corn Belt (page 30); more than half of those two states' farm production is in the grain and beans category. Over the hilly country that reaches from southern Indiana to central Georgia, the emphasis shifts to livestock—chiefly poultry and eggs in Georgia, more mixed in Tennessee and Kentucky, where beef and dairy cattle take the lead. Tobacco and horses, justly famous as Kentucky specialties, concentrate in the Bluegrass region, east of the mapped flight paths. Florida is king of citrus, of course; it is also very strong in vegetable crops and in the nursery trade.

Georgia and northern Florida are in the heart of the southern pine belt. Historically, the U.S. timber industry concentrated where extensive virgin forests were being logged. That lasted until the 1980s, when production fell off in the last such area standing, the Pacific Northwest. At that point, production shifted to where plantations of very young trees put on weight fastest: the Southeast. Much of the land now planted in rows of pines was previously farmed, but farms were suffering as soils became worn out, rendering the land affordable for investment in forestry.

Shallow seas covered most of this area from 400 million to 360 million years ago, leaving widespread limestones and dolostones. These weather—in fact, they dissolve in groundwater—to produce a family of landforms called "karst." We devote two articles in this corridor to karst. As you can see on this map, karst is widespread in the eastern states. Although our Kentucky Sinkhole Plain location is not under the mapped flight paths, you can expect to cross areas with sinkholes on most paths across western Kentucky and very likely in the adjacent states as well. Most hilliness under this corridor derives from differential erosion of different Paleozoic sediments, especially the limestones. The Valley and Ridge Appalachians break in on the scene dramatically in the 150 miles immediately north of Atlanta.

Karst regions of the eastern United States shown in green

As the Paleozoic seas retreated, beginning 360 million years ago, enormous rich coal beds were deposited in southern Illinois and Indiana and in western Kentucky. Although you may see some mining, this Illinois basin has been relatively inactive because its coal is high in sulfur. Power plants currently hold costs down by buying Wyoming or Appalachian coal rather than by adding the equipment that Illinois basin coal would need in order to meet sulfur emissions standards.

NORTHBOUND: **Start with p. 134**
SOUTHBOUND: **Start with pp. 24, 26, 30, 78**

Kentucky Sinkhole Plain and Mammoth Cave

LOOK FOR farmland pitted with small depressions and ponds; short creeks that end where they flow into a depression.

❶ 200-ft.-deep cockpit in the Knobs ❷ road to Mammoth Cave ❸ I-65 ❹ Park City, KY ❺ terminus (sink) of Little Sinking Creek ❻ sink of Gardner Creek ❼ area with several oil wells ❽ Louie B. Nunn (Cumberland) Pkwy. ❾ sinkholes ❿ terra rosa soil

NORTHBOUND: Go to pp. 78, 30, 26, 24

Large areas of south-central Kentucky's plateaus look like a case of the pox. Thousands of tiny ponds and even greater numbers of small depressions are sinkholes ❾ formed in Mississippian limestone and dolomite bedrock. Geologists refer to such landscapes as karst, in reference to the Karst region of Slovenia.

Clay-rich soil developing in a sinkhole may form a seal to make a pond. If this soil is disturbed, the pond may drain overnight. Surface creeks here tend to be very short. They go a few miles and then sink abruptly into the ground, carrying on as underground streams, collecting water that seeps through overlying sinkholes. Underground, the streams may erode immense networks of caves.

Freshly plowed fields in limestone areas often look pinkish. These *terra rosa* soils ❿ form after water has dissolved the carbonate minerals and carried them away, leaving clay minerals behind at the surface. Iron in the clays commonly oxidizes to reddish tints.

Both Gardner Creek ❻ and Little Sinking Creek ❺ sink in the Sinkhole Plain, the lowest area within the image at 600 feet above sea level. Dry sinkholes pitting the plain are between 10 and 25 feet deep. To the north, you can see the Knobs with its rougher terrain, largely forested and too steep to farm. In the Knobs and plateau areas, the limestone is capped with a layer of erosion-resistant sandstone 60 feet thick.

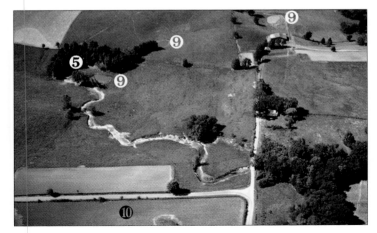

Valley floors between knobs are close to the 600-foot elevation of the nearby plain. Some valleys are entirely surrounded by ridges at 800-foot elevation. These are giant sinkholes, 200 feet deep ❶. Karst uplands riddled with giant sinkholes are called "cockpit karst," an old term alluding to pits for cockfights. Within the Knobs, the reverse is also found: freestanding hills with 200 feet of relief on almost all sides. Extreme cases of that pattern are called "tower karst"; the world's premier photogenic example is the green tower-shaped hills around Guilin, China. In contrast to south-central Kentucky's 50 inches of annual precipitation, Guilin gets 75 inches, and Jamaica's cockpits get still more. Extreme cases of karst all occur in high-rainfall tropical climates with thick limestone or dolomite beds.

But Kentucky is not outdone in the realm of limestone dissolution: It has a karst feature of national park status. The underground streams that originate as sinking creeks on the Sinkhole Plain flow northward to the Green River. Where they pass underneath the sandstone-capped plateaus northeast of the Knobs, they carved out an enormous network of caves on multiple levels, including the longest known cave in the world. Mammoth Cave was ranked third longest until 1972, when explorers in the nearby Flint Ridge cave system found a connecting passageway, establishing that the two are in fact one cave. To date, 365 miles have been mapped, but apparently greater distances remain to be explored.

There are many caves, many vertical passages, much overlap between different layers, and many entrances, so explorers are rarely more than several hours away from one entrance or another. Their project is to improve the accuracy of cave maps and then to seek out connecting routes between different entrances.

Because the sandstone cap layer is watertight, very little dripping of water from cave ceilings occurs here and therefore few stalactites and stalagmites.

Of the more than 130 species that live in Mammoth Cave, 42 are dependent on cave habitat. Their survival there is threatened by several kinds of pollution, including electric light, ozone, and septically polluted groundwater from the surrounding area.

Watts Bar Lake, Dam, and Nuclear Plant, Tennessee

LOOK FOR two white cooling towers below a dam, distinguishing this long, complex reservoir from many others in Tennessee and Kentucky. Look for the contrast between parallel ridges at the lake and random drainage patterns northwest of it.

Low altitude small plane photo, facing south ❶ Tennessee River ❷ Watts Bar Nuclear Plant ❸ Watts Bar Dam and Lock
❹ tugboat pushing two barges into lock while two barges it already took through the lock wait

Between Chattanooga and Knoxville, the Tennessee River backs up behind two dams built by the Tennessee Valley Authority (TVA), Chickamauga (1936) and Watts Bar (1942) ❸. In addition to flood control and locks for barges, these two dams, like the contemporaneous Bonneville and Grand Coulee dams in the Northwest, added electrical power generation far in excess of existing demand. There were two timely benefits from doing so: generating jobs to stem the Depression and generating electricity to win World War II. When the United States entered World War II in December 1941, the new dams gave the United States a critical edge over its enemies in aluminum smelting and therefore in aircraft manufacture. The world's largest aluminum factory during the war years was in nearby Knoxville, drawing its power from Watts Dam.

Today, the power capacity of TVA dams looks almost quaint. Just below Watts Bar Dam, look for the cooling towers of the Watts Bar Nuclear Plant ❷. Although one of its two units was never completed, the working one alone generates six times more electricity than the dam. All 29 hydroelectric dams in the TVA grid together produce only 9 percent of TVA power, 3 nuclear plants produce 30 percent, and 11 coal plants produce 61 percent. But those coal plants depend on the dams, whose locks enable barges ❹ to deliver coal right to their doorsteps from mines near the highest navigable reaches of the Tennessee. Barging is often the cheapest way to ship heavy loads.

Watts Bar Lake meanders within a straight linear trough bounded by long, straight ridges running north-northeast to south-southwest. The ridges on the southeast flank are skinny and tightly packed together. Generally, shales are found in the valleys; limestones, on the ridges. The ridges range in age from 513 to 460 million years. On the northwest flank, Walden Ridge is the southeast edge of the Cumberland Plateau, which continues to the northwest, cut by very crooked valleys. Shales and limestones on the plateau range from 385 to 318 million years old. Younger coal-bearing strata occur farther west. Walden Ridge shows the sharp transition between two major physiographic parts of the Appalachians—the Appalachian Plateau and the Valley and Ridge Province.

Parallel ridges in the Valley and Ridge increase in height to the north-northeast, emerging as peninsulas in the lake. Black Oak Ridge leads directly to the town of Oak Ridge and Oak Ridge National Laboratory. Both town and lab were built in 1942 in top secret, under a different name, as part of the Manhattan Project. A thousand farm families were evicted in a matter of weeks, over the livid protests of the TVA's director, who had big agricultural plans for this sleepy valley. Together with facilities in Chicago, New Mexico, and eastern Washington, the Oak Ridge lab developed the atomic bomb. Oak Ridge served as the design lab and factory for enriching uranium. Between that and the aluminum, we can say with only slight exaggeration that this is the valley where World War II was won. In 1948, the lab was reborn under its present name, dedicated to high-level scientific research for nonmilitary purposes.

The Tennessee Valley Authority is as remarkable and unique in U.S. history as the Manhattan Project. Part of Franklin Roosevelt's New Deal prescription for the Depression, it could have taken place only within a depression context. For Theodore Roosevelt and Gifford Pinchot, to whom the concept can be traced, conservation could really only work by integrating all aspects of watershed management under one agency. In addition to building and operating dams, locks, an 800-mile navigation channel, coal-fired power plants, nuclear power plants, and an electric transmission grid, the TVA was once in charge of forestry; agricultural education; fertilizer design and manufacture; fighting malaria, smallpox, forest fires, and soil erosion; and promoting all aspects of economic development in the Tennessee River watershed. One economic effort was a laboratory to develop technology for a porcelain industry using Appalachian clay.

Many conservative politicians saw the TVA as a toehold for socialism, with total centralized planning. However, the TVA became self-financing, and a substantial taxpayer, in 1959. In 2005, it facilitated the first new steel mill in the United States in decades, and it may soon become the first U.S. utility to build and operate a new-generation nuclear power plant.

Atlanta, Georgia

LOOK FOR the towers of downtown Atlanta, with its shift in street orientation; solitary, bare, white Stone Mountain 14 miles east of downtown.

Facing north-northeast, from an approach pattern ❶ I-75 and I-85, joined through the center of the image, divide from this point north ❷ Coca-Cola headquarters and Georgia Institute of Technology ❸ Bank of America Plaza, tallest skyscraper in the South ❹ Centennial Olympic Park ❺ Georgia Dome ❻ state capitol, with gold dome ❼ I-20

As a principal airline hub, Atlanta rivals and in many years surpasses Chicago and Dallas/Fort Worth in passenger volume. Even if you do not land in Atlanta, you may fly over it, as it is also a major air navigation point.

Although most central Atlanta streets form a grid on the cardinal directions, a small core district of streets runs on two diagonal alignments. The gold dome of the state capitol ❻ is near its southeast end, by a "spaghetti junction" of three freeways. West of the office towers, look for Centennial Olympic Park ❹, site of the 1996 Olympics and the Georgia Dome stadium ❺. Farther northwest is Inman Yard, one of the largest rail yards in the United States.

The green linear corridor of the Chattahoochee River runs southwest through Atlanta's western suburbs. Parallel ridges rise beyond the river. With luck, you will see the dendritic drainage pattern of streams on the river's southeast side, and the trellised drainages northwest of the river. The river follows the Brevard Fault here, marking the boundary between the Piedmont and Blue Ridge provinces.

The naked granite dome of Stone Mountain rises 800 feet above its surroundings 14 miles east of central Atlanta. The mountain's east face is carved into a sculpture of Confederate leaders Robert E. Lee, Jefferson Davis, and Stonewall Jackson, and their horses.

Atlanta is part of the metamorphic Piedmont Province. The fall line and beyond it the navigable rivers of the Coastal Plain are many miles to the east and south, and the Blue Ridge Province begins a few miles to the north. Railroad investors founded the city, foreseeing that its location at the south end of the Blue Ridge would inevitably put it on the main line between the Gulf and Atlantic coasts. Moreover, a low pass connects it to Chattanooga and the valleys of the Appalachian Plateau. The Georgia General Assembly established the Western and Atlantic Railroad in 1836 as a line running through the center of the state. The town at its northern terminus was named first Terminus and then, in 1845, Atlanta, short for Atlantica-Pacifica. That was looking forward quite a bit. Four years later, tracks connected Atlanta to Chattanooga.

Atlanta was a minor Confederate city during the Civil War. In 1864, General William Tecumseh Sherman's army marched down the rail line from Chattanooga, entering Atlanta after a series of battles in northern Georgia. After occupying Atlanta for two months, Sherman ordered the city burned before completing his notorious march to the sea.

After the war, Atlanta enjoyed a peacetime boom, including the rail connections envisioned by its founders. The earliest streets were aligned with the railroads. Later development followed the compass points.

The main rail line, and later Interstate 85, spurred the growth of a line of Piedmont cities, including Greensboro and Charlotte, North Carolina, and Greenville, South Carolina, with Atlanta the anchor. This line parallels the more easterly fall line of cities founded in earlier centuries when water transport ruled. Its dispersed development pattern over recent decades earned it the nickname "Spersopolis"; notice town after town strung out along each freeway. Near Atlanta, former farmlands have reverted to woodland, clearing the way for further development.

John S. Pemberton, pharmacist and holder of the French Wine Cola patent, contrived Coca-Cola from the kola nut and the cocaine leaf in 1886 in response to a county prohibition ordinance. He sold the Coca-Cola patent for $2,300 five years later.

In 1916, Gutzon Borglum was hired to carve a monumental sculpture to commemorate the Confederacy on Stone Mountain. He completed only Lee's head before he fell out with local backers in 1925; he went on to design and carve Mount Rushmore in South Dakota. The Stone Mountain project languished until 1963, when Walker Hancock resumed the work.

Atlanta's leadership in airports began early, with the country's first passenger air terminal in 1931 and the first air traffic control tower in 1939.

Metamorphosed sedimentary rocks underlie much of the area, locally intruded by granite bodies such as Stone Mountain. The Brevard Fault Zone in the northwest Atlanta suburbs is a major Appalachian feature, reaching from southern Virginia to northern Florida and separating the Piedmont and Blue Ridge provinces. The Brevard likely moved in several mountain-building episodes between 470 million and 300 million years ago. Granites intruded the Georgia Piedmont during the same time span. Stone Mountain's granite ranges in age from 325 million to 280 million years.

North Florida Karst

LOOK FOR small lakes, circular depressions, short streams.

❶ Wacissa, FL, 15 mi. east of Woodville ❷ Horsehead Spring and several nearby springs give rise to the Wacissa River ❸ Wacissa River ❹ Anderson Bay, a swamp ❺ a cluster of intermittent karst ponds; the area south of this road is swampy, with low-relief sinkholes, whereas to the north is a karst upland with knobs and deep sinkholes ❻ Aucilla River

Southeast of Tallahassee, we see a region of disappearing streams, circular depressions, and small lakes. The streams occupy narrow valleys and are not fed by networks of tributaries. Moreover, many streams literally spring from the ground, flow a distance, and then disappear without entering a lake or a visible depression. The depressions may be either green and wet ❹ or relatively dry ❺. Adjoining depressions often appear to be linked. Forested ridges may separate the depressions. Development is sparse. This is the Woodville Karst Plain.

A low escarpment, the Cody Scarp, cuts through the landscape, bounding the Woodville Karst Plain on the north. The landscape farther north is a mosaic of small farms, orchards, roads, and towns, with ponds and lakes filling many depressions. This too is a karst terrain, overlain here by clays and sands, accounting for the difference in appearance and land use.

Karst occurs where water-soluble rocks (typically limestone or dolostone) underlie the surface. Limestone underlies all of Florida, with a thin veneer of sand and clay on top of it in many areas.

The depressions visible here are sinkholes, which form where groundwater has dissolved the limestone. Rainwater absorbs carbon dioxide as it falls through the air, making rain slightly acidic when it reaches the surface. Percolating into the soil or subsurface, rainwater becomes groundwater. As it percolates through the soil, groundwater dissolves additional carbon dioxide given off by soil bacteria and decaying organic matter. Carbon dioxide concentrations within soil are 10 to 100 times greater than in the atmosphere.

By absorbing carbon dioxide, rainwater can become carbonic acid, which readily dissolves limestone's principal mineral, calcium carbonate. Dissolution continues until the groundwater is saturated with calcium and bicarbonate ions. Dissolution is most rapid where acidic water first encounters limestone: on the surface and in fractures or permeable zones connected to the surface.

Surface rocks control the number of sinkholes in an area. Where bare limestone occurs on the surface, as it does on the Woodville Karst, sinkholes are rare. Where 30 to 200 feet of sand or clay cover the limestone, sinkholes are very common, as is the case north of the Woodville Karst.

Three types of sinkholes are found: solution sinkholes, cover subsidence sinkholes, and cover collapse sinkholes. Solution sinkholes develop where little or no material covers the limestone. If an impermeable layer accumulates on the bottom of the sinkhole, a lake or a marsh will develop. The rolling topography around Woodville shows this pattern.

Cover subsidence sinkholes develop where enough sand buries the limestone that sand grains can fill the voids created by dissolution of the underlying limestone. As groundwater dissolves the limestone, sand grains slip down from above to take its place. The depression remains relatively shallow and well drained. Cover collapse sinkholes develop where clays and sands are thick enough to form a temporary bridge above the developing sinkhole. Eventually, the sinkhole opens to a width that the overlying material cannot bridge, and the surface collapses catastrophically. When this happens in a developed area, news crews rush to the site, with insurance adjusters close on their heels.

The Woodville Karst is known for something we cannot see from the air: underwater cave diving. Caves and other subsurface karst-dissolution features carry underground streams and rivers from areas of surface infiltration to discharge zones. Water in flooded Woodville area caves moves slowly south beneath the Florida Panhandle to discharge as freshwater springs in the Gulf of Mexico, suggesting that the cave network formed during the Ice Ages, when sea level was lower than it is today. A saltwater aquifer is already saturated with calcium carbonate and thus cannot dissolve limestone. In order to reach beneath present sea level, a cave network had to form when salt waters did not fill the aquifer as they do today near the Gulf coast. Such a time last occurred more than 10,000 years ago during the last glacial maximum.

Phosphate Mines, Florida

LOOK FOR large, white rectangular pits, some with green lakes; some with vegetation.

Fifty miles east of Tampa lies the American capital of phosphate production. We see the strip mines as large rectangular excavations revealing white bedrock ❸. Beside the largest pits, we often see tall processing plants ❺ converting the phosphate rock into phosphoric acid, superphosphate, or triple superphosphate. There are also large rectangular pits filled with greenish water—settling basins ❹ where tailings from the processing plant reside for a year or more—and rectangular fields similar in size to the strip mines. These are reclaimed strip mine pits ❷.

Railroad tracks lead from the plants to Gulf coast docks near Tampa. From there, the products are taken by barge across the Gulf and into the Mississippi River system and then to fertilizer plants in the farming regions of the South and Midwest. The very low cost of water transport makes Florida phosphate mining an economical enterprise.

Phosphate ore is composed of the mineral calcium phosphate apatite. In Florida, it occurs as a sedimentary deposit laid down 11 million to 3 million years ago. The deposits formed in two phases. In the late Miocene, the southern Florida area was a shallow marine shelf subject to deep-water ocean currents carrying a high concentration of phosphorus, which precipitated as apatite on the sea floor of the shelf. Later, the sea level fell, leaving the shelf exposed as dry land. About 3 million years ago, the seas returned, restoring the shallow marine shelf. The phosphorus in the underlying older rock dissolved and then precipitated a second time within the younger shelf sediments. Phosphorus is now more concentrated in the younger phosphorite deposits than in the older sediments.

In Florida, phosphate mines are concentrated around Lakeland. New mines are being developed south of Lakeland, where phosphate beds are found at greater depths beneath the surface. North of Lakeland, oval lakes mark the central Florida karst district. (See page 144.) Although phosphate beds also occur to the north, the shallow water table prevents economical mining. Eventually, shallow groundwater will also halt the phosphate producers' southward march. The location of strip mining is thus controlled in part by topography: Mines are located on a low plateau.

Reclamation of these phosphate strip mines is very slow because the tailings (waste) consist of very fine grains and clays suspended in a lot of water. Solids constitute only 5 percent of the tailings leaving the processing plant. After a year or more in settling ponds, solids constitute 20 percent or more of the tailings. The settling ponds can be topped up with more tailings until they dewater enough to pass as solid ground, or the tailings can be removed to an abandoned mine pit. In either case, pasture or other crops are planted on the reclaimed site.

Agriculture consumes about two-thirds of U.S. phosphate production. Modern fertilizers represent a refinement of the 17th-century practice of applying ground bones to the soil to replace phosphorus removed in the harvested plants. In 1838, the German chemist Justus von Liebig used sulfuric acid to make bone phosphorus more accessible to crop plants. In 1842, the English farmer John Lawes patented a process for using sulfuric acid with phosphatic nodules to make superphosphate fertilizer.

Phosphorus is a key element for plant and animal life. Apatite forms our teeth and skeletons. DNA incorporates phosphorus in its helix, and the energy cycle that powers our cells uses phosphorus. Florida phosphorus is an essential element in U.S. agriculture, and one may say without exaggeration that there is a little bit of Florida bedrock in each of us.

❶ Lakeland Linder Regional Airport, southeast of Lakeland ❷ strip mines in stages of reclamation ❸ strip mine ❹ settling basin
❺ North Poley Creek ❻ Willow Oak, FL ❼ Mulberry, FL ❽ phosphate processing plants
Photo taken in 2003; by 2007, ❸ was flooded, ❹ was dewatered, and mining was active just east of them.

Lake Okeechobee, Florida

LOOK FOR the one big lake in Florida, the canals and rivers feeding and draining it, and the broad, gently sloped levee containing it.

Facing east-southeast ❶ St. Lucie Canal (outflow) ❷ gas-fired Martin Power Plant with cooling pond ❸ Belle Glade, FL ❹ Canals draining the lake and the surrounding cropland, mostly sugarcane ❺ Clewiston, FL; cropland to southwest includes citrus orchards ❻ Okeechobee, FL ❼ Kissimmee River (chief tributary to lake) ❽ Herbert Hoover Dike; on the far shore it is right next to the lake ❾ glades (swamps) in Glade County ❿ Caloosahatchee Canal/River (outflow)

After the Great Lakes and Great Salt Lake, Lake Okeechobee is the next-biggest lake in the lower 48 states. That would be measured in surface area; it averages barely 10 feet deep, so in volume, it comes in behind Lake Tahoe and Crater Lake, which are almost 1,000 and 2,000 feet deep, respectively. Too close to sea level to drain quickly, it rises threateningly when a lot of rain falls.

A century of efforts to alter South Florida hydrology for the benefit of farms and cities has created a tangle of problems and dangers. The natural Lake Okeechobee had no conspicuous outlet. Its entire swampy south shore was the edge of the Everglades: A 20-mile-wide sheet of water oozed from the lake into the glades, flowing on south to the tip of Florida and dropping only around 10 feet in those 100 miles. Starting in 1905, developers dug canals ❹ to shrink the lake and drain the swamps around its south half, creating acreage for farming. They left an equal swath of swampy Water Conservation Areas between the new croplands and the coast, hoping that those would absorb floods the way the Everglades used to. Note the sharp transitions between three broad belts between the Atlantic and the lake: the metropolis along the coast, the undeveloped conservation areas, and the grid of sugarcane plots.

Settlers near the lake pushed up a 5- to 9-foot muck levee along its shore for protection, tragically underestimating the floods they faced. Hurricane winds can push this lake hard enough to raise its level 15 feet at the downwind shore while drying up miles of lakebed along the upwind shore. Hurricanes breached the levee in 1926 and 1928, flooding the settlements and leaving 3,000 people dead.

The Herbert Hoover administration set to raising the levees, which were later renamed the Herbert Hoover Dike ❸. Hoover didn't want to set a precedent of federal responsibility for flood control, so the levee project was repackaged as a navigation project. The lake, with the St. Lucie ❶ and Caloosahatchee ❿ canals, became an ocean-to-gulf ship canal with five locks. In the 1950s, after more hurricanes, engineers piled the levee still higher.

Seasonal droughts are a problem for Florida farmers; you may see a few center pivot irrigation circles southwest of the lake. Farming interests successfully argued to raise the lake a bit higher to provide more water for irrigation. Meanwhile, land to its south had subsided as drained peatland shrank and decomposed.

The lake was becoming a reservoir and the earthen levee reimagined as a dam—without being rebuilt as one. It was officially listed as a dam in 2005. But levees are not dams; levees are designed to far lower standards intended to deal with occasional floods, not with year-round water on one side higher than the dry land on the other. With year-round water pressure on it, groundwater under a levee slowly erodes "pipes" that undermine it. Pipes develop especially easily in water-soluble bedrock, such as the limestone here. Several times, the Army Corps of Engineers has leapt into the breach and plugged incipient blowouts in the dike. Dams also require spillways so that floods can overtop them without destroying them. This dike has none. A handful of canal outlets adding up to less than half a mile in width are asked to accept the storm overflows that once crossed the 30-mile-wide natural spillway into the Everglades.

In 2006, an expert review panel concluded that the dike has a 50 percent chance of failing within 4 years and a greater than 50 percent chance of failing within 30 years, even after all the currently planned improvements are completed.

Constraining Okeechobee's outflow has an unintended hydrologic consequence: Sea water invades parts of the Florida aquifer, locally ruining wells. In the past, much of the Okeechobee sheetflow seeped down into the south Florida aquifer, which slowly flows to the ocean, blocking sea water from flowing inland. The aquifer yields to the pressure of the saltwater when too much of the sheetflow is shunted into canals and too much groundwater is also pumped from the aquifer.

Unintended consequences also disrupt the region's ecology. West of Lake Okeechobee, the Caloosahatchee River, famous as a home of manatees and dolphins, is polluted by the fertilizers and pesticides in agricultural runoff from the Kissimmee drainage, the heart of Florida citrus country. Both the lake and the rivers are prone to algal blooms that secrete toxins and consume oxygen, leaving too little for fish.

The South Florida Water Management District has undertaken an enormous, complex plan to save the Everglades ecosystem without sacrificing the farms and urban systems that seem to conflict with it. It's a tall order.

Big Cypress Swamp and the Everglades, Florida

LOOK FOR water! Dikes, canals, sloughs, and islands.

West of Miami, planes fly over the northern Everglades and often the Big Cypress Swamp region near the west coast. Your view abruptly transitions to wetland at a north-south dike bounding the metropolitan area on the west. The world beneath the flight path is wet: a river without banks flowing south-southwest from Lake Okeechobee to the Gulf. The world here is also flat: Contour maps do not show elevation contours between Miami and the Gulf of Mexico but rather elevation benchmarks—five feet here, eight feet there, seven feet farther on.

Several habitats can be identified from the air, all controlled by small differences in elevation or soil. Sawgrass prairies ❹ occur along the banks of the larger sloughs and waterways and on dry land north of Florida Bay. Near the Gulf coast, cypress swamps develop in depressions. Pinelands grow on dry limestone ridges, notably on the Atlantic Coastal Ridge on the eastern margin of the Everglades. The characteristic habitats of the heart of the Everglades are sawgrass marshes, water lily sloughs, and the small but conspicuous scattered hardwood hammocks ❺ and tree islands ❻. These teardrop-shaped clumps are generally aligned north-south with the flow of water. They develop where very slightly higher ground enabled a few less saturation-tolerant species to grow. Over centuries, or even millennia, these plants build up peat that further enhances the tree islands' height advantage, allowing a varied, hardwood-dominated flora to persist.

Everglades geology is simple and young. Tamiami limestones are the oldest rocks, at 6 million years; they occur on the Gulf coast beneath northwestern Everglades National Park and the Big Cypress Swamp. The depressions favored by cypress are likely early-stage karst sinkholes. The Miami Oolite ("oh a light!") forms the low Atlantic Coastal Ridge running southwest from Miami. Oolites consist of carbonate grains formed in shallow tropical water. Longshore currents deposited the Miami Oolite in its coastal ridge alignment during the Ice Ages. The Miami Oolite also underlies the eastern Everglades but is replaced in the central Everglades by the Miami Bryozoan Limestone, composed of bryozoan skeletons.

Before the development of south Florida, the Kissimmee River flowed into Lake Okeechobee. The river was fed by the karst topography of central Florida to the west and north. The water moving from the lake across the Everglades to the coast covered more than 11,000 square miles.

Development has transformed much of the Everglades environment over the past 125 years. Dredging of the Everglades began in the 1880s, creating a network of drainage canals which was dramatically expanded between 1905 and 1910, yielding great expanses of farmland. Alongside the elevated Interstate 75 that runs west from Miami, drained marshes are now sugarcane plantations.

Coastal mangroves along the Atlantic were cleared and replaced by palm trees to improve the sea view from the hotels and resorts that began to appear in south Florida in the 1920s.

In 1948, the Army Corps of Engineers was charged by Congress to construct a system of roads, canals, levees, and dams across the Everglades. The resulting agency is now the South Florida Water Management District. Today, half of the original south Florida wetlands have been eliminated and with them 90 percent of the wading birds, manatees, Florida panthers, and a host of other species.

Preservation and renewal of the Everglades are thanks in large part to the efforts of two individuals: Ernest Coe and Marjory Stoneman Douglas. Coe was a landscape architect who proposed in 1928 that a national park be created in the Everglades. The park opened in 1947. That same year, Douglas published *The Everglades: River of Grass*, in which she identified the role of both Lake Okeechobee water and the Kissimmee River in the ecosystem of the Everglades. She actively campaigned through the end of the 20th century to expand the preservation and renewal of the Everglades.

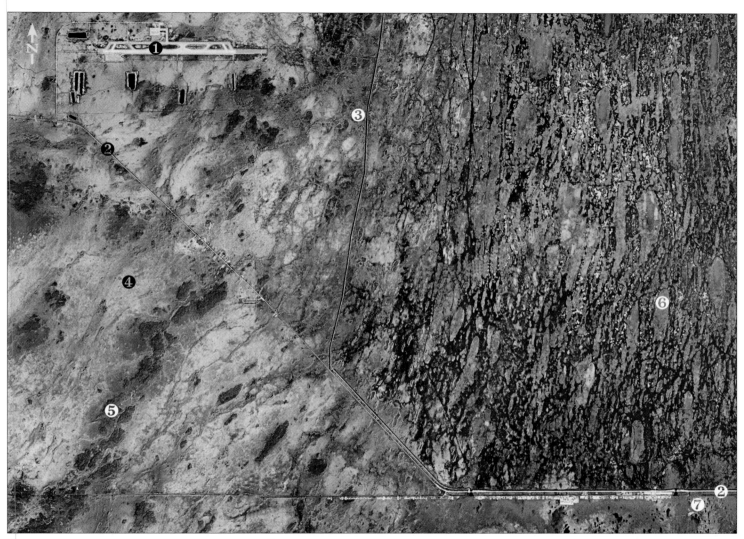

❶ Dade-Collier Training and Transition Airport ❷ U.S. Hwy. 41, the Tamiami Trail; in the image are Fifty-mile Bend and Forty-mile Bend
❸ levee dividing Big Cypress National Preserve (to west) from the wetter Shark River Slough in Water Conservation Area 3A (east)
❹ sawgrass prairie ❺ hardwood hammocks ❻ tree islands ❼ Shark Valley Visitor Center in Everglades National Park, which lies
south of Hwy. 41; the row of buildings westward is the Miccosukee Indian Reservation with tour guides, zoos, and cultural center

SOUTHBOUND: **Go to p. 134**
Big Cypress Swamp and the Everglades, Florida **151**

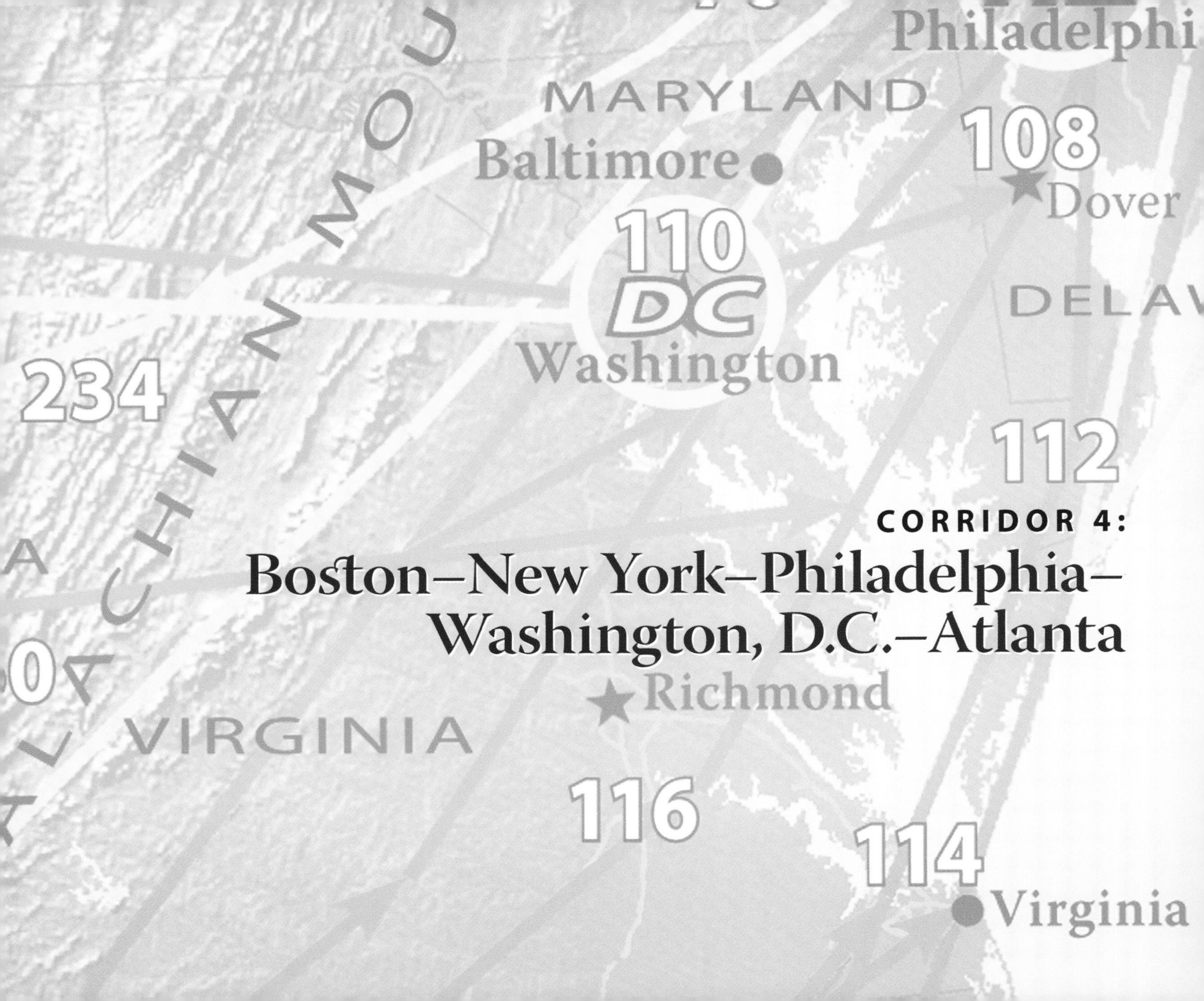

MARYLAND

Baltimore ●

108
★ Dover

110
DC
Washington

DELAW

234

112

CORRIDOR 4:

Boston–New York–Philadelphia–Washington, D.C.–Atlanta

★ Richmond

VIRGINIA

116

114

● Virginia

All the northeastern airports have essentially the same preferred path southbound to Atlanta; northbound, the preferred paths fan out from the very start, depending on their destination. Routes to JFK, LaGuardia, and Boston cross Norfolk, Virginia, and then stay near the coastline, whereas routes to Newark, Philadelphia, and Washington, D.C. are somewhat farther inland. Don't worry, though. Most features we describe in this corridor are either the cities themselves—large features visible from some distance—or regionally characteristic landform types. You don't have to fly over a precise correct location to recognize them.

A word you will read often is "province." Geologists divide the eastern seaboard, from the coast inland across the Appalachian Mountains to their far western edge, into five parallel bands they call provinces.

1. **The Coastal Plain Province** is, like most coastal plains, low and flat, with meandering rivers crossing its alluvial soils. Many of the rivers become saltwater-drowned valleys tens of miles before reaching the open sea. During each glacial stage of the Ice Ages, the sea level dropped by several hundred feet. The larger rivers responded by eroding their valleys deeper. When the ice melted, the sea rose again, turning these valleys into estuaries. The earliest English speakers recognized them as rivers, even though no one could have mistaken their water for fresh water or their tides for river currents.

2. **The Piedmont Province** is only modestly higher, but its roughened topography is obvious from the air. It has bedrock near the surface, keeping the majority of streams from forming meanders. The boundary between the Coastal Plain Province and the Piedmont Province is called the fall line, because many streams have rapids, or falls, where they cross it. The cities of Paterson and Trenton, New Jersey, Philadelphia, Pennsylvania, Washington, D.C., Richmond, Virginia, Raleigh, North Carolina, Columbia, South Carolina, Augusta, Georgia, and several others are on the fall line.

3. **The Blue Ridge Province** includes the highest Appalachian summits. (See page 164.) Together, the Piedmont and the Blue Ridge provinces represent the core of the ancestral Appalachian Mountains. For most of its length in Virginia, the Blue Ridge Province consists of a single, moderately broad ridge, Blue Ridge. Farther south, the province widens into a dissected mountain range, including the Great Smokies; then the province ends, just short of Atlanta; the other provinces continue. North of Virginia, the province becomes more intermittent and then indistinct, but geologists recognize it as far as southern Pennsylvania.

4. **The Valley and Ridge Province** may be the easiest to recognize, with its alternation of very distinct, mostly straight and parallel valleys and ridges. Some people think of it as "wrinkled" country. A continuous broader valley separates it from the Blue Ridge Province. Several rivers, including Virginia's fabled Shenandoah, each occupy a portion of this Great Valley's 1,200-mile length.

5. **The Appalachian Plateaus Province** is too far west to be seen from this corridor, barring unusual flight path deviations. Its broader summit ridges and dendritic stream valley patterns distinguish it from the Valley and Ridge.

The differences among the provinces derive from their geologic histories, as you will read on many of the following pages.

Boston Harbor Drumlins, Massachusetts

LOOK FOR small islands scattered across the harbor immediately east of Logan Airport; 12 large, white, egg-shaped structures on a peninsula by the airport.

Facing southwest ❶ Nantasket Beach ❷ Cohasset, MA ❸ Hingham Bay ❹ Peddocks Island ❺ Fort Warren on Georges Island ❻ Lovells Island ❼ Gallops Island; arrow indicates flow direction of ice sheet ❽ Deer Island Lighthouse; Deer Island itself, with wastewater treatment plant, is out of view below the image.

❾ Deer Island Waste Water Treatment Plant, with digesters in foreground

Logan International Airport perches on a peninsula in Boston Harbor, the lowest part of a basin excavated by ice sheets during the Ice Ages and later drowned by the post–Ice Age rise in sea level. Boston and its harbor alike are dotted with small, somewhat elongated hills called drumlins, which typically have a blunter end and a more tapered end, like an inverted teaspoon bowl. Similar drumlin swarms are found in other areas that were once near ice sheet margins (see page 276), but this is America's only swarm that emerges above sea level (barely) and forms islands. The peninsula under Logan itself is four former islands artificially joined to the mainland with fill.

Look closely; you will see that the small islands around Logan are drumlins reworked by wave action and sand; some are two or three drumlins connected by sand spits called tombolos. (Given a good view of Lovells Island ❻, you'll see at its center a drumlin hill tapering in the same direction as Gallops ❼ and Peddocks ❹ islands.)

As might be expected in Boston, the islands have colorful histories. They served as the sites of:

- Native American fishing camps, with archaeological evidence dated to at least 8,000 years ago
- an internment camp for Indians during King Philip's War and a graveyard for around half of them.
- a fish-drying business
- a Revolutionary War skirmish fought over hay
- shipwrecks, including the 74-gun *Magnifique* in 1782 ❻
- legendary buried pirate treasure
- a fort for coastal defense ❺
- a Civil War prison ❺
- the base for the 54th Colored Regiment, which was featured in the movie *Glory*
- a polio hospital
- a disabled children's hospital
- a poorhouse
- a school for orphans
- a reform school for boys
- a home for unwed mothers
- an Ellis Island–style quarantine for immigrants
- a graveyard for hundreds of sick and malnourished immigrants who did not survive quarantine
- World War II training camps and a command post for the harbor's minefield ❼
- quarries for granite and slate
- sewage dumps in the past, advanced sewage plants today
- brothels, gambling dens, and a ring for illegal boxing matches
- summer resorts
- a residential development designed by Frederick Law Olmsted but never built
- and a Nike antiaircraft missile base

With storms nibbling away at their gravelly edges, many of the islands have shrunk dramatically over the four centuries, along with their menu of permitted activities. Today, they are a national recreation area whose acreage of land roughly doubles most days between low tide and high tide.

A dozen 130-foot white "eggs" ❾ mark Deer Island, the closest island to Logan Airport. (A 1938 hurricane created a sandspit connecting it to the mainland.) The eggs are sewage digesters, part of the Deer Island Waste Water Treatment Plant, the innovative centerpiece of the cleanup that has already reduced pollution in Boston Harbor by 90 percent in the space of 17 years. Inside them, bacteria digest sewage sludge in much the same way that they digest food in your intestines. One by-product, methane, is captured and used to generate part of the plant's electric power. The sludge itself is pelletized and distributed to farmers as fertilizer. Final-stage wastewater goes into a new 9-mile tunnel out to sea. Fertilizer and wastewater both are certified squeaky-clean, at least by wastewater standards—rid of nearly all toxic pollutants, harmful bacteria, and even the chlorine that was used to kill the last remaining bacteria. Before the project began, marine life was rapidly disappearing from the inner harbor, and nearby beaches were frequently unsafe for swimming because of sewage contamination.

Narragansett Bay and Providence, Rhode Island

LOOK FOR a long, narrow estuary bounded by small cities and towns.

Dozens of marinas line Narragansett Bay. Even on a poor day, you are likely to see many small vessels underway ❿. The state of Rhode Island surrounds the bay; no resident is more than 25 miles from salt water. With 400 miles of coastline, the state calls itself the "Ocean State." On the limited Rhode Island acreage that can be called uplands, you will see small kettle lakes formed where large blocks of ice were entrained in the glacial moraine.

Along with most of the bays to the west in Connecticut, Narragansett Bay is not strictly a drowned river valley. The topography of Rhode Island is the product of deposition rather than erosion. Ice Age glaciers extended over Rhode Island several times. As the last glacier melted, the debris it carried settled on Rhode Island's bedrock. Within the debris were large blocks of ice, which also melted, leaving holes in the "till," or glacial debris, many of which became kettle lakes ❻. Till plains ❶ form the uplands north and west of the bay; an older till plain forms the bay's islands and eastern shores. Glacial outwash formed by the melting of the last glacier covers the lowlands west of the bay.

Paleozoic and older sedimentary rocks underlying Narragansett Bay include coals, sands, and claystones deposited in a basin between older granites. Sedimentary rocks do not resist erosion well; granites do. It is likely that streams draining the region north of the bay carved a valley in the sediments and that the valley was then deepened and eroded by Ice Age glaciers. As the glaciers melted, an ice dam formed near Newport, creating a lake approximately where the bay is now. The ice dam eventually burst, and the glacial till on the bay shore was reworked by running water to form the outwash plains. Over time, fluvial and glacial erosion cut a deep bedrock channel, now largely filled with glacial debris, beneath the bay and Providence River ❺.

In 1524, Giovanni da Verrazano wrote the first description of Narragansett Bay in a letter to Francis I, King of France. Verrazano visited the bay a few weeks after sailing into New York Harbor. He reported well-fed Algonquian natives exploiting the abundant fishery of the bay. He observed extensive cultivation onshore and described open "forests which could be penetrated even by a large army; the trees there are oaks, cypresses, and others unknown in our Europe. We found Lucullan apples, plums, and filberts, and many kinds of fruit different from ours." The native people used fire to manage the forests, maintaining brush-free thoroughfares.

The smallest state has the longest name: the State of Rhode Island and Providence Plantations. We shorten it to simply "Rhode Island." Roger Williams founded the colony in 1643. Williams was exiled from Massachusetts on religious grounds. Rhode Island became a home for dissenters, who founded the first Baptist church at Providence and the first synagogue at Newport. The state played an outsized role in both wars with the British. Native son Commodore Oliver Hazard Perry prevailed at the Battle of Lake Erie and sent the dispatch, "We have met the enemy and they are ours."

❶ till plain　**❷** Seekonk River　**❸** Providence　**❹** East Providence　**❺** Providence River　**❻** one of several kettle lakes in the vicinity
❼ I-295　**❽** I-95　**❾** Cranston　**❿** Narragansett Bay

Connecticut River Valley, Connecticut and Massachusetts

LOOK FOR a prominent river in the center of a broad, low-relief, agricultural valley; a system of locks and canals north of Hartford.

This 50-mile section of the Connecticut River valley, from a few miles north of Springfield, Massachusetts ❹, to the south edge of the Hartford, Connecticut, metropolitan area provides two landscape elements rare elsewhere in New England: flat land and rich soils. The valley rapidly became the principal farming center for the American colonies.

The Dutch explorer Adriaen Block sailed upriver as far as South Windsor, where he encountered the Podunk and Nawaas tribes in 1614. Hoping to avert the repressions they suffered from neighboring tribes, the Podunk later asked the Puritans to build a trading post at Windsor. The Puritans declined, but Pilgrims from Plymouth accepted, establishing Connecticut's first English settlement at the Farmington River confluence. English and Puritan settlers soon joined them. Tobacco was introduced from Virginia in 1640. River transport stimulated manufacturing here through the 18th century, but as the railroads developed in the following century, industry along the Connecticut declined. Skilled craftsmen departed to open factories in growing cities farther west.

Each town on the Connecticut was founded on high ground; the larger towns grew to surround areas of swamp, slough, and wet bottomland that still remain undeveloped. Railroads and highways are also located well away from the river bottomlands. The cities and towns are no longer confined along the river but spread into the surrounding farmland. You may see some plots covered by sheeting, a frequent practice on tobacco crops.

Away from the river, you may see pits with reddish brown walls, many of them filled by small lakes. Sandstone was quarried here and taken to New York and Boston for use in 19th-century brownstone houses.

Two parallel faults about 20 miles apart created this broad segment of the valley. About 200 million years ago, the faults dropped the valley down while raising the eastern and western uplands.

Sediments filled the resulting basin, as did several widespread lava flows. The eastern fault moved more than the western fault, so the lavas and sediments are tilted gently to the east within the basin. The valley floor rises westward to a long ridge and then drops steeply to the next valley. The Farmington River flows north in that valley at the foot of the steep slope west of Hartford, then turns and cuts a gorge through the ridge, flowing southeast to join the Connecticut at Windsor, six miles below Windsor Locks ❾.

The basin was likely filled with sediments when continental glaciers moved into Connecticut during the Ice Ages. The glaciers eroded the valley sediments; the highlands resisted erosion. As the climate warmed and the glaciers melted, the excavated river valley was dammed by glacial debris between Rocky Hill and Glastonbury, south of Hartford. Lake Hitchcock filled the valley for 185 miles upstream. Lake Hitchcock lasted 4,000 years. Glacial meltwater streams brought sediment into the lake, creating deltas along its margin. These small deltas persist today, providing the high ground under Enfield, Windsor, and other river towns.

The climate remained very cold and likely quite windy after Lake Hitchcock and two other big lakes downstream drained. The largest one filled the trough that is now Long Island Sound but was above sea level then. Windblown sand and silt covers the glacial drift in the valley and adjoining uplands, later developing into rich soils. As the climate warmed, the land was colonized first by spruce, then pine, and finally hardwoods.

Bottomlands beside the river are largely undeveloped for good reason: repeated flooding. The worst flood since European settlement followed a spring thaw in 1936, when many bridges along the river in Massachusetts were destroyed, and most of Springfield was under water. But this was not just a Connecticut River problem: Rivers from Pennsylvania to Maine flooded, leaving more than 400,000 people homeless.

❶ Connecticut River ❷ I-90, the Massachusetts Turnpike ❸ I-95 ❹ Springfield, MA ❺ Longmeadow, MA ❻ Thompsonville, 2 mi. south of the MA state line in CT ❼ Enfield ❽ canal ❾ Windsor Locks; the canal formerly had locks here

SOUTHBOUND: Go to pp. 6, 232, 68, 110, 112, 114

Valley and Ridge Province at Clifton Forge, Virginia

LOOK FOR a freeway and a railroad together crossing a section of long, parallel ridges with repeated S-shaped meanders in the valleys.

The Chesapeake and Ohio Railway ❻ and Interstate 64 ❽ make their way together along narrow river bottoms as they cross the Valley and Ridge Province in southwest Virginia. In places, the rail line leaves the river to tunnel beneath a ridge. The ridges run northeast-southwest, separated by narrow valleys. At Clifton Forge ❸, the Jackson ❷, Cowpasture ❼, and James ❶ rivers, meandering in multiple S curves, carve a valley wide enough for the highway to swing north of town while the rail line runs along the river on the south edge of town.

The ridges and valleys are the product of different rates of erosion on different types of bedrock. Erosion-resistant sandstones hold up the ridges, and easily eroded limestones and shales underlie the valleys.

The different rock layers produce different-textured drainage patterns. Near the Jackson River, the lower slopes are deeply incised by a dense network of small streams and rills ❺. This is typical of clayey or silty soils derived from underlying shale. In contrast, only a few streams cut into the upper slopes and ridge crests ❹. This is typical of land underlain by well-drained material, such as sandstone or limestone. In these rocks, a high proportion of runoff sinks into the ground, leaving little for the surface streams to carry. The ridge crest also shows karst sinkholes, typical of limestone. The densely spaced and widely spaced stream drainages thus mark contrasting rock units and can be used to trace a boundary for long distances, not following any contour but rising and falling across the ridges and valleys.

The rocks in this region were first laid down in flat sedimentary layers. In the Valley and Ridge Province the layers were folded during the Allegheny Orogeny 275 million to 260 million years ago.

As a fold develops, erosion removes the surface layer to reveal the older layer beneath. At Clifton Forge, the youngest, uppermost layers were deposited 415 million to 360 million years ago, whereas the oldest were deposited 490 million to 440 million years ago. The oldest layers crop out in the center of the folds, where the younger overlying layers were removed as the fold grew. Geologists call this an anticline; in profile, it looks like an arch, or a fold with the concave side down. Alternatively, if the youngest layers crop out in the center of a fold, surrounded by older layers, the fold is a "syncline," a fold with its concave side up, making a trough shape.

Folding in the Valley and Ridge Province during the Allegheny Orogeny resulted from a plate tectonic event: the collision between North America and Europe-Africa to form the supercontinent Pangaea. This was the last of three mountain-building episodes that formed the Appalachian Mountains.

We can thank 19th-century logging for making these rock layers visible. Logs were needed to fire the iron forge that gave Clifton Forge its name. The surrounding area had both iron ore and the limestone needed to refine it in a forge. Many blast furnaces were in use in western Virginia by the 1830s; the Civil War heightened and localized the demand for iron for weapons. The Lucy Selina furnace in Longdale Furnace ❾ made the iron plates that turned the USS *Merrimack* into the ironclad CSS *Virginia*. Timber was charred in local kilns to make charcoal, since cordwood does not burn hot enough for forges. The average forge consumed 300 acres of forest every year. A wood famine was looming when coal was substituted for wood in the late 19th century.

The Chesapeake and Ohio Railway was built partly to deliver coal to the forges in Virginia and partly to deliver the iron to markets on the Atlantic coast. The eastern and western divisions of the C&O met at the Clifton Forge rail yard and engine shop. The world's widest rail bridge was built across the Jackson River to serve the yard in 1923. By the end of that decade, the Appalachian iron industry collapsed as richer iron deposits went into production on the Great Lakes.

NORTHBOUND: Go to pp. 114, 112, 110, 68, 232, 6

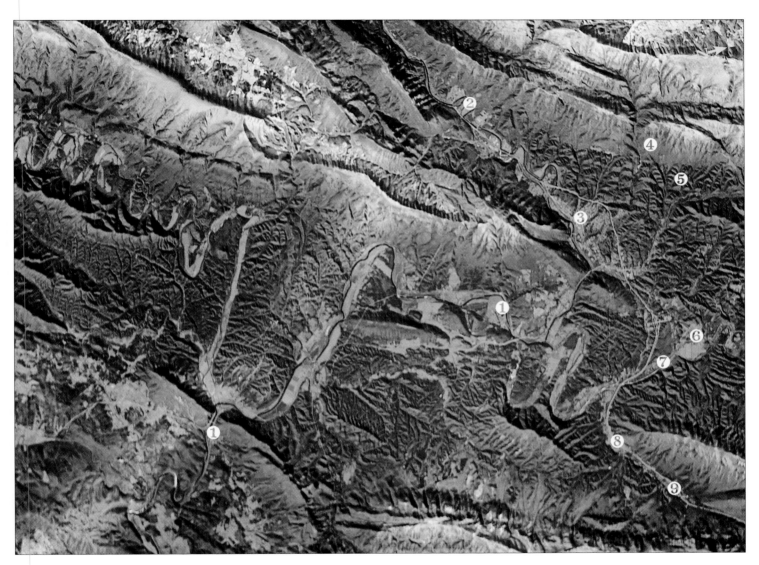

❶ James River ❷ Jackson River ❸ Clifton Forge ❹ busier drainage pattern on limestone ❺ relatively smooth drainage pattern on shale ❻ Chesapeake and Ohio Railway ❼ Cowpasture River ❽ I-64 ❾ Longdale Furnace

SOUTHBOUND: Go to pp. 116, 118

Valley and Ridge Province at Clifton Forge, Virginia **161**

Forest Pests

LOOK FOR red-brown patches in forests in spring or summer: Do they have yellowish tan edges?

A southern pine beetle "spot" infestation on a mountain slope in Georgia, showing yellowish "faders," reddish dead trees, and grayish trees killed first of all. Trees are visibly lined up in rows, indicating a plantation. Low-altitude small plane view.

A landscape-scale mountain pine beetle infestation in the Gros Ventre Range in WY, with the north end of the Teton Range in the background. Low-altitude small plane view, facing northwest.

NORTHBOUND: Go to pp. 118, 116

Patchy red-brown in western and southeastern conifer forests is usually the work of bark beetles. Trees can handle a few of these native critters laying eggs in their inner bark and, as larvae, feasting on it. With some regularity, though, beetle populations explode for a few years, locally or regionally, and kill many trees.

To tell whether red-brown patches are caused by fire or by beetles, look at their edges. Crazy-quilt patterns and abrupt edges, or edges that follow ridgelines, highways, or rivers, suggest fire. So does proximity to blackened stubble, of course. (Two other causes worth mentioning are red belt, page 285, and fungal diseases.)

Green giving way to red-brown via yellowish tan margins suggests beetles. The yellowish "faders" represent the most active part of the infestation visible from the air; they are full of munching larvae. An equal number of adjacent green trees are typically also infested. The red-brown trees have their dead needles hanging on but probably no longer have beetles. Gray areas of leafless dead trees are common at the core of beetle "spots" (and also of course in burns). Spot outbreaks are more characteristic of the Southeast than of the West, where dead trees are often more scattered. Depending on the time of year and the stage of the outbreak, entire mountainsides may contain yellow or red-crowned trees. Beetles can take trees from green to gray in the course of a single season.

Bark beetles are part of the larger forest health story. They are one mechanism by which firefighting leads to worse fires. Where forest managers neither allow fires nor thin the forest, trees may grow too dense for their own good. None are getting quite enough light and water, so they all become stressed and unhealthy, leaving them vulnerable to beetles.

Trees do defend themselves against beetle attack. For example, defense is a primary function of pitch, which can entomb a beetle in its own bore hole. Stressed trees have fewer defensive resources. Beetles can locate stressed trees by their smell; beetle scouts find vulnerable trees and then emit pheromones to attract others of their species. With easy food abundant, beetles are more likely to irrupt. In their wake, they leave a forest with many dead trees and dry limbs—a tinderbox awaiting a bolt of lightning to set it off.

No one knows how bad beetle outbreaks were before records were kept. Consensus holds that they occurred sometimes, but not as often as they have in the near-century of Smokey Bear and no-fire policies. The Southeast has seen few since 2002; Texas, Louisiana, and Arkansas have gone scot free since 1997. Meanwhile, the past decade was the worst on record in the West. Warming trends likely play a part. In the lab, all life stages of southern pine beetle are killed by air temperatures of 3°F; on the ground, the species apparently hits a northern range limit where most winters reach that temperature at least once a year. Global warming will likely bring beetle infestations north of the Ohio River wherever 3°F cold snaps become a rarity. Warming is also implicated in a recent mountain pine beetle outbreak all across interior British Columbia.

Of the many kinds of bark beetles, three *Dendroctonus* species are serious irruptive pests: The southern pine beetle ranges from Texas to New Jersey; the western pine beetle and the mountain pine beetle both range throughout the mountainous western states.

Autumn color in mixed hardwood-conifer forests is normally easy to distinguish from pest damage; it often includes scarlet, unlike dead needles of any sort. An exception might be in the western and north-central states where groves of quaking aspen in fall make yellow patches surrounded by green conifers. At their autumn peak, aspens are a clear lemon yellow. Patches of a deeper golden yellow may be larches—deciduous conifers whose needles turn color and drop every fall; you are likely to see larches only in Canada or under the northernmost Seattle–New York flight path on our map. Yellow larches usually make a heathery mix with evergreens, unlike the yellow aspens, which typically grow in pure stands and are common in every part of the Rockies. Yellow fall color localized along western streamsides is usually cottonwood, a relative of aspen.

Blue Ridge Province at Mt. Mitchell, North Carolina

LOOK FOR a high ridge with a fire lookout tower on its summit and a parking lot just north of the lookout.

❶ Slopes of Black Mountain; Mt. Mitchell summit is just out of frame ❷ Blue Ridge Pkwy. at Balsam Gap ❸ Dillingham, NC
❹ Barnardsville, NC ❺ Mt. Mitchell parking lot, view to south-southwest showing conifer mortality

The highest peak in the United States east of the Mississippi River is Mt. Mitchell. This 6,684-foot peak is the high point of the northwest-trending Black Mountain ❶, an extension of the Blue Ridge Province in North Carolina. The narrow two-lane road along the east and south flanks of Mt. Mitchell is the Blue Ridge Parkway ❷, running between Asheville, North Carolina, and Front Royal, Virginia.

Conifer forests, a southern refuge of the northern spruce-fir forest, cover the slopes above 5,000 feet elevation. On the ridgelines, conifers have died in large numbers over recent decades ❺. An invasive aphid-like pest is one cause. Air pollution is strongly suspected as a contributing cause, but the exact pollutant and mechanism are unclear at present. Lower elevations host a mixed forest with oaks and conifers.

Topography here is more irregular than the Valley and Ridge landscape seen to the west. Streams on the west side of Black Mountain flow to the Gulf of Mexico; those on the east flow to the Atlantic. They created deeply eroded, dendritic drainage patterns that vary in stream density across the region, creating distinct textures on different hillsides. Faults control the distribution of bedrock types. All are types of metamorphosed sedimentary rocks, each with its own drainage pattern that occurs discontinuously.

The oldest rocks in the Blue Ridge range from 1.4 billion to 1 billion years old. Geologists group many rocks of that age as a Grenville Province that resulted from the inferred assembly of a supercontinent, Rodinia. Rifting of Rodinia created the Iapetus Ocean and the continental fragments that became North America, northwest Africa, and western Europe. The rocks underlying Black Mountain and the Blue Ridge were deposited as sandstones and claystones off Rodinia's Iapetan shore about 750 million years ago. The Iapetus began to close by subduction, forming island arcs perhaps similar to the Mariana Islands in today's western Pacific. Three times over the next 400 million years, subduction brought pieces of continental crust into collision with North America and caused a mountain-building event, or orogeny, which included thrusting and metamorphism of rocks in the Blue Ridge Province.

Slices or sheets of the earth's crust traveled a net distance of perhaps 125 miles northwest on horizontal thrust fault surfaces. Mt. Mitchell rock was displaced to the northwest during each orogeny; the breadth of the thrust sheet it was part of varied.

The Blue Ridge shares metamorphic rocks with the adjacent Piedmont Province, but differs in having been lifted on thrust faults. The Valley and Ridge Province was also lifted and folded by thrust faults, although vertical movement there was less than in the Blue Ridge. Stream erosion attacked the unmetamorphosed sediments west of the Blue Ridge to create the Great Valley, enhancing the relief of the erosion-resistant Blue Ridge rocks. Rivers breach the northern Blue Ridge in several places, affording transportation routes between the Atlantic and the Midwest. No major rivers breach the southern Blue Ridge, resulting in a very different pattern of poorer transportation, later settlement, and inhibited development in the interior Southeast.

Supercontinents are not forever. Yet. Pangaea began to break up 225 million years ago. Sea floor spreading opened the Atlantic Ocean between the Carolinas and northwest Africa about 190 million years ago. Erosion stripped sediments from the Appalachians, redepositing them on the Coastal Plain Province and Atlantic shelf.

After more than 200 million years of erosion, you would think that the Appalachian Mountains would be worn down to a level plain by now. Many geophysicists think that the roots of mountain ranges have a low density, which allows the ranges to "float" on the mantle long after the end of their orogenic plate tectonic process. Others, however, think that the presence of high ridges and deep valleys today poses a profound challenge for the geophysicist: What plate tectonic process accounts for this topography? The range is too far from any plate boundary to be affected by presently understood tectonic processes. Possibly relevant are two crustal arches revealed by careful mapping at Cape Fear, North Carolina, and Selma, Alabama. They appear to extend inland, intersecting at Mt. Mitchell. Whatever process produces these arches likely leads to the present elevation of these mountains.

SOUTHBOUND: Go to p. 142

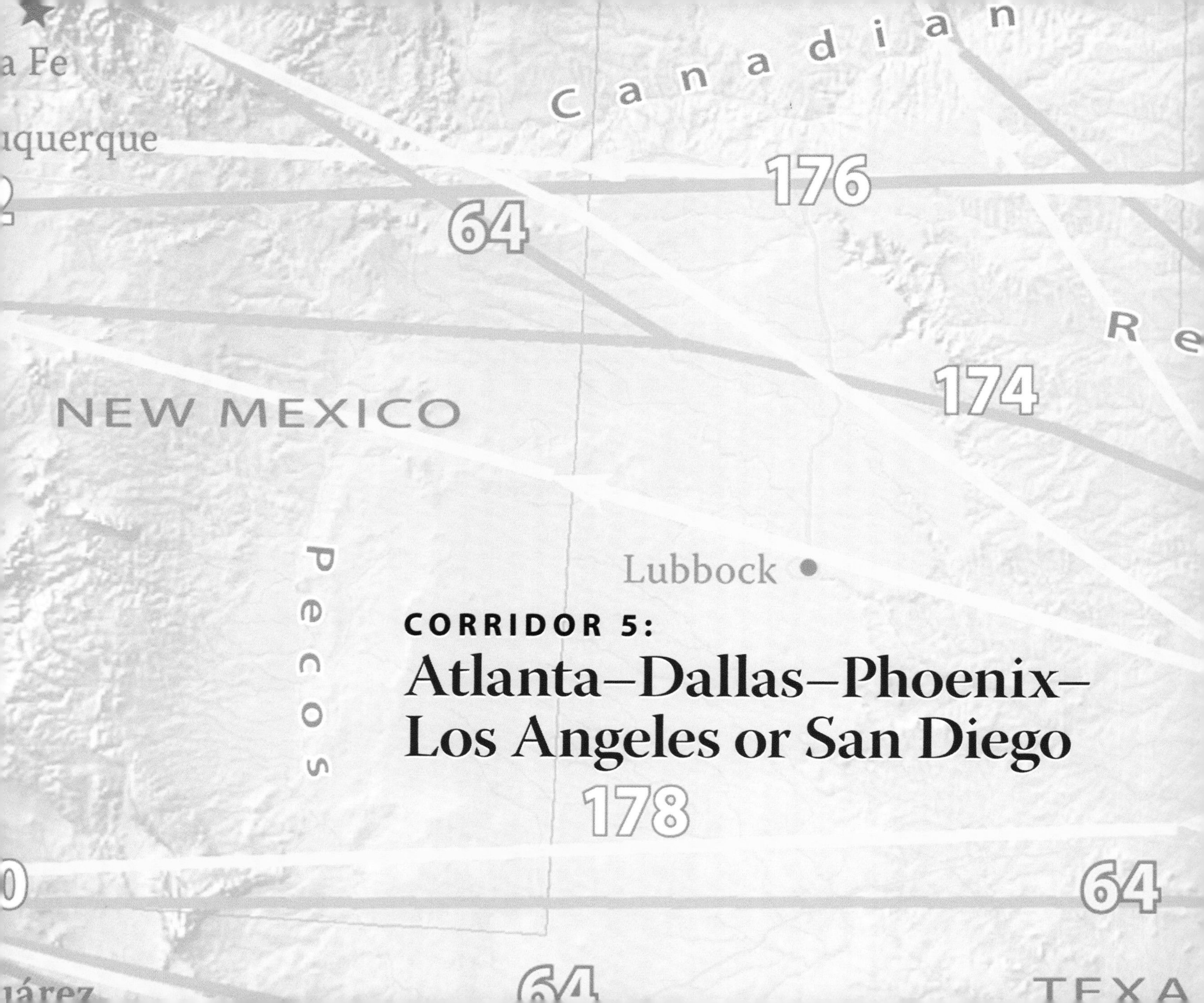

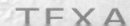

a Fe

uquerque

Canadian

176

64

Re

174

NEW MEXICO

Pecos

Lubbock •

CORRIDOR 5:
Atlanta–Dallas–Phoenix–Los Angeles or San Diego

178

64

árez

64

TEXA

These city pairs have no published preferred routes. Flights typically enter and leave the Los Angeles area via one of two heavily used NAVAIDS: Twentynine Palms or Thermal, near Indio.

Near the Atlanta end, flights to or from Los Angeles often route via Memphis. For the great distance in between, pilots usually plan a fairly straight-line sequence of NAVAIDS and may use the same routes in opposite directions. Look for the landscape out your window on the mapped lines first, but then scan all areas within 50 miles of either line. A small minority of flights deviate northward as far as Fayetteville, Arkansas, and Alamosa, Colorado, or southward as far as Montgomery, Alabama, and El Paso, Texas.

Between Dallas and the Southwest, southern routes via El Paso and northern routes via Prescott, Arizona, or Albuquerque, New Mexico, are equally common. Either way, you will cross dramatic geology well exposed, as most of it is too dry to be masked by either forest or agriculture.

All flight paths east from Dallas cross the continent's largest river, the lower Mississippi.

> I was taught to think I was the richest girl in Christendom because I lived so near to the river. The river belonged to us because we could go and look at its power and its beauty . . . The British feel about their royal family the way people in the Delta feel about the river.*

Or so Ellen Gilchrist remembers her upbringing. The Delta itself, a wide, flat plain patterned with countless meanders, may be just as impressive. The Mississippi lowlands display a complex history, including effects of

- Human engineering, 150 to 50 years ago, including levees and drainage of swamps.
- The end of the Ice Age 12,000 years ago, when rivers filled the basin with sediment and made sweeping changes in their courses, and sea level rose.
- A failed continental rift perhaps 600 million years ago.

Near Atlanta, you briefly cross the southern end of the Appalachians. Two of the four Appalachian provinces, or landform belts, are well displayed: the Valley and Ridge and the Appalachian Plateaus. Topography similar (and related) to the Valley and Ridge crops up in Arkansas as the Ouachita Mountains. (See page 242.) The Southeast tends to be green at all times of year, only partly thanks to the several pine species that dominate the forests; much of the herbaceous vegetation can be green in winter as well.

At some point crossing Texas or Oklahoma, you will see a dramatic transition between green and arid land. The location varies, depending on the season and on whether the year has been relatively rainy. In Arizona and New Mexico, either of two things can make the land green: irrigation or elevation. Irrigated valley bottoms, bright green in the growing season, are few and far between. The darker green of coniferous woodland, most typically pinyon pines and junipers, indicates elevated terrain. Higher habitats are just moist enough to grow trees, thanks to a combination of two effects: cool temperatures, which reduce evaporation; and orographic precipitation, which creates rain and snow where the prevailing westerlies rise to cross mountains. In the westernmost part of the flight, within 100 miles either way of the Colorado River, tree cover is close to nil.

— *Ellen Gilchrist, "Delta of Three Rivers," *Millsaps Magazine,* Fall-Winter 2000. www.millsaps.edu/pubrel/magazine/ fallwinter00/story3.html (1/15/07)

EASTBOUND: Start with pp. 66, 64, 62

The Appalachians's End, Northern Alabama

LOOK FOR boundaries between the Coastal Plain, the dissected plateau, and the parallel Appalachian valleys and ridges at their southern-most tip; coal mines, both active and retired.

Tuscaloosa lies on the Gulf Coastal Plain a few miles west of the Appalachian Mountains. Streams meander across the flat land. Dams impound the Black Warrior River, creating a serpentine lake reaching into the heart of Tuscaloosa.

Here at their apparent southern terminus, the Appalachians are represented by two of their provinces: the Valley and Ridge and, to its northwest, the Cumberland Plateau, one of the Appalachian Plateaus. Coal mines near Tuscaloosa exploit 300-million-year-old coal-bearing strata of the plateau's Black Warrior basin. The active mines are easy to identify by their parade of machinery and trucks. The abandoned mines commonly fill with water, forming small lakes with one or more straight shorelines.

Sandy sediments eroded from the Appalachians 100 million to 95 million years ago make up the eastern Gulf Coastal Plain. Loosely cemented, they are easily eroded. Small quarries and sand pits on low hills around Tuscaloosa extract sand for concrete.

Steep, narrow ridges at the south end of the Valley and Ridge rise east of Tuscaloosa to run northeast 1,200 miles. If you are flying east, you may be able to follow Interstate 59 as it turns between Rock Mountain ❻ and Shades Mountain ❹. These ridges mark the flanks of a giant fold of rock, the Birmingham anticline, which arched 290 million to 240 million years ago during the Allegheny Orogeny. Birmingham is in a valley formed by erosion of the anticline. Rocks on the upper surface of a fold tend to fracture under the stress of folding, leaving them weakened and easily eroded. As the fold continues to grow and after it stops growing, erosion removes the rock strata at the center of the anticline, creating an "anticlinal valley." Erosion-resistant sandstones underlie both Rock and Shades mountains, on opposite sides of the fold.

Red Mountain, the ridge extending from Shades Mountain to downtown Birmingham, contains hematite, a red iron oxide ore. The freeway roadcut in Red Mountain holds a city geologic park.

The top of Red Mountain bears the world's largest cast iron statue; it depicts Vulcan, and the nearby NAVAID that brings your flight this way is named Vulcan.

The Alabama iron industry predates Birmingham. Small iron foundries in northeast Alabama supplied cannon balls and other ironware for the Confederate army. Birmingham was founded in 1871 where coal, limestone, and iron ore all occur, making the city a combined mining and smelting center and a rail depot. However, the iron ore deposits around Birmingham were modest. Over the past 50 years, South American ore delivered by barge through the port of Mobile, together with recycled iron and steel, replaced locally mined ore in Birmingham's mills ❶.

The Appalachians seem to disappear beneath the Gulf Coastal Plain near Tuscaloosa. Similar-appearing mountains are seen in Arkansas (see page 242). For many years, geologists were uncertain of any connection between these ranges, which share rock strata of similar age and style of deformation. Oil and gas exploration, seismic, and well data published in the past 20 years revealed a buried continuity between the two ranges, resolving one question but posing another: Why did this ancient mountain range turn northwest beneath the Alabama-Mississippi state line?

The most widely accepted hypothesis infers that the coastline of the proto–North American continent featured a large bay, or embayment, in the area of the present-day lower Mississippi River. The Appalachian Mountains resulted when that continent and a proto-Europe-Africa continent collided, closing the Iapetus Ocean 240 million years ago. The map-view shape of the Appalachian chain reflects the shape of the continents. Iapetus closed first along the Appalachian margin, then later along the Ouachita margin. How exactly the closure occurred on an embayment between Alabama and Arkansas remains something of a mystery, buried deep beneath much younger sediments.

EASTBOUND: Go to p. 142

❶ Fairfield Works, one of five integrated steelmaking plants still operated in the U.S. by U.S. Steel ❷ rail line of Tennessee Coal and Iron, connecting the area's mines and mills ❸ Wenonah mine ❹ Shades Mountain, which had iron mines along much of its length ❺ a golf course ❻ West Rock Mountain ❼ I-59/I-20 ❽ Bessemer, AL, 40 mi. east-northeast of Tuscaloosa

The Yazoo Delta, Mississippi

LOOK FOR a large, flat agricultural region riddled with meandering streams, with a sharp eastern boundary provided by forested hills; clusters of rectangular ponds.

❶ Lower Auxiliary Channel, between two levees, a flood-control measure ❷ catfish ponds ❸ Wolf Lake, former meander loops cut off from the Yazoo River; note traces of earlier riverbanks concentric with the loops ❹ Yazoo River ❺ U.S. Hwy. 49 ❻ Panther Swamp National Wildlife Refuge ❼ Jonestown Cut-Off, an exercise in river straightening ❽ Yazoo City ❾ hills overlooking the delta

The Mississippi River below its confluence with the Ohio meanders its way through a plain called the Mississippi Delta. The name may be confusing. Far to the south, where the river empties into the Gulf of Mexico in Louisiana, it has built its current delta, the "Birdfoot Delta." (See page 298.) This inland region is "the Delta," the birthplace of the blues. U.S. Highway 49 runs on north from Yazoo City, Mississippi, to Clarksdale, purportedly where Robert Johnson went down to the crossroads to flag a ride and where, Taj Mahal sang, he lay around so long that his hambone spoiled. Parchman Farm, the lamented prison work farm, lies in a meander loop called Black Bayou at the center of the Yazoo Delta.

Mississippi's portion of this delta, between the Mississippi and Yazoo rivers, is the flattest well-watered region in the country. The Mississippi drops only five inches per mile over the whole stretch. At that almost subliminal gradient, a river unloads sediment continually and takes every possible opportunity to meander. A few days of thunderstorm weather in the Midwest will raise the Mississippi a few feet, turning the Yazoo ❹ and other tributaries into distributaries lazily flowing backward, spreading out across seasonal swamps and leaving more sediment.

The Delta was once at the head of a huge ocean bay. Deltaic sedimentation filled it to about 100 to 200 feet above present sea level. Glacial melting at the end of the last Ice Age alone was responsible for all the sediment near today's Delta surface, plus the loess on the adjacent hills.

Delta soil is about as rich as you can find—a point driven home by early promoters who compared its soils to those of the Nile Delta. But the land was swampy and prone to annual flooding. When three "cessions" of Indian holdings opened it to white settlement in 1820–32, settlers wanted only the highest ground, the natural levees along the rivers. Natural levees here may be hundreds of feet wide. They grow during floods because a current's sediment-carrying capacity is directly proportional to its speed. At any spot where the fast-flowing, muddy flood escapes its banks, it immediately slows sharply and lays down a new layer of mud.

As the first plantations proved outstanding for cotton, planters staked out any ground that was even a little bit elevated, and built levees ❶ to improve their odds. Cotton was the product almost exclusively, and most of the labor was slave labor. Yet the Delta was only partially cleared and drained before the Civil War, and wartime neglect allowed artificial levees to collapse and forest to encroach. After the war, speculators grabbed cheap land, only to abandon it when they found few buyers. Within 15 years, 51 percent of the Yazoo Delta belonged to the state, and less area was farmed than before the war. The Delta's population was largely African-American, as it is today. Campaigns to attract new small farmers were thwarted—in part by fears of racial tensions and yellow fever.

During the final third of the 19th century, northern railroad companies and speculators bought up Delta land, logged the forest, drained the swamps, and constructed railroads and levees. Bald cypress, lord of the back swamps, was the timber most prized and is unlikely to rule such vast tracts ever again. By 1920, large cotton plantations almost covered the Delta, presenting a picture close to what pre–Civil War planters envisioned, except that the cotton was picked by sharecroppers rather than slaves. Some prosperous years between 1895 and 1930 were followed by the Depression and a new round of depopulation.

The latter half of the 20th century brought crop diversification, culminating in an explosion of catfish ponds ❷ in the 1970s and 1980s. Catfish had always been popular in southern cooking. As demand began to outstrip the supply of wild-caught catfish, the idea of growing them in ponds developed more or less spontaneously. It proved profitable and in many ways preferable to the wild product. Almost all catfish Americans eat today is farmed channel cat, and we eat more of it than any other farmed fish. The Yazoo Delta has produced more than half of the nation's catfish in every year since 1987.

Farm catfish eat feed made from corn, soybeans, and fish meal. Not being fierce predators like salmon and trout, they eat much less fish meal, avoiding the objection raised in regard to salmon aquaculture that it yields less fish protein than it consumes. Catfish grow best in warm water near 84°F and can survive in up to 95°F water if it is well aerated. Algae aerate the water sufficiently by day, and powered aerators do the job on summer nights.

WESTBOUND: Go to p. 240

Dallas, Texas

LOOK FOR the green river plain through the center of town; multiple street alignments.

Facing south ❶ Trinity River ❷ levees ❸ Union Station ❹ Fair Park ❺ Cotton Bowl ❻ White Rock Lake ❼ Southern Methodist University ❽ Dallas-Love Airport

EASTBOUND: Go to p. 240

The Trinity River—a green, levee-confined floodplain much of the year—slides past Dallas. The river ❶ is not navigable here; it led to the founding of a town not by offering water passage but by obstructing land travel. In 1841 John Neely Bryan built a trading post on a bluff above the river where native trails converged to ford the river. Bryan abandoned Dallas for the California gold rush in 1849. Today, Union Station occupies his cabin's site ❸.

Dallas developed slowly until late in the 19th century. The street grids' discordant alignments are conspicuous from above. The first streets were laid out in 1844, at right angles to the river. A second street grid soon appeared, oriented at 45 degrees to north. Then a third grid appeared, oriented to due north. The three grids intersect in an angular net around downtown. But that was not the end of alignments! The first residential districts added other alignments to this maze as Dallas annexed them.

The coming of the railroads gave Dallas the boost required to distinguish it from its north Texas peers. The Houston and Texas Central Railroad connected Dallas to the Gulf coast in 1872. A link north to Sherman, Texas, connected Dallas with the Missouri-Kansas-Texas Railroad (M.K.T., or "Katy") in 1873, which in turn linked Dallas with Kansas City and points farther east.

In exchange for a $100,000 bonus and a right of way, the Texas and Pacific Railway was built across Dallas en route to Fort Worth and El Paso that same year. Within a few years, Dallas became a nexus of lines joining Midwest and Atlantic cities with the Gulf of Mexico and the Pacific. Rail-stimulated growth made Dallas the largest city in Texas by 1890, with a population exceeding 38,000.

The Trinity River, which overtops its banks most years, produced Dallas's worst flood in 1908. That disaster led Dallas to hire planner George E. Kessler to solve problems created by eight railroads, six stations, and a maze of tracks. Kessler's plan reduced the number of rail tracks in downtown, added the Union Station, and proposed a system of levees to confine the Trinity south and west of downtown—elements all in place within two decades. Much of the rest of the plan was not implemented. Among Kessler's 240 projects are plans for Cincinnati, Ohio; Indianapolis, Indiana; Cleveland, Ohio; Denver, Colorado; Syracuse, New York; and Kansas City.

A couple of miles east of downtown, the 277-acre Fair Park ❹ hosts the state fair each October. Like many Dallas amenities, the fair was created to lure tourists. More than 100,000 visitors came to the first fair in 1886, a crowning success for an exhibit of farm equipment, livestock, and horse racing. Kessler designed the core of permanent park lanes and buildings in 1904. Attendance exceeded 1 million people in 1916, and more than 3 million in the average recent year. It is the largest state fair.

The Cotton Bowl ❺ was built in 1930, followed by a collection of art deco buildings for the Texas Centennial Exposition. How did Dallas build these facilities in the middle of the Depression? In 1930, "Dad" Joiner discovered the 6-billion-barrel East Texas Oil field 100 miles east of Dallas. The regional Federal Reserve Bank, opened in 1914, made Dallas the natural financial center for oil development. Local banks profited by lending money for development of the east Texas field and later for development of the west Texas Permian Basin. (See page 178.)

The downtown core we see today, with its glass-clad towers and expansive parking lots, dates mainly from the oil boom and bust of the 1970s. The 1973 Arab oil embargo caused crude oil prices to quadruple. The 1978 OPEC production slowdown caused crude prices to double yet again. Domestic oil companies based in Dallas enjoyed strong cash flows, as did their local bankers. Most of the downtown towers date from this period. A coeval building boom heightened Houston.

Few of the new buildings were ever fully occupied. During the 1980s, suburban towns north and west of Dallas offered long-term tax abatements to attract employers. North of Dallas, a "telecom corridor" grew in Richardson. West of Dallas, a number of national headquarters relocated to Irving. As these early tax abatements expired, exurbs farther from central Dallas attracted companies with a new round of tax abatements and other incentives. Plano, Lewisville, and their far-flung siblings are employing modern versions of the growth incentives pioneered by the city fathers of Dallas a century earlier.

Caprock Escarpment and Llano Estacado, Texas

LOOK FOR red badlands, separated from a shallowly dimpled flat farmland by a sharp white-rimmed cliff incised in fractal-like patterns.

Few rivers disrupt the flat and featureless High Plains. The especially flat section known as the Llano Estacado, south of the Canadian River in the Texas Panhandle, does at least have crisply defined edges: the Mescalero Escarpment on the west in New Mexico and the Caprock Escarpment on the east in Texas.

In 1541, the explorer Francisco Vásquez de Coronado described plains

> so vast, that I did not find their a limit anywhere I went, although I traveled over them for more than 300 leagues . . . with no more landmarks than if we had been swallowed up by the sea . . . There was not a stone, nor bit of rising ground, nor a tree, nor a shrub, nor anything to go by.

Some believe that in order to have something to go by, he drove stakes into this featureless plain, the Llano Estacado, or "Staked Plain." Alternatively it could mean "Stockaded Plain": Early explorers were sorely challenged to find routes up the Mescalero Escarpment "stockade."

East of the Caprock Escarpment lie the Gypsum Plains. As you may infer from the topography, the difference between the two plains is vertical, a result of erosion removing a top layer of caprock. The Llano Estacado ❷, with its pastures and irrigated fields on brown or gray soil, sits on the caprock layer; then there are badlands ❺, with few signs of economic activity, where erosion is working away at the red layers below the caprock; then farther east, after a gradual transition, you see where the bedrock gives way to smooth, farmable topography.

Beds of red clay were laid down 250 million years ago all across the West Texas Permian Basin. For 200 million years, the basin was an arm of the ocean while the Appalachian Mountains rose to the east. Mountain building culminated in the assembly of the supercontinent Pangaea, stranding the Permian Basin as an inland sea that eventually evaporated, leaving red beds behind.

The strata above the red clays are sandstones interbedded with finer sediments. As the Rocky Mountains rose 11 million to 4 million years ago, rivers eroding them ran across the High Plains, depositing these thick, porous beds, the Ogallala Formation. (Below the surface, the Ogallala Aquifer supplies most High Plains irrigation water; see page 37). Prior to the Ice Ages, the Ogallala Formation likely reached from the Dakotas to the Gulf of Mexico. Much reduced by Ice Age erosion, it is still one of the most widespread formations in the United States.

Ogallala strata are not generally very hard, having been buried neither deep nor long. Here, however, they were converted into caprock, also known as hardpan. Over time, volumes of groundwater carrying dissolved lime flowed through these sands. It was arid here; the water that came close to the surface evaporated, precipitating calcium carbonate (lime), binding the soil with a strong white cement. On the Llano Estacado, hardpan can be over 60 feet thick. It forms the white cliff-top layer in our image ❶.

The shallow round depressions ❹ on the plateau resemble karst sinkholes, but these puncture sandstone, not limestone. Several explanations have been proposed, starting with ancient buffalo wallows. Field studies failed to unearth the substantial buffalo dung deposits predicted by that hypothesis. Most geologists now agree the depressions are deflation hollows scoured into an arid, more or less barren landscape by strong winds, most likely during the Ice Age.

Four million years ago, the Llano Estacado extended across the High Plains from the Rockies. Then the Pecos River captured the headwaters of the Brazos and Colorado rivers, cutting the Llano off from the Rockies as it eroded the Mescalero Escarpment. The streams carving the interfingered canyons in the Caprock Escarpment cliffs continue to advance on the Llano Estacado at rates averaging between four and seven inches per year. At that rate, they could finish their llano lunch in 2 million years.

Facing north ❶ Caprock Escarpment ❷ Llano Estacado ❸ Prairie Dog Town Fork of the Red River ❹ deflation hollow ❺ badlands

Amarillo, Texas

LOOK FOR a midsize city surrounded by irrigated fields, a large industrial facility to its northeast, and extensive gas field well sites to its west.

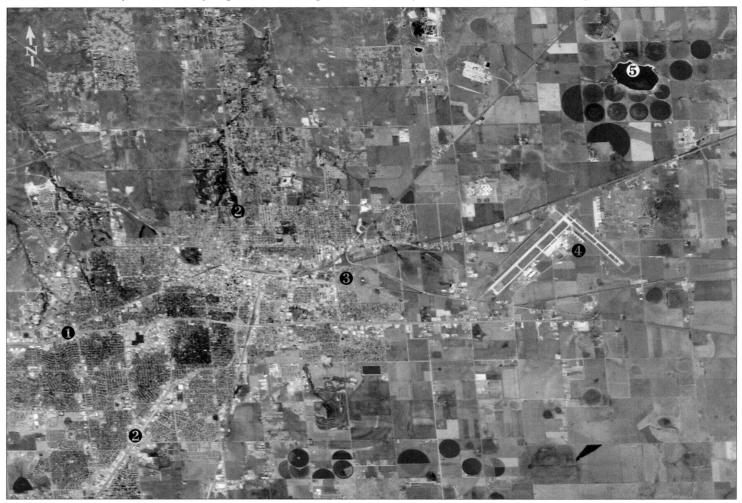

❶ I-40 ❷ I-27 ❸ old stockyards ❹ Rick Husband Amarillo International Airport ❺ McGee Lake; U.S. Department of Energy Pantex plant is just out of frame to right.

The Texas Panhandle is a flat agricultural landscape crossed by several small canyons and one larger one, Palo Duro Canyon. Flights often cross directly above the NAVAID at Amarillo, its largest town, so your only indication of your passage over Amarillo may be the inferred center of the diverging highways, the L-shaped runways at Amarillo International Airport, or the nuclear weapons assembly plant 20 miles to the northeast.

A group of Colorado City, Texas, shop owners founded Amarillo in 1887. J. T. Berry from Abilene platted the city, hoping to make it the commercial center of Potter County. A countywide election to identify the county seat inspired Berry to offer local ranch hands both a commercial lot and a residential lot if the town was chosen. The voters elected Amarillo, even though it was located at the county's southern edge.

Rail connections transformed many High Plains villages into boomtowns, as Berry and company knew well. They soon lured the Fort Worth and Denver City Railroad to Amarillo and built cattle pens and stockyards along its right of way. Three more railroads built lines to the city by 1903, making it the center of the cattle industry in the Panhandle and the adjoining states. Feedlots can still be seen along the rail lines.

Wheat became the Panhandle's second agricultural focus. Between 1925 and 1930, the gasoline-powered tractor replaced the steam tractor and horse over much of the southern plains. The new equipment broke millions of previously unplowed acres to plant wheat. By 1931, wheat production had increased by 300 percent, far in excess of demand. Farmers in eastern Colorado, western Kansas, and the Oklahoma Panhandle also planted new acreage in cotton, sorghum, and corn, all encouraged by the relatively generous rainfall of the 1920s. Drought struck in 1931, persisting until the fall of 1939. This region, known since then as the Dust Bowl, spawned repeated "black blizzards" of topsoil lifted by the winds and carried east across the United States, culminating on Black Sunday, April 14, 1935. Congress created the Soil Conservation Service a week later. Agricultural practices in the Panhandle today reflect the work of the SCS, now the Natural Resources Conservation Service.

Gas was discovered in the Panhandle in 1918; oil, in 1921. Before pipelines were laid, the railroads carried the oil to Amarillo. The refinery near downtown dates from this period. The Cliffside gas field north of Amarillo brought a surprise: large volumes of helium mixed with the methane. By 1965, approximately 96 percent of the world's helium was produced within 250 miles of Amarillo. Helium is an inert, nonflammable gas that is lighter than air. Aside from lifting balloons, it has more exotic uses in the space shuttle, nuclear fusion experiments, weapons development, lasers, and deep-sea-diving air supplies.

Helium has not always been so well regarded. In 1917, the entire U.S. supply of helium was stored in three vials at the University of Kansas. While a graduate student, C. W. Seibel concluded "with regret" in his thesis on the gas that it had no practical use. He was surprised when a U.S. Bureau of Mines scientist expressed interest in filling a blimp with it instead of hydrogen. Seibel provided a cost estimate exceeding $100 million, an impractical sum even for the military. Ten years after World War I, the United States produced helium for a small fraction of Seibel's cost.

Helium is thought to escape from the earth's mantle, probably via faults. Why so much helium is found in this region remains an interesting puzzle.

Amarillo's remote interior location earned it the Pantex ordnance factory in 1942. It produced bombs throughout World War II. In 1951, the second U.S. nuclear weapons assembly plant was built at Pantex; in time, it was left as the only one in the United States. In recent years, it has become a nuclear weapons disassembly plant.

Amarillo means "yellow" in Spanish. The town was first called Oneida, but its inhabitants renamed it Amarillo for a local lake and stream named by early traders. Whether the yellow was a tribute to the soil or to the spring wildflowers is a subject of local debate. Houses were painted yellow in honor of the name change. Fort Worth and Denver City Railroad records indicate that their employees abandoned the Spanish pronunciation from the beginning, saying "am-a-rillo."

Permian Basin Oil and Gas Fields, West Texas

LOOK FOR three large-scale geometries dominating the landscape midway between El Paso and Dallas: rectangles of dry farming, circles of center pivot irrigation, and grids of oil and gas wells.

Farming and ranching drew European settlers to west Texas in the mid-19th century, but the poor soils and arid climate gave them meager returns. Fortune cracked a smile in 1921 with west Texas oil, the first in a series of oil discoveries that transformed Texas and eastern New Mexico.

Small white rectangles mark well sites within the great rectangular grid of dirt service roads. In west Texas, you will see oil fields, typically with closely spaced wells, and gas fields with fewer, more widely spaced wells. Some well sites include small blue pools, a derrick, possibly some trailers, and a number of cars and trucks, all indicating ongoing drilling. Where this array of equipment is outside the grid of well sites, an exploration well is drilling. Where you see a flare of gas from the derrick, a well is testing.

Refineries ❷ are prominent near the larger oil fields and towns of the Permian Basin. Within the fields, gas-processing plants ❹ remove water, carbon dioxide, and sulfur dioxide from the produced gas. You may see the faint, straight trace of buried pipelines cutting through farms not overlying oil fields.

The land is flat, save for the Pecos River valley and the western margin of the Edwards Plateau. Elsewhere in Texas, early prospecting geologists could look to surface geology for hints of targets, but not on the flat west Texas Llano Estacado. Reports of oil seeps, along with water wells occasionally encountering oil or gas, drew the first wildcat promoters. Their central Permian Basin discoveries were made more by luck than by science.

Early gravity and magnetic surveys identified an anomaly in southeast New Mexico in 1928, enabling discovery of the Hobbs Field. That encouraged further development of geophysical methods in oil exploration, including reflection seismic surveys, which led to the Wasson Field, Texas, discovery in 1935. The field was not brought into production until late 1937 because of Depression-era low oil prices and the lack of a pipeline to the area. The onset of World War II created a robust market for oil, stimulating the development of many of the Permian Basin's largest fields. The basin is divided into the Midland Basin on the east, the Central Basin Platform, and the Delaware Basin on the west. The Wasson Field is within the Central Basin Platform.

Oil exploration revealed a deep basin of Paleozoic rocks (600 million to 250 million years old) beneath the Llano Estacado. Rocks of Permian age, 300 million to 250 million years old, produce the bulk of the oil and give their name to the region. Older, underlying rock units produce the bulk of the gas.

The Permian sediments, including organic-rich claystones, were deposited in a tropical marine embayment flanked by carbonate reefs. With burial and heating, the complex molecules of the organic matter broke down into the simpler molecules of oil and gas. When the basin filled with sediments at the end of the Allegheny Orogeny, large salt and gypsum playas, similar to those near the Great Salt Lake today, capped the marine beds. The Permian rocks are generally hidden by younger sediments but can be seen on the surface between the Guadalupe Mountains and the Pecos River valley. The rocks typically form red soils marked by white beds where the evaporites are thick.

West Texas Intermediate, or WTI, is a household word to investors, frequently heard on news reports. This crude oil, produced only in the Permian Basin, has served since 1983 as the market benchmark for sweet crude, with high gravity and very low sulfur content. Pipelines deliver it to refineries on the Gulf coast and in the Midwest, where it yields a higher proportion of gasoline than any other U.S. crude.

❶ Wasson Field oil well sites and their service roads nearly cover the image. ❷ oil refinery ❸ Denver City, TX ❹ gas-processing plant ❺ center pivot irrigation circle 1/2 mi. in diameter ❻ center pivot irrigation circle 1 mi. in diameter

WESTBOUND: Go to p. 36

Permian Basin Oil and Gas Fields, West Texas   **179**

El Paso, Texas, and Ciudad Juárez, Mexico

LOOK FOR two very different-looking cities divided by a river, at a bend wedged between the ends of two small but steep mountain ranges.

El Paso del Norte, the Northern Pass, sits where the Rio Grande glides between the Franklin Mountains of Texas and the Sierra de Juárez of Mexico. The Rio Grande changes course here from south-flowing to southeast-flowing en route to the Gulf of Mexico. The Franklin Mountains rise within the El Paso city limits to run 15 miles into New Mexico; beyond them, similar fault block ranges continue north 100 miles in series. Their east-dipping Paleozoic limestones tell us of an ocean covering this land from 600 million to 250 million years ago.

The Rio Grande ❶, about as wide as a three-lane road except during floods, separates El Paso ❻ from its twin city, Juárez ❸, Mexico. The river's floodplain is walled in cement, with a tall fence on the north side. Marked by a large Mexican flag, Interstate 110 provides the main border crossing ❼. From the air, the cities' contrast in urban development and density is striking. (See page 190.)

Texas joined the United States in 1845. The Mexican-American War broke out the following year, primarily over control of California. The 1848 treaty ending the war placed the new border on the Rio Grande from here south. Secretary of war Jefferson Davis — soon to become president of the Confederacy — wanted a southern, all-weather rail route from San Antonio to California. The route needed to pass through Tucson, which still lay within Mexico. South Carolina railroad promoter James Gadsden was appointed minister to Mexico and negotiated the Purchase named after him, acquiring 30,000 square miles for $333 each. The El Paso–Tucson line, interrupted by the Civil War, went unfinished until 1881, 12 years after the transcontinental line through Utah. The line linked newly discovered copper deposits within the Gadsden Purchase to eastern markets. Benefits to the cotton-growing Southeast fell far short of what Davis and Gadsden anticipated.

Biggs Army Airfield, marking a longstanding military presence here, adjoins El Paso International Airport ❺ on the north. Fort Bliss ❹ is immediately west of the airport and holds much land north and northeast of the city.

Two main rail lines enter Juárez from the south; in El Paso, a main line from Albuquerque meets the Southern Pacific main line. Downstream from the cities, irrigated fields line the river on both sides. In northwest El Paso, two tall smokestacks rise from the ASARCO smelter, which processed Mexican lead and copper ores from 1887 to 1998. The 612-foot stack was built in 1951, and the 828-foot stack in 1967, to reduce ground-level air pollution; air pollution litigation drags on in ASARCO's bankruptcy proceedings.

Although most people see the Franklin Mountains and the Sierra de Juárez, just five miles apart, as bulwarks of two geopolitical realms, geologists see them as paradoxical markers of opposing geological forces. The Franklins rose on normal faults, which occur where the earth's crust is under horizontal tension. The Sierra de Juárez rose on thrust faults, which occur where the crust is under compression. How can the crust be both stretched east to west and squeezed east to west in what is essentially the same place? The short answer is that compression happened first, raising the Rocky Mountains (including the Sierra de Juárez) and was soon followed by extension, raising the countless ranges (including the Franklins) that we group as Basin and Range.

The Basin and Range Province reaches from southern Oregon and central Idaho to Big Bend National Park in Texas. The Rio Grande Rift forms its eastern boundary, running north from where it is oldest and widest, in El Paso. There, the surrounding landscape is youthful, subject to earthquakes on its active Basin and Range faults. Before the Ice Ages, the Rio Grande flowed through a gap south of the Organ Mountains and then along the west side of the Franklins. About 1 million years ago, uplift of both the Organ and Franklin mountains diverted the Rio Grande into its present course.

EASTBOUND: Go to p. 36

❶ Rio Grande (Rio Bravo) **❷** Smeltertown, with ASARCO copper smelter **❸** Franklin Mountains **❹** Fort Bliss **❺** El Paso International Airport **❻** El Paso **❼** port of entry **❽** Ciudad Juárez

Rio Grande Rift at Albuquerque, New Mexico

LOOK FOR a broad valley flanked on the east by fault block mountains and less spectacularly on the west by small volcanoes with lava flows.

❶ Blackbird Hill, and Wind Mesa, a scoria cone and lava flow remnant, respectively, of the Cat Hills volcanics ❷ Ceja Mesa
❸ I-40 ❹ Albuquerque volcanoes ❺ Rio Grande ❻ I-25 ❼ Albuquerque ❽ Manzano Mountains ❾ Cañon de Tijeras
❿ Sandia Crest, 10,678 ft., with Sandia Peak Ski Area and Tram, in the Sandia Mountains

In the Rio Grande valley lies Albuquerque, framed spectacularly by the Sandia and Manzano Mountains on the east, the Jemez Mountains on the north, and the eastern margin of the Colorado Plateau on the west. The valley narrows southward between the western Sierra Ladrones and eastern Los Pinos Mountains. The Rio Grande meanders along its floodplain, a north-south depression darkened by alluvial soils and relatively dense vegetation. Interstate 25 is never far away. Just south of the Sandias, Interstate 40 descends from the High Plains through Cañon de Tijeras, crosses the river in town, and ascends westward past Ceja Mesa and a number of small volcanoes.

The Albuquerque Basin underlies the valley here. It is the central segment of the Rio Grande Rift, which reaches from El Paso to northern Colorado. (See pages 46, 93.) A rift valley is a depression of the earth's crust bounded by one or more faults that break through the crust. Along the faults, one block of rock moves downward, creating a basin where sediments can accumulate. Rifting began in the Albuquerque Basin 28 million years ago.

A series of faults runs along the bases of the Sandia and Manzano mountains, ❽❿ dropping the valley down on the west and lifting the mountains up on the east. A northeast-trending fault runs through Cañon de Tijeras ❾ beneath Interstate 40, separating the higher Sandia fault block from the Manzano fault block. Faulting has been active for a long time, allowing streams to carve deep canyons into the mountain fronts, and faulting continues to this day. Earthquakes are common here.

The west side of the rift is also bounded by faults. They show less total movement than those on the east, but they guided magma to the Albuquerque volcanoes ❹: 5 large scoria cones and 11 smaller vents in a line on top of the Ceja Mesa, on a surface built up by several slightly older basalt flows. Scoria is gas-charged lava erupted rapidly as a frothy liquid, then quickly solidified. The alignment of both the volcanoes and the vents of the underlying lava flows marks a fault now buried beneath the volcanic edifice.

Other small volcanoes occur on the west side of the basin, including the Cat Hills volcanoes ❶, above another fault on Cat Mesa, about 15 miles to the south of the Albuquerque volcanoes. The somewhat larger Isleta Volcano is east of the Cat Hills, crossed on its east side by Interstate 25. This composite volcano initially erupted in a lake then occupying the basin. The explosive reaction of water to hot lava created a circular volcanic ring, or "maar" volcano. Subsequently, both lavas and pyroclastic material erupted from the central vent to build the 300-foot-high peak.

Ceja Mesa ❷ separates the Rio Puerco and Rio Grande valleys for 70 miles. Sediments underlying the mesa were deposited by the Rio Grande, and the mesa top is inferred to represent the level of the Rio Grande 2 million years ago. A similar mesa stands on the east side of the valley below the Manzano Mountains. At one time, these mesas were likely parts of a continuous valley floor. During the past 10,000 years, the Rio Grande and other streams have been cutting into this older level of river sediments.

It appears that the basin alternately filled with sediments and then flushed them in accord with Ice Age cycles. Higher precipitation rates during glacial advances delivered sediment; then arid interglacial climates brought little sediment, and streams eroded the Ice Age beds. In the early 20th century, erosion increased because of overgrazing in much of the Albuquerque Basin. The incised stream and river banks we see today were carved then.

Albuquerque was founded in 1706, named for the Duke of Alburquerque, governor of New Spain from 1653 to 1660. (The first "r" was later dropped from the city's name.) The Santa Fe Railway chose its right of way through Cañon de Tijeras, reaching the Rio Grande in 1880. U.S. Route 66 followed the same path in 1926. The population of Albuquerque was less than 100,000 in 1949, when the Sandia National Laboratories were founded, but doubled in the next 10 years. Much of the present city was built during the past 30 years.

WESTBOUND: Go to p. 100

Chino Mine, New Mexico

LOOK FOR several open mines and tailings piles, with large buildings nearby.

Facing north ❶ Pinos Altos Range ❷ Hanover Mine ❸ tailings pile ❹ Chino Mine main pit ❺ Kneeling Nun

EASTBOUND: Go to p. 100

The Chino mine, 12 miles east of Silver City, New Mexico, is one of several large open-pit mines ❷❹ in southern New Mexico and Arizona. Long known as the Santa Rita Mine, it is one of the oldest and largest mines in the United States, its pit over a mile and a half across and 1,500 feet deep. Large tailings piles lie west and east of the pit, and smaller pits pock nearby ridges. The Kneeling Nun ❺, a prominent ridge, stands above the mine. Or kneels.

The Chino Mine extracts copper and molybdenum from igneous rocks at the end of the Kneeling Nun. It is one of the few operations in the United States that uses both of the two main techniques for processing copper ore. The more common technique, first developed for large-scale use at Utah's Bingham pit (see page 214) consists of concentrating the ore and then smelting it.

The Chino Mine also uses heap leaching and solution extraction/electrowinning (SX/EW). The copper ore occurs as small grains within a matrix of non-ore rock. Look for three-story-tall trucks within the pit, hauling ore to the mill. To extract the ore, the rock is crushed to sand and gravel in the mill, then placed on a leach pad and sprayed with sulfuric acid. The acid seeps through the leach pad, dissolving copper and other metal ores to yield "pregnant leach solution." The solution is pumped from the base of the leach pad to an SX/EW plant, which extracts a copper concentrate. The residual acid is reused at the leach pad. The copper solution, with additional sulfuric acid, goes to an electrowinning cell where an electric current precipitates the dissolved copper onto a cathode. The resulting copper is 99.99 percent pure.

Ore at Chino averages less than 1 percent copper: the other 99 percent of the material taken from the pit is waste, or tailings—the sculpted landscape surrounding the pit and processing facilities.

The tree-covered Colorado Plateau rises north of the mine and the Basin and Range Province stretches to the south. The Chino Mine and a number of other copper mines occur along the margin of a broad upthrown regional fault block known as the Santa Rita horst. Sedimentary rocks including limestone and dolomite underlie the region, ranging in age from 542 million to about 99 million years old. Various igneous rock types are also found, the products of several episodes of intrusion and volcanism between 75 million and 24 million years ago. The Kneeling Nun Tuff erupted from a caldera in the Black Mountains 34.9 million years ago.

The region's igneous rocks were generated by subduction of the oceanic Farallon Plate beneath North America. For a time, the Farallon Plate did not dive at a steep angle, as it does around the Pacific Ocean today. Instead, the plate seems to have sharply reduced its angle of descent once it entered the mantle, bringing it much farther east beneath the continental plate than is seen anywhere today. Where the Farallon Plate eventually reached greater depths, water it acquired from the Pacific Ocean escaped into the overlying mantle. With sufficient water at certain depths, some mantle material melts into magma which, being much less dense than the surrounding mantle, rises toward the surface.

As it rises, water escapes carrying dissolved elements, including sulfur, copper, gold, silver, and other metals. These metals are not water soluble under surface conditions, but they dissolve readily at the high temperatures and pressures deep underground. The rising water follows any fractures it encounters en route to the surface. A rising magma body commonly produces many such fractures above it. At shallow depths, the dissolved material precipitates, often in a predictable sequence: lead sulfide, then zinc sulfide, copper sulfide, silver, gold, pyrite (iron sulfide) and, finally, sinter. If it encounters limestone, the acidic sulfide-rich water will rapidly dissolve the rock and simultaneously deposit the metal sulfides to create a "skarn" ore deposit.

This process occurred at Chino and in the adjoining mining regions of the West around 50 million to 35 million years ago. In some locations, such as Chino, the ore deposit was later remobilized by circulating groundwater to form a "supergene" ("born on top") ore. Two types of ore deposit at the same site result from this process: the supergene deposit near the surface and the older skarn deposit some distance below.

Superstition Mountains and the Mogollon Rim, Arizona

LOOK FOR reservoirs, steep mountains, and deep canyons northeast of Phoenix.

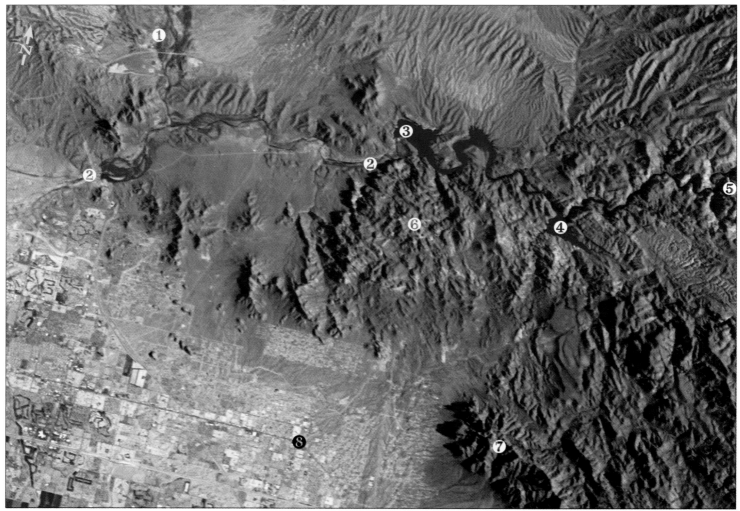

❶ Verde River ❷ Salt River ❸ Stewart Mountain Dam and Saguaro Lake ❹ Mormon Flat Dam and Canyon Lake ❺ Theodore Roosevelt Dam ❻ Goldfield Mountains ❼ Superstition Mountains, 5,024 ft. ❽ Apache Junction, due east of Phoenix and PHX

The Superstition, McDowell, and Mazatzal mountains northeast of Phoenix are a transitional zone between the Basin and Range Province and the Colorado Plateau. The Sonoran Desert, with its saguaro cactus, gives way here to pinyon-juniper woodland and ponderosa pine forests with increasing elevation. Several deep valleys extend fingers of desert into the plateau.

The Salt River ❷ begins on the plateau, flowing west through four impounded lakes on its way to the Gila River west of Phoenix. The Verde River ❶ flows southeast from near Flagstaff through the Verde Valley and the Tonto Basin of the transition zone. En route, the river passes through two impounded lakes. The two rivers meet northwest of the Superstitions about 20 miles east of Phoenix, where a dam diverts water into two main irrigation canals.

The prehistoric Hohokam initiated canal irrigation for crops in the Gila River valley in 200 BC. Nine hundred years later, their irrigation system included almost 250 miles of canals providing water for corn, squash, and cotton. These people left the valley around AD 1400, eventually replaced by the Pima, Maricopa, and Yaqui, who also built canals for irrigation.

Europeans did not settle the Phoenix region in significant numbers until after the Civil War. Arizona was unable to issue bonds for public works until it became a state in 1912. In 1901, a group of Phoenix-area residents formed the National Irrigation Association to lobby Congress. Theodore Roosevelt signed the 1902 National Reclamation Act, the first Progressive act of his presidency.

The Salt River Valley Water Users' Association (SRVWUA) formed in 1903 to realize the act's benefits. Using its members' farms as collateral, the Bureau of Reclamation obtained loans to build Theodore Roosevelt Dam ❺ in 1911. Revenues from the dam's power generation and water sales repaid the loans. Later, the SRVWUA built more dams below Roosevelt to create the 60-mile-long lake series we see today. The dams on the Verde and Salt rivers, the canals, and the power plants constitute the Salt River Project. The project fostered the development of the Phoenix area, first a "reclaimed" irrigated farmland and then as grassy suburbs.

The Superstition ❼, McDowell, and Mazatzal mountains comprise Precambrian rocks up to 1.7 billion years old partially buried by volcanic rocks erupted 30 million to 10 million years ago. Faulting disrupted these rocks 8 million to 2 million years ago as the Basin and Range opened. Volcanism resumed about 6 million years ago, continuing through the Ice Ages.

East of those mountains, the Salt River and its tributaries carve deep headwaters canyons in the Mogollon Rim, revealing layers of rock also seen in the Grand Canyon: cliffs of Redwall Limestone, Coconino Sandstone, and the Kaibab Formation. The Mogollon Rim is the southern edge of the Colorado Plateau, forming an escarpment 500 to 1,500 feet high. Northeast of the rim, the surface of the Kaibab dips northeast gently to the Little Colorado River, covered in places by 90-million to 60-million-year-old Mancos Shale and younger volcanic rocks.

The upper Salt and Verde river drainages have a more chronologically continuous set of rock units than the Grand Canyon. In each region a thick sequence of Paleozoic sediments was deposited over much older Precambrian rocks. Both regions were raised through the Mesozoic era and again during the Laramide Orogeny, shedding sediments into rivers that flowed northeast toward the Four Corners. The Grand Canyon's lack of younger rocks contributes to the difficulty of explaining how and when it was carved.

In the region around the Mogollon Rim, the outcrops of younger rocks suggest that a canyon 4,000 feet deep was carved into the Laramide-age Apache uplift by a northeast-flowing river. About 18 million to 15 million years ago, volcanic eruptions from large calderas, some in the Superstition Mountains, deposited enough volcanic material to disrupt the river drainage. A "Paleo Salt" river began flowing to the south, carving a new canyon through the Mogollon region. Basin and Range faulting was probably active at this time in the adjacent mountains. A new canyon 2,000 feet deep was eroded and then filled before the modern Salt River began to cut the present canyon system in the context of a new episode of faulting that began 8 million years ago.

Lake Havasu City, Arizona

LOOK FOR the only river of any size in this broad desert, widened into a blue reservoir wrapped around a thumb-shaped peninsula attached to a large development with curving streets and several golf courses.

Whether you approach from west or east, an almost hallucinatory anomaly awaits you at Lake Havasu City. You spend 15 minutes crossing some of the harshest desert landscape in the country, only to see a broad suburb suddenly unfurl.

World War II brought the first development to this remote site on the desert shores of the Colorado River. Shortly after Parker Dam's completion created Lake Havasu, an airstrip ❷ was built for pilot training. Soon, General Patton was training tank drivers here as well.

In 1964, Robert McCulloch, owner of McCulloch Motors Corporation, picked the disused Army base as a site for a two-cycle engine factory. He then decided to build a planned community around the core his factory workers' residences would provide.

The location suggested tourism and retirement as additional economic mainstays. Needing a bucketful of publicity to prime those two pumps, McCulloch hit upon one of American real estate development's grandest nonsequiturs: He bought the London Bridge, which was being replaced in 1968, had all its stones individually marked and shipped, bulldozed a new channel for it to cross in Arizona, and had it put back together, stone by stone ❸.

A few years later, McCulloch purchased another planned community development in its early stages. Though much smaller, Silver Lakes at Helendale, California, was perhaps more ambitious in excavating its lakes in the middle of dry desert. It is seen from the Las Vegas–Los Angeles flight corridor. (See page 63 for a photo.)

Today, Lake Havasu City almost rivals Panama City Beach, Florida, as a spring break destination for bikinitropic college students. The average daily high in March is an enticing 80°F. July and August average highs of 111°F make summer tourism problematic. The double-decker red London bus and extensive British-themed retail become especially surreal—or perhaps merely futuristic—when the mercury passes 110°F. Many homeowners are seasonal residents. Most outdoor time is spent on the golf courses or in or on the water. The sheer concentration of boaters has led to several fatal carbon monoxide poisonings near idling motors. Looking at air quality data on a broader scale in 2006, however, *Money* magazine rated Lake Havasu City's air the cleanest of any U.S. town.

Although the founding father loved to call his creation a planned community, planning innovations were a no-show, as were certain normal planning elements—a municipal sewage treatment facility, for example. In 2000, more than 90 percent of the city's residential sewage went through septic drainfields. Municipal water for southern California, meanwhile, was pumped out of the far side of the lake. The citizens, to their credit, did the right thing, voting overwhelmingly in 2001 to pay for a top-notch water treatment plant. The effluent water should be clean and plentiful enough to irrigate the town's verdure, consisting mainly of golf courses. Unfortunately, the system won't be complete until around 2010.

Also missing from the community plan was preservation of the local sport fishery. Striped and largemouth bass were stocked in this part of the Colorado before it was a lake, and the rising waters gave them a big habitat boost at first, by drowning the riverbank stands of cottonwoods. A legendary bass fishery bloomed briefly, then wilted. At the same time that those cottonwoods began to rot away, fertilizer runoff from the golf courses, together with leakage from the septic drainfields, sent several lake coves down the familiar path of eutrophication, algal growth, and deoxygenation. Remediation came late but strong, with the installation of more than 100,000 fish habitat structures during the 1990s. Although these benefit bass and catfish primarily, efforts to preserve the endangered native fish are under way as well.

Lake Havasu was created as a reservoir for the Colorado River Aqueduct, serving southern California. Its much deeper upstream companions, Lakes Powell and Mead, release enough water to keep Lake Havasu's shorelines nearly constant even while they fluctuate sharply themselves. (See pages 56 and 60.)

Facing north ❶ Colorado River (California-Arizona state line); the broad section in the foreground is Lake Havasu ❷ Lake Havasu City airstrip ❸ canal with London Bridge ❹ Lake Havasu City

❺ salt evaporator ponds at Cadiz Dry Lake, between Lake Havasu City and Los Angeles (see p. 62)

Calexico, California, and Mexicali, Mexico

LOOK FOR the dramatic contrast in urbanization and in crop colors between the two sides of the international border; look closely for canals and a river.

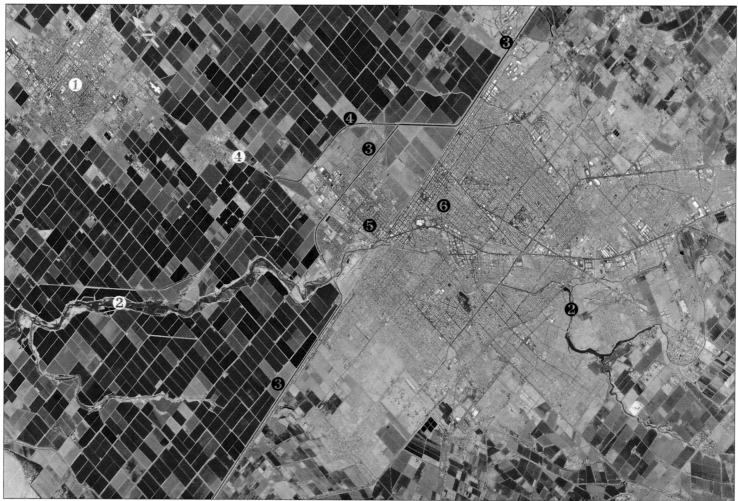

❶ El Centro, CA   **❷** New River   **❸** All-American Canal   **❹** Central Main Canal   **❺** Calexico   **❻** Mexicali

An arbitrary straight line splits this landscape asunder. It's not as if the land is naturally suited to irrigated agriculture on one side and to factories and dense urban population on the other. The difference derives purely from an international border line selected in 1848 by the victor nation in the Mexican-American War.

The color contrast is misleading. Although the U.S. side is more verdant because U.S. farmers, claiming the lion's share of Colorado River water rights, can afford to irrigate lavishly, the two sides—the Imperial and Mexicali valleys—are both agricultural breadbaskets, roughly comparable in production. Both concentrate on winter-season vegetables and (decreasingly) on cotton.

The big difference is the factories, or *maquiladoras*, on the Mexican side and the huge population they have attracted. This is the fifth-largest twin-city pair on the border, expected to surpass 1 million by 2010. Though smaller than Tijuana, Mexicali is the state capital of Baja California Norte.

The *maquiladora* industry grew in response to special trade agreements and the wage differential between the two countries—an average of $1.42 per hour (in one recent year) in *maquilas* versus a California minimum wage of $6.75. Nevertheless, Mexican industry languishes in competition with still lower-wage countries, such as Malaysia and Indonesia. Mexican law gave favorable treatment to *maquiladoras* that assemble products from U.S.-made parts and then export the products back into the United States.

Recently, two large gas-fired electric power plants were built west of the area in the image. Their plans to import gas from the United States and to export the majority of the electricity provoke suspicions that they were put here less for the low wages than for the weaker pollution laws. However, the plants easily met Mexican pollution standards and come close to meeting those that would have been required to site them in Calexico.

Near the two plants is Silicon Border, a new industrial park specializing in chip manufacture; its backers hope that its proximity to chip designers and to markets in California will overcome Asia's edge in wages. Another new facility capitalizes on California's proximity without needing to export anything: It's a major landfill to take U.S. garbage.

In Calexico, on the U.S. side, the big growth sector is retail: Mexicali residents commonly walk across the border to shop. Private schools also attract international day trips. Calexico's proportion of Spanish-surnamed citizens, at about 95 percent of the total, rivals that of Mexicali, which has Mexico's biggest Chinese community. The Chinese arrived around 1904, brought in by a U.S. company to work in irrigation canal construction.

This desert region gets its water from the Colorado River, 50 miles east. Two manmade streams deliver it: the All-American Canal ❸ on the U.S. side and the New River ❶, which winds around on the Mexican side as far as Mexicali, then meanders across on a northwesterly course. Both originated as U.S. enterprises: the canal by design, the "river" by fiasco—a story told on page 192. The New is one of the continent's most grotesquely polluted rivers. We'll spare you the details.

A clamor for a purely U.S. canal route arose after the 1907 fiasco on the New River. The All-American Canal opened in 1942. For a stretch east of these twin cities, this patriotically named canal closely hugs the border. Still farther east, it takes a jog through the Algodones Dunes, an enormous line of dunes blown up against the foot of the Chocolate Mountains. Watch for the construction of a twin canal alongside the existing one in the dune section. The old canal will be permanently shut down when (and if) the new, watertight concrete canal opens. The old earthen one loses 67,700 acre-feet of water a year through seepage into the sands. As of September 2006, however, the project was halted under a court order. Mexicali officials sued to stop it, because the seepage crosses the border and irrigates 400 Mexican farms and has done so since the 1940s. Calexico sided with Mexicali in the suit: The city council decided that its bread is buttered more on the Mexican side (via Calexico's retail sales and sales taxes) than on the U.S. side.

At 1,000 square miles, the Algodones Dunes are probably the biggest area of desert sand dunes in the United States, and certainly the closest to Hollywood. They have provided settings for "Sahara" scenes throughout the history of the movies.

Salton Sea and Imperial Valley, California

LOOK FOR a large, pear-shaped lake in a valley of rectangular, usually bright green fields, flanked by desert and mountains on both sides.

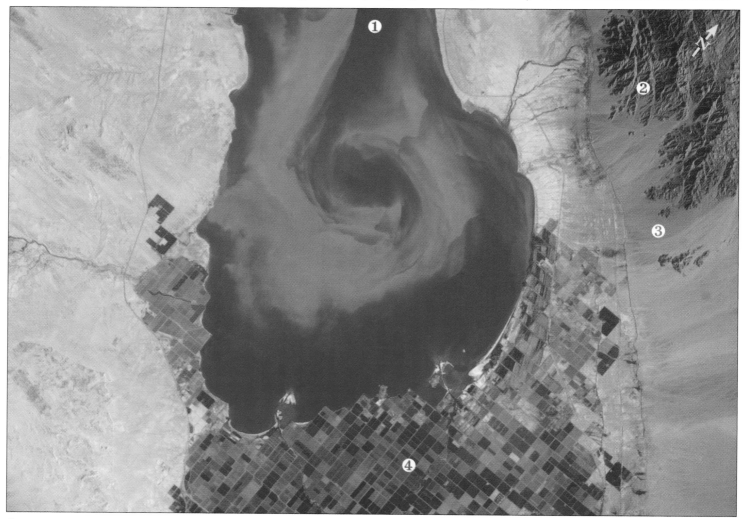

❶ Salton Sea, its surface patterned with an algal bloom (a feature that is not always present) **❷** two fault scarps, members of the San Andreas Fault system **❸** alluvial fans at the foot of the Chocolate Mountains **❹** irrigated crops of the Imperial Valley. Astronaut view.

Below sea level in southernmost California's interior valley, a desert blooms. Irrigated, it enjoys a 300-day growing season and copiously yields vegetables and alfalfa at times of year when no other U.S. farming region can. Its lowest part holds the Salton Sea, one of the country's largest lakes, which went from dry to wet a hundred years ago when irrigation ran amok.

Private developers created a land rush in 1901 by delivering Colorado River water to the part of the valley they were selling; they named it "Imperial." By choosing the lowest path, a detour through Mexico, they only had to divert water into old dry streambeds running down into the valley.

That wasn't as easy as it sounds, at least at first. The Colorado, as yet undammed, was extremely silty and variable in volume. Engineers would cut a break in its levee, only to see the new channel soon choke with silt—a perfectly normal event in active river deltas, like this one. As the flow dwindled, farmers already dependent on that water waxed irate and filed suits, and the increasingly rattled engineers cut ever-bigger outlets. In the winter of 1904–5, they gave the river (then enjoying its highest levels in the 27 years that records had been kept) a path it really liked. Within days, almost the entire flood-stage Colorado River flowed into the Imperial Valley, gouging 40-foot-deep canyons overnight.

Halting the torrent was beyond the ability of the soon-bankrupt developers. President Theodore Roosevelt saw no federal obligation to help, so the Southern Pacific Railroad shouldered the burden, dumping 2,481 train-car loads of rock and clay into the breach fast enough to stem the flow. But that was in 1907, two years after the diversion broke loose. The Salton Sea was a fait accompli.

It enjoyed one bass-rich decade as a freshwater lake; while at its bottom it was dissolving salt from ancient lake deposits. Farmers add more salt—4 million tons of it a year—via irrigation runoff; they have to, or their fields will become too salty to grow crops.

Today, it is considerably saltier than the ocean, too salty for some of its introduced ocean fish species. Rich in nutrients from fertilizer runoff, it could offer a highly productive fishery if salinity and nitrate levels were reduced and stabilized. Congress is studying how and whether to do that. The sea is important to migrating waterfowl, which have lost many wetlands elsewhere in California. Environmentalists now defend the accidental sea more often than they decry it as a corporate catastrophe.

Salton Sea boosters have long labored to refute the popular view of it as a modern accident. They have a point. A lake much broader and deeper than the present one came and went here in more or less random flip-flops through recent geologic history. To understand why, look at the geologic setting. The Coachella, Imperial, and Mexicali valleys constitute a big trough that dropped between faults of the San Andreas Fault system. It is continuous with the Gulf of California, a new ocean basin where two tectonic plates are pulling apart.

Picture, then, a longer version of the Gulf of California with the highly turbid Colorado River emptying into its east side and constructing a delta across the narrow gulf, cutting off its north end and creating a closed basin there. As in other deltas, this river split into multiple courses and shifted often. When the river (or a major portion of it) flowed down the north slope of its delta, it filled the closed basin until the water was high enough to spill over and flow out to sea. At such a highstand, the lake would inundate all the present Coachella, Imperial, and Mexicali valley croplands. But where the river emptied into it, the current would slow, causing sediment to drop and soon to divert the river into a new channel. When all or nearly all the river went straight into the Gulf again, the lake would begin to dry up. The river's entire flow might fill the lake in 12 to 20 years, and typical evaporation rates could dry it up completely in 53 years.

All that the canal diggers did was give the river a little nudge that flipped its switch; it would have happened sooner or later, in nature. If the Southern Pacific hadn't come along and saved them, their accidental lake would have grown to drown the land development they were working for. As it turned out, the development needed a lake of about this (smaller) size to serve as a drainage sump. Whether it can also sustain fish and fowl at reasonable cost remains to be seen.

WESTBOUND: Go to pp. 62, 64, 66

Salinas

Fresno

NEVADA

288

200

202

Visalia

268

Bakersfield

204 206 270

64

CORRIDOR 6:
San Francisco–Los Angeles

Santa Barbara

Even with flight times of barely an hour, this shuttle route offers a strong and varied show. With three airports at the north end and five at the south, as well as nearby regional airports, many combinations are possible. The FAA publishes no preferred routes. The resulting flight paths are distributed across a corridor 100 miles wide. Any attempt to show all the paths we have tracked would produce a very cluttered map, so we show only a few.

You will see pockets of highly productive irrigated agriculture—wine grapes, lettuce, spinach, strawberries, artichokes, and so on. Near each end of the trip, you will see a megalopolis expanding rapidly; here and there in the valleys in between, you will see small exurbs metastasizing. Away from the main highways, where driving in the rugged terrain is very slow, Coast Range hamlets experience little growth.

You may be surprised at how arid and undeveloped much of the land is, especially in the southern half of the corridor. Your aerial view reveals the true climate and natural vegetation more accurately than the agricultural valley views that drivers see from Interstate 5 or Highway 101. Aridity keeps the vegetation sparse, exposing the young, raw, active geology.

Most of the trip is over either the San Andreas Fault zone or west of it, over the slice of California that is attached to the Pacific tectonic plate, moving slowly northwest along the San Andreas Fault zone—the drifting continental fragment characterized in pop culture as "California falling into the Pacific Ocean." The mountains belong to either the Coast Ranges, which run northwest-southeast, or the Transverse Ranges, which run east-west. Both have a complex history of movement on many faults. Some of the faults may predate the San Andreas Fault in this area, but most have at least been affected by it. Many combine strike-slip (horizontal) movement with vertical movement.

The northwest-bound slice is continental crust material hitchhiking on an oceanic plate. It was formerly part of North America, but the East Pacific Rise on the Pacific Plate (oceanic crust sliding northwest) ripped it free of its parent. The Coast Ranges are firmly attached to the Pacific Plate; the piece of crust underlying the Transverse Ranges, however, rotates between strands of the San Andreas Fault. Picture spinning a pencil between your palms: Your palms represent the Pacific and North American Plates sliding past each other; the pencil represents this rotating block. The Transverse Ranges seem to have arrived at their present oblique angle to the coastline after at least 90 degrees of clockwise rotation. There may be smaller "crumbs" that rotated counterclockwise.

NORTHBOUND: Start with pp. 66, 270

South San Francisco Bay

LOOK FOR varicolored reddish sheets of water around the edges of the bay; broad salt marshes drained by curly tidal streams; geometrically elegant suburban and industrial developments on flat shore land.

Facing southwest on SFO approach ❶ Redwood City ❷ salt evaporation ponds ❸ Pacific Shores Center ❹ Bair Island ❺ Foster City

Sitting on the edge of your seat, forehead pressing the clear plastic, you're flying into San Francisco, and there it is! The fog-shrouded Golden Gate . . . the Transamerica Pyramid . . . the Bay Bridge . . .

Those are the hors d'oeuvres. The Bay Area is saving its best visuals for last: the surreal colors and fractal drainage patterns of the South Bay salt marshes and evaporation ponds. On the heavily used southeast approach to SFO, your last 140 seconds before bumping tarmac will display (through left-side windows) a small block of salt ponds ❷, Pacific Shores Center ❸, Bair Island ❹, and Foster City ❺. Similar features are close to SJC and OAK.

These muddy flats have a tortuous history of shifting human effects. The Ohlone Indians came down to gather salt from naturally occurring salt pans on the east shore. The Ohlone left several hundred middens, or shell mounds, near the shore, some exceeding 20 feet high and hundreds of feet long. Following Euro-American settlement, salt operations evolved over many decades, growing to industrial scale and eventually consolidating under Cargill, Inc.

Around 1860, Sierra Nevada gold miners set change in motion in the bay when they turned from panning for gold to hydraulic mining. They impounded mountain streams to create water cannons to blast entire ridges into gravel and finer sediment. Enormous sluice boxes sorted out the gold, leaving everything else to wash on down the rivers to the bay. The sediment began filling the bay, threatening shipping interests, which set dredges to work maintaining a navigable channel. Dumping of dredgings was unregulated; the bay was remodeled, willy-nilly.

By the mid-20th century, the sediments became assets: They could support enormous salt ponds or even new real estate. Bits of fill augmented San Francisco around the edges; the Army Corps of Engineers put out a document envisioning most of the bay converted to suburbs, and at least some developers answered its siren call. But where the corps calculated that the Foster City town site should prudently be filled to 8 to 12 feet above mean sea level, the developers found that too expensive. They countered with a design perforated with large curving lagoons, enabling rapid drainage, aided by pumps, from a surface just 4 to 5 feet above sea level.

No doubt the citizens love their lagoon marinas, and Foster City's Web site, as of 2006, proclaims this creative solution a smashing success, but it may prove to have been penny wise, pound foolish if this century brings a several-foot rise in sea level. That isn't the only hazard to worry about, either. Engineers have learned that fill soils are prone to liquefaction when shaken; buildings on fill face greater earthquake risk than does the rest of the Bay Area.

The 1959 Army Corps of Engineers report avoided the word "fill," preferring "reclamation"—an Alice-in-Wonderland term for converting a site to a completely new use. Californians appalled by the report responded with a Save the Bay movement, soon reversing the tide of human attitudes to the bay (and reclaiming the meaning of "reclaim"). In 1965, the state declared a moratorium on fill. In 1974, Congress established the San Francisco Bay National Wildlife Refuge, and in 2003, governmental bodies bought 15,100 acres of Cargill's South Bay salt ponds for restoration.

Cargill continues to operate a huge salt facility on the bay's east shore. The ponds' red hues consist of salt-loving algae (page 217). On the west side (the Silicon Valley coast, as it were), Cargill held on to a small block of salt ponds ❷ to sell to developers when the time is ripe. Celebrity neighbors are already in place: the Pacific Shores Center ❸ houses DreamWorks Animation SKG, birthplace of *Shrek 2*, *Madagascar*, *Shrek the Third*, *Madagascar 2*, and so on.

In the 21st century, scientists rule the marshes and many of the salt ponds. They are proceeding slowly, having seen how badly ecosystems suffer when engineering proceeds in advance of scientific understanding. Atlantic spartina, a giant salt marsh grass, was introduced here in an ill-advised restoration effort in the 1970s and may now be the worst of several invasive species. Flying low over the bay, you may spot spartina growing in dark green circles a few yards in diameter.

At least in the first decades, many salt ponds taken over from Cargill will remain salt ponds, now managed to maximize shorebird populations rather than salt. Dense populations of brine shrimp in the ponds feed many wild predators. Simply returning the bay to nature would incur a loss of desirable species that came to the salt ponds as their native habitats diminished elsewhere.

California Aqueduct and Kesterson Wildlife Refuge, California

LOOK FOR a squarish reservoir—the largest lake on the Coast Range/Central Valley margin south of the Sacramento River—with a small triangular reservoir right below it; east of there, at the heart of the Central Valley, a murky marshland full of sinuous sloughs.

Facing east ❶ California Aqueduct ❷ San Luis Wasteway ❸ Delta-Mendota Canal ❹ O'Neill Forebay ❺ San Luis Dam and Reservoir; from here southward, the next 180 mi. of the aqueduct are officially San Luis Canal, in a name switch simply reflecting federal as opposed to state management.

Facing east Kesterson Wildlife Refuge just east of Newman, CA ❻ San Joaquin River ❼ Salt Slough ❽ Mud Slough ❾ duck ponds with gun clubs

San Luis Dam is the fourth-largest earth-filled dam in the United States. (Oahe and Fort Peck, page 279, are larger.) The smaller dam on the O'Neill Forebay ❹, right below it, works upside down: The canal at its base flows *toward* the dam, where the water is pumped up into the Forebay. A larger canal, the California Aqueduct ❶, flows into the northern corner of the Forebay and out the southeastern corner. Water is pumped from the Forebay up into the San Luis Reservoir in seasons of plenty and flows back down in seasons of need. No significant flow enters the reservoir from its natural drainage, making it an "offstream reservoir" (again, the largest in the United States). The two reservoirs exist to even out the flow of water through the aqueduct. They are the keystone of the Central Valley Project, the world's biggest and most expensive water-moving project to date. It carries northern California water to the Los Angeles metro area and to San Joaquin Valley farmers.

Northeast of the reservoir is an anomalously wild area with meandering rivers and no highways or farms. That's the San Luis National Wildlife Refuge (no relation), by far the largest remnant of the original Central Valley wetlands.

Before plows and livestock arrived, the valley's flat floor invited its rivers to sprawl. Expanses of semiarid shrub/grassland intermingled with vast marshes of tall bulrushes. Both the marshes and the rushes are known locally as "tules" (TOO-lees). Some marshes survived as wildlife refuges: places for waterfowl to thrive and present abundant targets to hunters. The marshes still host many duck clubs, but the Fish and Wildlife Service now manages them for a broader set of native wildlife. At the same time, the federal Bureau of Reclamation, the 45 percent partner with the state in the Central Valley Project (CVP), saw the area as a link in its plan to manage irrigation water. In 1981 and 1982, the refuge—then called Kesterson—had a notorious close brush with death.

The chief agricultural destinations for CVP water lie along the western flank of the southern valley—the tan-colored area on page 198. This area, some of the driest in all the valley, had never been farmed much or valued highly, as its soils tend to become salty if irrigated. Local landowners organized the Westlands Water District and campaigned for the Central Valley Project, which would improve their prospects a hundredfold. They got it. As a part of the project, the bureau planned the San Luis Drain ❷, parallel to the San Luis Canal but flowing the other way, to carry salty drainage to the Sacramento River. The bureau built the drain as far as Kesterson, only to stop when Bay Area political forces protested against contaminated water entering their bay. The bureau went into a holding pattern until the issue could be resolved, digging ponds in the Kesterson refuge to absorb the drainage. Ten years later, a majority of birds hatched there had hideous fatal deformities. The drainage water was contaminated with more than common salt.

Coast Range streams flow into the Westlands only to evaporate before reaching a larger body of water. Some Coast Range rocks are relatively rich in selenium, an element necessary in trace amounts for both plant and animal health but toxic at higher levels. Selenium is naturally concentrated in alluvial soils where Coast Range creeks dry up. Beginning in the 1970s, irrigation water dissolved the selenium and carried it through the San Luis Drain to Kesterson, where it became increasingly concentrated as it worked its way up the food chain.

The media loved the story of birds poisoned in their own refuge. Before long, courts and politicians forbade the bureau to dump irrigation drainage into either the refuge or the Sacramento River. However, the bureau is still obligated to dispose of the farmers' drainage so that they can farm as promised by the terms of the Central Valley Project. After 25 years of scientific studies and expensive proposals to deal with this Gordian knot, the refuge appears surprisingly healthy, but disposal of selenium remains an unresolved problem.

A solution may involve retiring substantial acreage of selenium-tainted Westlands farmland. That would make economic sense: At the rates Los Angeles is ready to pay for water, $1 million worth of water grows $900,000 of crops there. The farmers believe—with a certain amount of support from court decisions—that not only the water rights but also the absurdly low prices they pay for water are now their property. As one farmer, C. W. "Bill" Jones, told a reporter, "You can't have agriculture without subsidized water." Farmers elsewhere might have a few things to say about that.

Big Sur, California

LOOK FOR an 88-mile stretch of steep coastline undeveloped except for a perched two-lane highway, with large landslide scars; brownish, smooth kelp patches interrupting the pattern of ocean waves.

❶ Monterey Bay   ❷ Monterey   ❸ Carmel   ❹ Point Lobos   ❺ CA Hwy. 1   ❻ Point Sur   ❼ Big Sur Valley and Sur-Nacimiento Fault
❽ highest part of Santa Lucia Range. Astronaut view about 35 mi. wide.

Nowhere else in North America will you find such a legendarily spectacular stretch of coastline within 250 miles of 25 million people yet with so little development. How many parking lots do you see? Multistory condos or hotels? Marinas? Swimming pools? Beach umbrellas?

Beaches are scattered, skimpy, and few. The Santa Lucia Range drops steeply to the sea, barely leaving room for the winding two-lane road. Bulldozers and blasting crews modify such topography elsewhere on the California coast; why not here? The difference was that most of this coast was designated a national forest at a time when no one saw wild scenery as a gold mine. Big Sur held very little land attractive to miners or even to the most eccentric farmers, so there are few inholdings. By the time value was ascribed to recreational land, Big Sur had a passionate band of advocates ensuring that the Forest Service did not sell.

An 82,000-acre estate complete with "castle" was established in 1919 by publisher William Randolph Hearst. In 1957, the Hearst Castle was donated to the state. In 2004, the state bought all nearby development rights from his heirs, except for 27 mini-estates and a midsized hotel. These, if they come to pass, will be at the south end of the undeveloped coastline.

Landslides have repeatedly wiped out parts of the precarious Highway 1 ❺. Repairs often consisted of bulldozing more earth off the top of the slide so that it slid down, reducing the slide's slope enough for repaving to proceed—fighting fire with fire. This method made the slide scars big enough to see from your aircraft window. Unreliable (if not downright hazardous) road access undoubtedly dampens the ardor of any would-be developers.

In the 1930s, Big Sur was so remote that the perseverance there of a few dozen sea otters remained a secret among a few locals, while the world's mammalogists declared the California sea otter an extinct subspecies. Otters like to do their relaxing in kelp beds, which calm the surface movement of waves. Look for patches of kelp just offshore: brownish-green gaps in the regular pattern of waves. Kelp beds were missing during the 1930s because sea urchin populations, without enough sea otters to keep them in check through predation, exploded, and overgrazed the kelp. We owe the return of kelp to the recovery of California sea otters. With protection from the fur trade, the otters' population rebounded by 1980 to more than 2,000 between Big Sur and Monterey Bay. After 1990, otter numbers mysteriously faltered. The prime suspect is a disease carried by house cats and delivered to the bay in sewage.

The Santa Lucias are part of the Coast Ranges. Elsewhere, California's Coast Ranges are built from marine sediments of the Franciscan mélange crumpled against the edge of North America in a long-lived subduction zone. The Santa Lucias, in contrast, are part of Salinia, a terrane carried north along the San Andreas Fault zone after transform motion replaced subduction. Salinia comprises 1.7-billion-year-old metamorphic rocks intruded by 100-million-year-old granites. The latter formed in a magmatic arc where the oceanic Farallon Plate subducted beneath North America, possibly a southern continuation of the Sierra Nevada volcanic arc. The highest Santa Lucia peaks ❽ expose nearly white granite.

In addition to moving past each other at the San Andreas Fault zone, the two crustal plates push against each other, causing thrust faults. As Salinia slid northward past the main belt of Franciscan rocks, more westerly Franciscan rocks were thrust up onto its western edge along the Sur-Nacimiento Fault, which runs close to the shoreline: onshore in places and offshore in others.

Big Sur ("South") as a place name originally referred to a river and its short valley ❼ on a segment of the Sur-Nacimiento Fault. The Big Sur aura expanded to embrace the entire wild coast for 88 miles between the two closest towns, Carmel ❸ and San Simeon.

The Big Sur and smaller coastal valleys are the southernmost refugia of the coast redwood. The Santa Lucias today are clothed less in conifers than in dry grassland and chaparral, an evergreen shrub community that goes up in flames cyclically. To walk from those hot, dry slopes into the shady redwood groves is to experience cognitive dissonance—a dissonance that the redwoods share, as they are out of place here, left over from cooler times. They persist here thanks to coastal fog and to the shade of other redwoods. If a grove is logged or burnt down, redwood stumps will resprout, but the sprouts will not thrive or produce a new grove in the present climate, let alone the future climate.

San Benito Mountain and New Idria, California

LOOK FOR a bluish white-tinted mountain range rising immediately west of the Central Valley, southeast of San Jose.

Facing northeast ❶ Silver Creek ❷ San Carlos Creek ❸ New Idria Mine ❹ Idria Peak, 4,655 ft. ❺ San Carlos Mines and Peak, 4,845 ft.; note road up this side of the mountain ❻ San Benito Mountain, 5,241 ft., highest peak in the south Coast Ranges

Among all the coast ranges overflown south of the Bay Area, the highest range jumps out at you: It's a different color. Surrounded by reddish tan sedimentary bedrock, San Benito Mountain ❻ and its neighbors have bluish white bedrock instead, with less green vegetation cloaking them than the surrounding area.

This may be California's biggest patch dominated by the state rock, serpentine. Soils derived from it are more difficult for plants to grow in, so reduced plant cover is characteristic. The soils tend to weather to a red color, but this is not apparent from high above San Benito; what is apparent here is the color of unweathered serpentine, the bluish green that reminded someone long ago of snakeskin.

Serpentine regions have a host of interesting and unusual minerals. This particular patch has economically important deposits of cinnabar, or mercury ore, which turned these mountains into a mirror image of the California gold rush. Mercury mines yielded some of the era's greatest fortunes.

Gold mining is a pick-your-poison proposition. After you've exhausted the loose sedimentary placer deposits, which are separable with the help of plain water, you need a solvent to separate gold embedded in the rock of lode deposits. Pick mercury, arsenic, cyanide, or two of them for a one-two punch. Mercury, also called quicksilver, predominated from Roman times through 1880 and still does today among artisanal gold miners in many developing nations. Cyanide predominates at the industrial scale. (See page 44.)

When Spain's colonies were rife with gold mines, the king kept the colonies on a short leash by monopolizing Spanish mercury. That worked until enterprising sailors began smuggling Chinese mercury in the mid-1700s. Mercury became no less precious than gold. In 1845, a Mexican Army captain filed a mercury claim near Misión San José. He recognized cinnabar, a red pigment the local Indians used for face paint. Both his mine, later named New Almaden, and gold discoveries near Los Angeles were quickly reported to Washington, helping to ensure that California would become part of the United States as spoils of the Mexican-American War.

Soon after the famed Sutter's Mill gold nugget was found in 1848, quicksilver prospectors scoured the Coast Ranges. High on San Benito Mountain in 1854, they founded the New Idria ❸❺ mining district, which became the biggest U.S. mercury district, producing until 1972. The world's two greatest mercury districts up to that time were Almadén in Spain, for which the Romans fought Carthage, and Idrija, in Slovenia. You might fly close enough to see the ghost town of Idria; if not, note the miners' roads winding up over the top of the range.

Mercury is one strange metal, the only metal that is a liquid at household temperatures and a gas at temperatures easily achieved over a campfire. To separate it from ore, you distill it: You bake the ore and catch the oozing liquid metal and the emitted vapors, which condense into a liquid and run down the surfaces of your still. Mercury dissolves gold, a metal that shirks most chemical bonds. One way to reseparate the gold-mercury amalgam is to bake it. The mercury vapors can again be caught in a retort and reused, a sensible practice followed in today's corporate smelters but often neglected in the wilds. Forty-niners held a shovelful of pasty amalgam over a campfire; today's artisans use a propane torch.

Mercury's toxicity was obvious in the 1850s. A visitor to the smelters wrote that the workers' "leaden eyes are the consequence of even these short spells, and any length of time continued at this labor effectually shortens life." Dead trees and fish and sick cattle were also noted, yet wanton release of mercury into the streams and mercury vapor into the air continued unabated in California, as it does in parts of the Amazon basin today. Many Sierra Nevada streams remained dead for decades.

Once released, mercury persists and spreads, becoming a diffuse global pollution problem. The mercury atoms bioaccumulated by any particular swordfish (a food pregnant women should avoid) were released over several centuries and in every part of the world. Many governments now ban the use of mercury in herbicides, in paint, in thermometers, in hats (hence the term "mad as a hatter"); some ban it in tooth fillings or regulate emissions of mercury from coal-fired power plants. Yet its use in gold mining goes virtually unhindered. Impoverished gold miners often work beyond the reach of the law, and efforts to educate them about safe alternatives are left mainly to private nonprofits. Individual gold miners release around 500 tons of mercury per year—more than 25 percent of the world's total releases and two to five times the weight of the gold it yields.

Morros and Mo-tels, San Luis Obispo, California

LOOK FOR a valley town bisected by an east-west line of small rounded hills, a few miles inland from the Pacific.

San Luis Obispo lies in an idyllic Coast Range valley studded with an east-west row of anomalous, more or less round crags: the Morros ❹❺❻❼, also known as the Seven Sisters or the Nine Sisters. As there are 12 of them, we prefer Morros, Spanish for "hillocks." From the air, you can see the pale gray color of their rhyodacite lava summits contrasting with the muddy Franciscan sediments of the nearby mountains.

The town originated as a Spanish mission settlement in 1772. The word "Obispo" (bishop) clarifies that this mission was named not for the canonized King Louis IX of France but for Louis of Toulouse, who died at age 23 after renouncing his claim to the throne of Naples in order to be a priest. Padre Junípero Serra founded a mission here after the valley proved itself a fertile hunting ground for grizzly bears. Starvation was threatening the Monterey mission; Padre Serra sent a hunting party back to a valley his men had once dubbed "the plain of the bears" when passing through. The party returned with four and a half tons of bear meat, and the mission was saved.

You may spot an M, for Mission College Preparatory High School, on Cerro San Luis Obispo, the Morro most central to the town. The westernmost Morro lies a few feet out into the Pacific, connected to the beach by a small sandspit. It's called Morro Rock; both the bay and its town are named Morro Bay. The tallest Morros lie between Morro Bay and San Luis Obispo.

The Morros are volcanic necks—magma that solidified in conduits underneath volcanoes and was later exposed by differential erosion of the softer surrounding volcanic debris. (Ship Rock, page 98, is another.) These volcanoes erupted between 26 million and 22 million years ago when the San Andreas transform movement replaced subduction as the plate margin process along this part of the North American margin.

Geologist Tanya Atwater infers that a block of crust containing part of the south Coast Ranges ripped from the North American Plate and rotated like a ball bearing caught between North America and the northwest-moving Pacific Plate. It rotated clockwise by about 130 degrees over the past 20 million years. Its mountain ridges run east-west, in contrast to the north-northwest to south-southeast orientation of the Coast Ranges proper: the Transverse Ranges of Santa Barbara, Ventura, and Los Angeles counties (the Sierra Madre, Santa Ynez, Santa Monica, San Gabriel, and San Bernardino mountains).

The Morros lie in the "bearing grease" between this rotating "ball bearing" block and the two pieces to its northwest: Salinia (see page 201) and the marine and coastal sliver that includes the Point Reyes peninsula, western San Francisco, and a few coastal bits of Big Sur. The block, or microplate boundary, faults are largely hidden under valley fill sediments surrounding them.

Islay Hill ❹, the largest among the quite small Morros continuing east from Cerro San Luis Obispo ❺, was not named by homesick Scottish islanders drowning their sorrows in distilled peat smoke. Malt whiskey aficionados might have influenced the spelling, but the word, originally transcribed "yslay," is a local native word for a wild cherry that grows there. (It's pronounced ee-SLY, as opposed to EYE-la for the Scottish island.) "Islay" may turn up on a wine label some day, as San Luis Obispo is a nascent wine-growing region.

San Luis Obispo gave birth to the first motel, or at least to the word "motel." The Motel Inn, built in 1925 in charming Mission style, still stands, complete with red tiles and mock bell tower. Its original neon sign flashed "Hotel" and "Mo-tel" alternately, lest the neologism's meaning be lost on any passing motorist. It was only natural for the motel to be conceived on Highway 101 ❸, which followed the path of the old Camino Real of the mission friars and was a focus of the early days of automotive touring for pleasure. By the 1960s, most traffic between the Bay Area and southern California had moved over to Interstate 5 in the Central Valley.

Facing south-southwest ❶ Shell Beach, on Pacific Ocean ❷ Point San Luis ❸ U.S. Hwy. 101
Four Morros: ❹ Islay Hill, about 780 ft. ❺ Cerro San Luis Obispo, 1,292 ft. ❻ Bishop Peak, 1,546 ft. ❼ Chumash Peak, 1,268 ft.
❽ San Luis Obispo ❾ California Polytechnic State University

San Andreas Fault on the Carrizo Plain, California

LOOK FOR a small, straight mountain range just east of an arid basin encrusted with white salt in its lowest portion; if you are close enough, look for the fault line near the western foot of this range.

The 1857 Fort Tejon earthquake, one of the largest recorded quakes on the San Andreas Fault, redecorated the Carrizo Plain, making it perhaps the world's most popular site for photos of active strike-slip faults. The photos show a row of stream ravines all displaced 33 feet to the right in 1857 ❸. The fault line is straight, perpendicular to the stream ravines, and parallel to the main ridges and valleys in the vicinity, which all relate to the fault.

The San Andreas is a zone of faulting a few hundred feet wide. Typically, most of the movement on the fault is along the main fault strand, with less movement occurring on other, minor strands.

The main strand can jump to the left or right, resulting in small jogs in the fault line. You may be able to spot places where the line jogs or steps to the left. Small hills often mark these spots where blocks have pushed up between strands of the fault. On the other hand, where the fault line jogs to the right, the blocks sink to form small, narrow valleys; small lakes, or sag ponds, fill some of them.

West of the fault, on the floor of the Carrizo Plain, white-crusted playa lakebeds are conspicuous. They're generally lakes in the winter, dry flats in summer. Alkaline and salty minerals have accumulated in them, giving the water varying chemical compositions that support assorted populations of bacteria, which in turn shade the water in different tints. Huge numbers of shorebirds frequent these lakes at some times of the year. Except for this occasional lake, the plain is a very dry place and looks nearly barren from the air.

A few miles west and southwest of San Francisco International Airport, two narrow lakes next to I-280 fill parts of a long trough on top of the fault. Two Spaniards who explored here on St. Andrew's Day in 1773 named this valley Cañada de San Andrés. The civil engineer who named the fault unfortunately adopted a "Germish" translation that first appeared on an 1877 county map. San is Spanish; Andreas is German. Put those together with "fault" and we've got, let's see, Spermglish? These two lakes are reservoirs, not sag ponds. They may be your best location to spot the San Andreas Fault on flights between San Francisco and the North or East.

On flights using San Jose, Oakland, Burbank, or Orange County airports, you may fly right over the Carrizo Plain or over other unmistakably straight valleys farther north in the Coast Ranges; those look a lot like this one and also mark the San Andreas Fault. Valleys form by erosion where rock is weak or fractured because of repeated fault movement through the rocks. Movement occurs mainly during earthquakes, when a segment of the San Andreas, or an associated fault, breaks. The Carrizo Plain segment has apparently been "locked" since 1857, unlike the Parkfield segment immediately to its north, which has "crept" with many small and medium-sized earthquakes. The movement of the San Andreas Fault was first understood to be purely horizontal, or strike-slip, in the 1950s. Even then, the amount, timing, and cause of the movement remained moot. The 1960s plate tectonics revolution in geology finally made sense of the San Andreas Fault.

For students of plate tectonics, the San Andreas is an exciting example of a well-defined plate boundary that's visible. Most plate boundaries are under oceans; the few that are on land often make large mountain ranges, like the Himalayas and the Alps, where a plethora of faults and even small separate pieces of plates within extremely rugged terrain make the precise plate boundary difficult to locate. The San Andreas Fault separates the North American Plate from the Pacific Plate. Los Angeles, on the Pacific Plate, creeps toward San Francisco, on the North American. Looking at the two plates, geologists calculate their relative motion at 2.2 inches per year. The San Andreas Fault moves only 1.4 inches per year, so the remaining 0.8 inch must slip elsewhere. Geophysicists studying this plate boundary think that it may be getting ready to jump to a new line roughly along the California-Nevada border. If it does, San Francisco will become part of the Pacific Plate, joining Los Angeles on the journey to the Northwest.

Farther south, the same plate boundary creates a small ocean basin with a sea covering it: the Gulf of California, separating Baja California from the Mexican mainland.

SOUTHBOUND: Go to pp. 270, 66

Facing east ❶ Temblor Range ❷ Carrizo Plain with salt-crusted playa ❸ line of creek valleys offset (west side northward) by fault movement on the San Andreas Fault; it is subtly visible between the two dotted lines ❹ Central Valley

Facing northwest, a close-up of the line of creek valleys offset by fault movement, about 5 mi. past (or south of) point ❸ in the above photo. Low-altitude small plane view

222

Salt L

NEVADA

UTA

24

CORRIDOR 7:
Chicago–San Francisco

Carson
City

220

6

288

Flights between Chicago and the Bay Area tend to stay in a narrower corridor than do some other long hauls across the West and are joined in this corridor by the majority of flights between the Bay Area and New York or Philadelphia or Boston. Even bee-line routes enabled by the new navigation equipment will track between our mapped lines much of the way. The FAA also publishes a northerly preferred option, crossing Lake Oahe, South Dakota, and the Wind River Range in Wyoming; Boston or Toronto flights would be more likely than Chicago flights to take it. As westbound flights approach the California-Nevada line, they fan out, crossing the Sierra Nevada and the Central Valley on various transects, depending on which airport they're headed for.

On the Great Plains, you are likely to see at least three kinds of evidence for strong wind: crop stripes and two kinds of hills named for their constituent windblown particles. Neither Iowa's Loess Hills nor Nebraska's Sand Hills are supported by bedrock.

The corridor crosses both the Rockies and the Sierra Nevada without typically seeing their highest parts, and it crosses Utah's canyon country well away from its national parks. All the same, the landscapes offer a feast of mountains and canyons.

This corridor alone shows a full transect of the region geographers call the Great Basin and geologists call the Basin and Range. Great Basin describes a region whose rivers do not reach any ocean. Rivers, without getting very big, run for tens of miles only to enter a lake, or a playa, from which the water evaporates at least as fast as the streams can deliver it. This process makes the lake salty and sometimes alkaline; the salts become conspicuous as white crusts on dry lakebeds (playas). In wet seasons or years, the playa may become a lake again, or the lake may rise and expand, but drier seasons return, and the body of water shrinks and may dry up. During the Ice Ages, wet times persisted for tens of thousands of years, and the Great Salt Lake achieved truly Great Lake dimensions; it even found an outlet to the sea, briefly. The Bonneville Salt Flats in Utah are a playa of that oversized lake, called Lake Bonneville.

Closed basins like this are common in arid regions. Any tectonically active region on land will raise ridges that produce some closed basins. Given a reasonable amount of rainfall, rivers will tend to fill a basin with a lake until the lake overflows, focusing erosion on the outlet until the lake drains completely. In this manner, most of the world ends up draining to the seas via river systems. Sizable natural lakes are exceptions to the rule. Entire regions of America lack them. The two most extensive kinds of region that have a significant cover of natural lakes are glaciated regions and, paradoxically, dry regions like the Great Basin.

This region is arid because it lies downwind of the Cascades and Sierra Nevada, a long, unbroken mountain crest that crosses the prevailing westerly airflow, creating heavy orographic precipitation on its western slopes and leaving little moisture in the air mass for its next several hundred miles east. Except for orographic precipitation on a few high Rocky Mountain ranges, climates remain arid from the Sierra almost to Iowa. Most crops you will see are irrigated. The many mines and oil or gas wells you will see are the chief economic use of the land.

"Basin and Range" describes a pattern—covering all of Nevada and large portions of Utah, Oregon, Idaho, Arizona, and beyond—of linear north-south mountain ranges separated by somewhat broader, nearly flat valleys. These are fault block ranges; some are additionally considered metamorphic core complexes. These ranges rose within the last 20 million years as part of a process of extension, or stretching, of the earth's crust. It may be more accurate to say that the basins sank rather than that the ranges rose; geologists speculate that the preexisting condition was an "American Altiplano," a very high plateau. The Great Basin is still a plateau, with most of its flat valley floors at least 4,000 feet above sea level.

EASTBOUND: Start with pp. 196, 64, 198

WESTBOUND: Start with pp. 24, 26, 28, 30, 32, 34, 36, 38, 40, 284

Flaming Gorge, Wyoming and Utah

LOOK FOR a long L-shaped reservoir, dammed at the south end, in dry red-rock country. (The cross-line of the L is narrow.)

❶ Flaming Gorge Reservoir ❷ two hogbacks ❸ Flaming Gorge Dam ❹ Green River ❺ Browns Park ❻ Uinta Mountains.
Astronaut view 35 mi. wide

EASTBOUND: Go to pp. 284, 40, 38, 36, 34, 32, 30, 28, 26, 24

The Green River flows entirely through arid lands, after initially receiving its water mainly from nearby mountains. Spring snowmelt and early-summer thunderstorms coincide to produce a great May-June peak in runoff. Flaming Gorge Dam ❸ manages to even out the monthly flows but with unanticipated effects on riverbank contours and river habitats. At least two fish species are threatened because of the change, and the Army Corps of Engineers is studying flow regimes that might encourage their survival. Stabilizing the banks has also invited an invasion of saltcedars, a noxious nonnative tree. Downstream from Flaming Gorge Dam, the Green is joined by the Yampa, a nearly equal river without major dams; below their confluence, June flooding still occurs.

Aside from saltcedars, greenery is in scarce supply on the Green in Utah. Among several possible etymologies, we like to think that fur trappers named the river after its verdant riparian strips upstream in Wyoming, where they found their buck-toothed quarry. The upper basin became a trappers' mecca in the 1820s, the scene of their legendary annual rendezvous. All of southwest Wyoming is at least 6,000 feet above sea level and wide open, with harsh, windswept winters. Trappers wishing to tough out a winter here in order to trap when the pelts are thickest typically followed the example of the local Shoshonè people, repairing downstream to Browns Park, a relatively sheltered stretch of valley at 5,400 feet ❺. This Shangri-La cradled perhaps the northernmost instance of maize farming in the West between about 300 and 1600. In the early 1800s, it became one of the first white settlements in the Rockies.

At the east end of Browns Park, the river turns south, entering the canyon of Lodore. Dinosaur National Monument was established here in 1915 to protect the richest Jurassic fossil site ever found. In 1938, its 80 acres were augmented with 203,000 acres of spectacular canyonland on the Green and Yampa rivers.

In 1950, a proposal for dams in Dinosaur National Monument provoked the nation's second great dam controversy. In the four decades since the first controversy (over flooding California's Hetch Hetchy valley), Hoover, Bonneville, Grand Coulee, and most of the Tennessee dams had been built, and dams had an impregnable status in public opinion. But with Dinosaur's canyons in the balance, and inspiring stands taken against these dams by Frederick Law Olmsted and Bernard De Voto, the Sierra Club and others drew a line in the sand. After a five-year public relations war, dam proponents compromised: The Green would run forever free in Dinosaur National Monument but would be dammed instead at Flaming Gorge and Glen Canyon (page 57). Although this can be spun as a transformative victory for the environmentalists—as the birth of the environmental mass movement and the end of knee-jerk approval of dams—many environmentalists commenced decades of cursing themselves or one another for sacrificing two canyons just as worthy of reverence as the ones they saved.

Completed in 1964, Flaming Gorge Dam stands 502 feet high. The reservoir has yielded lake trout trophies over 50 pounds.

The Uinta Mountains ❻ rise immediately south of the reservoir, running east-west—an anomaly among Laramide uplifts and most western ranges. The Uintas lack sharp summits and resemble a giant whaleback. Ice Age alpine glaciers cut steep-sided valleys, in some cases extending far enough to breach the encircling hogbacks. Along the northern base of the range, the hogbacks ❷ stand as high as 800 feet above the valleys. The higher one is Madison limestone; the outer one, Weber sandstone; both are much older rocks than the Dakota Hogback sandstones. (See pages 43, 44, 89.)

The Uintas visibly force the river's eastward turn in Flaming Gorge, yet it doesn't circumvent them; it cuts right through the uplift's core 40 miles east, raising the old riddle of how the river cut through the mountain range. It was here that John Wesley Powell, at the beginning of his Grand Canyon voyage, coined his "antecedent stream" hypothesis, which he later applied to the Grand Canyon as well: The river was there when the mountains began to rise and kept pace in cutting its canyon as they rose.

Closer study, though, showed that the Green has been in the canyon of Lodore less than 7 million years. As the Uintas rose around 50 million years ago, a huge lake filled southwest Wyoming. After Basin and Range extension took over in the region, faults opened the Browns Park valley, drawing the drainage there, and perhaps on southeast to the Yampa, circumventing the entire uplift. With help from timely fault-driven subsidence of the Lodore area, a Yampa tributary eroding headward could then have "captured" the Green from a Browns Park that was higher than it is now.

Desolation Canyon and the Uinta Basin, Utah

LOOK FOR a river in shallow meandering canyons, crossing uninhabited reddish country; areas dotted with natural gas well pads.

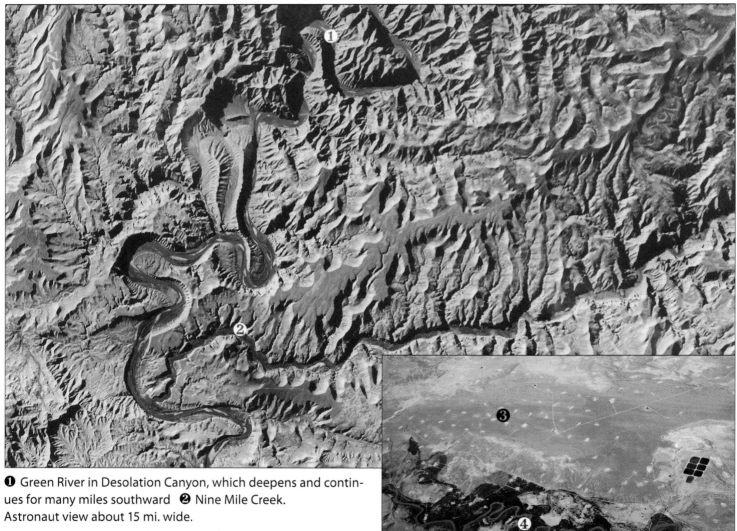

❶ Green River in Desolation Canyon, which deepens and continues for many miles southward ❷ Nine Mile Creek. Astronaut view about 15 mi. wide.

Facing north-northwest ❸ gas wells ❹ White River

Flights between the Bay Area and the Northeast typically cross the Green River either at Flaming Gorge Reservoir (see page 210) or in Desolation Canyon ❶. The colorful red and orange surroundings expose many of the same Paleozoic and Mesozoic sedimentary rocks that crop out from Arizona to South Dakota.

The stretch of the Green River known as Desolation Canyon is fast becoming a fabled destination for river rats. The typical float trip in inflatables goes 84 miles without passing under a single bridge or by a single town. It offers whitewater but is usually less challenging than, say, the Grand Canyon or the Middle Fork of the Salmon River in Idaho.

Whitewater travel as recreation was born on the Green. John Wesley Powell embarked on his famous Grand Canyon trip at Green River, Wyoming, in 1869. That was for science, of course, not for fun; yet Powell was soon back for a second trip, and his vivid account was widely read. In 1909, a Utah man named Nathaniel "Than" Galloway, having designed boats and developed new techniques for running the Green and Colorado, was hired as the first professional whitewater guide on a trip undertaken for pleasure. Inflatable rafts arrived as military surplus after World War II.

Note how the canyon sinuously snakes across the desert bedrock. The very existence of these "entrenched meanders" tells of big changes in the not-too-distant geologic past. A river confined to a bedrock canyon cannot form meanders; they form only in loose sediment, where stream gradient (the angle of the water's descent) is very low. These meanders must have been made by a Green River winding across a gentle plain whose surface soils were subsequently stripped away. Canyon-cutting began just a few million years ago, probably following a change in course that sharply steepened the Colorado River's overall gradient. (See page 49.) "Base level" is the elevation at the mouth of a river, either a lake or the ocean. It can change for a number of reasons: falling sea level, capture by another river, or major faulting that alters the river's course. After such a drop in its base level, a river's speed and its erosive power increase; the enhanced erosion slowly works its way upstream.

The giant whaleback shape of the Uinta Mountains—among them King's Peak, Utah's highest point, at 13,528 feet—rises to the north. Hogbacks frame the range intermittently; the main one on this south side is Madison limestone and the other, where there are two, is Round Mountain limestone. Lowlands all around the Uintas were filled with huge lakes between 70 million and 45 million years ago, when the Laramide fault blocks first raised the Rockies. Rapid uplift led to rapid erosion in the mountains and to rapid deposition of sediment in the lake basins. Plants flourished in a subtropical climate, adding copious organic matter to the lake sediments, now known as the Green River Formation—and every geology student knows what can happen to organic matter in sedimentary rocks. The Green River Formation has yielded substantial oil and gas, especially in this corner of Utah and adjacent parts of Colorado. Most well pads ❸ you see just east of Desolation Canyon produce gas; the Uintas' south flank has oil wells. The Bureau of Land Management anticipates thousands of additional wells by 2020.

Far greater hydrocarbon reserves—allegedly greater than Saudi Arabia's—are found in Green River oil shales, in a waxy solid form that can be extracted only with high heat. This could be done at 950°F in enormous retorts next to gargantuan open-pit mines, devastating the local landscape and releasing almost twice as much carbon dioxide as an equivalent amount of conventional crude releases over its product cycle. To be cost-effective, it would probably require oil prices above $90 a barrel, perhaps much higher.

Alternatively, Shell Oil has tested an innovative technique avoiding open-pit mines. Shell lowers electric heaters into wells, heats the shale beds to 650°F over a period of a year or two, and captures the natural gas and the lighter oil fractions that are forced out first. Shell claims that this yields five times as much energy as it consumes, would be competitive at oil prices of $25 a barrel, and would be relatively clean. Although it looks promising, it still needs large-scale testing and thorough study of water issues—both the potential for contamination and the total consumption of local water. The Colorado River's water is already fully allocated among 30 million people in two nations.

Bingham Canyon Mine, Utah

A smokestack 1,215 feet tall at the foot of the Oquirrh Mountains marks the smelter for the Bingham Canyon open-pit mine: the site, more than any other, where mechanized pit mining was first developed. It produces primarily copper but also gold, silver, and other ores.

Ore rock is crushed to small grains within the pit. A conveyer system takes this gravel to the small company town of Copperton, east of the pit. There, a concentrator separates the copper minerals from the host rock in a process known as "beneficiation." After receiving the concentrate by pipeline, the smelter roasts it to remove arsenic and sulfur dioxide; then furnaces convert it from 30 percent copper to first 98.5 percent "blister" copper and then 99.5 percent "anode" copper. A two-mile rail line takes that to the refinery, which produces 99.9 percent copper ingots, plus the precious metals.

The rock removed from the Bingham pit is about 0.6 percent ore; the large piles of gray, yellow, orange, and red material surrounding the pit are non-ore waste. Tailings also cover the landscape around Copperton, and the refinery produces slag.

Bingham Canyon was first settled in 1848 by Thomas and Sanford Bingham, who started a cattle ranch. After the Binghams moved to Weber County a few years later, the canyon was exploited primarily for timber. In 1863, soldiers from Salt Lake City's Fort Douglas discovered gold and silver ore in the canyon. Other discoveries followed, but they were not rich enough to pay off when wagon transport of the ores was taken into account. In 1873, a rail line to near the Oquirrhs made mining profitable and led to the development of milling and smelting.

A welter of mining claims covered Bingham Canyon and adjoining land near the end of the 19th century. Boston Consolidated Mining Company and the Utah Copper Company bought up the claims, speculating that large-scale mining would be feasible. In 1898, Daniel Jackling and Robert Gemmell proposed to exploit the low-grade deposits with two novel techniques: large-scale mechanized open mining and large-scale "flotation separation beneficiation" to separate ore from waste. The concentrator at Copperton is the successor to Jackling's original plant. By 1910, the mining and refining facilities at the north end of the Oquirrhs comprised the largest industrial mining facility in the world. It kept growing and produced one-third of the copper used by the Allies during World War II.

The Oquirrh Mountains ❶ are a range within the Basin and Range Province. Interpreting the processes responsible for ores at Bingham Canyon has proved difficult. Limestone, sandstone, and shale strata under the northern Oquirrhs are 315 million to 500 million years old. Thrust faulting and folding during the subsequent orogenies deformed the ancient sediments before intrusion of igneous rocks about 40 million years ago. The Bingham pit exploits a porphyry copper deposit created during that intrusion. "Porphyry" describes igneous rocks with two very different sizes of crystalline grains. Feldspars are typically the extra-large grains. Porphyries often occur within "granitic" rocks, coarse-grained igneous rocks composed of feldspars, quartz, mica, and other minerals. Ores occur at Bingham Canyon in both the porphyry intrusion and the surrounding Paleozoic limestones. The ores form distinct patterns within the intrusion: Copper ores formed an upside-down cup shape near the top of the stock. Gold occurs both in zones of highest copper concentration and in areas without copper.

Facing west ❶ Oquirrh Mountains ❷ Stansbury Mountains ❸ Tooele Valley ❹ the open pit of the Bingham Canyon Mine ❺ tailings

Great Salt Lake, Utah

LOOK FOR tinted polygons and a long tint-accented causeway at the north end of the lake.

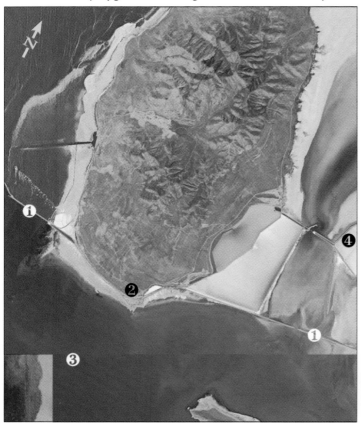

❶ causeway ❷ Promontory Point ❸ main body of Great Salt Lake ❹ salt evaporation pans. Astronaut view about 11 mi. wide.

Facing north-northeast ❺ abandoned grade of historic railway; Promontory Summit is out of frame to the left ❻ Wellsville Mountains, on the Wasatch Fault ❼ Bear River Migratory Bird Refuge marsh ❽ Brigham City

Great Salt Lake is intriguingly colorized by natural responses to two industries. Around Willard Bay, the lake's northeastern arm, it's hard to miss the salt evaporation pans ❹, which range from white to orange to red in sharp contrast to the deep blue lake. As water evaporates from these impoundments, the concentration of salt increases; red salt-loving algae flourish and then are concentrated by evaporation. Eventually, it gets too salty even for these algae. Individual pans shift through many reddish shades, ending up bright salt white, as the impounded water evaporates.

A network of dikes divides the shallow water into geometric forms. As the water level drops, a secondary network of roads emerges, dividing the pan into smaller pans. On the very whitest pans, where all the water has evaporated, look for heavy equipment that comes out to remove the product. The salt is primarily sodium chloride—plain table salt—with many commercial uses.

The larger, northwestern arm of the lake gets pinkish with the same algae. A railroad causeway ❶ cuts this arm off from the main lake. With no tributaries to supply fresh water, its water level dropped while its salinity rose.

Beyond the salt pans, close to the mountain front, you can see a marsh ❼, part of the Bear River Migratory Bird Refuge. Tucked in between the refuge and the Wasatch Range is Interstate 15/84. Most of Utah's populace and most of its industry are found between the lake's east shore and the Wasatch Front.

The base of the mountains ❻ marks the Wasatch Fault, one of the biggest and most active in the Basin and Range Province (most of Nevada and Utah). This fault extends 250 miles from the Utah-Idaho line south to Nephi, Utah. It is a "normal fault": One side (the mountains) moves up, and one side (the lake basin) moves down, in response to the earth's crust stretching, or extending. In cross-section, the fault plane arcs to the west beneath the lake. In typical earthquakes on long normal faults, only one segment of the fault moves in each earthquake. Ten segments occur on this fault, including individual segments at Brigham City, Salt Lake City, and Provo. Flying over, you can see these segments because large valleys in the Wasatch Front separate them. The last major earthquake on the Wasatch Fault, with about 10 feet of movement, came 400 years ago on the Provo segment.

The first transcontinental railroad was completed when the east-building Central Pacific and west-building Union Pacific railroads met in 1869 at Promontory Summit, at the north end of the peninsula dividing the lake's two northern arms. The Union Pacific started from Omaha, crossed Nebraska and Wyoming, and descended through the Wasatch Front in the narrow valley it now shares with I-15/84 above Ogden. The city is named for William Butler Ogden, who financed the Union Pacific.

Current bridge technology could not span the lake, so the route skirted the lake's northern end, necessitating sharp curves, ups, downs, and a 700-foot climb to the desolate summit, where a tent encampment sprang up to accommodate passengers laying over between trains. The two companies ran their own trains on their own tracks only, forcing the layover.

Today, the Promontory Summit right of way is abandoned, as are the few towns that mark it. Rail companies long contemplated a time-saving level route across the lake—a route through Promontory Point ❷, the peninsula's tip, as opposed to Promontory Summit, site of the golden spike. A combination causeway and trestle, finally built in 1903, proved more difficult than it looked. The lake's salt-crusted mud floor sank unpredictably, swallowing sections of rock fill and sometimes dunking trains. Still, the causeway served heavy traffic for decades.

In 1959, a sturdier causeway ❶ with no trestle replaced it, thus cutting off (and reddening) the northern lake. This heavy-duty causeway proved no more reliable than the old one. In the 1980s, a series of wet years raised the lake to rail level, washing out sections of causeway over several months. Occasionally, six-foot waves crashed into trains.

Lack of an outlet, which makes the lake salty, also makes it difficult to regulate. Actually, it has an outlet, but the outlet is several hundred feet above present water level. The lake rose to its outlet level for centuries at a time during the Ice Ages, developing wave-cut terraces. (Look for a terrace marked by gravel pits directly above the Salt Lake City International Airport; other than that one, Lake Bonneville terraces are easier to see on mountains in northwest Utah than in the Wasatches.) Utahns are not eager for moister climates to return and give their lake an outlet again.

Bonneville Salt Flats, Utah

LOOK FOR flat, white lake bottom north of Interstate 80 and west of the "oasis" town of Wendover, Utah.

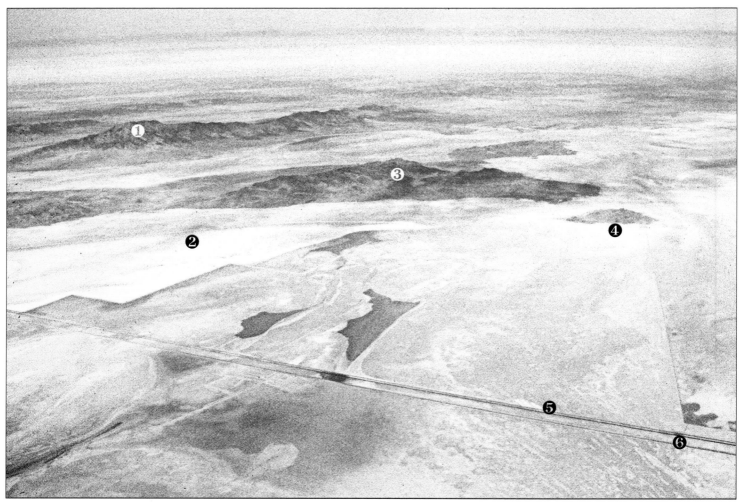

Facing northwest   ❶ Pilot Range   ❷ Bonneville race track on Bonneville Salt Flats   ❸ Silver Island Mountains   ❹ Floating Island
❺ I-80   ❻ Western Pacific rail line, now part of Union Pacific Railroad

The brilliant white flatland at the west end of the Great Salt Lake Basin is known to motor speed enthusiasts as the Bonneville Salt Flats. A straight racetrack ❷ runs for more than 10 miles parallel to the base of the Silver Island Mountains, and a circular or oval track is also prepared in most years. Both are prepared in summer and can disappear under a shallow lake late in the year. A network of canals and levees defines the potash salt evaporator pans south of the interstate (and west of the area in the photo).

The salt flats are within the West Desert Basin, a sector of the Great Salt Lake Basin separated by a low divide from the Great Salt Lake for perhaps 10,000 years. Lake Bonneville filled the entire region during the Ice Ages, and you may be able to see its ancient shorelines on slopes above the flats. Two rivers flow year-round into the lake, but the West Basin has no perennial streams. Consequently, the brines in the West Desert Basin are denser, have a different chemistry, and have formed a more substantial salt crust.

William Randolph Hearst, the newspaper magnate, first drew attention to the Great Salt Lake Basin as a potential racing site in 1896, when he sponsored a transcontinental bicycle race as a publicity stunt for his papers. The race passed through the salt flats.

In 1914, Teddy Tezlaff drove a Blitzen Benz across the flats at 141.73 miles per hour, an unofficial land speed record. A racetrack was established in 1912, but early races failed to attract spectators to the remote locale. Speed records in the early automobile era were set in France and Great Britain, and on beaches in Florida. In 1925, a race across the flats between a Central Pacific passenger train and a Studebaker driven by Ab Jenkins drew national attention when Jenkins won the race by more than 10 minutes. In 1935, Malcolm Campbell set the first of Bonneville's many official records, covering 1 mile at an average speed of 301.129 miles per hour. Later racers broke 400, 500, and 600 miles per hour at Bonneville. Since 1983, new land speed records have been set in northwest Nevada's Black Rock Desert, including a speed of 763.035 miles per hour in 1997, which still stands as the record as we go to press 10 years later. We note with interest, however, that Bonneville still claims the land speed record for a barstool.

The hard, flat surface of the Bonneville Salt Flats provides good traction to racing vehicles and is strong enough to support vehicles weighing 10 tons. During the winter and spring, precipitation over the flats and adjoining mountains creates a shallow lake. Streams draining the mountains carry dissolved minerals, which precipitate on the lake as it evaporates during the dry and windy summer months. The resulting surface salt layer is more than a foot thick. The salt rests on a thick layer of carbonate mud and is interbedded with thin layers of gypsum (calcium sulfate). The layers are porous, and dense brines commonly occur beneath the salt surface.

The layer is not as thick today as it was 100 years ago; nor is the racetrack as long. A survey in 1921 found the salt layer to be as thick as three feet in many places on the flats. A survey in 1998 found it to be a foot thick in most places. Potash mining south of the interstate began in 1939 with the construction of brine canals. This process is responsible for the slow loss of the salt layer on the racetracks. An agreement between the Bureau of Land Management and the mine's operator appears to have remedied the problem. In recent years, brines collected in the canals are piped to a plant in Wendover, where potash (potassium chloride) and magnesium chloride brine are removed. The residual brine, rich in sodium chloride, is returned in the winter months to the racetrack area where it precipitates salt during the summer months.

Jedediah Smith reportedly crossed the flats while returning from an 1827 expedition to California. Joseph Walker mapped the Great Salt Lake Basin in 1833 and named the flats for his boss, Captain Benjamin Bonneville. John Frémont's 1845 expedition crossed the flats while seeking a shorter route to the Pacific than the Oregon Trail. Lansford Hastings then promoted the route across the flats as the "Hastings Cutoff" to California. In 1846, the Donner-Reed party took the cutoff and became mired in the carbonate muds beneath salt on the north edge of the Bonneville flats. The delay placed the party in the Sierra Nevada when winter came on, and early snows stranded them with tragic results. The following year, nearly all migrants chose Oregon over the Hastings Cutoff, but the discovery of gold in January 1948 reversed California's eclipse.

Wheeler Peak and the Snake Range, Nevada

LOOK FOR a high mountain distinguished from others in Basin and Range country by a road switchbacking up its east side; a contrast between this pair of relatively domal mountain ranges and the numerous asymmetrical, linear, north-south ones.

The well-named Basin and Range Province consists of broad basins separating several hundred mountain ranges. Ice Age lakes occupied most of the basins, leaving flat sediments across their centers and beach sands along their shores. The Snake Range separated Spring Lake, on its west side, from the southwestern arm of huge Lake Bonneville, which extended northeast beyond Ogden, Utah, and south to Cedar City. On the many linear ranges, north-trending faults track the valley-slope margin on the steeper of the two flanks.

The Snake Range, in contrast, is a broad dome about equally steep on the east and the west. Look for the road cut high on the east side of 13,063-foot Wheeler Peak ❸, Nevada's highest. (This area became Great Basin National Park in 1986.) Sacramento Pass ❷ divides the range into northern and southern segments. Metamorphosed Precambrian and Paleozoic rocks make up much of the Northern Snake Range ❹; younger sediments and plutonic rocks make up the Southern Snake Range ❸❻.

Southern Nevada averages less than 15 inches of annual rainfall. The Snake Range's upper slopes catch 35 inches of rain each year, nourishing alpine plant communities, whereas the midslopes support a montane conifer community. Here, the ancient intermontane bristlecone pine perseveres. In 1964, the U.S. Forest Service permitted a researcher studying the ages of these trees to cut down a single live bristlecone in order to count its annual rings more accurately than can be done by boring a core sample. He chose one on Wheeler Peak and counted 4,844 rings, which would have made "Prometheus" the oldest living thing if he hadn't just made it a dead thing. Now the oldest known bristlecone is in California's White Mountains, on the west side of the Basin and Range.

The montane and alpine zones are "island" refuges for plants and animals in a "sea" of basins that grew too hot and dry for them. During the Ice Age, similar communities extended from the lower edge of permanent snow down to the valley floor lakeshores. As the climate warmed, they retreated upslope, a process that contin-ues and appears to have accelerated during the past century.

Sagebrush/grass communities cover the Spring Valley and the lower slopes of the Snake Range, as they do a greater portion of the Basin and Range than any other community type. Livestock overgrazing has led to more shrubs and fewer grasses. The Snake Valley floor, with dry lakebed soils too salty and alkaline for sagebrush or most grasses, supports a shadscale community.

Three types of mountains are seen in the Basin and Range: volcanoes, fault blocks, and metamorphic core complexes. Volcanoes are familiar to most people, and fault blocks are a topic in introductory geology and geography courses. Metamorphic core complexes, on the other hand, are taught in few courses and a generation ago were little known even among geologists. After 30 years of study, the precise cause of these mountains remains hotly debated, though it seems clear that they result only where extension (stretching) of the earth's crust reaches an extreme degree.

In regions of mild extension, such as the Albuquerque Basin (see page 183), relatively simple "normal" faults break the crust to allow the basin to widen. In regions experiencing greater crustal extension, one master fault can penetrate the crust, extending for miles at a low angle. Material above the master fault fragments into an array of small fault blocks. Deep below the surface, rocks are metamorphosed by the high temperature and pressure that prevail at depth. A fault cutting these rocks will shear them, creating a distinctive metamorphic fabric visible to a trained eye from the air. (The mountains rising behind Palm Springs, California, show such a fabric.)

With sufficient crustal extension and time, erosion removes the material above the master fault , allowing the thinned crust below the fault to bow upward isostatically in a large-scale dome. The domal shape of the Snake Range and other core complexes reflects the doming, or folding, of the master fault, which runs just below the minor ridges and peaks of the range.

Facing north-northeast ❶ Spring Valley ❷ Sacramento Pass ❸ Wheeler Peak, 13,063 ft., Southern Snake Range ❹ Mt. Moriah, 12,050 ft., Northern Snake Range ❺ Ipabah Peak, 12,087 ft., Deep Creek Range, Utah ❻ Mt. Washington, 11,658 ft. ❼ Snake Valley ❽ Baking Powder Flat, an alkaline dry lake bed

Ruby Mountains, Nevada

LOOK FOR a tall, north-south range with an extensive alpine landscape crowning its ridges.

The Ruby Mountains differ from neighboring ranges in north-central Nevada: the Rubies are taller and often snowier. Look at the shape of the upper valleys. You will see steep walls bounding U-shaped upper valleys, and the occasional small lake. These are classic features of glaciated alpine landscapes. Nevada's "Swiss Alps" are a range approximately 100 miles long and 10 miles wide, with 10 peaks exceeding 10,000 feet high and hosting the largest area of alpine tundra in Nevada. The "rubies" of the range are red garnets found in metamorphic rocks.

Big and Little Bald mountains lie just south of the Rubies, separated from them by the 6,790-foot Overland Pass, which is crossed by dirt road. A large open-pit gold mine is on the west flank of Big Bald Mountain.

Note the fates of streams draining this range. The western streams leave the canyons and valleys, combine into larger streams, and flow north into the Humboldt River, Nevada's longest ❶. It runs west across northern Nevada before terminating through evaporation in the Humboldt Sink, about 70 miles from Winnemucca, Nevada.

Most east-slope streams leave the canyons and disappear into porous alluvium ❺. White patches on the flat valley floor are salt deposits left by the evaporation of ephemeral lakes that occupy the valley after a rainy spell. At the south end of Ruby Valley, however, 200 springs feed a large marsh area on a terrace above the valley floor—the Ruby Lake National Wildlife Refuge.

Normal faults bound both sides of the range, giving it straight margins. The faults are covered in part by debris shed from the range, and so they are less prominent than some faults in the Great Basin, such as those near Salt Lake City. (See page 217.)

Metamorphic rocks and granite rocks underlie much of the Rubies and adjoining ranges, giving the bedrock its gray color. The geology tells a complicated story, one that is typical of much of the Great Basin. Marine limestones, sandstones, and claystones were deposited 650 million to 300 million years ago. These rocks were buried under younger sediments and were metamorphosed, which converted the limestones into marble, the sandstones into quartzites, and the claystones into slates. These rocks were next folded and then intruded by Mesozoic and Eocene granites, but the granites and metamorphosed sediments probably remained buried under younger sedimentary rocks.

At that time, the region was underlain by unusually thick continental crust, which geologists envision created a high plateau here. The crust was not able to bear its own mass, and so it collapsed, or spread out toward its western margin. The crust fractured along many more or less parallel faults. One side of each fault dropped and the other rose, creating Basin and Range topography. A few places, including the northern Ruby Mountains and the Snake Range (see page 220), suffered extreme stretching; a surface layer of rocks slid to the west, allowing the deep rocks to rise to the surface as a metamorphic core complex. The metamorphic core of the Rubies was exhumed from a depth of eight to nine miles.

Metamorphic rock units in the northern Rubies grade to unmetamorphosed sediments southward. At Big Bald Mountain, these rocks bear micron-scale gold particles. The open-pit mine you may see there is at the southeast end of the Carlin Trend of gold deposits. These deposits occur as gold flecks too small to see with the naked eye. They were deposited in the sediments by hot fluids circulating around the Eocene granites when they were emplaced.

Granites are solid rock bodies that result from the slow cooling of silica-rich molten magma. As the magma crystalizes, its elements that cannot form minerals dissolve in the superheated water circulating through the magma. The water and its dissolved load may travel some distance through subsurface faults, fractures, and rock pores before cooling precipitates the gold and other dissolved elements. In the Carlin Trend, metals typically precipitated within microscopic pores in ancient sediments.

Facing northeast ❶ Humboldt River where headwater streams from the Ruby Mountains enter it ❷ Ruby Dome, 11,387 ft.
❸ Lamoille Canyon ❹ East Humboldt Range ❺ disappearing streams ❻ King Peak, 11,034 ft. ❼ Overland Lake

Pyramid Lake, Nevada

LOOK FOR the largest, deepest-blue lake in the western Nevada desert north of Reno. (Don't confuse this lake with Lake Tahoe, which is surrounded by forests, roads, and houses, south of Reno in the Sierra Nevada.)

Deep, blue Pyramid Lake presents a strong contrast to other lakes nearby. Most Nevada lakes occupy relatively narrow basins bounded by one or more mountain ranges and appear white, light green, or gray; you may be able to see the lake bottom.

Look along Pyramid Lake's shore for ridges parallel to the present beach. Many are partly vegetated. These ridges are older beaches, formed when the water level was higher.

Tufa mounds dot the lakeshore, some sitting next to the lake, some on older beaches at a distance from the present shore. The largest one ❺ lies just off the eastern shore, about halfway up the lake. Its pyramidal shape gives the lake its name. A number of springs flow on the lake floor, carrying dissolved calcium carbonate and diverse other minerals. As the spring waters cool in the lake waters, the dissolved minerals precipitate, forming tufa deposits under water around the springs' vents. All the visible tufa precipitated in lake water during times of higher water levels.

The Truckee River flows into the lake through a small delta at the south end. The Truckee rises at Lake Tahoe, flows east through Reno, and then turns north to Pyramid Lake. In high-rainfall years prior to 1950, the Truckee delivered enough water to cause Pyramid Lake to overflow and fill the adjoining basin, forming the ephemeral Winnemucca Lake. Irrigation was introduced after World War II, diverting a large portion of the river's water. Look for center pivot irrigation circles in the Truckee valley east of Reno.

Springs occur around Pyramid Lake along active faults that have moved during historic times. Rocks of the eastern Lake Range and western Virginia Mountains are moving up while the Pyramid Lake area drops down. Recent fieldwork also found a horizontal component to the faults' motion. The mountains west of the lake are moving north relative to those on the east side. The faults bounding the Pyramid Lake basin are thus strike-slip faults, just like the San Andreas Fault in California, and, like the San Andreas, they are part of a zone of faults all moving in the same direction.

The Pyramid Lake basin is on the boundary between the Sierra Nevada and the Basin and Range Province. The boundary extends from southern Oregon to the Mojave Desert, where it joins the San Andreas Fault. The Sierras are moving north along the boundary, and the extension occurring within the Basin and Range stops at this boundary. The boundary zone, termed the Walker Lane, includes Walker Lake, seen from the more southerly flight paths east of the Bay Area. Basins east of the Walker Lane, such as Winnemucca Basin, trend north or northeast, whereas those within the lane often trend north or northwest.

Today, Pyramid Lake accommodates a modest trout population. Before World War II, the lake held the Lahontan cutthroat trout, probably the largest trout in the world. Avid trout fishermen, especially those employed in Hollywood during its golden era, flocked north in quest for it. These visitors caught virtually all the large individuals, and by 1941, the Lahontan cutthroat trout was extinct within the lake. But were Hollywood moguls solely responsible?

The Truckee River was incorporated in the Newlands Project, the first major reclamation and interbasin water transfer project. Derby Dam was built across the Truckee in 1905 to divert 50 percent of the river's water for irrigation in the Carson Sink. Reduced streamflow increased Pyramid Lake salinity and eutrophication and also for many years eliminated the entire spawning habitat of a fish species found only in Pyramid Lake. After the cui-ui (*Chasmistes cujus*) was placed on the endangered species list, the Pyramid Lake Paiute tribe used the listing to regain control over the lake's management, including reintroduction of the Lahontan cutthroat trout and recovery of the cui-ui.

Facing east ❶ Pyramid Lake ❷ Lake Range ❸ Nightingale Mountains ❹ Virginia Mountains. The Pyramid is near the far shore, just out of frame on the right.

Earthbound view facing west ❺ the Pyramid

WESTBOUND: Go to p. 266

Eastern Central Valley Orchards, California

LOOK FOR orchards, which combine the dark green of forests with the regular fine lines of crops; streams that divide as they descend the valley slope westward.

Grid-textured dark green plots are orchards. ❶ Calaveras River ❷ Bellota, CA ❸ Mormon Slough ❹ plant nursery operation
❺ Linden, CA; the Linden VOR, a navigational aid crossed by many flights east from the Bay Area, is just out of frame at top right

EASTBOUND: Go to p. 266

It's a simple plan: Coast Ranges, Central Valley, Sierra Nevada. It's what you'll see if you fly from west to east anywhere within 200 miles of the Bay Area. For 10 to 20 days each winter, the valley may look like a bed of cotton. Although the valley is the world's top cotton-growing area, that isn't cotton, it's tule fog. The rest of the year, the fog stays on the coast; the Coast Ranges protect the valley from moisture, the sun shines, and temperatures range from warm to scorching.

The prevailing airflow rises to cross the Sierra, the highest mountain range in the lower 48 states. The Sierra rises gradually on the west side; the airflow does the same, releasing most of its moisture over this 50- to 70-mile western slope. Most of the rain and snow falls between October and April, but the snow is still melting and coming down the mountainside through May, June, and July.

What does that make the Central Valley? A big, flat, warm, sunny near-desert with a magnificent water supply. What do humans do when presented with such a fine paradox? Farm it.

The top seven farming counties in the nation are here. They include the major producers of dairy products, grapes, fruits, nuts, and berries. California grows at least 98 percent of the U.S. crop of almonds, walnuts, pistachios, plums, nectarines, cling peaches, olives, persimmons, and raisins—and most of those orchards and vineyards are in the Central Valley. The valley may freeze for a few nights in winter, so the crops that do best here love sun but also need a token winter. That would be most temperate-zone crops. The Central Valley produces more wine than Napa or Sonoma and nearly all the table grapes and raisins. As urban sprawl ripped out thousands of acres of orange and avocado trees in southern California, farmers found or created the right varieties to grow these crops in the Central Valley as well.

The photo features orchards, dairy farms, and a nursery ❹ at the transition from valley to Sierra foothills. If this were the Mediterranean, farms and vineyards would cover those foothill slopes, but with so much flat land nearby, these hills are left as cattle range.

Where the main watercourse in the photo leaves the foothills, dividing into two branches, the contrast between the straightened Mormon Slough ❸ and the curvy Calaveras River ❶ looks like an example of a diversion canal versus a river, but it is not. Both are

there in the earliest written descriptions of the valley. They join the San Joaquin River 2 miles apart, 16 miles downstream at Stockton.

Around 1900, sediment built a bar across the Calaveras where it and the Mormon Slough part ways. The bar, likely a product of gold mining upstream, directed all the water down the slough except during spring floods. Riverbank and slough-side farmers both wanted the water; one faction would build a diversionary weir to bring more flow their way; then the opposing faction would tear it down at night. Meanwhile, Stockton urbanites, striving to end a series of downtown floods, leveed Mormon Slough with little success. So in 1930, they dammed the river upstream of the split. (The higher dam you may see 14 miles farther up was built later.) The riverbank farmers then irrigated from other sources, accepting the dry river bed; indeed, some grew dependent on driving their tractors across it and sued the Water District when it began sending some water their way again in 1955.

Stockton is the third-largest Central Valley city, after Sacramento and Fresno, and officially an ocean port: The river is dredged for seagoing vessels up to this point.

The Calaveras River and Mormon Slough are the southernmost rivers listed as critical habitat for chinook salmon. They are also early toeholds for two threatening invasive species: the Chinese mitten crab and the New Zealand mudsnail. The former, a delicacy in China, burrows into streambanks and can cross land when it needs to. Scientists have listed several possible threats from it, though it has not inflicted catastrophic economic or ecological harm yet. The mudsnail is another story, having completely taken over many miles of streambed, covering them at densities up to 500,000 snails per square yard. Yes, it's tiny; it looks like a black coating. Between these threats and those that come from both urban and agricultural runoff, survival for the salmon looks dicey, at best.

The valley has the state's fastest population growth, largely by migration to its cities from other parts of the state. At the same time, it has the highest rates of both unemployment and poverty, concentrated in small towns where Latinos make up 50 to 90 percent of the population.

Sacramento, California, and Its Delta

LOOK FOR a large city with broad new suburbs on the east bank of a meandering river; a straight ship canal and a swath of rice fields and wetlands both paralleling the river on its west, south of the city.

❶ Yolo Bypass, the floodway, largely planted in rice **❷** Sacramento River **❸** Sacramento Weir, a spillway from the river into the Yolo Bypass **❹** American River **❺** I-80 just east of Davis **❻** Deep Water Ship Channel **❼** turning basin **❽** Sacramento, with expanses of new subdivisions, especially to the south

EASTBOUND: Go to pp. 196, 64, 198

The entire area south of Sacramento and southwest to the far edge of the flat Central Valley is laced with watercourses confined by levees. Many of the islands are 25 feet below sea level; a neighborhood can be named Del Paso Heights for reaching a dizzying 60 feet above sea level.

The low water-laced area is the Sacramento River delta. This bay head delta is neither triangular like the Nile's nor a birdfoot like the Mississippi's, but like them, it's a large sea-level area of river-sediment islands outlined by multiple river channels that separate and rejoin. Both the delta and the Central Valley belong almost equally to two rivers: the Sacramento ❷ draining from the north and the San Joaquin draining from the south.

Look for the straight Deep Water Ship Channel ❻, carved out in 1963 parallel to the Sacramento River, south from West Sacramento. The channel heads at a triangular ship-turning basin ❼ lined with several docks and a rice elevator. A huge pile of bright blond wood chips ready for shipping to Asian paper mills was usually present for many years, but no wood chips were exported from here in 2006; if you see such a pile, chip exports have resumed.

From the turning basin to where the ship channel rejoins the Sacramento River at Rio Vista, a wide swath of grasslands, rice paddies, and other crops lies on its west flank. This is the Yolo Bypass ❶, a floodway built to protect Sacramento from flooding by taking overflow from the river. This floodway also serves as wetland habitat and a premier rice-growing area.

The bypass is exhibit A of enlightened floodplain management at Sacramento. The other kind is far more conspicuous: new suburbs on the floodplain. Growth here in the fastest-growing metro area in California is fueled partly by stratospheric real estate prices in the coastal cities: Around Sacramento, people can buy the same house on the same-size lot for two-thirds the price of a Bay Area house and still be within driving distance of their old haunts and friends.

Buyers doubtless notice that their new neighborhood is walled by levees and may assume that if local government allows the development, the government must be responsible for flood protection. In fact, no government entity here owns or ever built a system of levees. Most levees belong to small districts and were built by individual farmers, some more than a century ago. These old levees contain scores of spots weakened by erosion, burrowing beavers, or buried, rotting wood. The chief government role has been to examine the levees and to certify that breaching them would take a flood of the size calculated to come along once in a century. That vague level of certification is lower than the certification New Orleans's levees enjoyed before Hurricane Katrina.

At least one scientist here gives the area worse than 50-50 odds of experiencing Katrina-scale flooding within the next 50 years: Jeffrey Mount was on the state's Reclamation Board when it decided to start reviewing development proposals for adequate flood-protection plans. Governor Arnold Schwarzenegger responded by replacing the entire board and asking the federal government to fund levee repair. The right to develop is apparently impregnable.

California's tax structure intensifies the pressure to allow urban growth. Counties are dependent on property taxes for revenue. Proposition 13, a 1978 voter-initiative law, prevents most property tax increases. So county governments often feel that they'll have no money for new expenses, such as improved flood control, unless they allow new tracts on floodplains in order to increase their tax base.

California has seen many serious floods during its relatively brief recorded history. Wet winters here are several times wetter than dry winters. The worst floods happen when a wet winter has built up the snowpack in the Sierra Nevada, and then a tropical Pacific storm system brings heavy rainfall combined with abrupt warming. The rain falling on the deep fresh snow melts it so fast that the daily runoff into the streams can equal two or three times the rainfall.

A hundred years ago, vast marshes were the heart of the delta. Dominant plants included giant bulrushes that the Spanish called tules. By 1930, most of the tules were drained and converted to highly productive agriculture. As farming compacted and oxidized the peaty soils, island surfaces sank below sea level. To continue farming, the farmers had to build levees.

WESTBOUND: Go to pp. 198, 64, 196

Cincinnati

Ohio

Riv...

Charleston ★ WEST

236 VIRGIN...

Lexington

...TUCKY

238

CORRIDOR 8:
New York–
Washington, D.C.–Dallas

Flights we have tracked follow the preferred routes between New York and Dallas more often than not. Although all NY airports have the same westbound preferred route—soon joined by the preferred route out of Boston—they have very different routes eastbound: to Newark and Philadelphia, the route is over Texarkana, Memphis, Nashville, then bending eastward at Beckley, West Virginia, to pass near or even east of Washington, D.C. To LaGuardia and JFK, the route is to Birmingham and Atlanta, where it joins the routes from Atlanta to LaGuardia or JFK, crossing lower Chesapeake Bay (Corridor 4). Flying via Atlanta is longer, consuming more fuel and time, so don't be surprised if your flight takes a more direct route instead; yet we have seen flights take the Atlanta route at least sometimes. Dallas to Boston has two preferred options: the Atlanta route or one more northerly than any of the others, via Little Rock, Cleveland, and Albany.

This corridor could perhaps be nicknamed Mississippian. The great river is its most prominent feature. Aside from that, when you are not over its sediment-covered plain, you spend much time over hilly plateau country, commonly with bedrock of the age geologists call Mississippian. Limestone bedrock produces regions of karst topography both east and west of the Mississippi plain. (See pages 137–39.) Karst processes make the land hilly even where the strata lie flat.

Coal beds of similar age make this flight corridor the coal-mining corridor. (Carboniferous, meaning "coal bearing," is the name European geologists use for rocks of Mississippian and Pennsylvanian age.) In many places, coals are interbedded with limestones; deposition of limey and organic-rich sediments took turns over long cycles, when the region was a basin behind a high mountain range, an ancestral stage of the Appalachians. The east-west compression that later raised the final Appalachians crumpled the basin into folds, more intensely at the eastern side, less so in the west. You will see the result as three landform provinces under your flight, all three of them bearing coal:

- The Valley and Ridge, with strong, tall, parallel ridges and relatively broad valleys
- The Appalachian Plateaus, with narrow crooked valleys in chaotic patterns and broad or sometimes even flat-topped ridges in between
- The karst plateaus of western Kentucky and Tennessee, similar to the preceding but gentler, with shallower valleys and broader ridges or even small plains in between

Valley and Ridge topography also crops up in Arkansas as the Ouachita Mountains. The same two styles of plateau and karst topography replace it northward; you would see that sequence from flights between Dallas and Chicago.

There is little truly flat land under this corridor. Cotton and rice grow prolifically in the only two broad flat areas: northeast Texas and the Mississippi valley. A flight path slightly north of the mapped westbound path will take you over Kentucky's rolling bluegrass country, where the nation's wealthiest-appearing farms raise thoroughbred horses. The sedimentary bedrock there is unusually rich in calcium phosphate, which reaches the horses via the grass, contributing to strong muscles and bones. The karst plateau supports diverse but seldom lucrative small farms wherever it is flat enough. West Virginia and eastern Kentucky, in the Appalachian Plateau, have very narrow valley bottoms, where farming has always been a tough proposition.

EASTBOUND: Start with p. 172
WESTBOUND: Start with pp. 6, 68

Nazareth, Pennsylvania

LOOK FOR a midsize town with a triangular-oval racetrack.

Facing northeast ❶ Nazareth ❷ limestone quarries ❸ cement factories ❹ Nazareth Speedway

EASTBOUND: Go to pp. 68, 6

Nazareth sits within the Lehigh Valley of eastern Pennsylvania. Just south of the business district, the triangular-oval racetrack and grandstand ❹ distinguish this from nearby cities. The Nazareth Speedway once boasted the world's fastest one-mile track.

The Lehigh Valley is Pennsylvania's portion of the Great Valley, the easternmost feature of the Valley and Ridge Province. This topographic low receives local names as it runs southwest from Pennsylvania to Alabama. After a small gap, a similar topographic low extends north through the Hudson Valley into Canada. The Lehigh Valley is bounded on the north by Blue Mountain, also known as Kittatinny Mountain, and on the south by South and Lehigh mountains.

Limestones underlie the Lehigh Valley, giving it karst features. (See pages 138, 144.) Only a few streams enter the valley from its flanks because most streams go underground; small spring-fed lakes fill shallow sinkholes surrounded by brush or timber. Limestone quarries ❷ dot the valley, some active and others filled with water. Cement plants ❸ sit beside the larger quarries. Quarries are seen throughout the valley, up to the base of Blue Mountain.

An abandoned rail line hugs the base of Blue Mountain, running near active slate quarries and abandoned iron mines. The slate quarries concentrate where the Lehigh River cuts through Blue Mountain at Slatington, about 15 miles west of Nazareth. The iron mines are in narrow valleys near the base of Blue Mountain. These and others along South Mountain fed the colonial iron industry in Bethlehem, only to be abandoned in the 19th century when the much richer Michigan iron deposits were developed.

Nazareth and environs were part of the original land grant to William Penn. Five thousand acres were sold in 1740 to George Whitefield, who established a school and hired German Protestant dissidents from Moravia to run it. Whitefield sold the property to the Moravians a year later. After successfully introducing wheat farming to service the growing market in Bethlehem, the Moravians developed Nazareth as a center for Moravian education.

The large German-speaking population drew Christian Frederick Martin to Nazareth in 1838. Trained as a cabinetmaker, in 1833 he had emigrated from Germany to New York, where he founded the Martin Guitar Company. He left New York to live within familiar society in a landscape similar to his homeland.

Nazareth's best-known citizen is racecar driver Mario Andretti. His family came from Italy after World War II. Look for the small dirt ovals where Andretti began racing in 1959.

David Saylor introduced Portland cement to the United States in 1872, when he built his first plant five miles southeast of Nazareth. Named for a building stone quarried along the English Channel, Portland cement is made from limestone containing silica, clay, aluminum, and iron oxides. The Lehigh Valley is underlain by just such a rock. The limestone is heated in a kiln to 2,732°F to create a clinker that is ground very fine and mixed with gypsum. When mixed with water, the product sets as a hard cement. It is ubiquitous in highway and building construction.

Some quarries exploit slates found in the 450-million-year-old Martinsburg Formation. Slates are metamorphic rocks created by heating and intensely folding the clay-rich sedimentary rocks shale and claystone. The clay and other sedimentary grains recrystalize during metamorphism to create the very strong cleavage. Slate is best known as a roofing material and as a garden paving stone.

Lehigh and South mountains are part of the Reading Prong. Its rock units formed along the eastern margin of an ancient North American continent. The Iapetus Ocean, predating the present Atlantic Ocean, once separated New England and parts of northern Europe from North America. The limestones found in the Lehigh Valley suggest that it was then located within the tropics and away from major rivers. The slates suggest that the Iapetus first deepened so that clays and sands were deposited onto the older limestones. A line of volcanoes developed in New England at this time and soon collided with North America as the Iapetus Ocean closed during the Taconic Orogeny, creating a major mountain range in New England and Canada. The rocks of the Reading Prong moved westward as great sheets sliding away from the rising mountains. The sheets divided into large segments that overrode each other in thrusts, intensely folding the claystones and shales so they recrystalized as slates.

WESTBOUND: Go to p. 70

Spruce Knob, West Virginia

LOOK FOR parallel valleys and ridges; different drainage patterns on the flanks of the ridges.

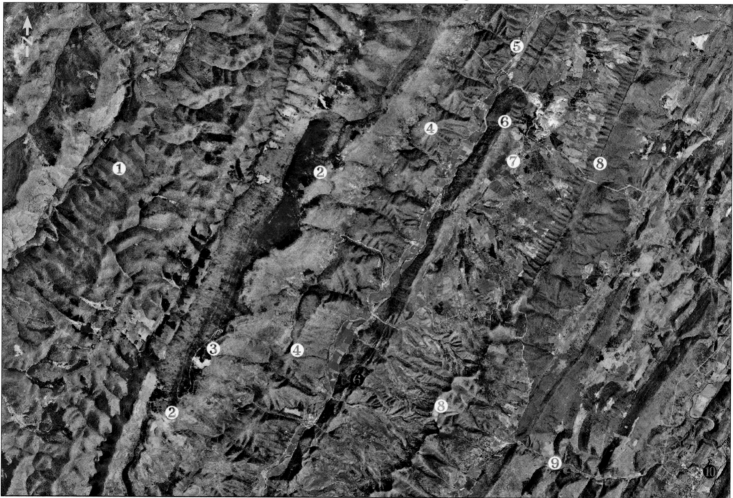

① Allegheny Plateau Province ② Spruce Mountain, on the Allegheny Front, dividing provinces ③ Spruce Knob ④ Fore Knobs
⑤ North Fork South Branch Potomac River, and U.S. Hwy. 33 ⑥ River Knobs ⑦ Germany Valley ⑧ North Fork Mountain
⑨ U.S. Hwy. 33 ⑩ Franklin, WV

EASTBOUND: Go to pp. 110, 70

Spruce Knob, the highest point in West Virginia, is not prominent. Ask a flight attendant to have the pilot announce when your plane is over this small culmination on Spruce Mountain ❷.

Spruce Mountain is on the Allegheny Front, the boundary between the Allegheny Plateau ❶ and the Valley and Ridge Province. East of Spruce Mountain, tight folds in the underlying rocks create parallel narrow valleys and ridges trending northeast. East of this image with its narrow ridges, the broader highland of Shenandoah Mountain is followed by the Shenandoah Valley segment of the Great Valley, and then by the Blue Ridge. Spruce Mountain also lies on the major drainage divide: The Allegheny Plateau west of it drains to the Ohio River and the Gulf of Mexico, whereas the Valley and Ridge east of it drains to the Potomac River and the Atlantic Ocean.

Local drainage patterns often reveal the type of underlying bedrock: Zones with widely spaced streams typify resistant rocks, such as sandstone; zones with closely spaced streams typify easily eroded rocks, such as claystone or shale. These distinctive zones extend for miles along the ridges and valleys. Identical drainage pattern zones sometimes wrap around the end of a valley or a ridge and merge, indicating the axis, or centerline, of a fold.

The Wills Mountain anticline ❹❺❻❼❽ is an arch of layered rocks running northeast-southwest. This fold is the western boundary of the Nittany anticlinorium, an enormous arch stretching 185 miles from central Pennsylvania to southern Virginia. To the east and parallel to Wills Mountain is the Middle Mountain syncline. (A syncline has its concave side up, like an arch inverted.)

Hard sandstones cap most mountaintops in this region: Spruce Knob is 315-million-year-old Pottsville Sandstone; Seneca Rocks (just out of image frame north of ❺) is 440-million-year-old Tuscarora Sandstone. Both are remnants of once-widespread rock layers extending south from New York. These sedimentary rocks record the history of the Iapetus Ocean, a vanished ocean that once separated Laurentia, a proto–North American continent, from a proto-European continent. Ancient limestones of the Germany Valley ❼ were deposited off the east coast of Laurentia in clear tropical waters. Beginning perhaps 475 million years ago, an island arc formed over a subduction zone that consumed part of the Iapetus crust to the east. Bentonite clays found here derive from ash erupted from the arc's volcanoes. Eventually, the island arc collided with North America, causing the Taconic Orogeny. Over a 10-million-year period, this mountain-building episode first occurred in Newfoundland, then in Alabama, then in New York, and finally in Quebec. The relative timing of these points of collision reflects the shapes of both the Laurentian continent and the island arc.

In the Spruce Knob area, the collision created a deep ocean trough between 465 million and 440 million years ago. The trough filled with deep-water sediments until the Tuscarora sandstones were deposited in a near-shore, shallow marine setting. Similar sandstones of this age are found in small outcrops from New York to Alabama.

To the east, sediments underlying Shenandoah Mountain record a second collision event. The Acadian Orogeny migrated from Newfoundland to Virginia between 325 million and 300 million years ago when Laurentia collided with another island arc. Once again, a deep ocean trough formed and also filled at first with deep-water sediments and then with increasingly shallow water sediments until finally, deltaic and river plain sediments filled it completely. Geologists call these sediments, first described in New York, the Catskill Delta.

All these rock layers lay horizontal when they were first deposited. The folding and faulting we see from the air resulted from the Allegheny Orogeny, the collision between Laurentia and Europe/Africa. These continents came together 290 million to 240 million years ago to form Pangaea, the supercontinent that also included India, Antarctica, and South America. This final collision squeezed the crust bearing the Taconic- and Acadian-related sediments. The crust broke along almost horizontal planes, known as thrust faults. Sections of crust slid to the west, riding over the crust there to form the Blue Ridge. Farther west, the layered rocks responded to the compression by folding into the anticlines and synclines seen throughout the Valley and Ridge Province.

WESTBOUND: Go to p. 160

Mountaintop Removal Coal Mining, West Virginia

LOOK FOR flattened mountaintops; most are either grassy fields or bare dirt and bedrock, with or without busy draglines and trucks.

Kentucky

West Virginia

Virginia

Hobet 21 Mine, west of Danville, WV. Low-altitude small plane view.

map of mountaintop mining permits as of 2005

EASTBOUND: Go to p. 160

Coal has a big future: There's a lot of it left to mine, whereas petroleum is depleting. Whenever we hear about another coal mine disaster—miners asphyxiated, immolated, or buried deep in a coal shaft—we may think, "Do miners still have to lead that dangerous, claustrophobic life down in a coal shaft? It seems so 19th century; isn't there a way to mine coal without going underground?"

There is. Called mountaintop mining officially, but mountaintop removal by its critics, it upsets many people in the region more than the old mine shafts do. Basically, it's open-pit mining reshaped to remove flat coal seams in mountainous terrain.

Coal is found in the Appalachian Plateaus of eastern Kentucky and Tennessee and western Pennsylvania, Virginia, and West Virginia. You can see both mountaintop removals and contour mines throughout the region, where the layers of sedimentary rock lie flat. They are mountains because tectonic forces raised them higher than the lowlands to the west, forming a plateau. With plenty of rainfall, streams have dissected the plateau in a dendritic pattern of steep-sided valleys.

A few of those flat sedimentary layers are coal seams. They reach the surface where they intersect valley slopes. You could walk around a mountain and find the same seam surfacing at close to the same contour the whole way. In this region, you'll see many places where a bulldozed bench, like a large road cut, follows a contour around a mountain. That bench is a "contour mine," a minimal strip mine that gets only a little of that mountain's coal.

More coal can be extracted by mining far into a seam, removing much of it before the mountain collapses into the mined layer. Afterward, it would be too dangerous to mine additional seams above or below that one. The only way to get multiple seams or 100 percent of one seam is to use explosives and heavy earthmoving equipment to remove the entire "overburden"—the portion of the mountain lying above the coal seam—then remove the coal.

And then what? Put the overburden back where it came from? Yes, that's the concept. Mine reclamation is supposed to restore the "approximate original contour," and to plan for a postmining use, usually wildlife use, rangeland, or industrial development. For some proposed uses, companies can get a variance and leave the mountain flat-topped. Mining boosters argue that flattened mountaintops are just what West Virginia needs, since it suffers a lack of flat ground for industry. To prove the point, the state has put up a prison here, a high school there, but private enterprise has declined to build anything substantial. Grass is the easiest thing to grow on the sites; hence, "rangeland."

A few problems come to mind. If all the tailings are returned to the mine, they're still simply broken rock. The mine owner can find some fine dirt to spread over the surface, but forest recovery is slow without topsoil, organic matter, mycorrhizae, or a network of roots to hold the slope in place. Pile it back up to a steep slope, and sooner or later, it will slide. Every year, Appalachian homes—and lives—are taken out by mining-related landslides or mining-related flooding. As you can see from the air, almost all the communities and farms are in the narrow river valleys, so they're all vulnerable. Disastrous floods made the news in 2001–4, but most years see some floods.

Then there's the "swell factor." If you garden, you know that when you dig a hole, it makes a pile of dirt bigger than the hole, because you've added air space between pieces of dirt. It's the same with mountaintops: Pile them back up to almost their original height, and you still have 35 percent of the overburden to find a home for. So mine operators fill creek valleys with it. Miles of creek headwaters disappear under rubble, sending sediment downstream in the creeks and rivers, making them more subject to flooding and less able to support fish and other wildlife.

The people of the Appalachian coal region have accepted dangerous mining jobs for more than a century. These jobs allowed them to continue living in their beautiful mountain country. Now the hours spent on the job may be safer, but the mountains are being flattened by monstrous machines, and the dangers of coal mining follow residents into their bedrooms at night. Not surprisingly, populations are shrinking in the affected counties.

With political will and higher coal prices, reclamation after mountaintop removal can become less polluting and less hazardous. But it's difficult to imagine how it could ever truly restore the natural landscape and ecology.

Coal Mining at Elkhorn City, Pike County, Kentucky

LOOK FOR open-pit coal mines, steep mountains, narrow ridges, and narrow valleys.

❶ contour coal mines ❷ Russell Fork ❸ Chesapeake and Ohio rail line ❹ Elkhorn

Elkhorn City is a small town in the eastern Kentucky coal region ❹. Steep mountain slopes, narrow ridges, and narrow valleys characterize the area. Flat land is limited: Only the valley floors support agriculture. The region lies on the Cumberland Plateau, one of several plateaus within the Appalachian Plateaus Province of the Appalachian range. Rock layers on the plateaus have not been intensely folded or faulted but lie almost flat, enabling miners to exploit the coals in a variety of ways.

Coal mining here can be classed as mountaintop mining, contour mining, or underground mining. Mountaintop mining excavates any rock lying above the coal seam, depositing the "overburden" in an adjoining valley. (See page 236.) The coal seam is excavated and removed by trucks. Restoration of the mine and adjoining valley fill typically includes reforestation but remains readily identified by the contrast with older, established forests. Contour mining ❶ begins on the mountainside where the coal seam is exposed. The mine follows the coal seam into the mountain, using large-scale augers to excavate the coal. Look for flat steps, often two or more such steps running in parallel along the same mountainside.

Underground mines have surface facilities, including ventilators and elevators, supporting the operation. A rail line may service the facilities, which can be located anywhere: a valley floor, a ridge top, or on the mountainside. Highly mechanized underground mining systems have largely supplanted manual "room and pillar" mining. The two common systems are narrow "continuous miners" and very broad "longwall" systems.

The east-facing Pottsville Escarpment bounds the Cumberland Plateau. To its east, the Pine and Cumberland mountains run northeast-southwest along the Kentucky-Virginia border. These westernmost mountains of the Valley and Ridge Province were formed during the Allegheny Orogeny 240 million years ago.

Eastern Kentucky's coals, sandstones, and claystones were deposited 320 million to 300 million years ago. Fossils in the coals include ferns, seed ferns, calamite trees, and cordaite trees, indicating that these rocks were deposited in a humid and possibly tropical setting. Similar conditions extended from Alabama through Pennsylvania and west into Illinois. Fossils within the claystones include corals, trilobites, snails, clams, and fish teeth, all indicating a sea, which must have invaded and covered the older coal-forming environment.

That marine transgression affects our lives today. Coal, a major source of power in the United States, poses major environmental problems, including acid mine drainage, acid rain, and ash. As sea water flooded the land, sulfur dissolved in it combined with the plant material that later became coal. When the sediments were buried, the sulfur combined with iron to form pyrite. Mining exposes the pyrite to either surface water or groundwater, causing the pyrite to break down into iron and sulfur ions. The sulfur ions combine with water to form a weak acid, the acid mine drainage that wreaks havoc on streams and rivers.

Most of the pyrite remains in the coal, to be broken down when the coal is burned as fuel. The sulfur combines with oxygen and leaves the smokestack as sulfur dioxide, which in turn combines with water vapor in the air to form an acid, which falls as acid rain. Eastern Kentucky's coal beds record at least three marine transgressions. Coals lying directly below the marine claystones have the highest sulfur content.

As for the ash, it results from burning coals containing thin beds of silt or sand, which break down into fine particles that are borne aloft in the hot smoke.

Eastern Kentucky is a relatively isolated region of the United States. Underground coal mining began in Pike County when railroads connected it with more populated areas in 1880. Production grew rapidly between 1904 and 1918 as more rail lines were completed and the United States used more coal. Surface mining began in 1944 and today accounts for only about one-third of the county's production. Although we may see extensive activity and scars while flying over the region, considerably more activity remains out of view underground.

WESTBOUND: Go to pp. 138, 140

Crowley's Ridge and the Mississippi Delta in Arkansas

LOOK FOR a very long north-south stripe of forest—a subtle ridge—dividing a flat agricultural plain, west of the Mississippi River.

Facing north ❶ L'Anguille River ❷ Crowley's Ridge ❸ Cherry Valley, AR ❹ Birdeye, AR ❺ Straight Slough, next to the levee bounding the floodway on its west side ❻ Cross County Ditch ❼ levee, with road on top, bounding the floodway on its east side ❽ Oak Donnick–St. Francis Bay Floodway ❾ St. Francis River (meandering just to the right of and then below the frame)

EASTBOUND: Go to pp. 140, 138

If I can't find her in West Helena,
she must be in East Monroe I know.

—Robert Johnson, "Dust My Broom"

As a cradle of blues music and as a landform, the Mississippi Delta is in Arkansas and Mississippi about equally, along with small parts of three other states. West Helena lies at the southern tip of Crowley's Ridge ❷, a 148-mile arc of up to 200-foot relief, the chief interruption of the flat terrain. In the photo, open croplands flank the forested ridge. In the 1820s, the reverse was true: Settlers avoided the swampy bottoms, traveling and settling on the ridge. Settlers prescient enough to recognize the swamps' agricultural potential laid claim to them, drained them, and became wealthy.

Some swamps remain. Fifteen miles west of the ridge in the photo lies Bayou De View, a swamp so little visited that the ivory-billed woodpecker may have persevered in it undetected for 60 years. Scientists had considered the species long extinct, and many are still skeptical of the 2004 sightings.

Before the Ice Ages, the Mississippi occupied the valley west of the ridge; the valley just east of the ridge, now occupied by the St. Francis River, held the Ohio; and the present Mississippi course was occupied by the Tennessee. The three joined below the south end of the ridge. During each peak of Ice Age glaciation, sea level was hundreds of feet lower than now, enabling the rivers to cut a deep, broad valley. When the ice melted, the rivers would swell and carry staggering loads of glacial sediment.

In this stretch, the Mississippi's gradient decreased, causing it to dump sediment and build up both its own bed and natural levees on both sides until its bed was higher than the adjacent floodplain. After each flood, the river could not return to its raised former channel. That basic cycle forms all river deltas, so this is a true delta in terms of process and in the way that streams split and fan out.

Eighteenth- and 19th-century settlers saw many floods. To protect their crops and homes, the settlers made the levees higher and more nearly continuous. It wasn't enough. The 1927 flood—described by Memphis Minnie in the much-covered song "When the Levee Breaks"—was the biggest flood in U.S. history by most measures. It inundated 26,000 square miles and left at least 246 people dead. In response, the Army Corps of Engineers expanded its flood-control measures beyond levees, building dams, short-circuiting river loops, and selecting areas as "floodways" ❽ to relieve some of the water pressure on levees. Yet levees remain the key bulwark. A modern Huck Finn rafting down the lower river would see little but levees the whole way.

Draining swamps failed to erase the phantasmagoric patterns of ghost meanders, which you see when flying over many parts of the plain. More recently, several meander loops were cut off, primarily to shorten travel times for boats. The abandoned loops are conspicuous on the ground as oxbow lakes and on a map as strange loops in the state lines—the river's course at the time of first surveys versus its course today.

The Delta's deep alluvial soil and its warm, humid climate make it one of the nation's most productive farming regions for cotton, sugar, soybeans, rice, and catfish. Crowley's Ridge, in contrast, has windblown soil, a remnant of a broad loess deposit that the shifting rivers removed from the rest of the delta. Fault movement raised the ridge above flood levels, preserving its thick loess, so that 20-some feet of post-Ice Age fault uplift led to much greater relief.

The fault is part of the New Madrid Fault Zone, which in 1811 and 1812 produced the most powerful quakes ever recorded in the lower 48 states. Geologists long puzzled over massive quakes so far from mountains or from other earthquake zones. According to one hypothesis, the Mississippi Embayment (the underlying valley of the lower river) may have originated as a rift valley that failed more than 600 million years ago. A supercontinent was breaking up—not Pangaea but one before it, called Rodinia. This rift was one line along which the stresses tearing Rodinia apart expressed themselves. But after splitting by some tens of miles amid copious earthquake and volcanic activity, it seized up as stress was relieved at other rifts. It has been a midcontinent ever since, yet it remains a zone of weakness in the continental plate. Although no one knows why, the region is under measurable north-south compressive stress. Rift-weakened zones here and near Charleston, South Carolina (see page 124), may focus the stress to cause earthquakes.

Hot Springs, Arkansas

LOOK FOR a small city just south of a wishbone-shaped set of small, sharp ridges. The distinctive reservoir in the photo can help locate it.

The city of Hot Springs ❹ sits in a wide, flat-bottom valley surrounded by the northeast-trending ridges of the Ouachita Mountains. The impounded Ouachita River ❷ forms Lake Hamilton ❺ to the south and west of Hot Springs. The town takes its name from 47 warm- and hot-water springs nested within a wishbone-shaped set of ridges just northwest of the town center. They include Hot Springs Mountain directly above town, West Mountain to the southwest, Indian Mountain to the northeast, and North Mountain to the northwest. A thrust fault lies on the northwest flank of Hot Springs Mountain, carrying the 414-million- to 345-million-year-old Arkansas Novaculite and the 450-million-year-old Big Fork Chert north and over the younger rocks of the narrow valley northwest of Hot Springs Mountain.

The springs issue from a sandstone layer at the bottom of a section of shales 310 million to 305 million years old. Fractures in the novaculite and chert associated with the deep-rooted thrust fault provide the plumbing for the hot springs. Molten rock magma lies close to the surface beneath some hot springs, but not most of them in the United States, and not here. At sufficient depth, the earth is hot anywhere. Hot-springs regions are scattered across the mountainous West but are rare in the East and rarest of all in the central states. Such regions require a system of faults or fractures through which the water can rise thousands of feet quickly, without cooling down completely. At Hot Springs, Arkansas, isotope studies indicate that water emerging from the springs fell as rain about 4,400 years ago. It spends most of that time trickling down and comes up again in a matter of days.

Flights between Dallas and mid-Atlantic cities appear to cross the same mountain range twice. You wouldn't know that from maps, which identify the Ouachita (WASH-ĭ-tah) Mountains here and the Appalachian Valley and Ridge Province in the east, but you can't miss the resemblance. Both consist of parallel narrow ridges and valleys. Streams form a trellis pattern, primarily running parallel to the ridges, but here and there carving water gaps through the ridges and capturing the adjoining valley's drainage. Although not as high, the Ouachitas are as steep as the Appalachians. Many of the resistant rock strata that stand tallest are novaculite, a pure form of chert, which made the best arrowheads in the East and today makes the best natural whetstones.

The Ozark Plateau lies north of the Ouachitas, just as the Appalachian Plateaus lie west of the Valley and Ridge. The folds in the Ouachitas formed during the Permian, 300 million to 250 million years ago, the same era when the Valley and Ridge Province folded. Features analogous to the Blue Ridge and the Piedmont may lie buried to the south beneath Texas and the Mississippi valley. After many years of speculation, oil and gas industry well and seismic data now offer a picture of the Appalachian-Ouachita connection. The Appalachian range plunges beneath the Gulf Coastal Plain in Alabama, extends northwest beneath the broad Mississippi River valley, and pops up again as the Ouachitas and Ozark Plateau. These features continue west into Oklahoma, disappear beneath the Red River valley, and reappear yet again in west Texas as the Marathon Mountains.

In 1541, Hernando de Soto came across the springs and learned from local Indians gesticulating at him that the springs had healing powers. The springs' reputation attracted French, and later American, settlers. Congress decided to acquire and preserve this famous resource in 1832, even before granting Arkansas statehood. That would make it by far the oldest national park, though with no Park Service to run it then, it had to wait until 1921 to become Hot Springs National Park.

In 1946, a Texan named William Jefferson Blythe Jr. met his unfortunate end in a car crash. Three months later, in the small town of Hope, his widow gave birth to their son and named him William Jefferson Blythe III. In 1950, Mrs. Blythe married a man named Roger Clinton, and two years later, they moved to Hot Springs. The boy eventually took the stepfather's surname as well. Although in later years, he liked to say that he was from Hope, Hot Springs, the hometown he doubtless remembers better, justifiably also calls the 42nd president a native son.

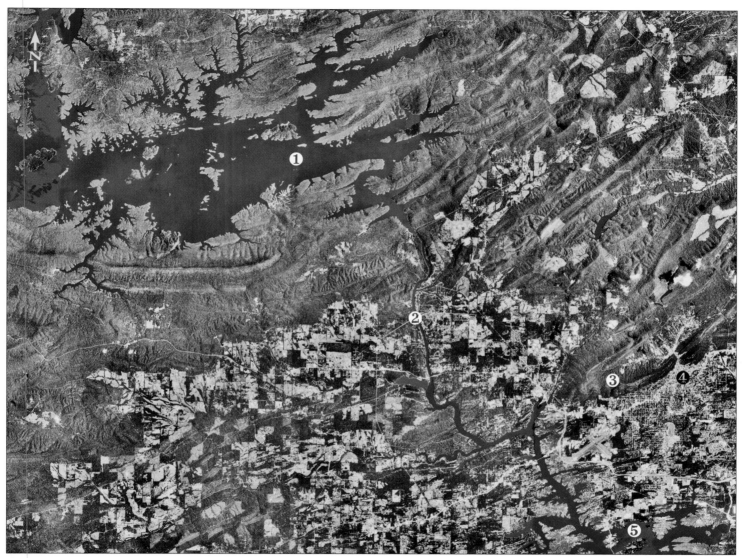

❶ Lake Ouachita, with its many arms presenting a display of trellised drainages **❷** Ouachita River **❸** valley containing most of Hot Springs National Park between ridges intersecting in a wishbone shape **❹** city of Hot Springs **❺** Lake Hamilton

WESTBOUND: Go to p. 172

PACIFIC

OCEAN

Colu

Sm

250

Portland
PDX

64

64

Salem ★

288

CORRIDOR 9:
Seattle–Portland–
San Francisco or Los Angeles

252

OREGON

254

256

These flight paths are in the vanguard, as of 2007, of the trend toward flying along straight lines largely independent of NAVAIDs. Hurricanes and major thunderstorms are rare; so are detours to avoid severe weather. Nevertheless, there are commonly two widely separated options for each direction; for example, flights from Los Angeles to the Northwest most often start out either north to Bakersfield or west to Santa Barbara and then Salinas, before beelining to near Portland or Olympia.

The topographic theme of this corridor is two parallel mountain chains, one coastal and one inland, separated in most places by a broad agricultural valley. Many subduction-related mountain systems answer that description. The mountains from Seattle to northern California all result from a single subduction zone and encompass at least five dramatically distinct ranges. But in central and southern California, the San Andreas Fault system creates very different mountains that together have few analogs elsewhere.

As for the intervening lowlands, California's Central Valley is the nation's most intensely productive agricultural region, known for vegetables, nuts, grapes, tree fruit, berries, rice, cotton, and dairy. Its northern counterpart, the Puget-Willamette Valley, is known for grass seed, nursery plants and bulbs, grapes, and dairy.

Conifer forests cloak the mountain ranges. These forests are not to be passed over lightly: They're not only the world's tallest forests, with the world's most massive individual trees, but also the most productive plant communities by biological measures.

(Those measures would be biomass per unit area and annual increase in biomass per unit area.)

Science has not definitively explained either why broadleaf trees are outgunned here or what kinds of steroids the conifers are on. The first answer may relate to the wet and mild winters alternating with dry and sunny summers. In most of the world's favorable climates, broadleaf trees enjoy a strong edge, relegating conifers to the frigid zones, the harsh mountain climates, and the pioneer stages in plant succession. Evergreen trees gain only a slight advantage in getting a little photosynthesis done in the seasons when deciduous trees are leafless. But in this west-coast climate, summer commonly has periods so dry as to shut down a lot of the photosynthesis, making off-season photosynthesis more critical. Support for that explanation comes from the unusual number of broadleaf evergreen trees, such as live oak and bay laurel, in coastal California; they outweigh deciduous trees there, coming in second after conifers. On the other hand, the most productive forests here, where redwoods or Sitka spruce grow, are in the coastal fog belt, a part of the region where summer drought rarely curtails photosynthesis.

We can't discount the notion that some uniquely impressive genes just chanced to evolve in Pacific Coast conifers. However, scientists have identified one natural growth-enhancing supplement, of which the supply is already severely depleted: salmon. (See page 253.)

NORTHBOUND: Start with p. 66

Puget Sound, Washington

LOOK FOR overall north-south elongation of hills, lakes, and arms of the sea in western Washington; ferries (large white boats that look the same at both ends).

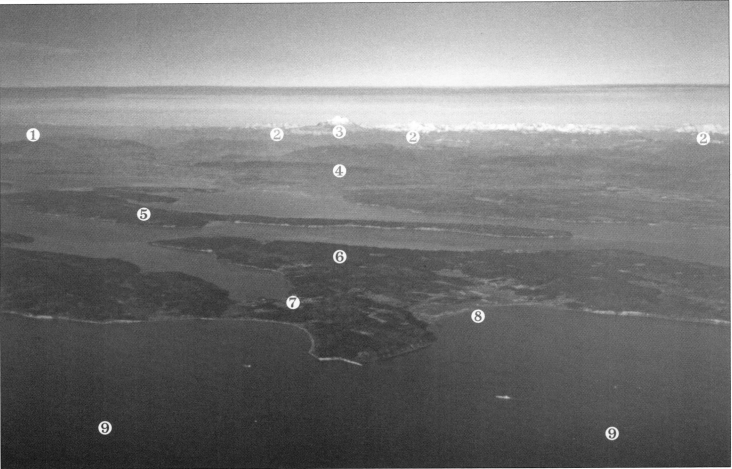

Facing northeast ❶ mountains in British Columbia (nonvolcanic) ❷ North Cascades (nonvolcanic) ❸ Mt. Baker (a volcano) ❹ mainland ❺ Camano Island ❻ Whidbey Island ❼ Freeland, WA ❽ Useless Bay ❾ Admiralty Inlet, a northward extension of Puget Sound, with the South Whidbey Island Fault under it, parallel to Whidbey Island

Most of Washington State's population congregates around this intricate inland waterway, which made a sweeping transition, over the past century, from an economy of timber, paper, and shipping through a wartime burst of shipbuilding to a hip culture of jetliners, software, Internet commerce, crunching guitars, and three-dollar coffee. Seattle is home to Boeing, the only U.S. corporation still building jetliners, and the airport closest to downtown is Boeing Field, which primarily serves for launching and landing the merchandise.

The nation's biggest ferryboat system crisscrosses the sound on 10 routes, carrying 65,000 passengers and 30,000 cars on an average day. More than 25,000 people live on islands with no bridge connection. Whidbey Island ❻ has a ferry to the metropolis at its south end, one to the Olympic Peninsula at its middle, and a two-bridge connection to the mainland via Fidalgo Island at its far north end.

Puget Sound can be thought of as a larger version of Narragansett Bay. Both are complexly branched inlets between long north-south ridges shaped by south-flowing ice sheet lobes. The Puget Lobe, 16,000 years ago, was more than 5,000 feet thick at Washington's northern border and more than 2,000 feet thick (three times the Space Needle's height) above most Seattle real estate. The Puget Lobe left massive deposits throughout the area it covered—1,200 feet thick at Tacoma, for example. Surface material across the Puget lowlands is glacial drift, with a few exceptions. North of the South Whidbey Island Fault Zone are outcrops of older metamorphic rocks similar to those found in the North Cascades. The few bedrock outcrops south of the fault zone are volcanic or sedimentary. Young mudflow deposits fill the valleys descending from Mt. Rainier. (See page 248.)

Seattle's hills are glacial drumlins. They aren't as numerous or elongated as Wisconsin and New York drumlins (see page 276), partly because early developers here flattened them, to varying degrees. Queen Anne Hill may be easiest to spot, as it stands just north of the Space Needle; about as wide as it is long, Queen Anne Hill consists of two Siamese-twin drumlins.

The Puget Lobe advanced and retreated at least five times over the course of the Ice Ages. Only the most recent incursion into Washington, lasting from 19,000 to 15,000 years ago, is easy for geologists to read. Each time, the lobe originated in Canada, where Puget Sound continues under different names as the waterways separating Vancouver Island from the British Columbia mainland. Dozens of mountain glaciers flowed into that northern trough from both sides, joined a similar coalition of glaciers descending the Fraser River valley, and headed south, eventually reaching a little farther than the present-day southern tip of salt water, near Olympia. Washington's own mountain glaciers were already in retreat at this time, reflecting a warming climate. But the huge mass of ice accumulating at those colder, more northerly, source areas in Canada kept pushing the Puget Lobe south.

To either side of Puget Sound, you see mountain ranges that still have glaciers. The North Cascades ❷ and the volcanic Cascades (including Mt. Rainier) form the eastern flank. The Olympic Mountains, on the west, are made of sea floor sediments and basalts scraped off on the edge of the continental plate as the oceanic plate they were on subducted into the earth's interior. Crammed into an indentation between two stout exotic terranes (the North Cascades and Vancouver Island, pages 292 and 328), they became an almost round mountain range, with ridgelines in arc patterns.

Thick glacial sediments make it difficult to discern bedrock structure under the Puget Trough. Over the past two decades, geologists have identified the South Whidbey Island Fault ❾, and the Seattle Fault crossing east-west through downtown Seattle. The latter is a thrust fault under north-south compression, pushing its south side up and over its north side. The outlines of land and water reflect this. Downtown Seattle, where Puget Sound widens and the land narrows, is at the southern edge of the sinking block; the wide peninsula of West Seattle is on the rising block. The Seattle Fault ruptured about 1,100 years ago in an earthquake whose magnitude was at least 7, but this wasn't discovered until 1992. The Northwest coast's propensity for large earthquakes was underestimated until recently, because no Big Ones happened to come along within the 200-odd years of written history here.

Mt. Rainier

LOOK FOR—oh, forget it. If you have to look for it, it's not showing.

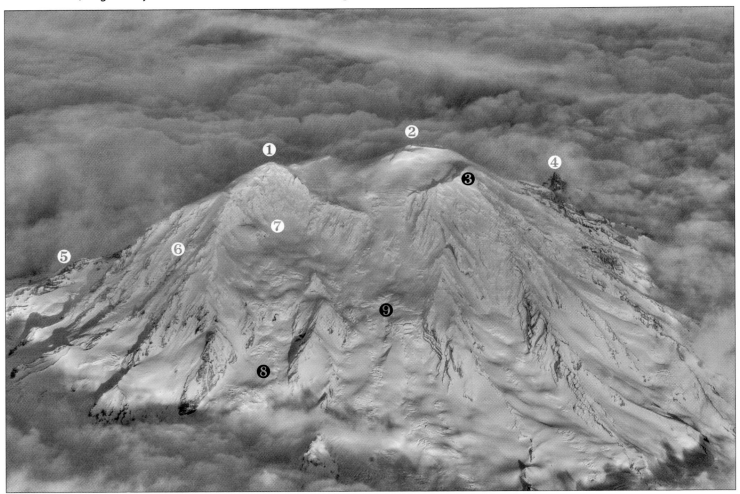

Facing east-northeast ❶ Liberty Cap, 14,112 ft. ❷ the summit crater and Columbia Crest, 14,411 ft. ❸ Point Success, 14,158 ft.
❹ Little Tahoma Peak ❺ Ptarmigan Ridge ❻ Mowich Face ❼ Sunset Amphitheater ❽ Puyallup Glacier ❾ Tahoma Glacier
The top of the cloud layer is at around 6,500 ft.

Mt. Rainier rises to 14,411 feet of elevation. On four different sides, its slopes drop more than 2 vertical miles to valleys nestling at its feet 10 miles away. (Sea level, for that matter, is only 42 miles away.) It's the most impressive mountain in the lower 48 states. Definitely. If our word or your own eyes don't convince you, it's the runaway winner according to two mathematical measures—"prominence" and "spire measure"—for rating impressive mountains. Mt. Shasta is more massive and about as high, but Rainier's beetling, crevassed glaciers make it appear higher and, over time, have also made it steeper in reality. It is the most heavily glaciered mountain in the lower 48. Its lodge, Paradise Inn, received more than 1,000 inches of snow in a single winter. (A U.S. record at the time, it was subsequently bested by Mt. Baker in the North Cascades.)

In an average year, around 10,000 people set out to climb Rainier—several hundred on a favorable day. A little more than half reach the top. On some routes, all it will take you is a professional guide, excellent fitness, and good luck with the weather. The "easy route" takes two days, gaining about 5,000 feet the first day, then gaining 4,000 feet and descending 9,000 feet on the second; a handful of Übermensch types have sweated it out in one day. Most years, a few climbers die, and several are rescued.

Another superlative often heard is that it is the most dangerous mountain in the United States. That's not about climbing accidents; it's about a volcano. The Cascades, a subduction-related arc running from northern California to southwestern British Columbia, include a dozen volcanoes bearing evidence of activity within the past 10,000 years. What makes Rainier more dangerous than the rest is the sheer mass of ice on its slopes and the number of people living on what might be called its floodplain.

In the past 10,000 years, Mt. Rainier generated at least 60 "lahars" (la-HARs, an Indonesian word for mudflows). These consist of rock, largely fine particles, such as volcanic ash, mixed with water to a consistency and color resembling wet concrete. They flow down river valleys at speeds in the range of 15 to 100 miles per hour, picking up boulders, cars, and anything else along the way. When lahars stop flowing, they set up like concrete, making rescue of buried victims impossible.

Entire ridges and slopes high on the mountain consist of lahar ready-mix just a little too dry or frozen too hard to slide down the mountain, yet. Many kinds of events can trigger lahars. Rising magma within the mountain can melt ice and cause a lahar. Eruptions of ash, mixing with melting glaciers, can form a lahar. Rising magma can bulge the mountain's flank outward until it collapses, sending rock into the valleys to mix with rivers and form a lahar.

Those triggers involve volcanic activity, which offers advance warning via the network of seismographs and GPS sensors set up for this purpose. Alternatively, lahars can start without any volcanic activity. This happens because the mountain's lava flows are locally subjected to acidic hot watery fluids percolating out from its interior, turning rock very gradually into clay. At some point, perhaps after a lot of rain or a hot afternoon, it gives way without warning.

Hotter, flashier kinds of eruptions will come sooner or later; potential hazards include lava flows or pyroclastic clouds. Even in the event that hot lava, ash, or gases trigger them, lahars pose the greater danger to the Seattle and Tacoma metro areas, where more than 150,000 people live on top of old Mt. Rainier lahars—the best available indicators of where future lahars may go.

Mt. Rainier is a composite volcano, built by eruptions of lava flows (primarily andesite) and pyroclastic debris over a period of about half a million years. The current summit, a crater about one-quarter mile across, is likely less than 2,000 years old ❷. It erupted small volumes of pumice several times between 1820 and 1894.

Dangers notwithstanding, Washingtonians experience Mt. Rainier first and foremost as a glorious talismanic Northwest presence. Flights in and out of Seattle are usually well below cruising altitude when they pass the mountain, enhancing your view. If you take a path southeast of Seattle (or east of Portland), you may see another volcano, Mt. Adams, resembling Rainier but broader and 2,000 feet lower. Mt. Adams is near the Cascades' eastern edge, where grassland replaces forest because of the rain shadow effect. North-south flights in good weather display a whole sequence of snow-laden volcanoes, a line of celestial guardians. The next two to the south, after Adams, are the pointier Hood and Jefferson. Mt. St. Helens is not "in line" but due west of Adams and almost 4,000 feet lower.

Mt. St. Helens, Washington

LOOK FOR a prominent mountain west of the main line of high Cascade volcanoes and somewhat shorter, broader, and often grayer. If you fly close, its amphitheater shape and devastated surroundings are unmistakeable. It may emit a puff of steam. Or more.

Facing south **❶** Mt. Hood, OR **❷** approximate pre-1980 height of Mt. St. Helens **❸** a nearby lava dome **❹** Spirit Lake **❺** eroded 1980 pumice plain **❻** landslide debris. Low-altitude helicopter view, February 1, 2005.

Facing east-southeast **❼** glaciers **❽** new dome **❾** old dome. Low-altitude helicopter view, October 22, 2006.

Until this mountain woke us up in 1980, most residents of the other lower 48 states were unaware of something Alaskans and Hawaiians have always taken for granted: We have active volcanoes, and they affect people's lives. As we write this, Mt. St. Helens is steaming fairly often and pushing magma up in a lava dome at a faster rate than it did in the early 1980s. The geologists studying it think that they understand the mountain well enough to feel safe flying low over it—much closer than your flight will go. If the steady, stodgy lava dome growth were to give way to another explosive eruption, they are confident that they would detect warning signs—distinctive gas emissions, tremors, and bulges—several days in advance. Pilots getting the word from geologists to circumvent volcanoes or ash clouds is a routine event in some parts of the world—anywhere between Anchorage and Jakarta, for example.

Before 1980, Mt. St. Helens had a smooth symmetrical shape reminiscent of either Mt. Fuji or an ice cream cone: It was conventionally seen as the best-loved, most graceful, and implicitly least dangerous of Northwest volcanoes. On the contrary, its smoothness was a sign of relatively recent volcanic activity: Mt. St. Helens's flanks were not gouged by glaciers, because they were too new.

A few glaciers did survive the 1980 eruptions, and a few others that melted away have reappeared. The inset photo shows how close a glacier can be to hot lava without melting.

As you can see, a big bite of the ice cream is missing, blasted into small bits on May 18, 1980, along with some of the mountain's "beloved" status. Dust encircled the globe, and coarser ash an inch deep blanketed central Washington, but the majority of the missing bulk is spread out as a giant landslide deposit across many square miles north of the peak, including the foreground of the photo.

The eruption took place when the pressure of magma rising in the center of the mountain bulged the north slope outward until it collapsed in a landslide. That took a heavy lid off the pressurized, gassy magma in the center, which responded by exploding with the force of 500 Hiroshima bombs. An eruption proper ensued, lasting nine hours and concluding with the formation of a lava dome. That first dome lasted a week. A smaller eruption on May 25 blew it up and replaced it with another dome; that cycle repeated four times before the present "old" dome persisted ❾.

You can still see large areas of trees lying on their sides and others floating in Spirit Lake ❹. Seared and flattened by the hurricane-force shock wave in front of the magma explosion, they lie aligned with the curves the wind took, following the topography.

The mountain slept from 1986 to 2004. On October 1, 2004, a new dome ❽ began growing next to the old one. Lava towers and fins are pushed up out of the earth, only to be toppled and buried as the eruption progresses. The old dome steadily creeps northward, shoved aside by rising magma. For several months, the new dome grew at an average rate of 2.5 cubic yards per second. That rate could produce a mountain as high as the pre-1980 one by 2050. Cascade volcanism encompasses a gamut of lavas and eruptive styles. Southwest of Mt. St. Helens stands a fairly young lava dome ❸ that was never part of a big mountain. To the east are small cinder cones and broad, low-relief shield volcanoes.

Most tall Cascade volcanoes are composite volcanoes built up over a long time in many layers—some layers being lava flows, others "pyroclastic" flows blasted into the air as ash or other particles.

Many tall Cascade volcanoes likely had at least one explosive eruption in the past; to reach their present height, they must have gone back to rebuilding with lava. If 1980-style explosions predominated, we wouldn't have many tall peaks. The slow growth of Mt. St. Helens over the past two decades gives us some sense of the long periods required to build these peaks.

Patch Cuts at Saddleblanket Mountain, Oregon

LOOK FOR forested landscapes perforated with patches that look bare, or white in winter, or very fine-grained and paler.

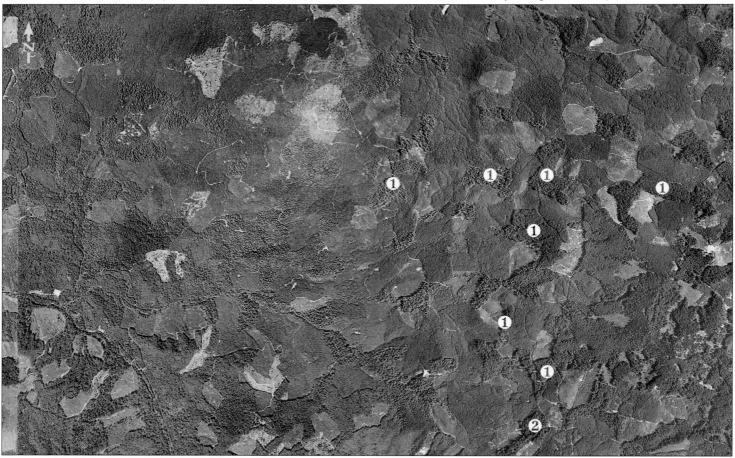

❶ patches of virgin old growth that were part of a proposed old-growth timber sale on Forest Service land east of Eugene, OR
❷ site of the four-year tree-sit operation

Patch cutting is hard to miss in many parts of the forested West. Unlike the East, the West still has small but substantial portions of its forests in never-logged virgin condition. Trees there are commonly 200 to 500 years old; some of the second-growth forest (land that was logged only once) has also regrown into a semblance of a natural native forest, with trees more than 50 years old. But the great majority of northwestern forest is slated to be treated as cropland, growing only one or a few conifer species for just a few decades before the batch is harvested.

The photo encompasses a 1999 timber sale that was to include patches of old growth with some trees older than 700 years ❶. Activists maintained "tree sits" ❷ on platforms high in eight of the trees for more than two years, preventing logging while they organized opposition to the sale. The Forest Service rescinded the sale.

In the 1970s, popular and congressional outrage arose regarding the vast vistas of stumps rapidly replacing old-growth forest in the Northwest. Over time, the Forest Service modified its practices in the region, replacing clear-cutting with patch cutting. Patch cuts are simply smaller clear-cuts, typically 20 to 30 acres. Visually and ecologically, smaller is a little better; but too many patch cuts is not a big improvement over too many large clear-cuts. Seeing cuts from a jetliner makes it easy to grasp what constitutes too many.

The photo is in the western Cascade Mountains in Oregon. A new crop of seedlings grows fast enough here to look like a forest again from the air in about 20 years. So, wherever you see a patch that looks bare or white in winter or paler green with a finer texture, assume that the patch was logged within the past 20 years. Such patches take up more than 50 percent of this view, when they should take up 5 to 10 percent. If logging is kept up at this average rate—one-fortieth of the forest annually—the result will be no trees older than 40 years to log. How is that lumber going to compare, in either quantity or quality, with the 250-year-old trees logged in the 1980s? Recent generations of Americans have been taking far more than their share of the timber resource, leaving a small share for their grandchildren; in other words, they have logged at unsustainable rates.

So far, we've looked at the forest only as a source of lumber. How does forest land on a 40-year harvest rotation compare with its predecessors as a forest? All the stages in the maturation of a forest have different components. Where you eliminate the middle-aged and old stages, you lose many components. The forest becomes less resilient in the face of challenges, which are likely to accelerate with climate change, introduction of exotic species, and loss of native species.

In recent years, logging has fallen off sharply in the Northwest's national forests. Many affected people angrily blame the spotted owl or the environmentalists rather than the long-term impact of logging at unsustainable rates. If the nonwilderness old-growth forests were made available tomorrow for logging at 1980s rates, they would all be gone in a few years, leaving the supply as meager as it is now. Why not let another generation, another century even, have a say about keeping a meaningful fraction of the old forest?

"Sustained yield" officially governed Forest Service logging rates for decades. The calculations for allowable cut, however, were flawed. They assumed that future trees will grow faster than past trees, thanks to anticipated progress in silviculture. Neither recent experience here nor centuries of logging on other continents support that assumption.

Trees achieve their greatest sizes and growth rates in the world in the Pacific Northwest and northern California. That's puzzling when you consider that the region gets much less sun and rather less rainfall during the growing season than many tropical and subtropical forests. One contributing factor has been identified, and it suggests that trees may grow more slowly in the future. Before Pacific salmon populations melted away under the onslaught of fishing, dams, water pollution, and habitat destruction, spawned-out salmon annually fertilized parts of North America with approximately 8 million tons of high-nitrogen fertilizer: their own bodies. Bears and other animals that ate the dead fish spread the nutrients a mile or more from salmon streams. No other known transfer of marine nutrients onto the land compares with this. There's been no measurement of how quickly its benefits are dissipating as salmon dwindle; trees grow too slowly, and the sweeping change from virgin forests to managed ones makes it difficult to isolate the effects of lost salmon runs. But there can be no commercial substitute for 8 million tons of free fertilizer.

Hanna Nickel Mine, Riddle, Oregon

LOOK FOR open-pit mine with bright red-orange soils capping ridge crests.

Facing west ❶ Hanna Nickel Mine on top of Nickel Mountain ❷ mine tramway line ❸ rail siding and tailings

Flying between the Pacific Northwest and San Francisco, you can track your progress by the tall volcanic peaks of the High Cascades on the eastern horizon. If your seat is on the western side of the plane as you fly above western Oregon, route tracking is more problematic south of Eugene and the upper reaches of the Willamette drainage. Nonetheless, the well-forested landscape does provide some clues. North of Eugene, the Willamette Valley separates the Coast Ranges from the volcanic pile of the Cascades. South of Eugene, the Coast Ranges and the Cascades appear to merge into a single mass of tree-covered peaks and valleys. The grid of clear-cuts, young second-growth, and older second-growth forest may suggest that this is a playground for the timber industry.

The Willamette River drainage ends south of Eugene, replaced by the Umpqua River drainage. Look for the broad lowland surrounding a river flowing north or northwest. You may see the timber town of Roseburg, with its mills and log yards, in a narrow valley of the Umpqua about 70 miles south of Eugene.

As you fly south of Roseburg, note the orientation of the highest ridges. When you first see the ridges trending southwest, you will know that you are now above the Klamath Mountains. Note the forest cover. Some ridges will be thickly forested or intensely logged; others will appear as thinly forested savanna and of no interest to the loggers. Look for the soil color wherever the vegetation is sparse. You will see red and orange soils on some sparsely vegetated ridges, as well as darker gray and brown soils on other ridges. The variety of soil color and supported vegetation reflect strong differences in the underlying bedrock.

Twenty miles south of Roseburg, look for a large red-orange scar on the ridge above the logging town of Riddle, west of I-5. This is Hanna Nickel Mine ❶, the only nickel mine in the lower 48 states. If you see large machinery and trucks operating on the site, you will know that the price of nickel is relatively high. Look for ore cars on the rail siding ❸ at the base of the mountain and a parade of ore carriers on the road between the active pits and the siding. If the open pit is empty and the blacktop road is free of traffic, you will know that nickel prices are at a long-term average price or worse.

This mine and a smelter were opened during World War II and continued in operation until the 1970s. Falling nickel prices led to the mine's closure, the sale of the property by Hanna Mining Co., and the dismantling of the smelter. Recently, the mine opened in response to higher prices. The ore is taken by rail to the coast at Coos Bay and sent to refineries in Asia.

The Klamath Mountains are quite different from either the Coast Ranges or the Cascades. In many ways, the geology of the Klamaths is similar to the foothills of the Sierra Nevada range. The Klamaths are underlain by belts of distinctive rock units forming large arcs that swing southwest from Roseburg to the coast and then swing southeast into northern California. These rock units represent several island arcs formed in the Pacific Ocean 245 million to 165 million years ago. Some arcs may have first formed at a great distance from North America and then were carried across the Pacific as that ocean plate subducted beneath the continent. These arcs were intensely deformed when they collided with North America. Today, we see the result of this process as the diverse array of bedrock and soils in the Klamaths.

The nickel ore strip near Riddle exploits a soil formed by weathering a peridotite bedrock. Peridotite, rich in iron, magnesium, nickel, and oxygen, is thought to be common in the upper mantle but is quite uncommon in the crust. The island-arc collisions brought these peridotite fragments of the mantle to the surface when they created the Klamaths. Groundwater dissolved the nickel at the top of the weathering zone and then precipitated the nickel ore garnierite at the base of the weathering zone. Much of the iron and magnesium weathered from the peridotite was carried away by the groundwater, thus leaving behind a nickel-enriched laterite soil. (Nickel laterite is a specific soil in the group called serpentine soils, noted for their harsh effect on many plants. Sparse patches with reddish soil are also seen in many California mountains. See pages 203, 265.) Refining nickel from laterite is energy intensive; as electricity costs have risen in the Northwest, refining of both nickel and aluminum laterite ores has become less competitive in the world metals market.

Crater Lake, Oregon

LOOK FOR a large, nearly round lake rimmed with high cliffs; conical Wizard Island near its western edge.

Facing east-southeast ❶ grasslands of the upper Klamath Basin ❷ smoke emanating from a forest fire ❸ Mt. Scott
❹ valley filled with pyroclastic flow from the crater-forming eruption ❺ Grouse Hill ❻ Llao Rock ❼ Wizard Island

The Oregon High Cascades march from north to south like a line of battleships at sea: Mt. Hood, Mt. Jefferson, Three Fingered Jack, Mt. Washington, the Three Sisters, Broken Top, Diamond Peak, Mt. Thielsen, Mt. Scott, and Mt. McLoughlin. These tall volcanoes sit on top of a great heap of older, mostly smaller, volcanoes that constitute the great volume of the Cascades.

Crater Lake lies within the caldera basin formed when Mt. Mazama erupted about 6,845 years ago. Five miles in diameter and 1,932 feet deep, the lake is the deepest one in the United States and the seventh-deepest lake in the world. Mt. Scott, at 8,929 feet the highest point in Crater Lake National Park, stands 2 miles east-southeast of the rim ❸. You will likely see snow on this volcanic mountain, as it receives an average of 533 inches annually. Rather than filling up until it overflows at the basin rim's low point, as most freshwater lakes do, Crater Lake fills until seepage through the somewhat porous caldera flanks reaches a rough equilibrium with the precipitation input. The seepage reappears as numerous springs on the outer slopes below the rim.

Most likely, your flight will pass either west or east of Crater Lake, providing a profile view. Looking at the north and south sides of Mt. Mazama, imagine two lines extending upward to a point where the sides might have met above the lake. This reveals a mountain profile similar to the higher Cascade volcanoes, with a precollapse summit around 12,000 feet. Mt. Mazama probably resembled some of today's younger Cascade stratovolcanoes, such as Middle Sister or South Sister. The other tall peaks have pointed profiles, the result of erosion during the Ice Ages.

A composite volcano is one that erupts over time from several vents, some producing lava flows and others pyroclastic debris, which bursts into the air and more or less solidifies before landing as fragments. The larger fragments fall near the vent; the finest fragments are carried away on the wind. A stratovolcano can be thought of loosely as an extra-large composite volcano.

Mt. Scott first erupted 420,000 years ago. About 30,000 years ago, a new eruptive phase included both explosive eruptions and flows of viscous lavas. The final active phase began 7,100 years ago, producing thick, viscous lava flows on the northwest side of the crater, including Grouse Hill and Llao Rock ❺❻. At that time, Mt.

Mazama was a major stratovolcano, visible from northern Oregon to northern California.

Its demise began with pumice and ash erupting from a vent above the present-day lake. After erupting about 6 cubic miles of magma, the summit of Mt. Mazama collapsed into the partially emptied magma chamber, opening the ring fracture we now see as Crater Lake's walls. A final eruption of ash through the ring fracture released another 4 to 6 cubic miles of magma.

In this "Plinian" eruption, water vapor with carbon dioxide and other gases drove the ash upward. (The eruptive style is named after Pliny's classic description of the eruptions of Mt. Vesuvius that buried Pompeii in AD 79.) The very finest ash flew over 18 miles up, and winds carried it far to the northeast. "Ash" refers to a size range of lava particle, from fine grit to sand. It settled in deposits 15 inches thick 125 miles away, and 2 inches thick more than 600 miles away. The heavier material fell back to Earth, blanketing the volcano and the nearby landscape. Gas and ash temperatures were over 570°F, so hot that the fine-grained particles fused together into a welded rock when they came to rest on the ground. The welded pyroclastic rock is found in many valleys around Crater Lake ❹.

Three vents erupted cones within the new caldera. The tallest of these remains 760 feet above the lake surface as Wizard Island ❼.

Composite stratovolcanoes do not necessarily end in caldera eruptions, as did Mt. Mazama and Newberry Volcano 70 miles to its northeast. At the end of their eruptive history, most stratovolcanoes persevere as high cones, requiring countless millennia to erode away. Not all the tallest Oregon Cascades are stratovolcanoes, however. Three Fingered Jack, Mt. Washington, North Sister, Diamond Peak, and Mt. Thielsen are tall shield volcanoes, meaning that they were built of lava flows without substantial pyroclastic contributions.

You may see Upper Klamath Lake south of Crater Lake, even from flights flying west of the Cascades. Klamath Lake occupies a graben (a structural valley dropped by fault movement) along the western margin of the Basin and Range Province. The Cascades extend west of Crater Lake about as far as I-5, where they give way to the Klamath Mountains.

Mt. Shasta, California

LOOK FOR a plain, northwest of this volcano, which you can't miss, covered with hummocky hills and scattered ponds and lakes.

Facing east ❶ Hotlum cone ❷ Misery Hill ❸ Whitney Glacier ❹ Shastina ❺ Sargents Ridge ❻ Whitney Creek
❼ Southern Pacific rail line; use ❻ and ❼ to correlate the two photos ❽ Black Butte

Facing southeast ❾ Lake Shastina ❿ ancient debris deposit with hummocky hills and small lakes fills the lower half of the photo

At 14,161 feet above sea level, Mt. Shasta rises 10,000 feet above the surrounding landscape. It is the largest Cascade volcano, with a volume close to Japan's Mt. Fuji. Four cones combine to make the present peak. Each cone was constructed by multiple eruptions from one vent over centuries or possibly millennia. The eruptions appear to have followed a sequence beginning with andesitic lavas, followed by pyroclastic flows sending fine ash down the volcano's flanks, and finishing with construction of a steep-sided dome of viscous dacite lava. The product of this lengthy, layered process is called a composite volcano.

The oldest of the four cones, perhaps 200,000 years old, is Sargents Ridge ❺, due south of the summit. The Misery Hill cone ❷ then erupted from a vent near the summit between 100,000 and 30,000 years ago. Shastina ❹, the apparent second summit northwest of the main summit, erupted between 9,700 and 9,400 years ago. The present summit, named the Hotlum cone ❶, last erupted in 1786. Black Butte, at the western foot of the mountain, looks like a cinder cone but is in fact a cluster of overlapping dacite lava domes. Interstate 5 wraps around the west side of Black Butte ❽.

After the winter's snows have melted, Shasta's glaciers are conspicuous even by moonlight against the dark volcanic rock. The Whitney Glacier ❸, descending northwest from near the summit, is California's longest.

Mt. Shasta is older even than the Sargents Ridge cone, many pieces of which are in plain view. Look at the valley north of the peak, with its countless hummocky hills, large impounded lakes, and many small lakes and ponds ❿. This landscape puzzled geologists for many years. Mt. St. Helens ended the mystery in 1980 when it erupted by first losing its north side in a massive debris avalanche. That event gave geologists a new model for interpreting similar deposits; Shasta Valley's hummocky landscape was perhaps the first to be recognized as an ancient debris avalanche. Mt. Shasta collapsed sometime between 380,000 and 300,000 years ago. The deposit extends almost 30 miles northwest of the mountain. Before this deposit was deciphered, many geologists doubted that it was possible for a landslide to move an enormous mass of rock 20 times farther, horizontally, than the landslide slipped vertically.

On clear days, shield volcanoes capping the Cascades are visible to the east. This low-relief type of volcano, constructed of fluid lava alone, was compared to a shield by Italian geologists who coined the term. These are small shield volcanoes, especially if compared to those that built the Hawaiian Islands.

The clump of white domes and spires southwest of Shasta, above Interstate 5, is Castle Crags, a granite pluton emplaced about 160 million years ago. These peaks, and much of the adjacent Klamath Mountains, were heavily glaciated until about 10,000 years ago, as shown by their U-shaped valleys beneath narrow ridges. Glacial horns, formed where glaciers scoured a peak from three or more sides, inspired the name Trinity Alps for the most glaciated part of the Klamaths.

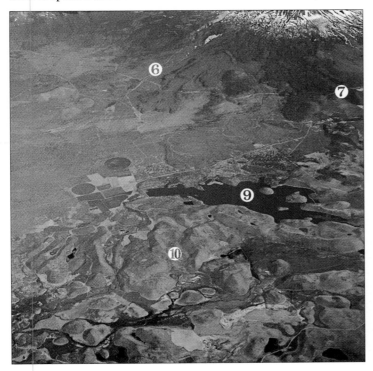

Klamath Mountains

LOOK FOR a broad mountainous area, usually with snow on its higher ridges; valleys are too narrow for farming and form chaotic drainage patterns.

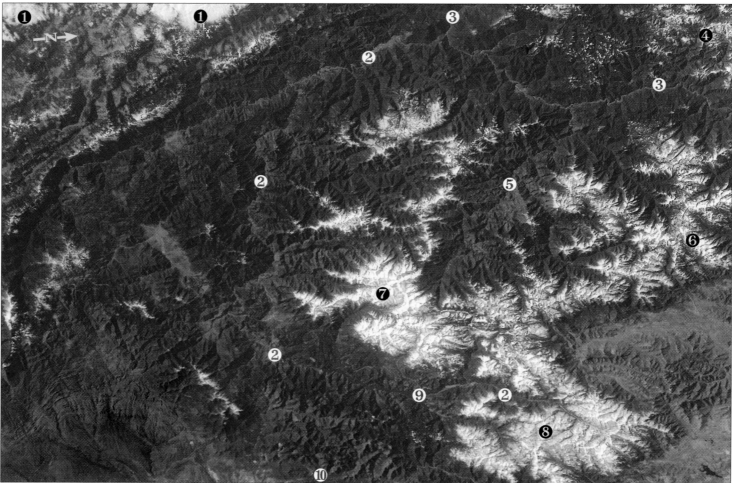

❶ coastal fog over the Coast Ranges ❷ Trinity River ❸ Klamath River ❹ Siskiyou Mountains ❺ Salmon River ❻ Marble Mountains ❼ Trinity Alps ❽ Trinity Mountains ❾ Clair Engle Lake ❿ Shasta Lake. Very broad astronaut view about 80 mi. top to bottom.

Most flights from Seattle or Portland to the Bay Area cross 330 miles of jumbled, forested mountains between Eugene, Oregon, and Ukiah, California. The northern third of this stretch is interrupted by the Umpqua and Rogue valleys, with some sizable towns and bits of agriculture and industry, but the southern two-thirds is so devoid of flat terrain that it has never been developed for any commercial activity other than logging, mining, and a little recreation. It's almost surreal to cross 200 verdant miles of nearly uninhabited land in the nation's most populous state. This is nothing like Death Valley.

If your window looks east, you can measure your progress with distant views of the Three Sisters, Crater Lake, Mt. McLoughlin (a Fuji-like straight-sloped volcano), Mt. Shasta, and the north end of the Central Valley. If your window looks west, look for the transition between the California Coast Ranges ❶, whose major rivers and ridges all trend north-northwest to south-southeast, and the southern Klamaths ❹❻❼❽, whose rivers carve a maze of arcs. The Coast Ranges have extensive areas of tan grassland high on the ridges, owing partly to logging history on private land and partly to alkaline heavy clay soils.

The geologic difference between the two is profound. The Coast Ranges represent an accretionary wedge: sea floor sediments scraped onto the North American Plate from the down-going oceanic Farallon Plate at a subduction zone 165 million to 20 million years ago. The north end of the San Andreas Fault moved northward along the subduction zone, raising the present northern Coast Ranges on a network of strike-slip and thrust faults during the past 5 million years. Some of the sediments have resurfaced after brief burial deep enough to convert them to high-grade metamorphic rocks. Almost all the rocks here at the north end of the Coast Ranges are sediments (either metamorphosed or not) deposited under sea water less than 200 million years ago.

In the Klamaths, on the other hand, geologic complexity seems equal to the square of the drainage pattern complexity. There are rocks of every broad class, with ages ranging from over 400 million to 145 million years. The complexity is somewhat reduced by interpreting all the rocks as four island arcs, each with attendant offshore sediments. Sediments may have traveled a long distance on an ocean plate before coming to rest in an accretionary wedge. Each island arc accreted to North America when subduction closed its intervening sea and is now identified within the Klamaths as at least one terrane bounded by major faults.

If it's winter or spring, snow marks the highest ranges for you. In this image—a broad astronaut view showing most of the California Klamaths in February—elevations above about 5,400 feet are white. Remembering that your view is from much closer to the ground and more oblique, look for shapes in the white ridge patterns to help identify mountains you are looking at. The Klamaths include several sizable mountain groups with well-known names of their own: the Siskiyou Mountains ❹ (maximum elevation 7,533 feet), Salmon Mountains (including the Marble Mountains, ❻ 8,302 feet), Trinity Alps ❼ (9,001 feet), Scott Mountains (8,542 feet), and Trinity Mountains ❽ (9,037 feet). Klamath peaks are higher than the Coast Ranges of either Oregon (maximum 4,097 feet) or California (8,094 feet north of Bay Area, 5,857 feet south). The Trinity Alps have a few active glaciers that appear durable enough to survive a couple more decades of global warming.

Gold and chromite have been mined in the Klamaths, but neither industry is very active today. As in the Sierra Nevada, gold deposits are associated with Mesozoic granitic intrusions. The gold was mined from stream deposits, using water sluices, dredging, and hydraulic mining. Mining scars can be seen in river valleys west of the three large reservoirs.

Chromite deposits are associated with serpentine areas, which are scattered through much of California's Coast Ranges, northern Sierra Nevada, and Klamaths. The Klamaths have by far the most. Among states, California has produced the most chromite and has the most serpentine, which it honors as the official state rock. Chromite mining here boomed during World War II, when cheaper foreign chromite was inaccessible; then it tapered off and ceased in the 1960s. The mineral is used to make chrome steel alloys. Platinum, which is also often found near serpentinite, has turned up in northern California beach gravels. There may be platinum mines in the region's future.

Lassen Peak and the Modoc Plateau, California

LOOK FOR a tall peak with snow fields, smaller volcanoes nearby, and a large impounded lake south of Lassen.

Facing west-southwest ❶ Central Valley ❷ Brokeoff Mountain ❸ Mt. Diller ❹ Red Rock Mountain ❺ Lassen Peak ❻ Chaos Crags ❼ Sulphur Works ❽ Bumpass Mountain ❾ Reading Peak ❿ 1914 mud flow

The southernmost major volcano in the Cascade Range, Lassen Peak rises above the northern Central Valley. Smaller volcanic domes surround the peak, part of a line of volcanoes running northwest to Mt. Shasta. Cascade volcanic rocks replace or cover the northernmost Sierra Nevada surface rocks north of Lake Almanor and Susanville. Smaller volcanic cones and lava flows of an entirely different volcanic province, the Modoc Plateau, lie east of Lassen Peak, extending north into Oregon and east to the Basin and Range Province at Honey Lake.

The 10,457-foot Lassen Peak is seen at a distance of 25 to 50 miles from many common flight paths. Until Mt. St. Helens's 1980 eruption, Lassen was celebrated—to the point of national park status—as the only volcano to erupt in living memory within the lower 48 states.

Lassen vented steam and ash for a year beginning on May 30, 1914. A year later, lava erupted into the peak's crater, soon sending a 10-mile-long lahar, or hot mudflow, down the east flank ❿. Two days later, an ash eruption culminated in a 4-mile pyroclastic flow, while mudflows swept down several valleys around Lassen. Pumice erupted next, raising a cloud 5 miles above the peak, and winds carried fine material 300 miles east. Small eruptions continued until the summer of 1917. Today, the only signs of activity are clouds vented from fumaroles on Lassen's western flank.

The taller composite volcanoes of the Cascades stand on the remains of older volcanoes. Lassen Peak erupted onto the remains of Mt. Tehama, a stratovolcano active between 600,000 and 400,000 years ago. Remnants of Tehama form the higher peaks just south of Lassen: Brokeoff Mountain ❷, Mt. Conard, Mt. Diller ❸, and Diamond Peak. These summits form an 11-mile-diameter circle marking the location of a caldera formed by the collapse of Mt. Tehama. Lassen Volcano National Park's Sulphur Works ❼ occupy the center of this circle, probably representing the remains of Tehama's principal vent.

East of Lassen, the cinder cones, small composite cones, shield volcanoes, and lava flows comprise the Modoc Plateau. The lavas are mostly basalt, a very fluid lava able to flow long distances from its vent zone. We see very few streams or lakes on the Modoc Plateau, because precipitation percolates down through the fractured basalt, leaving little water on the surface.

Some geologists speculate that these basalts erupted as the North American Plate passed over a plume of hot material rising from deep in the mantle. The Columbia River basalts of Oregon and Washington represent a major eruptive event, perhaps "announcing" the arrival of the plume at the base of the crust 16 million years ago. A portion of the plume could have flattened out under the base of crust and eventually emerged rather far afield, such as on the Modoc Plateau. Yellowstone, a "supervolcano," is seen as the plume's current location. There is no shortage of counterarguments about various aspects of the hypothesis, providing one of geology's more interesting ongoing controversies.

Streams are more abundant on the relatively impermeable rock of the Sierra Nevada. Lake Almanor Dam impounds the upper north fork of the Feather River. On its completion in 1914, Lake Almanor became the largest man-made lake in the world, driving the largest hydroelectric power plant in California. (Much larger lakes and dams were made in the 1930s and later, including Oroville Dam downstream on the same river, which remains the tallest hydroelectric dam in the United States.) Such an engineering feat would not have worked on the permeable volcanic bedrock just a few miles north on the Modoc Plateau.

The Sierra Nevada granitic and metamorphic rocks that crop out south of Lassen Peak are similar in age and composition to the rocks of the Klamaths; geologists long supposed that they share common origins. The Sierran rocks generally trend north-northwest over 300 miles from Sequoia National Park to Lake Almanor. The Klamaths form a great arc west-northwest to the Pacific, bending north across the California-Oregon line. (See page 260.) Any connection between these two provinces, however, is buried under the lavas of Lassen Peak, the southernmost stratovolcano in the Cascade Range.

Coast Range Ophiolite at Antelope Valley, California

LOOK FOR thin parallel ridges along the Central Valley margin; just west of them in the Coast Range, look for sharply defined patches of sparse tree cover on reddish soil.

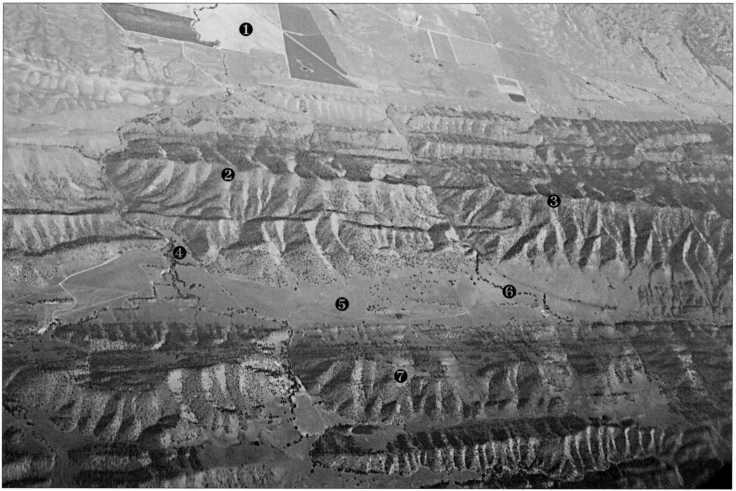

Facing east-southeast ❶ Central Valley, west of Williams, CA ❷ Three Sisters, 1,932 ft. ❸ Cortina Ridge ❹ Freshwater Creek
❺ Antelope Valley ❻ Salt Creek ❼ Oat Hills

Flights between the Bay Area and Seattle or Portland may fly either down the center of the Coast Ranges or along the margin between it and the Central Valley. For 120 miles, the valley margin is a distinctive strip of parallel low ridges and narrow strike valleys. Like parallel ridges in Pennsylvania (see page 12) and elsewhere, these were produced by differential erosion of the softer layers in a tilted stack of sedimentary rocks. Here, the sedimentary rocks—the Great Valley Sequence—descend to the east for several miles deep under the Central Valley floor and turn up on the other side in a few places in the Sierra Nevada foothills. There's a deep valley between the coast and the Sierras, structurally speaking; a lake or an arm of the sea filled it for much of its history. During those times, it filled with sediments, leaving it with a flat floor and no bedrock or even cobbles to obstruct a plow for tens of miles.

Just west of the low ridges ❷❸ lies a narrow valley ❺; beyond it, the Coast Ranges go on farther than the eye can see, even from 36,000 feet. The low ridges look almost barren; they're too arid for trees, because they're rain-shadowed downwind of the higher Coast Ranges.

A set of rocks known to geologists as the Coast Range ophiolite underlies the Antelope Valley just west of the low ridges and continues a short distance up the Coast Range slopes. Ophiolites comprise half a dozen rock structures found together in a particular sequence. Geologists noticed this recurring pattern in the Alps and gave it a name as early as 1813 but could not begin to see its meaning until they developed plate tectonics theory. They now recognize ophiolites as cross-sections of ocean crust that were ripped from their normal context within a subduction zone and eventually became exposed at the surface.

Ophiolites contain areas rich in an uncommon mineral called "serpentinite" for the snakeskin appearance of its greenish surface. Ophiolites were named after serpentinite, using the Greek word for "snake" in place of the Latin word. Serpentinite and its relatives (also found in ophiolites) have iron and magnesium levels more typical of the earth's mantle than of the crust.

Plants, of course, evolved mostly in soils derived from rocks typical of the earth's surface; soils with more magnesium and less calcium present serious challenges to most plants. At a transition from serpentine-derived soil to the surrounding area, the percentage of tree cover commonly doubles or triples. The serpentine soil may support sparse chaparral or widely scattered trees of only one or two species, where the adjacent normal soil supports a nearly closed forest canopy.

Try to spot sharply defined patches of differing tree density within the western part of the Coast Ranges. Serpentine soil often looks distinctly redder, as greenish serpentines with iron weather into reddish soils. (See page 254 for reddish serpentine soils around the Hanna Mine.) Ophiolites of similar age, also bounded by outcrops of Great Valley Sequence, continue for 300 miles south. At San Benito Mountain, exposed serpentine bedrock retains a conspicuous pale blue-green cast. (See page 202.)

During the Mesozoic, the Pacific off North America may have resembled today's Pacific off the Asian coast: chains of volcanic islands both large and small, all dragged hither and thither by a shifting complex of subduction zones. Approximately 170 million years ago, a new subduction zone developed along the California margin, persisting while the San Andreas Fault progressively shortened it over the past 30 million years. For all the years in between, sea floor sediments were getting scraped off onto the edge of the overriding continental crust. Those sedimentary rocks, now variously deformed and metamorphosed, are seen today as the Franciscan Complex, comprising much Coast Range bedrock from Crescent City in the north down to San Luis Obispo in the south.

Between this site and the Bay Area, flights pass east of Clear Lake, a large natural lake. A chaparral-covered lava dome, Mt. Konocti, rises 2,960 feet from its southwest shore. It's the youngest and northernmost in a string of volcanoes ascribed to magma leakage through the San Andreas Fault. The most recent activity was around 10,000 years ago.

SOUTHBOUND: Go to pp. 228, 226, 64, 196, 198

Yosemite National Park and the Sierra Nevada

LOOK FOR the unique form of Half Dome overlooking a deep valley; elsewhere, look for other rock domes, deeply fractured white granites, and much darker rocks near the eastern crest of the range.

❶ Yosemite Valley just east of Yosemite Village ❷ Half Dome ❸ Tenaya Lake on Tioga Pass road ❹ Vogelsang Peak ❺ Evelyn Lake ❻ Ireland Lake ❼ paternoster lakes ❽ Lyell Glacier on Mt. Lyell, 13,114 ft., highest peak in Yosemite National Park

NORTHBOUND: Go to pp. 198, 196, 64, 226, 228

Whether in summer or winter, the Sierra Nevada peaks stand white above their timbered western foothills. In winter and spring, it's the snowpack, which lies so thick it takes until June to melt, even in California; in summer and fall, it's the white granites of the Sierra batholith.

Forests extend to 9,500 feet before giving way to alpine meadows, so the many narrow, deep valley floors on the west slope are well forested. Yosemite National Park holds two of these valleys; two others are in two spectacular national parks at the south end of the range, unperturbed by any busy jetliner routes.

The Sierra Nevada is an enormous fault block raised by normal faulting on its eastern margin above the Long and Owens valleys. Flying across the southern part of the range, you can hardly miss the impressive eastern escarpment: near Mt. Whitney, it's the highest-relief fault scarp in the country. The fault block's western flank, in contrast, is a broad, gently sloping ramp, incised here and there by rivers.

The Sierra batholith is a vast agglomeration of small plutons of granitic rock intruded between 120 million and 90 million years ago. They originated as magma (molten rock) above the subduction zone where the oceanic Farallon Plate slid beneath North America. Water in the down-going ocean plate escaped into the overlying mantle, causing some of the mantle to melt. The magma was less dense than its surroundings, so it rose. No doubt some of it produced an arc of volcanoes, but probably 90 percent of the magma froze while still in the upper crust, becoming the white plutons we see today.

Narrow valleys bearing strings of small lakes run north to south near the Sierra crest; they are called "paternoster" lakes ❼ for their resemblance to rosary beads. Dark gray and reddish brown rocks cover the granite over some large areas near the crest. These "roof pendants" are all that remain of the preexisting crust that formed a "roof" covering the plutons when they crystallized. The pendants were metamorphosed by the heat given off by the magma bodies as they pooled below the pendants. Rocks of the same age and composition as the pendants also occur west of the Sierra batholith, where they are covered by forest. Lode deposits of gold, silver, and other ores were carried into the roof pendants by fluids escaping the cooling plutons.

Most geologists agree on the Sierra's origins (more than 80 million years ago) as a fairly typical subduction zone volcanic arc; what it's been doing ever since is mired in controversy. Some geologists interpret it as the western side of a "North American Altiplano," or high plateau, that extended to the Rockies. If they are right, the plateau developed 50 million years ago along with the Laramide Rocky Mountains, east of the plateau. The inferred plateau began to collapse, and the Basin and Range began to open on its normal faults, about 13 million to 10 million years ago. About 5 million years ago, the Sierran block tilted westward as its eastern side rose on faults. Soon, erosion removed the volcanic cover from the Sierra batholith, as well as much of the old roof rock separating the batholith from the volcanic rocks.

As it cooled, the batholith was fractured by either mountain-building stresses or thermal stresses. Streams eroded such valleys as Yosemite ❶ and its northern sibling, Hetch Hetchy, following these northeast- to southwest-trending fracture systems. The characteristic granite domes formed as the volcanic and roof rocks eroded away. Losing this overburden permitted the granite to expand, opening many cracks. These tend to split the rock mass into sheets parallel to the overlying topography; sheets forming beneath mountains mimic the convex shapes above them and may eventually form domes.

During the Ice Ages, even a California summer could not melt all the snow that winter dumped on the Sierra. An ice cap formed; individual glaciers diverged from the cap and flowed down the valleys, widening them. Several pulses of glaciation occurred until about 10,000 years ago. However, not every glacial pulse filled every valley to its brim. Hetch Hetchy, for example, was probably filled to its top during the last glacial advance, but Yosemite was not. Consequently, the glacier filling Hetch Hetchy did a better job of cleaning up the inevitable rock falls. As you fly over the Sierra, notice how some valleys are lined with rock debris and others are not, reflecting the depth of ice filling each valley during the last Ice Age.

Tulare Lake, California

LOOK FOR a sector of the southern Central Valley where the fields are gray-hued and extra large; tiny square ponds in corners of fields.

Facing north-northeast ❶ Stratford, CA ❷ Kings River, between two levees ❸ fields abandoned due to salinity ❹ Corcoran, CA
❺ field, at the heart of the Tulare Lake Bed, 1 mi. × 2 mi. ❻ California Aqueduct ❼ I-5 ❽ evaporation pond 1 mi. long

San Joaquin Valley farmland—the southern half of California's Central Valley—has three different "looks." The eastern half was settled and cultivated first and remains densest in towns, roads, and plots of diverse crops, including vineyards, fruit and nut orchards, and green vegetable truck crops, many of them green even in midwinter. With these high-value crops, small farms can prosper: The majority are 40 acres or smaller. Sun-Maid and Sunkist are farmers' co-ops, not big corporations. The eastern half has slightly more rainfall than the western half, but few Central Valley farms get by on rain; nearly all depend on irrigating with the rain and snow that fall abundantly in the Sierra Nevada.

In contrast, the western 40 percent of the valley looks tan and monotonous—huge one-mile-square fields with few roads, barns, or farmhouses. Even during a green season, a geometry of blank squares dominates the view. Important crops here include cotton, vegetables, melons, alfalfa, barley, and wheat.

Toward the south, look for a grayish area, round in outline, where fields are even bigger: 1 by 2 miles or 2 by 2 ❺. When the valley was first platted, no one cared to own this part. The tan quadrants were too far from water, and the gray ones were under the waters of Tulare Lake, then the largest freshwater lake in the West. Most land was snapped up in the early 1900s by a small number of large farm operations. The largest, the J. G. Boswell Co., has varied in size, often holding around 160,000 acres, equal to 25 miles long by 10 wide. (Try counting out 25 squares by 10.)

Irrigation via canals and artesian wells started in the 1850s in the San Joaquin Valley, soon followed by pumping of groundwater. By 1888, almost a thousand miles of canals were built; the lake was shrinking as its tributary rivers were diverted, and the valley was producing more wheat than any other area in the world. Farmers dared to plant wheat in ever lower parts of the dry lakebed, despite losing entire crops to floods during the occasional wetter winter.

The 1888 *Business Directory of Tulare County* described the lake as "a great, unsightly mud-hole . . . [It is] devoid of a single element of beauty and its uses are few." With boosters like that, who needs critics? Few mourned in 1899 when the lake went dry. That may not have been the first time: It had always expanded and shrunk seasonally by hundreds of square miles and by 28 feet in depth in historic times. Only at its highest levels did it ever spill into the San Joaquin River and drain to the ocean. This occurred rarely, but often enough to keep the water fresh and rich with fish, supporting a lucrative fishery through the 1880s.

When shallow lakes evaporate under a hot sun, salts concentrate. Extensive saline lake deposits attest to much larger lakes here during the Ice Ages. Salt also accumulates in irrigated soils that give up their water mainly via evaporation and transpiration. Irrigators must provide more water than the roots will soak up, so that some water can drain away, carrying the dissolved salts. In some parts of the valley, a shallow layer of impermeable clay defeats such precautions by holding the saline drainage close to the surface, in the root zone. As early as the 1890s, entire quarter-section farms became too salty for crops and were retired.

Irrigation drainage is too full of herbicides, pesticides, and fertilizers to return to local streams and rivers, so evaporation ponds ❽ now serve as dumps for the contaminated water. Loud air cannons are used to scare birds away from the toxic ponds.

In this arid corner of the continent, with its large human population, water is in short supply. Population growth and global warming may exacerbate the shortage. Much of the farming here—the cotton and alfalfa, especially—is extremely water- and chemical-intensive. More than 250 gallons of water are consumed in growing the cotton for a cotton T-shirt, and the entire crop is sprayed with herbicides at harvest time simply to make the bolls pop open for easier picking by machines. Cotton would not be grown here in a free-market economy: The water would be too expensive. Several nations would grow more cotton in regions well supplied with water and workers but are discouraged by the low cotton prices driven by subsidized U.S. cotton.

J. G. Boswell, whose namesake company produces more cotton than any other grower in the world, remarked to his biographers in their 2003 book, *The King of California*, that "there probably won't be any cotton growing in California ten years from now."

SOUTHBOUND: Go to p. 206

Historic Oil Fields at Taft, California

LOOK FOR oil fields and refineries at the south end of the Central Valley.

Facing northwest ❶ Sierra Madre Mountains ❷ Temblor Range, with Carrizo Plain and San Andreas Fault beyond it; see p. 206 for a view of them from the opposite side ❸ Taft, atop Midway-Sunset field ❹ Elk Hills ❺ California Aqueduct ❻ South Coles Levee field ❼ North Coles Levee field ❽ Kern River ❾ I-5

NORTHBOUND: Go to p. 206

Kern County is in the southern San Joaquin Valley, enclosed by the Tehachapi Mountains on the east, the San Emigdio Mountains on the south, and the Temblor Range ❷ on the west. Each is part of a larger mountain chain. The region's commercial center, Bakersfield, is the hub of the state's oil industry.

Four of the eight largest onshore oil fields in the United States are found here. Taft sits on top of the 2.75-billion-barrel Midway-Sunset field ❸. The 676-million-barrel Buena Vista field and the 1.53-billion-barrel Elk Hills field ❹ lie northeast of Taft, and the 1.24-billion-barrel Belridge South field lies to the northwest. If your view is to the east, you will likely see the 1.76-billion-barrel Kern River field and its many siblings around Bakersfield.

California's first oil-exploration well was drilled in 1861 in Humboldt County, in the state's far northwest corner. Three years later, oil mining commenced near Bakersfield, in the form of open pits dug to collect asphalt from a seep. Two years later, a refinery was built near McKittrick to produce kerosene, then the preferred fuel for lighting. No commercial oil well was drilled in the state until 1875, when the Pico Canyon discovery was made in Los Angeles.

An exploration well finally hit oil in Kern County in 1887, yielding 10 barrels per day. Two years later, the Midway-Sunset field was discovered west of town, but its early production of 30 barrels per day from 16 wells did not even hint at its size.

The region's oil boom began with the 1899 discovery of the Kern River field. Within four years, California became the leading oil-producing state in the United States. In these early decades, the Kern River field produced more oil than the state of Texas. Kern County dominated U.S. production until 1923, when three newly discovered fields in the Los Angeles Basin flooded the world market with crude. (See page 67.)

These early California fields were easy to find, once the appropriate drilling technology developed. It required little more than placing wells on crests or flanks of hills, as the surface topography in this region closely reflects the subsurface anticlines, which hold the oil. Seismic data were not used to explore here until 1936, a decade after it was introduced in the flat landscape of Texas.

Oil forms where organic-rich rocks are buried deeply enough for heat to break down the organic material. The Monterey Formation is among the most organic-rich rocks in the world and did not require burial as deep as many other organic-rich formations. Deposited between 12 million and 9 million years ago, the Monterey now lies 15,000 feet beneath much of the San Joaquin Valley, yielding oil and gas. Hydrocarbons are lighter than water, so they rise through tiny pores found in many underground rocks. If the hydrocarbons encounter a nonporous layer, they spread out along its base, and if this layer is folded into an anticline, the hydrocarbons fill the arch to form an oil and gas pool. In the San Joaquin Valley, the anticlines are still arching upward, slowly lifting the ridges.

On the west side of the valley, oil fields occur on northwest-trending ridges formed by the very active San Andreas Fault, which runs through the Temblor Range about 10 miles west of Taft. (See page 207.) Movement along the fault created the ranges and valleys west of the San Joaquin Valley.

The oil produced in Kern County and much of California is "heavy," yielding relatively little gasoline when refined. In this respect, west Texas crude is far superior. California oil is also viscous, resisting flow toward the well bore. Look for small steam plumes above some of these oil fields. In 1961, field operators began enhancing production by injecting steam down some wells to heat the oil so it would flow readily. You may also note a surprising number of electric power lines around the fields. Since 1980, steam has been put to work turning electric turbines before injection into the field. The cogenerated electricity is enough to power 1.5 million homes.

SOUTHBOUND: Go to p. 66

Historic Oil Fields at Taft, California   **271**

Great Falls

284

MONTANA

Helena

M O U N T A I N S

Billings

CORRIDOR 10:
New York, Chicago, or Minneapolis–Seattle

288

Yellowstone
Lake

R O C K

162

Jackson

As on Corridor 1, a wide array of flight paths are flown on these itineraries, primarily because your pilot will try to ride the jet stream eastbound, or to avoid fighting it westbound. If you have a chance on the day before you fly, look at a jet stream forecast online, and think about what path you would choose if you were the pilot. (Try http://squall.sfsu.edu/crws/jetstream.html; if that address is no longer current, search for "'jet stream' maps 'North America'" with a search engine.)

In the eastern half of the country, paths are generally tied to NAVAIDS and to published routes; that is to say, if you aren't on the line we show as a NY–SEA path, you may find yourself for a while on what we show as a path between some other pair of cities.

In the western half of the country, pilots are freer to take long beelines between distant NAVAIDs; a great many combinations are possible. To give you a good chance of seeing our subjects, we looked for subjects that are widely distributed in the north-south direction.

Regardless of flight path, you will spend more than an hour over four of the least densely populated states: Wyoming, Montana, and the Dakotas. (Only Alaska is more sparse.) Perhaps no single window frame view on Corridor 10 is as glaringly deserted as some farther south, such as the Bonneville Salt Flats; however, these four states are a big piece of terrain, much bigger than Texas, without a single city of 150,000.

Ice Age glacial landforms are seen all across the continent at these latitudes: the Finger Lakes, the Great Lakes, drumlins in five states, the Loess Hills, broad ice lobe-scoured valleys, alpine glacier-scoured U-shaped mountain valleys, and the giant ripples and scars of catastrophic megafloods. There's no better place to see them from than a window seat on a clear day.

Seattle or Portland flights don't find the western mountains as tidily arranged as flights between California and the East Coast. The latter cross the western mountains as three fairly well-organized belts: the big Sierra Nevada fault block in California, the Basin and Range fault blocks, and the Laramide Rocky Mountain ranges in Colorado, western Utah, and northern New Mexico.

Farther north, it's less predictable. Depending on where you cross the Cascades, you may see either a range of volcanoes or a broad, complex range of jagged metamorphic spires with two taller volcanoes. In Idaho, you may see a few large Basin and Range fault blocks or, more likely, the remarkably broad maze of erosional valleys and ridges carved in the Idaho batholith. In Montana and Wyoming, some of the many north-south ranges are Laramide-age Rocky Mountain uplifts. Some, including the Tetons, are narrower, younger Basin and Range fault blocks. And some are sets of close parallel ranges on Rocky Mountain thrust faults older than the Laramide faults; these find their closest relatives in the Canadian Rockies. To geologists, both these and the Laramide fault blocks are parts of the Rockies, since both resulted from thrust faulting in a compressional environment; the Basin and Range fault blocks, in contrast, rose later, when the environment had become extensional. But in Montana and Wyoming, the young extensional mountains mix with the older compressional ones, and residents call all of them the Rockies.

EASTBOUND: Start with pp. 246, 248

WESTBOUND FROM NY: Start with pp. 6, 8, 10, 12, 316, 16, 20; WESTBOUND FROM CH: Start with pp. 24, 26

The Niagara Escarpment at High Cliff, Wisconsin

LOOK FOR thin dark green lines (forested west-facing slopes) on Lake Winnebago's east shore and northward on either side of the valley draining the lake, continuing on the peninsula separating Green Bay from the main body of Lake Michigan.

Facing northeast and southeast, middle-distance and close-up low-altitude views of High Cliff overlooking Lake Winnebago.

EASTBOUND TO CH: Go to pp. 26, 24; **EASTBOUND TO NY:** Go to pp. 20, 16, 316, 12, 10, 8, 6

A long ridge separates Lake Michigan from the long, straight valley containing Green Bay and Lake Winnebago. The gentle slope on the Lake Michigan side is the tilted surface of a thick layer of relatively hard dolostone. The steeper slope overlooking Lake Winnebago is that same hard layer's edge, the Niagara Escarpment. West of it, erosive forces removed the dolostone and the softer layers underneath it—predominantly shale with some sandstone and limestone. Erosion stripped down to the next layer of hard dolostone, which slopes equally gently up to a similar (though lower) ridgetop on the other side of Lake Winnebago. This type of geologic structure—an erosional ridge with very little slope on one side and much steeper on the other—is known by its Spanish name, *cuesta*.

This particular cuesta goes many times farther than the far end of Green Bay. In some places, such as High Cliff State Park, the escarpment is a steep cliff. It's about 300 feet high here but achieves as much as a thousand feet of relief elsewhere. Many other sections are too subtle to see from the air. Its overall arc, however, makes a line so strong that you could hardly miss it from space. It's the big arch you see on maps around the tops of Lakes Michigan and Huron. It's the peninsulas and islands that separate Green Bay from Lake Michigan proper; then it runs east along the Upper Peninsula; then it is the peninsulas and islands between Georgian Bay and Lake Huron. It bequeaths a string of lovely waterfalls across southern Ontario before bending sharply east along Lake Ontario's southern shore to where, at long last, it achieves fame: The water draining out of Lake Erie drops over it in Niagara Falls.

The falls are no longer right at the escarpment. They started there 10,000 years ago when the ice sheet left the area but eroded their way upstream by about eight miles, leaving those eight miles of river in a gorge. From Niagara, the escarpment continues eastward a few dozen miles. For several miles eastward from Lockport, New York, the architects of the Erie Canal put the canal halfway up the escarpment slope in order to keep it at the best elevation to minimize the number of locks.

The escarpment's layers are made of sediments that settled to the bottom of a shallow sea during Silurian and Ordovician time (500 million to 435 million years ago). For long periods, sand and clay predominated; those layers eventually became sandstone and shale. At other periods, the sea was clear and warm as recorded by fossil-rich limestones (calcium carbonate). Later, magnesium-bearing fluids circulated through the limestones, altering them to dolostone, a magnesium carbonate.

All the layers were deposited as horizontal beds in the Michigan Basin, centered on Michigan's Lower Peninsula. Geologists dispute the tectonic cause of this intracratonic basin. The kinds of tectonic boundaries usually associated with the formation of basins were hundreds of miles away when the Michigan Basin formed. One group of hypotheses invokes forces from the earth's mantle; the other group infers crustal compression applied from a distance.

The escarpment developed over millions of years by a process of differential erosion and cliff retreat. We don't know how much farther out the escarpment was when it first appeared. There may originally have been streams parallel to the scarp face, but cliff retreat eventually had a life of its own: Weathering would eat out the soft rocks on the lower cliff; then the hard rocks immediately above, unsupported, would fall; and all the while, even small streams, given enough time, could carry most of the debris away. But to clear all the loose material away, leaving the smooth planes we find today both on top of the scarp and stretching out from its foot, required an ice sheet. Although neither a fault nor a glacial feature, the escarpment did get its finishing touches from the glaciers.

The Lake Winnebago area, including the gentle terrain on top of the escarpment, was completely covered by ice sheets at least twice during the Ice Ages. At various times when the ice sheet was less extensive, the two cuestas here directed the flow of a lobe, a broad glacier extending like a tongue out in front of the ice sheet. This lobe carved the valley deeper, with Lake Winnebago as the result.

Near the foot of the lake lies the city of Appleton. Nearby small towns include Kaukauna, Kimberly, and Neenah—names better known as brands of quintessential Wisconsin products: cheese and paper.

Drumlin Fields, Wisconsin and New York

LOOK FOR dozens or hundreds of very small hills all elongated in the same direction; in New York, look east and south of Sodus Bay, the largest long inlet in the Lake Ontario shore; in central Wisconsin, look southwest of a C-shaped lake. From high altitude, crop and forest outlines may show the parallel grain, if the topography itself is too subtle.

A mere 14,000 years ago, an ice cap more than a mile thick covered most of North America's northern half. The ice spread and flowed outward under its own weight, fastest near its southern edge, eventually grinding its way onto areas too far south to have accumulated ice from their own snowfall. Minnesota, Michigan, Wisconsin, New York, and New England all received a thorough glacial dermabrasion, removing several hundred feet of surface material, on average. Ohio, Indiana, Illinois, Iowa, and the Dakotas were each about half covered.

The ice left its mark in many ways. Some are best seen down on the ground; others, from your plane window. Most obvious are the lakes, which come in a wide variety of shapes and sizes: the 5 Great Lakes; deep fjordlike lakes in upstate New York, Montana, and Washington; nearly 12,000 shallow, fairly round lakes in Minnesota. Then there are gravelly ridges fitting several patterns: moraines, eskers, kames, and drumlins. Of these, little drumlins (from a Gaelic word for "hilltops") may be globally the least common, but where they do occur, they swarm. (Geologists call drumlin areas "swarms," or more often, "fields.") Wisconsin and upstate New York have the most drumlins: whole counties of them.

Drumlins near each other are elongated in one direction, the direction the ice was flowing. New York's drumlins mark where an ice stream—a "river" of flowing ice within a more static ice sheet—flowed south from what we see today as Lake Ontario and then curved eastward toward Oneida Lake, which fills a basin presumably carved by the same ice stream.

A majority of Wisconsin is covered with glacial rubble ("till," or glacial drift, or ground moraine) to depths of 100 feet or more. Essentially, every little dip or bump of Wisconsin topography got its shape from the ice sheet, except in the unglaciated southwest corner, the Driftless Area.

Wisconsinites built their state capitol on a drumlin. Farmers are so proud of them that they highlight them for us with plowing and cropping patterns, as you can see: The fields, unlike the roads, run parallel to the drumlins. Drumlins pebble the entire area between Madison, Milwaukee, and Lake Winnebago. A little smaller on average than New York's drumlins, they're pretty subtle to see from cruising altitude. The photo shows an especially dense and elongated swarm just southwest of Beaver Dam Lake, an artificial lake shaped like a backward C. You might not be able to tell that these are hills, but you can't miss the texture of scouring in a southwesterly direction, thanks to the way the farmers have accentuated it. (For a very different view of drumlins, see page 154.)

Drumlins are found near what was the outer edge of an ice sheet lobe at the time of its farthest advance. Exactly how they form is a mystery. Dissection reveals coarse and fine glacial sediment in concentric layers; however, a few hills with bedrock cores have been identified as drumlins. The end that faced upstream is usually steeper; the downstream end is tapered, approximating a perfectly streamlined shape.

The shape seems intuitively sensible by analogy to rivers. We know that where a river carrying suspended sediment slows down, it will drop some of the heavier sediment. One theory is that melting ice sheets similarly drop the sediments to form drumlins, while continuing to flow around them and to shape them. Another theory sees them as old end moraines that have been multiply breached (and the residual fragments streamlined) by glacial erosion.

Yet another hypothesis infers that drumlins were formed by water: As an Ice Age ended, meltwater under great pressure beneath the ice sheet would squirt downstream, leaving detritus piled up in streamlined shapes around any obstructions, whether of bedrock or simply rubble frozen to the substrate. A variation on that hypothesis suggests that subglacial lakes built up until the pressure was great enough to float the ice sheet slightly, initiating a floodlike release of meltwater. Such sheet floods, if they ever happened, might have formed drumlins.

❶ old Chicago and Northwestern rail line, marking the northeastern edge of the Dodge County, WI, drumlin field ❷ Rakes Bay, a western tip of Beaver Dam Lake ❸ main body of Beaver Dam Lake ❹ Lost Lake ❺ Beaver Dam, WI ❻ U.S. Hwy. 151

WESTBOUND: Go to pp. 28, 30, 32, 64

Drumlin Fields, Wisconsin and New York

Lake Oahe, South Dakota

LOOK FOR what looks like a wide north-south river in the middle of South Dakota; this impounded river, or reservoir, is usually below its full level, exposing bare, muddy banks.

Lake Oahe, in one of its widest parts, 30 miles north of Pierre, SD, taken when the lake was nearly full, showing a slender margin of pale mud. The west (north) bank is in the Cheyenne River Indian Reservation.

EASTBOUND: Go to pp. 64, 32, 30, 28

Most stretches of the Missouri River seen from flights between Seattle and the Northeast take the form of six long reservoirs. Lake Oahe is longest, at 231 miles, and Oahe Dam is one of the world's largest earth-filled concrete-surfaced dams. Although the lake is popular for boating and fishing and generates a moderate amount of electricity, it has done poorly in terms of its three main purposes.

The primary objective was a flourishing barge industry on the lower Missouri. (The dam builders blithely sacrificed upper-river barge traffic by building dams without locks. Flatboats and steamboats once plied the Missouri to halfway across Montana, but they faded away with the advent of rails in the 1860s.)

Six feet is the minimum channel depth for the U.S. barge industry; the Mississippi and Ohio have nine feet. A lengthy and expensive effort, beginning in the 1890s, to dredge a nine-foot channel from St. Louis, Missouri, to Sioux City, Iowa, enabling barges to reach the upper Missouri from New Orleans or Cleveland, was abandoned when the dry 1930s showed that at the river's lowest flow, channelization alone could not guarantee even six feet.

The Army Corps of Engineers proposed to guarantee it with dams. Fort Peck Dam in Montana was in use by 1940, storing water when it was plentiful and releasing it when needed for barge navigation. Fort Peck proved insufficient, but corps calculations showed that five more dams would do the trick. They do, fleetingly: The goal was an eight-month barging season, but recent dry years have seen that cut to less than three.

Few barges ply the Missouri. Barges typically carried fertilizer up in the spring, grain and beans down in the fall. Even before the barge season got so short, pilots found themselves struggling to make decent headway upstream; straightening and narrowing the river had increased the speed of the current. Damage inflicted on many port facilities by the flood of 1993 was the last straw. In recent years, total cargo barged on the Missouri was less than 1 percent of Mississippi River barge tonnage.

The dams' second objective was flood control. But with many undammed small tributaries entering downstream from the lowest dam, there have been six flood years since the reservoirs were all filled, climaxing in 1993 with the most expensive river flood in U.S. history. The Army Corps contends that damages would have been twice as bad without the flood-control structures, a contention that is challenged by some. Reshaping the river's cross-section to benefit navigation made it less able to accommodate high water.

The dams' third objective, and the main one for Dakotans, was irrigation. There is a conflict between diverting water for irrigation and sending it downstream to keep barges afloat. The corps resolved this Dakota versus Missouri issue by enlarging the reservoirs, but still the farmers ended up with only about 1 percent of the Oahe-irrigated acreage first proposed by South Dakota's governor. Droughts shrank the lake from a record high in 1997 to a record low, well under half full by volume, in 2006.

Farmers plowed and planted wherever engineers liberated floodplain land below the dams, but an equal acreage of equally fine bottomland lies drowned under the reservoirs. Most of that bottomland is on Indian reservations and was the only valuable resource on those reservations. The politically powerless Indians were not only relocated but bitterly impoverished, losing their livelihoods and receiving pitiful cash compensation. Congress has been working to make amends over the past decade.

It all fits a pattern: Throughout the big dam-building era (1920 through 1980), dam boosters greatly overestimated dams' economic benefits. There was only rudimentary understanding of how rivers can be manipulated and how they can't; many staggering long-term costs were not even a blip on the radar.

On the Missouri, three vertebrate species—a sturgeon, a tern, and a plover—are listed as endangered or threatened following the loss of the fluctuating, shifting river's ecosystem, which supported many times the number of waterfowl, fish, and amphibians that its tamed version supports today. The Army Corps is now addressing habitat loss with two "spring pulse" releases, mimicking on a smaller scale two high points in the river's natural annual cycle. This new plan, implemented in 2006, will cost money, anger a lot of river users whose share of the water will drop, and still face long odds of saving the endangered fish and birds.

Northern Black Hills, South Dakota and Wyoming

LOOK FOR a broad area of forested hills surrounded by arid ranch land, well to the east of the Rockies.

❶ inner hogback ❷ Red Valley, holding I-90 ❸ outer or Dakota Hogback ❹ Sturgis, SD, famed for Harley-Davidson gatherings ❺ edge of the High Plains; Bear Butte is 4 mi. north of here ❻ U.S. Hwy. 14 to Deadwood and Lead

Facing northwest, with Sturgis around the bend in the distance ❼ Bear Butte

The Black Hills share many elements with the Rocky Mountain Front Range. Metamorphic and granitic basement rocks more than 2 billion years old lie near their center, encircled and partially overlain by concentric rings of younger strata, including the long Dakota Hogback ❸. As in Colorado, gold discovered here led to a 19th-century gold rush.

The Black Hills are a Laramide uplift, similar to others in the Rocky Mountains, though well to the northeast of the Rockies. The Black Hills form a dome 130 miles long and 60 miles wide. The Powder River basin, with its abundant coal reserves, lies to the west; the Missouri Slope on the plains to the northeast; and the Badlands and Pine Ridge to the east. Small volcanic features, including Bear Butte ❼ in South Dakota and Devils Tower in Wyoming, dot their northern margin.

The Dakota Hogback is a ridge of erosion-resistant sandstone dipping into the High Plains. The steepness and sharp definition of the Dakota Hogback vary from one locale to another, ranging up to the Stonewall, as shown on page 88. Easily eroded red siltstones and shales of the Spearfish Formation underlie the Red Valley, a classic "strike valley ❷." "Dip" and "strike" describe the orientation of layered rocks. Although horizontal when originally laid down, the layers dip after folding or faulting. "Dip" is the compass direction a ball would roll in if placed on the upper surface of a layer, and "strike" is the compass bearing at right angles to the dip. Northeast of the Black Hills, the hogback dips to the northeast, and thus strikes southeast-northwest. The Red Valley runs parallel to the strike of the Dakota Hogback; hence, it is a "strike valley." When we fly over mountain landscapes, a straight valley we see is often a strike valley underlain by easily eroded rocks. The Red Valley differs from straight strike valleys in completely encircling the domal Black Hills uplift, earning its nickname, "the Racetrack." No river, Red or otherwise, completes a lap around the track.

Sedimentary rocks deposited 360 million to 250 million years ago now rise to a dissected plateau above the west side of the Red Valley. More than one-third of Black Hills sediments are water-soluble rocks, including limestone, dolomite, gypsum, and anhydrite, yielding the characteristic dry streams and sinkholes of an arid-region karst landscape. In order to kill buffalo easily, the Sioux would stampede them into the sinkholes; "buffalo jumps" were the only efficient way to hunt buffalo for the thousands of years before horses came to the plains. The largest such sinkhole, Vore Buffalo Jump, is now an archaeological preserve. Older bones show that mammoths and other Ice Age mammals enjoyed the hot springs of a sinkhole near Hot Springs, South Dakota, where archaeologists have excavated 55 mammoths since 1974, making this the world's richest mammoth deposit. Two of the six largest recreational cave systems in the world are here.

The town of Lead (pronounced "leed"), South Dakota, and the Homestake Mine, closed in 2002, are the most visible development in the northern Black Hills. More than 95 percent of the gold recovered from the Black Hills was mined within 10 miles of Lead. With more than 40 million ounces of gold extracted, the Homestake is among the world's largest gold mines. The gold was emplaced primarily during the formation of its host metamorphic rocks 1.7 billion years ago.

The Treaty of Fort Laramie, in 1868, placed the Black Hills within a Great Sioux Reservation, off limits to non-Indians without prior permission of the Sioux. A defiant General George Custer led cavalry through the Black Hills for military scouting in 1874 and discovered gold, precipitating an illegal gold rush. The U.S. government offered to buy the Black Hills for $6 million, a figure the Sioux found insufficient for their sacred lands. In 1876, the United States asserted a new claim to the Black Hills, sending Custer with 260 men to enforce it. The Battle of the Little Bighorn ensued; several thousand Sioux, Cheyenne, and Arapaho, led by Crazy Horse and Sitting Bull, enjoyed their most famous victory. Afterward, they were unable to obtain enough ammunition to fight a battle of that scale again.

Should your flight take you over the central Black Hills, your pilot may point out Mount Rushmore with its sculpted faces of Washington, Jefferson, Lincoln, and Teddy Roosevelt. Nearby, a larger carving of Chief Crazy Horse is emerging from the face of Thunderhead Mountain. Both monuments are in granite about as old as the gold at Lead.

Emptying Plains at Golden Valley County, North Dakota

LOOK FOR increasingly sparsely distributed crops, fence lines, farmhouses, and towns.

Golden Valley County. The whitish mottling is most likely saline deposits, which form through evaporation of groundwater that has risen to the surface from deep soils. Mottled soils also occur throughout the glacial till region due to surface moisture differences between coarser and finer till material.

Unless emptiness mesmerizes you, northern Great Plains landscapes may fail to hold your attention. It doesn't take long to see that much of the flat land is gridded with crops, yet towns, roads, and even farmhouses are few and far between. The reality is even emptier than the appearance, since many farmsteads, stores, and homes stand vacant. The population has declined for decades: 49 of North Dakota's 53 counties had fewer people in 2006 than they did in 2000; 30 had fewer than half the number they did in 1930. Population per square mile in some counties falls below 1, meeting the 1880 Census Bureau definition of "vacant land."

Few regions today suffer persistent depopulation. Take a minute (or take half an hour) to consider why people are leaving this region and whether anything can or should be done about it.

Farming on the plains today needs fewer workers and more machines and gasoline than it used to. In the 1870s, when Laura Ingalls Wilder's neighbors flocked to the Dakotas, they staked out 160-acre homesteads under the Homestead Act of 1862. Later Homestead Acts in 1909 and 1916 upped the homestead to 320 and then 640 acres, inspiring more land rushes. (Many 1870s settlers had given up and moved on by 1890.) Today, anything less than 1,000 acres is a small farm. If a working couple finds 1,000 acres too few to support them, they may buy out a neighbor and work 2,000 acres. With more sophisticated equipment, farmers keep working later in life than in the past: A majority are over 55. The household economy may leave no room for grown children. A growing part of farm income comes from renting sites for wind turbines, which require little labor.

But the decline in workers per acre farmed is not the whole story. Even in a farm state, only a small fraction of workers earn their living farming. There's no job shortage in North Dakota; it has one of the lowest unemployment rates in the country and a strong education system. It has cultivated industries that can exist anywhere, such as call centers, bank account processing, and software development. "Value-added agricultural products" help some farmers prosper. A farmers' cooperative, the Dakota Growers Pasta Company, ranks third nationally in pasta manufacture. If wheat is the crop that first came to your mind, you're only partly right: North Dakota is second only to California in crop diversity. Sunflowers, canola, soybeans, flax, and sugar beets are all big, as is beef ranching. Unlike in California, neither farmers nor counties here specialize rigidly; they adapt to changing prices by switching crops.

Yet jobs have failed to stem the exodus. Jobs alone don't resolve other issues most American twentysomethings would think of if asked why they don't move to North Dakota: Lifestyle. Landscape. Climate. Malls. Movieplexes. A sizable, nearby cohort of potential friends and dates.

When settlers flooded North Dakota in 1875, there wasn't such a contrast between urban and rural amenities. Generations of Americans took the isolation of rural life for granted; most important, hordes of people were literally hungry to move anywhere where cultivable land was there for the staking. Many were immigrants. Among America's immigrants and would-be immigrants today, motivated farmers can doubtless be found, but there's no free land. Logic suggests that if today's farmers retire without their heirs taking over the farms, corporations may buy the land and hire immigrants to work it. Some farm subsidies hasten that outcome by conferring advantages on larger farms.

Critics of the subsidized farm economy propose an alternative future. Northern Great Plains agriculture has always been dicey; some argue that it runs in the black only when climate cycles and commodity price cycles align in its favor, hanging on at other times thanks to subsidies—free homesteads and subsidized railroads in the 19th century; irrigation projects, import quotas, and direct subsidies in the 20th. Rising energy prices steepen the odds against farming, since petroleum and natural gas are raw materials for fertilizers, as well as fuel for farm machinery and for shipping products to distant markets.

In this view, it is unwise to prop up money-losing farms with subsidies when the same money could buy the land and restore it to native prairie and wildlife including bison, yielding a sustainable (albeit smaller) beef industry. First presented by an East Coast academician couple as a "metaphor" they called the Buffalo Commons, this vision has taken on nonmetaphorical life. Some ranchers have switched from cattle to bison. A buffalocentric cultural movement makes Native Americans the only group with net migration *into* North Dakota over recent decades.

WESTBOUND: Go to p. 62

Striped Crops near Windham, Montana

LOOK FOR crops in north-south stripes; a roughly flat layer of clouds west of a mountain range, ceasing abruptly along the range crest except for a few tendrils reaching eastward within valleys.

❶ Windham　❷ U.S. Hwy. 87 between Great Falls and Lewistown, Montana　❸ center pivot irrigation circles

The chinook wind, perhaps the most famous wind on the continent, concentrates on the edge of the plains at the foot of the Rocky Mountain Front from Colorado north. How can we see any evidence of this wind from 35,000 feet? Look which way the crops are striped.

This is dry country, close to the dry limit for growing wheat, thanks in part to the chinook (shih-NOOK). Scattered center pivot irrigation circles reveal where farmers have given up on dry farming. But most of them still farm dry, by the traditional fallow method, dividing their land into halves and leaving each half fallow, or unplanted, in alternate years. The fallow method saves some of this year's rain in the soil for next year's crop. Rain leaves the surface soil in four ways: It can soak downward to become groundwater, run off on the surface, evaporate, or be taken up by plants and transpire into the air through the plant's leaves. Transpiration is the greatest of the four fluxes here. Leaving a field fallow eliminates transpiration, except for a bit that goes on in weeds. About half of a year's rain may still be in the soil the following spring when the wheat seeds begin to grow.

Farmers can divide up fallow land in any manner, but dividing it in stripes crosswise to the direction of the strongest winds minimizes soil loss to wind erosion. The chinook blows from the west, so these stripes run north-south. You may also see a few fields with diagonal stripes, perhaps intended to counter chinooks channeled by local valleys.

The chinook blows mainly in the winter, for several hours to several days at a time, between 10 and 40 days a year—not enough days to ensure success to a wind farm. More remarkable than its strength are its warmth, dryness, and abrupt starts and stops. If it displaces a cold continental air mass, the mercury can rise with breathtaking speed—commonly 40°F in 15 minutes. Loma, Montana, holds the world record for temperature change within a 24-hour span. It warmed up by 103°F, to 49° from -54°, during a chinook in January 1972.

Nicknamed "snow eater," the chinook can melt or evaporate several inches of snow per hour. Farmers in the region hate chinooks for stealing their snow before it can melt and soak into the ground. Ranchers love them because by clearing the snow, they enable livestock to graze in winter. Most locals appreciate a little relief from -54°F weather; others get migraines.

In short, the chinook is a mixed blessing. It defoliates conifer trees in swathes called "red belts" on the slopes of the Rocky Mountain Front by sucking all the moisture out of the needles while the ground is still frozen. The needles' moisture can't be replaced as it evaporates. Some afflicted trees will die, but many will pull through on the strength of their spring crop of new needles. You may see big patches of red-brown forest in the Rockies. If they're on the eastern slope of the mountain front, they could be red belt. (Bark beetles, page 163, are more widespread culprits.)

Early fur traders called the winds chinooks because they come from the western side of the mountains, the home of Chinook Indians. Ironically, these traders were at Fort Vancouver, near present-day Portland, Oregon, where the word "chinook" applies to a wet westerly. In time, the term migrated east to where the same air masses turn dry. Originating as warm, wet air masses above the Pacific, they cause rain and snow on the western slopes of mountain ranges they cross.

Air cools as it rises higher crossing the mountains and warms as it descends to lower elevations. Cooler air holds less water vapor than warmer air, so these already water-saturated Pacific air masses are forced to relinquish moisture as rain or snow when they rise over mountains. Heat is released from droplets as they change state from liquid to solid snowflakes. This warming effect partially counteracts the cooling owing to lift, so a wet air mass reaches the mountain crest relatively warm, by Montana winter standards; then it drops steeply down the eastern slopes. Descending warms it further, increasing its vapor-holding capacity and making it a strongly drying wind.

Is there any way we can see this wind in action? If you see flat clouds backed up against the western side of the mountain crest, extending cloud tendrils through the passes and just a short way down valley on the east slope before vanishing, that's a chinook. The vanishing tendrils are turning into dry winds.

Mission Range and Valley, Montana

LOOK FOR a linear north-south mountain range rising at the east edge of a relatively broad agricultural valley holding a natural lake as broad (but not as long) as the valley.

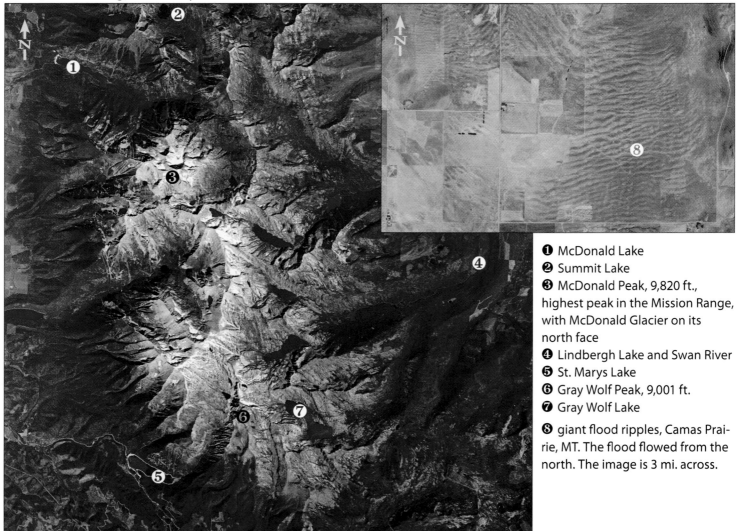

❶ McDonald Lake
❷ Summit Lake
❸ McDonald Peak, 9,820 ft., highest peak in the Mission Range, with McDonald Glacier on its north face
❹ Lindbergh Lake and Swan River
❺ St. Marys Lake
❻ Gray Wolf Peak, 9,001 ft.
❼ Gray Wolf Lake

❽ giant flood ripples, Camas Prairie, MT. The flood flowed from the north. The image is 3 mi. across.

EASTBOUND: Go to p. 62

At least 31 named mountain ranges and intervening valleys constitute the mountainous one-third of Montana, often making it difficult to locate your flight. The best way for us to help locate you at the latitude of the Mission Range is to describe several ranges in sequence.

Flying west, you can't miss the change from Great Plains to Rocky Mountains, as long as you aren't misled by several isolated smaller mountains that break the plains in central Montana. The Rockies begin with a 45-mile-wide expanse of wilderness ranges. This section as a whole has no accepted name but is known locally as "the Bob," short for the Bob Marshall Wilderness/Scapegoat Wilderness.

Its western rampart, the distinctly linear Swan Range, faces on its west the Swan Valley—mostly forested, with a highway and a string of lakes down the center. The lakes are renowned for loons; the forests, for western larches. The world's largest larch tree lives here. Larches are deciduous, dropping all their needles every fall, so the valley should be dark green mottled with golden yellow in early October and dark green mottled with lighter green in spring. The Mission Range rises west of this valley.

Flying east from Seattle, a prolonged, rather shapeless mass of forested Idaho mountains begins at Coeur d'Alene Lake in its narrow north-south glacial valley. After you cross the Bitterroot Mountains (at the Idaho-Montana line), the terrain gradually gets lower, gentler, and drier. Mountains give way to hilly open grassland.

Watch for a ranchland valley marked by numerous east-west ripples ❽. These ripples formed under the Missoula floods (see page 291), just as ripples form in the sand of a riverbed, only these are 600 times bigger. For viewers on the ground, they are there in plain view, yet were too big to see as water ripples until geologist J. T. Pardee saw them in aerial photographs.

The hilly grasslands are followed by the Mission Valley, an attractive agricultural valley about 10 miles wide. The valley is named for one of Montana's oldest settlements, formed in 1854 around the Jesuit mission of St. Ignatius. Northward, the valley gives way to equally broad Flathead Lake, squarish-looking in the distance. Other lakes in the mountains under this flight path are either much smaller or more than five times longer than their width. Lakeshore retreats line Flathead Lake, one of three mother lodes of the current Montana gold rush—the rush of urbanites buying second homes. The boom towns Kalispell, Whitefish, and Columbia Falls lie north of the lake.

This valley continues north another 900 miles into Canada, where they call it the Rocky Mountain Trench, a nearly straight gash visible from space. Flathead Lake marks (and was created by) the terminus of a lobe of the Cordilleran ice sheet that flowed down the trench. Looking up the valley from its south end, you can visualize the great tongue of ice that shaped it.

The Mission Range from its crest west is on the Flathead Indian Reservation. Only lightly visited, the mountains support the largest grizzly bear population between Glacier and Yellowstone national parks. The Mission Range is a fault block range trending north-south overall. West-flowing alpine glaciers gouged their valleys, leaving high east-west ridges. Where the valleys open westward onto the Mission Valley, they hold finger lakes ❶❺, some dammed by glacial moraines, some by concrete.

Given a close, clear view, you can detect a fine-lined horizontal texture and rich reddish and ochre-tan colors in the higher ramparts. These are Belt sedimentary rocks around 1.1 billion years old. They bear almost no fossils, as there was little or no life on land and only soft-bodied life in the sea when these sediments settled to the floor of a lake or inland sea. They piled up 10 miles thick, indicating that the basin sank 10 vertical miles while sediment deposition kept pace. That's profound subsidence and prodigious deposition. It must have been in a tectonically active setting, perhaps the breakup of a supercontinent. Remarkably, from that time on, the major portion of these sedimentary beds remained nearly flat for 1.1 billion years, even while being raised as mountains.

Although the rocks are ancient rocks, the Missions are one of Montana's young ranges and are still rising. Their orientation and activity suggest that they may be a northern outlier of the Basin and Range system, which stretches south to Mexico.

WESTBOUND: Go to p. 232

Forest Fires and Burns

LOOK FOR smoke; patchy textures in western or southeastern forests, including areas with a whitish or blackish stubble of dead trees.

Facing east-northeast ❶ Chiwawa River ❷ Twin Lakes ❸ White River ❹ Dirtyface fire, July 31, 2005, on Dirtyface Peak, WA ❺ Lake Wenatchee. (This particular fire was in the North Cascades, numeral 292 on the map, but the forest fires you see will be at various other locations—primarily in the Southeast and the West—suggested by a scattering of the numeral 282 across the map pages.)

The reddish brown color of dead needles mixing with the greens of America's conifer forests is a common sight. Its two most frequent causes are fires and insect pests, notably bark beetles. (To tell the difference, see page 163 on bark beetles.)

You can sometimes see flames at night from 35,000 feet. By day, a fire typically masquerades as a plume of smoke, usually coming from a broad patch of forest, grassland, or sagebrush steppe.

Fire's lasting effects on forests are visually more interesting, varying according to the type of fire. Some fires stay "cool" and close to the ground, consuming grasses and brush and scorching the mature trees only superficially. The latter will benefit almost immediately, invigorated by the reduced competition. Effects of these ground fires are visible from your window only if it is an open forest, with trees far enough apart to reveal the blackened understory. Ponderosa pine forest, a scenic and widespread forest type in the West, is adapted to a fire regime of light underburning every 15 years or so. If it doesn't burn, it will be either replaced by other species or, more likely, destroyed by fire because the younger trees become "ladder fuel," carrying fire up into the canopy.

Fires are hotter where there is a lot of dry brush or perhaps dead saplings in crowded, unhealthy stands. Surface fires here scorch many of the mature trees badly enough to kill them. The needles will turn red-brown and stay on those trees for a year or so.

The third and hottest kind of forest fire is a crown fire, which leaps from tree to tree, incinerating the needles and branches of the mature trees and most vegetation underneath as well. Immediately afterward, the trees would look like black stubble against a dull background. In most cases, the background will green up again in the next growing season. Gradually, over a decade, the charcoal sloughs off the trees, and the stubble of blackened trunks turns white against a green background.

Even the biggest, catastrophic wildfires typically burn in a patchwork of differing fire intensities, yielding, after a few decades pass, a patchwork of forest types at various stages of postfire development. This patchwork of differing age structure and species composition is ideal for wildlife habitat and forest health.

Wildfires in the Rockies burn mainly in July through September. In fall through spring, when the forests are cooler, moister, and less vulnerable, forest managers light prescribed fires. From high above, these look like wildfires. If all goes well, they stay cool and don't become crown fires. Occasionally, prescribed fires become wildfires, as one did at Los Alamos, New Mexico, in 2000.

Such lapses don't shake forest scientists' faith in fire as a tool. Its ecological benefits include increased species diversity and enhanced food for wildlife. It can also be good for human economics and safety, because it makes catastrophic fires less likely by removing undergrowth before it gets big enough to turn low fires into crown fires. Fires are inevitable, and people are better off with the controlled kind, even though a small percentage get out of control.

Fires are also increasingly common in sagebrush steppe. Sagebrush is completely flammable and not adept at resprouting after fire. Sagebrush increased over the past century because of overgrazing and fire suppression. Before settlement, the sagebrush community did best in places where it avoided fire, places so dry that the shrubs grow too far apart to spread a fire and too dry for many potential fire-spreading herbs to fill in the spaces between sagebrush plants. More broadly, sagebrush persisted because scattered individuals escaped the patchy fires. Most fires came during a dry year after a couple of wet years that fostered an herb understory. The native grasses of sagebrush country are perennial bunchgrasses that grow in stout clumps, often too far apart to spread a fire.

The invasion of cheatgrass from Europe changed all that. This annual grass germinates in the fall and grows rapidly in the spring, setting seed and dying by early summer. The flammable dead plants are often dense enough to spread fire. After a fire, cheat often takes over, with its lightweight seeds wind-carried from unburned areas. Sagebrush plants that escape one cheatgrass fire may succumb to another fire within a year or two. More than 100 million acres of sagebrush steppe are estimated to have been lost to this process.

Forest fire smoke is a bane of air travelers who like views and a thorn in the side of environmentalists. Fire is natural, it was a crucial Native American land-management practice, and it's good for nature in a way that ultimately is good for people. At the same time, the smoke is air pollution, just as harmful to our breathing and to our nature viewing as a lot of kinds of air pollution that we rail against. We just have to grit our teeth, squint, and suffer in silence.

WESTBOUND: Go to pp. 248, 246

The Channeled Scablands, Washington

LOOK FOR a pattern of grayish uncultivated land in strips crossing central Washington.

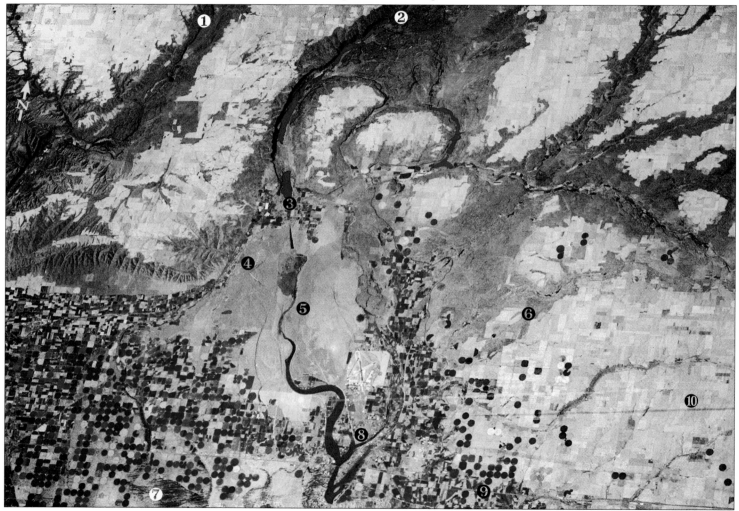

❶ Moses Coulee ❷ Dry Falls, in Grand Coulee ❸ Soap Lake, WA ❹ Ephrata, WA ❺ coarse fan deposit below coulees ❻ Black Rock Coulee ❼ sand dunes ❽ Moses Lake, WA ❾ I-90 ❿ jet contrail and its shadow. Astronaut view about 50 mi. across.

Of America's great geologic wonders, the Channeled Scablands were last to be recognized for what they are, and they remain underappreciated—precisely because they're almost too hard to wrap your mind around until you see them from 35,000 feet up. Any flight between Seattle and points east, weather and daylight permitting, offers you this vantage that geologists were so long denied. (The photo, an astronaut view, shows several dark "scabs." From 35,000 feet, you will see fewer of them at a time.)

The Scablands are scars from catastrophic floods that ripped across the region time and again as Ice Ages waned. In the photo, the gray areas—scabland channels called coulees ❶❷❸—are Columbia River Basalt with little or no soil on it. There's scant moisture to be gleaned from this thin soil whose sparse grasses and sagebrush can support a little grazing, at best.

The golden fields are wheat growing on deep Palouse loess (rhymes with "caboose puss"). This soil, some of the best for wheat in America, holds moisture so well that irrigation isn't needed—even here, with less than 15 inches of precipitation a year. (The photo was taken in August, with winter wheat golden or stubble, and irrigated crops green.) Loess is soil delivered by the wind. Ice Age glaciers ground bedrock into rubbly debris and dragged it out onto valley floors; winds picked up the fine clay and silt and spread them as loess 2 to 40 feet deep across the Columbia Plateau. Then the floods came and scoured away the loess and any older soil under it, right down to 15-million-year-old basalt bedrock in those gray channels but left it intact on the intervening plateaus. Southeast of the Scablands lies the Palouse, a region of deep loess now legendary for rolling hills painted with contour-cropped wheat.

The green lower-left quarter of the photo was the bottom of a short-lived lake that backed up where each flood had to squeeze through a narrow gap in low mountains south of the image. Floods arrived turbulently, probably stripping most soil, then settled down, depositing layers of debris. As you can see, the result of this unfair trade—a gravelly mix of flood sediments in return for rich loess—is deep but fast-draining soil that supports crops only if irrigated. The gray barren area on both banks of Moses Lake is an alluvial fan where the deluge spreading out from a canyon dropped sediment too coarse to yield a soil ❺.

The last flood was about 14,000 years ago. The biggest floods lasted a couple of weeks, emptying in that span a lake holding as much water as Lake Erie plus Lake Ontario. The peak flow rate was 10 times that of the greatest weather-related flood on record, or double the normal flow of all the world's rivers added together. All the gray channels in this photo were raging torrents at once, but still they could hold only a fraction of the total flow, which found additional channels and narrower coulees both east and west of these.

In short, these floods were totally out of scale with floods as we know them. Flying over the evidence, we can picture a child throwing a bucketful of water at a sand castle to watch it obliterate parts of the castle. If you have clear air and low-angle sunlight, you may discern giant ripples in flood deposits alongside the Columbia River. (See page 286 for other ripples from the same floods.) Several ripples are roughly half a mile long, the diameter of the irrigation circles. Imagine Niagara Falls so full of water that its surface has scarcely any vertical drop but looks more like a mountain creek flowing over a submerged log; that's what the aptly named Dry Falls ❷ looked like at times.

The flood source, called Lake Missoula after one small part of what it covered, formed each time the ice sheet in British Columbia extended a huge lobe south into Idaho, damming the Clark Fork and Flathead rivers. Some mechanism (plausibly involving the tendencies of ice to float and to get "rotten" as it melts) burst the ice dam again and again at intervals of a few decades. (Valleys in eastern British Columbia held large fjord lakes under the ice sheet, some of which may also have drained catastrophically across Washington.) Since the glacier tongue kept flowing south even while its front was melting and weakening, it kept rebuilding the dam and refilling the lake. A short while later, the deluge would reach the plateau area of eastern Washington, where it would divide into a broad net of channels, then recombine, pond in big backwater lakes, and find its way down the Columbia Gorge to the sea.

WESTBOUND: Go to p. 252

North Cascades, Washington

LOOK FOR the mountain range immediately east of Seattle becoming increasingly high, steep, snowy, and actively glaciated northward; two volcanoes (one quite distant) stand slightly higher than the nonvolcanic remainder.

Facing north ❶ Whitechuck River valley ❷ Glacier Peak volcano, 10,541 ft. ❸ Suiattle River valley ❹ Fortress Mountain 8,674 ft.; beyond it, hidden by clouds, higher mountains of the Bonanza, Dome, and other groups go on and on ❺ Sauk River valley ❻ Mt. David fire lookout site ❼ White River valley 1 mi. above ❸ on page 288. Snow conditions of November 8, 2006.

Facing north ❽ Sloan Peak, 7,835 ft., above the Sauk River valley just west of main image. Low altitude small plane view.

EASTBOUND: Go to p. 252

This **800-square-mile sea** of glacier-draped, precipitous peaks may come as a surprise if you are unfamiliar with the Northwest, especially if you happen to take a relatively northern path.

Most flights between Seattle and the East display Mt. Rainier out the south windows (see page 248), and the next major volcano in the High Cascades chain, Glacier Peak, more or less distant out the north windows ❷. These great volcanoes stand amid hundreds of smaller but steeper nonvolcanoes with varying amounts of snow. From midwinter to midspring, everything above treeline should be either dark bare cliffs or white; areas of snow persist year-round. The area from Glacier Peak to just past the Canadian border is the North Cascades, the most rugged U.S. area outside of Alaska, with the deepest snowfall and by far the most glaciers.

The majority of eastbound flights from Seattle see only its milder margins or may see its heart in the distance if the sky is really clear. A common Seattle approach, though, crosses the Cascades at the latitude of Chelan, offering north windows excellent views from well below cruising altitude. Chelan lies at the foot of Lake Chelan, a 55-mile-long fjord lake with more than 9,000 feet of relief between its bottom and adjacent mountains. Routes between Seattle and Europe or between Vancouver and the Midwest typically cross the heart of the North Cascades.

The combination of cloudy, wet weather, deep snow, alpine glaciers, and steep spires is no coincidence. Durable high-grade metamorphic rocks stand as most of the highest peaks. A "horn," or Matterhorn-like summit shape ❸, is created by alpine glaciers carving from three or four sides. Alpine glaciers have abounded in the area for at least 2 million years, carving the river valleys into U-shaped profiles. During interglacial stages and the present Holocene, sizable glaciers persisted. During several Ice Ages, the Puget lobe of the Cordilleran ice sheet covered the entire Puget Sound lowland but rarely pushed far into the adjacent Cascades. If it had, it would have softened their contours considerably. East of the Cascade Crest, some areas display softer relief where they were briefly overridden by the Okanogan Lobe. If you can spot a salient outlying peak on the western side of the range, envision it as a "nunatak," or isolated peak surrounded by glacial ice.

Today, the Cascade glaciers are melting back. Scientists measure their shrinkage from year to year to monitor the progress of global warming. If warming continues, they will disappear, though they will likely outlive the much smaller glaciers of Montana, Wyoming, Colorado, and California. The reason glaciers are bigger here than in the Rocky Mountain states is not that it's colder. On the contrary, it's milder but much wetter. The heaviest precipitation anywhere in the contiguous 48 states falls on high mountain slopes in western Washington. Most of that precipitation falls as snow, since winters are much wetter than summers. Over the winter of 1998, Mt. Baker Ski Area in the North Cascades received 1,140 inches of snowfall, the U.S. record for any weather station. Greater amounts no doubt fall on some of the region's glaciers, where they aren't measured daily. Where each year's new snow exceeds the amount that can melt away, a glacier forms.

Throughout the Pacific Coast states, prevailing airflow comes from the west, picking up moisture over the ocean. Orographic (mountain-generated) precipitation falls mainly on the windward side of mountains. Air passengers often see clouds piled up against the westward sides of mountain ranges; the air is more or less clear and dry to the east.

On clear days, you'll see that glaciers and snowfields are more abundant west of the Cascade Crest, and you may be able to see that the topography is steeper there. Rapid erosion by glaciers and raging mountain rivers accelerates the rate of uplift in a mountain range. Orographic rainfall inequality persists for all the years that the mountain range does, causing the western side of the Cascades to rise faster than the eastern side. Picture a floating block of plywood: The glue lines between sheets of wood are perfectly level, right? If you then take the block over to the saw and gouge several deep valleys into the top of the left-hand side of the block and then set it back into the water, the gouged side will float higher than before, so that the wood ply layers slope downward toward the intact right side. Mountain ranges tilt similarly because the earth's tectonic plates "float." Accelerated erosion from above and uplift from below combine to produce steep terrain.

WESTBOUND: Go to pp. 248, 246

300

296

SIANA

Baton Rouge

Mobile

300

New Orleans

Pe

298

ALA

298

CORRIDOR 11:
Florida–Texas

GULF OF MEXICO

Most flights between Texas and any Florida airport from Orlando south cross the Gulf of Mexico. The routes go close enough to the tip of the Mississippi's Birdfoot Delta and the Chandeleur Islands to offer views of them from at least one side of the aircraft, if clouds do not intervene. Storm-avoidance routes are needed frequently, as Florida has more tornadoes than any other state, as well as more hurricanes. When skies are fair, they often carry a thick haze of humidity.

Even through haze, though, the Louisiana coastline is a remarkable sight, a maze of curved bayous and straight canals painted on a landscape devoid of vertical relief and all but devoid of elevation above sea level. The land was formed by deltaic processes: a slow dance of land and sea advancing and retreating. The land advances at the active delta lobe; the sea advances upon most former delta lobes, primarily because delta sediments gradually compact, squeezing water out, under their own weight. The sea advances dramatically during each major storm; the delta makes up that difference, and a little more, over the rest of the year.

That was in the past. Today, the sea advances without respite. It has consumed about 40 square miles of Louisiana per year over the past 50 years. Various human actions inadvertently tipped the balance:

- Jetties at the Mississippi mouth succeeded in getting the river to help maintain its own depth for shipping, but they shoot the "mudstream" off the continental shelf; its sediments are needed to provide the bulk of land-building material.

- Levees and the Old River Control Structure (see page 301) prevent the river from switching to a new delta lobe, a natural event that would also distribute more sediment locally and less to the deep Gulf.
- Canals, built primarily as paths for oil industry barges, strengthen the flow of sea water inland, especially the storm surges that draw sediment out to sea. The canals also admit saltwater and sulfides, in some places killing marsh vegetation that formerly fortified the land against storm surges.
- Dams far upriver capture sediment that would otherwise contribute to delta building here.
- Sea level is rising because of global warming, which by the best estimates is partly natural but primarily human-caused.

Scientists and government have worked together to design projects that might halt the loss of southern Louisiana, but they come with a staggering price tag, most of which has yet to be appropriated.

Port activity you see along the Louisiana and east Texas coasts mostly serves offshore oil and gas in the Gulf, which plays a major role in U.S. production. Decisions will be made about either expanding or moving those facilities, depending on prognoses for the future habitability of coastal communities. Perhaps they will evolve into artificial islands.

Westward, oil continues as a major theme in the Texas portion of the corridor, especially in the refineries and port facilities near Houston.

WESTBOUND: Go to p. 46

Mobile Bay, Alabama

LOOK FOR a wide bay extending north from the Gulf, with several rivers and their deltas entering the bay at its northern end; the port facilities along the western side of the bay.

❶ Mobile River ❷ Tensaw River ❸ Middle River ❹ I-65 ❺ Apalachee River ❻ I-10 ❼ Mobile Bay ❽ Chickasaw ❾ Blakely Island ❿ Mobile

Upper Mobile Bay comprises a maze of channels and low islands. Some channels are dredged by the Army Corps of Engineers for shipping access to the port of Mobile and to cities upstream. McDuffie Island, at the south end of the port, handles coal. The intermodal port just north of downtown transfers containers between ships and trains. Across Mobile Channel, Blakely Island's docks handle petroleum, iron ore, and half of the wood products moving through the Gulf ❾. The tanks on Blakely store petroleum; the bay also has a refinery—one of three in Alabama—in the northern suburb of Chickasaw ❽. Carnival Cruise Lines make Mobile a port of call.

The delta at the north end of Mobile Bay is fed by the Mobile River ❶, which in turn is fed by the Alabama, Tombigbee, Black Warrior, Coosa, Tallapoosa, and Cahaba. This drainage basin covers 44,000 square miles in four states and supplies one of the greatest water yields per square mile among U.S. river drainage basins.

The delta begins where a river ❶ divides into distributary streams ❷❸❺. The river gradient decreases and the river slows. Sediments carried by the river drop out in increasing quantities. The Mobile and Alabama rivers meander above the delta, and the distributaries do so within the delta. Rivers erode their banks on the outer edge of meander loops and deposit sediment on the inner banks. Parallel arcs of older meanders within the largest meanders show that they are growing. Islands develop, some with small interior lakes. Low levees separate the islands from the channels. During floods, levees are often breached, flooding the islands. Minor splays or channels may connect the interior lake with a channel. Over time, the meandering channels will fill the entire bay.

One might wonder why this large drainage area has not already filled the bay. The delta is surprisingly small for the volume of sediment arriving annually, suggesting that perhaps the drainage basin is young and has not been feeding the delta with sediment for as long as other rivers with larger deltas on the Gulf.

The Mobile Bay and delta lie in a remarkably straight-margined valley. For many years, geologists inferred a graben, or block of crust dropped between two faults, underlying them. That hypothesis was tested by the oil industry. Exploration under the Bay and adjoining Gulf used a dense grid of seismic data and many wells. In 1979, the wells discovered the "Norphlet Trend," a deep gas play (more than 20,000 feet below the surface) with higher pressures and temperatures than the industry had ever seen. The fields did not begin production until 1988, as they required new engineering techniques to handle the heat and pressure.

The oil geologists and geophysicists found no data confirming a graben, so a new hypothesis was formulated to account for Mobile Bay: The river was redirected here during the last glacial maximum, 18,000 years ago. At that time, much of the world's water was tied up as ice in continental glaciers. Consequently, sea level was 200 feet lower than today, putting the Gulf coastline 60 miles south of its present position. River systems entering the Gulf nearby were established much earlier and had built up the fluctuating shoreline with sediment for millions of years, so their gradients as they crossed the exposed shelf were low, reflecting equilibrium developed during earlier glacial maxima. The newly developing Mobile River had a steeper gradient, so its upstream tributaries eroded headward farther than did other rivers. The Mobile Bay drainage basin grew during the last glacial maximum as its streams cut through drainage divides upstream and captured streams from adjoining basins. Throughout that time, its sediments dropped mainly at the river mouth, 60 miles south, so at Mobile Bay it was free to carve a deep valley. Finally, melting glaciers raised sea level and flooded the newly eroded valley. The present delta was deposited within the last 18,000 years.

Mississippi Birdfoot Delta and Chandeleur Islands, Louisiana

LOOK FOR a long north-trending arc of sandbars; a crowfoot-like splay of leveed river channels crossing tidal flats.

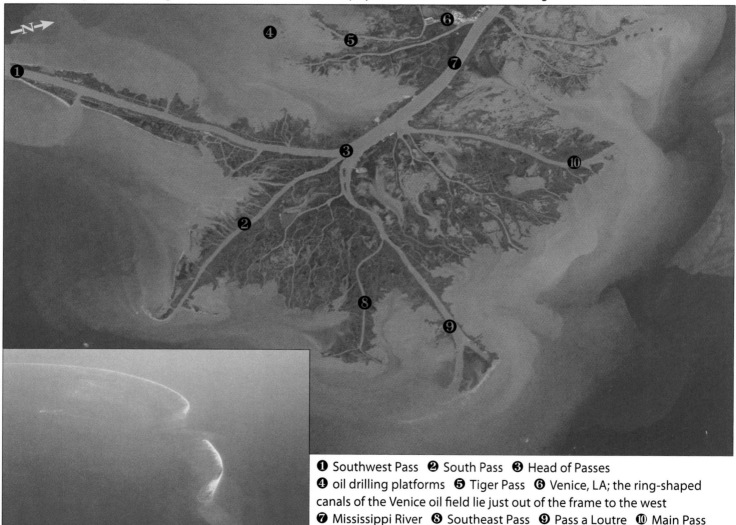

❶ Southwest Pass ❷ South Pass ❸ Head of Passes
❹ oil drilling platforms ❺ Tiger Pass ❻ Venice, LA; the ring-shaped canals of the Venice oil field lie just out of the frame to the west
❼ Mississippi River ❽ Southeast Pass ❾ Pass a Loutre ❿ Main Pass

Facing north: Chandeleur Islands, with Chandeleur Sound behind them

Southeast of New Orleans at the river hamlet of Pilottown and the Head of Passes ❸, the Mississippi River divides into a distributary system, delivering its waters and sediments into the Gulf of Mexico via the modern delta lobe descriptively called the Birdfoot. Fort Jackson and Fort St. Philip were built to defend New Orleans in the early 19th century at Plaquemines Bend, 15 miles above the Head of Passes. Fort Jackson is now below sea level; Fort St. Philip lies in flooded ruins across the river.

The Chandeleur Islands sketch a graceful arc between the Birdfoot and the coast of Mississippi. The islands you see will appear a bit different from this photo, because they are heavily reworked by each passing hurricane or tropical storm.

Change is the norm here. The Chandeleur lighthouse, originally built onshore near the north end of the islands in 1848, was destroyed in 1852 by storms and was rebuilt. Destroyed again by a hurricane in 1893, it was rebuilt in 1896. In 1998, Hurricane Georges passed over the islands, removing so much sand that the lighthouse was left in open water. The islands were rebuilt by sediment carried by longshore drift in the following seven years, but the lighthouse remained about 100 feet offshore. In 2005, Hurricane Dennis passed over the islands, removing more sand and leaving the lighthouse farther offshore. Hurricane Katrina swept up a few weeks later, removing so much sand that the lighthouse foundered and now is gone. An Air Force radio tower marks the site.

The larger islands display some vegetation: light green cordgrass and dark green mangrove. The mangroves host thousands of Magnificent Frigatebirds during the summer. In the absence of tropical storms, the islands acquire sand carried by longshore drift from the delta. The net trend over the past hundred years has been to shift the islands north and west, toward New Orleans.

The Chandeleurs are vestiges of an earlier Mississippi delta lobe. The Mississippi River has delivered enormous volumes of sediments to the Gulf of Mexico for 150 million years, piling sediment more than 10 miles thick. The Mississippi began building its modern delta southwest of Baton Rouge about 8,000 years ago. About 5,000 years ago, the river cut a new, shorter channel to the Gulf, building a delta lobe due south of Baton Rouge. Like other lobes before it, this shortcut turned itself into a long route as it built out into the Gulf. After 1,000 years, the Mississippi cut yet another, shorter channel to the Gulf, eastward beneath the future site of New Orleans. Without continued delivery of new sediments, the older lobes subsided beneath the Gulf, once again offering possible shortcuts. About 2,500 years ago, the Mississippi abandoned its southeastern delta for a new route to the Gulf, again due south of Baton Rouge, and that one was abandoned in favor of the current channel about 1,000 years ago. The process of successive delta deposition and abandonment has not finished. Geologists anticipate that the river will again flow due south of Baton Rouge to build yet another delta lobe before long. Indeed, today, about 20 percent of the river flows down the Atchafalaya River to the Gulf.

The Chandeleur Islands mark the eastern margin of the old St. Bernard lobe, the eastward delta lobe that was active roughly 4,000 to 2,500 years ago. When the river switched to a path west of the modern Birdfoot lobe, it cut off the St. Bernard lobe's supply of sediment, and the sands and muds of the St. Bernard lobe compressed under their own weight. The surface subsided beneath sea level, creating the saltwater bays named Lakes Pontchartrain, Maurepas, and Borgne, north and east of New Orleans. The St. Bernard lobe's outer margin also subsided, but sand drifting over to it from the Birdfoot lobe has kept bits of it—the Chandeleur Islands—above sea level. Dredging of the Mississippi River channel over the last century, together with the many dams upriver, especially on the Missouri, has sharply reduced the flow of sediment to the Gulf. This reduction in inputs makes it unlikely that the Chandeleur Islands will recoup the mass they lose during storms.

Only a network of pumping stations and canals built and maintained by the Army Corps of Engineers prevents the Atchafalaya from capturing a larger share of the Mississippi's flow. (See next page.) This system has not yet been tested by a tropical storm stalling over the lower Mississippi River for a week or more. Once the Mississippi takes the shorter route to the Gulf, the Birdfoot Delta will subside beneath the Gulf, and a new set of marginal islands may develop south and west of the Chandeleur Islands, which will sink beneath the waves.

Ports of Louisiana, near Baton Rouge

LOOK FOR port facilities scattered along the Mississippi River: seagoing ships, wharves, strings of barges tied up, grain elevators, oil tank farms. Also look for channels crossed by dams right where they leave the river's west side.

For more than 250 miles, the lowermost Mississippi River is a long, strung-out port interspersed with riverside farms and the occasional town. Although no divisions are apparent, the river is divided administratively into four ports: Baton Rouge (85 river miles long), South Louisiana (54 miles), New Orleans (33), and Plaquemines (80) down in the Birdfoot Delta. South Louisiana alone transfers more tonnage than any other U.S. port, and the four collectively are in a dead heat with the other top three ports in the world (Singapore, Rotterdam, and Shanghai). Different front-runners pull ahead from year to year.

The scene doesn't look like the world's busiest port. Rail yards and truck parking lots are scarce to nonexistent. Port facilities ❾ are outnumbered by bucolic riverside farms distinctively patterned in long, skinny, often tapered fields ❿ that splay out like fans around river bends (or around oxbow lakes, or even around bends that no longer have water in them at all). Centuries ago, when the river still occupied each of those bends, the original settlers laid out these "long lots," giving each farm a little piece of riverbank in the traditional French pattern. Slender plots became slenderer still when landowners died and their heirs divided their inheritances.

The ports look deceptively low-key for the simple reason that their chief cargos arrive in barges and pipelines. The top exports are grains. Soybeans, corn, wheat, and rice grow in the nation's heartland and float here on barges via the Missouri, Mississippi, Ohio, and Tennessee rivers. These port facilities transfer them from barges to seagoing vessels, perhaps after storage in grain elevators.

Crude oil is the top import. The oil refining and petrochemical industries, as well as the oil and gas pipelines, became concentrated long ago in southeast Texas and Louisiana, close to the oil fields and to ports. When the United States shifted from exporting to importing crude, the oil-related industries were still here, so this is where imported crude is delivered and where many of its refined and petrochemical products then ship from. Houston, for

the same reason, is the second-highest-tonnage U.S. port, whereas Los Angeles and New York/New Jersey, handling more manufactured goods than raw commodities, rank highest in number of containers shipped. Transferring bulk cargoes to and from ships is thoroughly mechanized, requiring only a handful of workers and enabling most Louisiana port facilities to be scattered along the river, well away from urban centers.

Economic inertia—specifically, the desire to keep all the port activities right where they are—forces the Army Corps of Engineers to lock horns with the Mississippi River in a unique water project. All 250 miles of port are on the river's delta; it is in the nature of the lower Mississippi, following the dictates of gravity, to jump its banks and pursue an entirely new course, building a new delta lobe, every thousand years or so. (See page 298.) Continuously depositing sediment, the river builds natural levees that raise it above the surrounding plain. The river breaches these levees during floods and does not climb back up into its old bed when the flood subsides. Man-made levees postpone river course changes while inexorably raising the river's channel ever higher above the plain, as you can see from your window with the right light.

The Mississippi apparently found its next course 150 years ago. It was gradually shifting its flow from the old to the new until 1963, when the Army Corps intervened. The corps built and operates four dams ❷❺ parallel to the river's west bank to prevent more than 30 percent of Mississippi water from falling out of the main riverbed and into those lower channels—except when floods threaten. Then the floodgates open.

A few miles west, the two channels ❹❼ join the Red River ❻, a Mississippi tributary prior to 1831. Together, they become the Atchafalaya (a-CHA-fa-LIE-a) River ❽, flowing south on a much shorter path to the Louisiana Gulf coast. Shorter is also steeper and inevitably preferred by the river. Many knowledgeable observers think that Ol' Man River will have his way sooner or later, forcing the engineers to reconceive the ports of Louisiana.

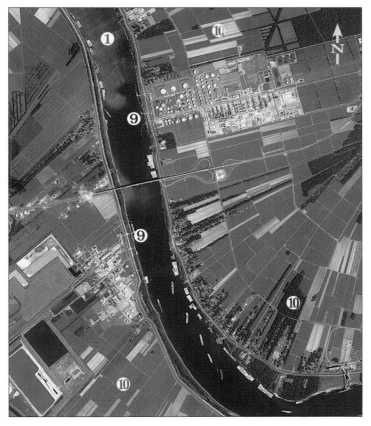

❶ Mississippi River ❷ Old River Control Structure, the main floodgates for outflow to the Atchafalaya ❸ Louisiana State Penitentiary, Angola ❹ Outflow Channel to the Atchafalaya ❺ Old River Lock ❻ Red River ❼ Old River, a long bend that the main river channel occupied until it was diverted at Shreve's Cut-off in 1831; one leg of the Old is now the barge canal, while another is drained except for a few lakes. ❽ Atchafalaya River ❾ port facilities just east of Donaldsonville, LA ❿ long lots

Houston, Texas

LOOK FOR widely separate clusters of industrial and office buildings; a waterway with refineries southeast of the center city.

Facing east-northeast ❶ I-610, the inner loop freeway ❷ I-10 ❸ Buffalo Bayou flanked by refineries and tank farms ❹ Gulf Freeway I-45 to William P. Hobby Airport ❺ I-45 ❻ Memorial Parkway ❼ Memorial Park ❽ The Galleria ❾ Rice University and Medical Center ❿ Reliant Astrodome. Astronaut view about 7 mi. across, showing only the central part of the metro area.

Flights using William P. Hobby Airport cross Houston, the fourth-largest city in the United States, affording passengers a panorama of freeways, tollways, heavy industry next to residential development, disparate collections of office blocks, and the Houston Ship Channel. Very little is old. Downtown Houston, with its hotels, convention center, arts district, and sports stadia, is near the original site of the city. Houston's largest shopping mall, The Galleria ❾, lies 5 miles west; Reliant Astrodome ❿ is 4 miles south. NASA's Johnson Space Center is about 20 miles southeast, a location rarely seen from commercial flights. Buffalo Bayou ❸ flows east through central Houston, widens into the Houston Ship Channel, and empties into Galveston Bay.

In 1836, a few months after the Texas army won independence from Mexico at San Jacinto, the brothers Augustus Chapman Allen and John Kirby Allen founded Houston at the "navigable limit" of Buffalo Bayou. They hired Thomas and Gail Borden to lay a grid of 80-foot-wide streets, including the 100-foot-wide Texas Avenue. (Gail Borden later invented condensed milk.) The brothers named the city for the president of Texas and hero of the Battle of San Jacinto, Sam Houston, and persuaded the Texas legislature to make their town the capital of the Republic. Two years later, the same legislature moved the capital to a more central location, Austin.

As Texas has no major navigable rivers, early settlements were on or near bays of the Gulf of Mexico. Early farming developed along river floodplains. Coastal towns competed to provide external markets for agricultural products, such as cotton, grains, and hides, and to provide manufactured goods to the plantations and farms. Before the Civil War, a regional rail network developed around Houston to move freight between its port and the landlocked interior. Rail construction halted during the war and resumed in earnest only after 1875, when Houston was finally connected by rail to the Midwest, Northeast, and West Coast.

The flurry of railroad construction created a market for the timber of the Piney Woods. Main rail lines through east Texas enabled mills to build a system of local logging railroads. At the end of the century, lumber was the state's principal manufacture. Beaumont, 90 miles east of Houston, became the lumber center; Houston, the financial and trade center. As with earlier farm-market towns, Houston used its rails to deliver raw materials from the hinterland to the Gulf while sending finished goods to the logging towns.

The U.S. Congress designated Houston a port in 1870 and two years later appropriated $10,000 to improve the ship channel. Large ships would dock at Galveston to transfer their loads to smaller vessels bound for Houston, where the loads would be transferred onto carts or trains. A commercial rivalry between Houston and Galveston lasted until 1900, when it ended in an abrupt cataclysm, the hurricane that swept Galveston away, leaving 8,000 dead. Seeing the advantages of an inland port, Congress appropriated $1 million to deepen the Houston Ship Channel to 25 feet.

In 1901, the Spindletop oil field was discovered outside Beaumont. Major fields at Humble and Goose Creek followed in 1905 and 1908. Oil soon fed two entirely new industries that grew on the shores of the ship channel: refining and petrochemicals. Sinclair Oil built the first large refinery in 1918. Today, 10 oil refineries yield the full array of transportation fuels, and 13 ethylene plants yield the variety of plastics we take for granted. Almost half of U.S. commodity petrochemicals are made in Houston. Almost all this activity ❸ is located along the ship channel.

Houston is known among planners and developers for its rejection of zoning. The city planning commission proposed zoning ordinances in 1929, only to see the city council reject them then and again in 1948 and 1962.

Nonetheless, the city is not entirely unplanned. A master plan recommending construction of limited-access highways was adopted in 1942. The plan identified rights of way for both the Gulf Freeway (part of I-45) and Memorial Parkway ❹❺. By the time they were completed a decade later, additional freeways were planned or proposed. In 1952, planners drew the Beltway 8 route through country well removed from developments then under way. Freeway planning continues. The present highway system, comprising concentric loops connected by more or less radial arteries, follows the philosophy, if not the exact plan, adopted in 1942. As you fly above the Houston freeways, observe traffic flow and judge for yourself whether this form of regional planning is effective.

Bryan, Texas

LOOK FOR a university campus; rural areas with both farm and forest land.

❶ TX Hwy. 6　**❷** Bryan　**❸** Texas A&M Research Annex　**❹** Brazos River　**❺** Easterwood Field　**❻** Texas A&M University

From Dallas south to Houston, flights cross a variety of natural regions devoted to agriculture. The Dallas–Fort Worth area lies on the blackland prairie, the southern extension of the midwestern tall-grass prairie. Prior to cultivation, urbanization, suburbanization, and exurbanization, the flat uplands held prairie with few trees, and the rivers and streams were bordered by oak, elm, cottonwood, and pecan. The soils are weathered from limestones.

To the south, the post oak savanna develops on uplands wherever the soil is derived from sand or claystone. Although the tall-grass prairie also develops here, scattered short post oak and blackjack oak trees distinguish the savanna from blackland prairie.

Houston lies within the zone of Gulf coast marshes and prairies where the sandy soils are just above sea level and so are poorly drained. Tall-grass prairie and post oak savanna occur locally, with post oak, live oak, acacia, and honey mesquite in the savannas. Your flight may take you east of Houston into the East Texas Piney Woods. The uplands' mixed forest includes loblolly, shortleaf, and longleaf pines, whereas diverse hardwood species dominate the stream courses. The lumber industry has planted fast-growing slash pine over thousands of acres.

Blackland prairie and post oak savanna were both widely converted to cotton and grain cultivation between 1850 and 1950. Today, only half of the blackland prairie and even less of the savanna are used for crops. Livestock grazing has increased, and much of the present farm production is for livestock feed.

In this setting, it is not surprising to find Texas A&M University ❸, the state's oldest public higher education institution. In 1862, the U.S. Congress passed the Morrill Land-Grant Act to encourage states to found schools "where the leading object shall be, without excluding other scientific and classical studies and including military tactics, to teach such branches of learning as are related to agriculture and the mechanic arts." The act allotted 30,000 acres of federal public land to each senator and representative. Texas was entitled to 180,000 acres, but there were no federal acres within the state, so it received 180,000 acres of federal land in Colorado and sold them for $0.75 an acre. The state legislature appropriated $75,000 for construction of the first campus buildings on land donated by citizens around Bryan, the Brazos County seat.

Upon opening in 1876, the university offered no courses in agriculture. Within three years, a farmers' protest led to the removal of the first president and faculty and the adoption of a mandatory agriculture and engineering curriculum. The student population responded unfavorably, declining from 500 to about 80 students in 1883, when the University of Texas opened in Austin. Texas A&M languished until 1887, when the Texas Agricultural Experiment Station was founded there. The two universities were funded by the Texas Permanent University Fund, consisting mainly of vast underutilized acreage, so they were cash-strapped until oil was found on Fund lands in 1923. With their oil royalties, they built strong programs in petroleum engineering and in geology.

Texas A&M rests on Paleocene sediments, 65 million to 55 million years old. Few outcrops interrupt the rolling country around Bryan, except along the banks of the Brazos and its larger tributaries. Geologists at A&M claim that these are the best-studied outcrops in Texas. More than simply being available to students, they are a good place to test one of the most interesting geological hypotheses of the past three decades.

In 1980, Luis and Walter Alvarez reported anomalously high iridium concentrations in sediments at the Cretaceous-Paleocene boundary. The two hypothesized that only an extraterrestrial object, such as an asteroid, could deliver so much iridium to one small band of sediment and that the impact of an asteroid on Earth at that time (65.5 million years ago) accounted for the disappearance of the dinosaurs. One test of these ideas required an uninterrupted section of sediments deposited continuously over a period encompassing the iridium layer. North America's best such outcrop is on the Brazos River ❹ near Bryan; hence the intense interest of geologists in the location. The impact-extinction hypothesis was widely debated within the geological community, until a new data set provided its confirmation. In 1990, oil industry data revealed an impact crater in the Gulf of Mexico north of the Yucatán Peninsula. Exploration wells drilled in the area confirmed its age to be the same as the end of the dinosaur era, the end of the Mesozoic Era, and the beginning of the Cenozoic Era and flourishing evolution of the mammals: 65.5 million years ago.

San Antonio and Austin, Texas

LOOK FOR the subtle topographic rise, and series of large reservoirs, of the long Balcones Escarpment, trending northeast-southwest between these two cities and generally parallel to and west of Interstate 35.

San Antonio ❶ San Pedro Springs ❷ Alamo ❸ Alamo Bowl ❹ San Antonio River ❺ I-35

Austin ❻ Robert Mueller Municipal Airport (closed) ❼ Lyndon Baines Johnson Library and Museum ❽ University of Texas ❾ Texas capitol ❿ Colorado River

These two Texas cities lie on the Balcones Fault zone, the source of freshwater springs that supported both native and early European settlements. The fault zone, from north of Fort Worth southwest past San Antonio to Del Rio, divides the Great Plains from the Gulf Coastal Plain. It produces the east-facing Balcones Escarpment, visible from the Colorado River ❿ south. The Texas Hill Country, stretching west from the escarpment, can be thought of as the relatively well-watered eastern part of the Edwards Plateau. Westward, the plateau receives less moisture from the Gulf of Mexico, and the trees of the Hill Country give way to prairies and then steppe.

Limestones underlie much of the Hill Country, forming a low-relief karst landscape with springs, disappearing streams, dry valleys, and caves. Cretaceous rocks of the Edwards Plateau are more resistant to erosion; the younger Gulf Plain sandstones and claystones are not, but they do maintain surface streams and rivers.

San Antonio, with five Spanish missions, became the capital of Spanish Texas in 1773. Spaniards founded San Antonio de Béxar Presidio in 1718; Canary Islanders founded San Fernando de Béxar nearby in 1731. The city's population declined during the 1810–13 Mexican War of Independence but rebounded sufficiently to warrant the siege of Béxar in 1835 and the siege of the Alamo ❷ in 1836, during the Texas Revolution. After Texas joined the United States, the city grew rapidly, aided by immigrants from central Europe.

Spanish colonists brought cattle, but not the Texas longhorn hybrid, which arose later, after English cattle breeds were introduced. During the Civil War, millions of cattle roamed wild across central Texas. Postbellum San Antonio became the point of departure for cattle drives to the Midwest.

By 1877, it was the largest city in the state and had a German-speaking majority population. Rail service reached San Antonio that year, bringing a wave of newcomers from the southern states, followed by an additional wave from Mexico after the 1910 Mexican Revolution. San Antonio missed out on the oil booms that fed Dallas and Houston early in the 20th century. Both active and retired military bases around the city date from World War II and have been a major economic driver ever since.

Interstate 35 ❺ runs north from the Mexican border at Laredo, through the centers of both San Antonio and Austin. Trucks comprise a quarter or more of the traffic, a significant fraction being international trucks taking advantage of NAFTA. A 12-lane toll road may be built in response to the growth of both I-35 cities and international traffic.

Austin was founded in 1839 specifically to be the capital of the Republic of Texas and to bear the name of Texas's founder, Stephen F. Austin. The site was chosen for its central location on the Colorado River ❿ in an area with abundant flowing springs. The original plat was 14 square blocks centered on Congress Avenue, running from the river up to the site of the future capitol building. Subsequent streets ran in diverse directions. Sam Houston, the second president of Texas, disliked Austin, ordering the capital moved first to his namesake town and later to Washington-on-the-Brazos. In 1845, a Texas constitutional convention agreed to join the United States and reinstated Austin as the state capital. In 1881, the legislature finally came up with funds for a capitol building by selling 3 million acres in the Panhandle. Standing 15 feet taller than the U.S. Capitol, it is the largest state capitol building ❾.

Austin's population doubled in the four years 1871–75, when it was the westernmost Texas rail depot, only to decline as the railroads reached farther west. The population grew again by 66 percent during the Great Depression, supported by the growing state government and university, by exceptional WPA largesse, and by a powerful congressman. Two of Lyndon B. Johnson's earliest legislative coups were dams to create Lake Austin and Lake Travis.

The University of Texas, four blocks north of the capitol, is the fifth-largest university in the United States and hosts the most-visited U.S. presidential library, Johnson's ❼. It was not heavily visited in its first years. The retired populist president then promoted his facility by opening it during home football games. Announcements in the stadium remind fans that the library across the street has many clean restrooms.

WESTBOUND: Go to p. 64

Yates Oil Field at Iraan, Texas

LOOK FOR a speckly white net of oil pad service roads just west of a north-south canyon in an otherwise little-developed arid expanse.

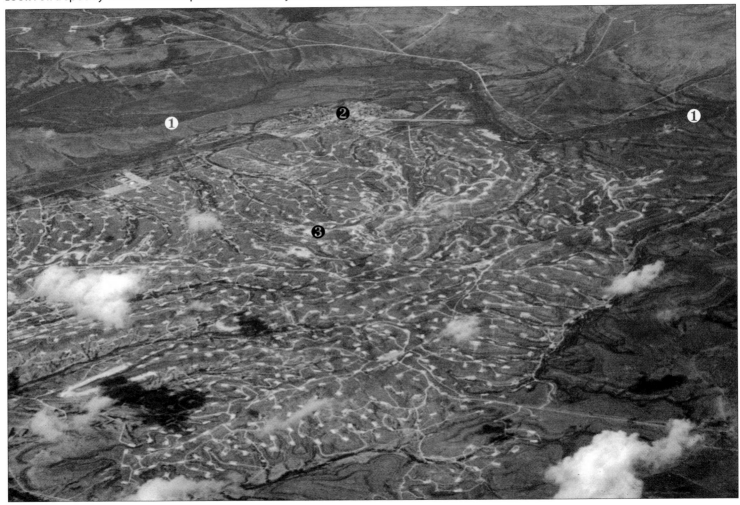

Facing northeast ❶ Pecos River ❷ Iraan ❸ oil well pads and service roads of the Yates Oil Field

EASTBOUND: Go to p. 64

The Pecos River runs south from New Mexico in a broad floodplain until it reaches the resistant Cretaceous sandstones and limestones of the Edwards Plateau. There, the river and its tributaries carve broad canyons with meandering patterns similar to those farther upstream, indicating that the channels predate plateau uplift.

Saltcedar, or tamarisk, lines most stream banks. This small Eurasian tree was introduced to the United States as an ornamental in the early 19th century and was later used to stabilize riverbanks in the arid West. Now the tree causes problems beyond merely spreading aggressively: It sucks large volumes of water out of streams and deposits large volumes of salt. Saltcedar thickets along the Pecos reduce the river's flow so much that various government bodies are trying to eradicate it. If you see naked banks on the Pecos, you will know that their efforts were locally successful.

The small town of Iraan ❷ sits beside the Pecos ❶ about 10 miles northwest of Interstate 10. Just southwest of Iraan, you cannot miss the Yates Oil Field, with hundreds of well pads and a net of white dirt service roads ❸. Iraan and this giant oil field are both named for the ranchers whose land sprouted gushers: Ira and Ann Yates.

The white limestone beds around Iraan lie almost flat. The first oil geologists in the area saw that they form a slight arch rising to a crest under the present network of well pads. (If the sun is very low, you may be able to see the gentle slopes.) Such arches, or anticlines, are ideal traps for oil and gas.

For many years, Texas oil producers "knew" no oil was to be found west of the Pecos, yet a small oil field at Big Lake, about 30 miles northeast of Iraan, sparked some hope in wildcatters. The conventional wisdom was overturned on October 28, 1926 when the Ira G. Yates 1-A well hit oil 992 feet beneath the surface. The remarkably shallow well produced 450 barrels per day, enough to encourage drilling a second well, which produced 3,440 barrels per day, and further wells with three more near-surface hits. In June 1927, the sixth well in the field flowed 500 barrels of oil per hour from 1,045 feet. Two years later, a Yates well would produce a world record rate of 204,672 barrels per day. Today, we know that the Yates field fills the anticline on the Pecos with more than 1.25 billion barrels of oil.

It takes a remarkable reservoir to yield such prolific rates. Most oil fields store oil in small pores between grains of sand or in minute fractures in solid rock. The narrow pores and fractures limit the percentage volume of oil within the rock and the rate of flow through the rock. The Yates field stores oil in wide fractures and small caves, yielding spectacularly higher volumes of oil and production rates.

The Yates field holds a special place in history, reaching from Iraan to Iran and the rest of the world. Following the rapid spread of railroads across the West, political opposition arose to the railroads' exercise of their freight oligopoly. Texas established a railroad commission to regulate railroads, terminals, wharves, and other transportation companies in the state.

When the first 18 Yates wells proved sufficient, in 1928, to pump oil faster than the first single pipeline could carry it away, the commission concluded that it, rather than the pipeline company, should get to decide how much oil each well owner could ship. It set a "fair" quota for each well, taking the maximum production rate of each well and lowering all by an equal percentage to fit the pipeline capacity. The commission even told the oilmen exactly how deep they could drill.

The commission soon expanded this far-reaching concept, the pipeline "common carrier," to embrace "prudent oil field practices," after the new East Texas oil field reduced the cost of oil to pennies per barrel. In the ensuing decades, the commission moved to support oil prices by restricting Texas production.

The example did not go unnoticed. Juan Pablo Pérez Alfonso studied the Texas Railroad Commission while in exile following the 1948 coup in his native Venezuela. In 1960, he and Abdullah al-Tariki of Saudi Arabia convened a meeting of oil exporters to respond to reduced oil prices imposed on them by Standard Oil. Thus was born OPEC, the Organization of the Petroleum Exporting Countries, closely modeled on the Texas Railroad Commission.

WESTBOUND: Go to p. 180

CORRIDOR 12:
Boston–Chicago

St. La

64

LAKE ONTARIO

NEW YORK

276

Rochester

Syracuse

314

Buffalo

Albany

316

16

Poughkeepsie

PENNSYLVANIA

10

14

12

Scranton

8

gstown

The FAA preferred routes for this city pair are the one eastbound and one westbound route on our map. Portions of these routes are also frequently used by flights between Chicago and Toronto or between Boston and Toronto, Buffalo, Detroit, or the West Coast, as well as between New York and many points west. The result is a lot of traffic over the NAVAIDs near Troy, Rochester, and especially Jamestown, New York.

This corridor almost exclusively crosses areas that were covered by ice sheets more than once in the past 2 million years. As we are generally near the margins of the farthest glacial advances, the time spent under ice was brief in proportion to the entire Pleistocene. The five Great Lakes, certainly the largest features of Corridor 12, display especially deep ice sheet erosion. In terms of longer-term geologic history, the western part of the flight is over the Michigan Basin, and the rest is over the Appalachian Mountains. Even though you are in the densely populated Northeast, you will see plenty of forest, largely thanks to the hilly, thin-soiled Appalachian topography.

Westbound flights frequently fly right over Niagara Falls. From the air, it may be even more difficult than from the ground to ignore the utterly urban context of this famous natural wonder. Nevertheless, it is an impressive waterfall. It can be the world's largest waterfall if the issue is framed just right. It has the greatest year-round average natural flow of any waterfall with a clean vertical drop. "Natural" is the key word, restricting the discussion to the average flow of 120 years ago. Currently, more than half of the Niagara River's flow bypasses the falls, diverted into tunnels to generate electricity in both Canada and the United States. In theory, the flow could be brought back with the flick of a few switches. (The two nations should declare an annual Biggest Waterfall Day during Victoria Falls's dry season and turn on the taps.) Flows are thoroughly regulated, with different rules for night, day, summer, winter, the tourist season, and so on. Regulations accommodate withdrawals of water from four Great Lakes upstream, as well as ship traffic through the locks of the Welland Canal, a portion of the St. Lawrence Seaway that you cross a few minutes west of the Niagara River. It is lit up at night, as are the falls.

Diversions maintain a 9:1 ratio between water volume over the Horseshoe Falls and the American Falls, whose share would dwindle without help. Even with help, the American Falls don't carry enough current to sweep away the blocks of dolomite that crumble from the brink. You may be able to see a talus slope of blocks about halfway up the falls, whereas the Horseshoe Falls drop into a deep plunge pool with sufficient turbulence to move the debris on downstream. Yes, that's the horseshoe-shaped one.

The falls exist thanks to at least two things: the same erosion-resistant Silurian dolostones lying on top of softer shales that are seen throughout the 650 miles of the Niagara Escarpment (see page 274); and their recent Ice Age history. Dolostone counts as an erosion-resistant rock over short time scales like this rapidly retreating waterfall, even though over longer scales, it dissolves and produces karst topography. The falls were born about 12,300 years ago as the ice retreated from the area and have eroded their way 8 miles upstream over those years, creating an 8-mile gorge with rapids and whirlpools.

This great river is the St. Lawrence, of course, although the four short interlake sections have other names: the Niagara, Detroit, St. Clair, and St. Marys rivers.

EASTBOUND: Start with pp. 24, 20
WESTBOUND: Start with p. 154

Mt. Monadnock, New Hampshire

LOOK FOR a gentle mountain in the shape of a horseshoe opening to the north, standing apart from any comparable mountains.

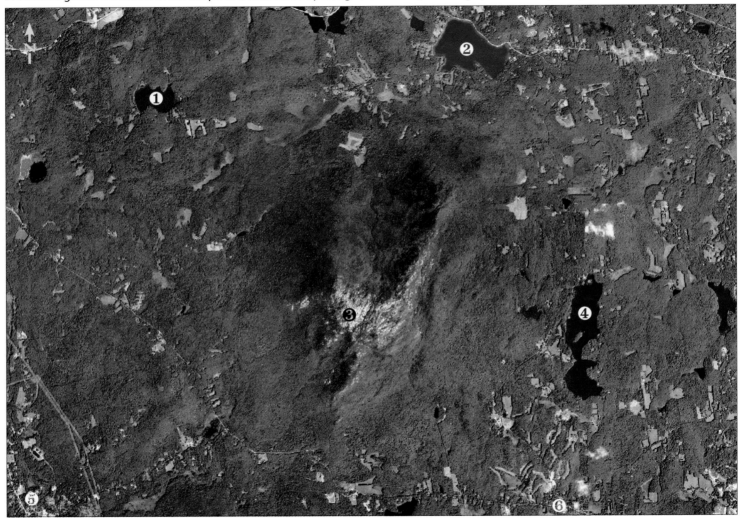

❶ Stone Pond **❷** Dublin Pond **❸** Mt. Monadnock **❹** Thorndike Pond **❺** Troy **❻** Jaffrey Center

EASTBOUND: Go to p. 154

From Mt. Monadnock's summit on a clear day, you can see all six New England states, including office towers in Boston. The summit is the most popular mountaintop hike in New England. ("Most-climbed" or "second-most climbed mountain in the world" are oft-repeated phrases in New Hampshire, but they ignore China's similar claim for Tai Shan; we would hate to argue with the Chinese over who puts more feet on the ground. Tai Shan is but one of five Taoist pilgrimage sites called the Five Great Mountains.)

The geologist William Morris Davis introduced the Algonquian word *monadnock* ("mountain standing alone") into English (or at least into geologist-speak) as a common noun for any mountain isolated on a plain.

Irregular ponds and lakes fill swampy depressions in the surrounding forest. Forest covers all but the highest ridges, which are bare rock. Forest covered them as well when the Europeans first arrived in the 17th century. They cleared the forest for pasture and lit fires repeatedly to maintain open fields. Rain stripped the soil from the summit and deposited it downslope. Forest recolonized the peak after grazing ended in the 19th century.

Thin, rocky ridge crest soils on Monadnock support a community of dwarf shrubs, notably the delicious New England low-bush blueberry. A little lower, red spruce mixes with dwarf shrubs on the upper slopes. The surrounding lowlands support sugar maple, beech, and yellow birch. Small swamps near the ponds and lakes host stands of Atlantic white cedar with red spruce and other conifers.

Sugar maples star in the New England fall color show, which some lucky readers will catch from the air. No other place in the world paints with fall foliage as brilliantly as northeastern North America. The intensity demands a particular combination of frosty nights with sunny days, leading to concern that it may be diminishing, or at least moving north into Canada, with global warming. Sugar maples have declined overall for several decades.

The contrast between New England's thin, stony soils and the upper Midwest's thick, rich soils motivated generations of pioneers. Both regions' soils developed since the time when thousands of feet of ice covered them. Along with different bedrock and different climate, end-glacial events played a big role.

Glaciers that overran mountainous New England first deepened the valleys and then filled them with rock debris. As they melted, the glaciers left long lakes that collected sediments before the majority of them drained. Where the lakes lasted long enough, lakebed sedimentation sorted the glacial debris, leaving some valleys with relatively fine soil on top, without the cobbles and sand characteristic of upland soils.

The deglaciating Midwest had vastly larger temporary lakes; on nearly flat terrain, modest amounts of debris can dam a really big lake. The lakes drained and dried up, and before vegetation took hold, prevailing west winds picked up the finest sediment particles, blowing them as dust and eventually dropping them as great drifts of loess. Plains west of the Missouri were a net donor of loess; a large area east of the Missouri was a net recipient of fabulous loess soil many feet thick. New England's lakes could not compare as loess source areas. Few of New England's soils ever overcame their coarse origin as glacial till.

The roots of the ancient Acadian mountains dominate New England: the granitic White Mountains on the east; folded and thrusted metamorphic rocks across Vermont and into New York. The flight path from Boston to Chicago, south of most of those mountains, crosses rocky hills geologically equivalent to the southeastern Piedmont Province. The mainly granitic and metamorphic rocks date from the Acadian Orogeny, a mountain-building episode caused by the collision of an island arc with North America.

Early Paleozoic sediments laid down on the western margin of the Iapetus Ocean were buried and metamorphosed by heat and pressure. Later, the granitic White Mountains backbone of New Hampshire and the primarily metamorphic Green Mountains backbone of Vermont rose as parallel large arches. They are still topographically elevated today, with the Connecticut River flowing down a narrow structural trough between them.

New England's mountains are part of the Appalachian chain; they share an Acadian-Orogeny Piedmont with their southeastern counterparts. High Appalachian ridges from Alabama to Pennsylvania (and on, after the gap, to Nova Scotia, West Africa, and Spain) record the later Allegheny Orogeny, when Iapetus finally closed, forming the supercontinent Pangaea. When Pangaea broke up, rift volcanism broke out north of Monadnock, leaving Mesozoic granites and minor volcanic rocks in the White Mountains.

WESTBOUND: Go to pp. 154, 312, 276, 20, 24

Troy, New York

LOOK FOR a straight north-south river joined from the west by a meandering smaller river paralleled by a canal with locks.

❶ Mohawk River ❷ Erie Canal; aside from short stretches like this one that needed locks, the eastern portion of the canal consisted of the Mohawk River ❸ Hudson River ❹ Cohoes, NY ❺ Troy

EASTBOUND: Go to pp. 24, 16, 316, 314, 158, 154

Troy sits on the east bank of the Hudson River just downstream from its confluence with the Mohawk River ❶ and upstream and across the Hudson ❸ from Albany. Canals and lock gates near the confluence mark the eastern terminus of the Erie Canal ❷. Competition between the canal and railroads—also visible along both rivers—provided the pivotal drama of several decades of U.S. economic history.

Jesse Hawley, a miller in Geneva, New York, proposed a canal linking the Hudson River with western New York and the Great Lakes. The proposal drew support from New York City's mayor DeWitt Clinton, who arranged funding for "Clinton's Folly" after he was elected governor. The canal opened from Troy to Buffalo on October 26, 1825. Travel time between New York City and the Great Lakes dropped by half, shipping costs, by 90 percent. The canal soon became the premier trade route west of the Appalachians, making New York City the premier U.S. seaport.

A year later, the state chartered a railroad alongside the canal, and it began offering service between Albany and Schenectady in 1831. The Mohawk and Hudson's "DeWitt Clinton" steam engine cut the two-day barge trip between Albany and Schenectady to one hour. (The Mohawk and Hudson merged into the New York Central Railroad in 1853.) The railroads were ultimately the undoing of the canals. Branch rail lines opened into undeveloped areas that canals could not reach. Once freight was on a train, it was rarely reloaded onto a barge. The developers of New York's railroads—Vanderbilt, Gould, Harriman, and others—went on to develop the transcontinental railroads.

A field guide concerned with geology cannot overlook Troy's other claim to fame: It was the birthplace of American geology. In 1830, Troy and London were possibly the two principal centers of geology in the world. Amos Eaton wrote the first local geology treatise published in the United States. He may have been the first to lead a geological field trip. After studying the geology of the Erie Canal in 1823–24, he laid out a precise nomenclature for New York rock formations. At the Rensselaer School (now Rensselaer Polytechnic Institute), which he founded in 1824, he trained a cadre of pioneering geologists, including James Hall, the first New York State geologist. Hall's geosyncline theory of the origin of mountains held sway for a century until toppled by the plate tectonic revolution in the 1960s.

The Hudson rolls past Troy at an elevation of 50 feet. Behind Troy, the land rises 400 feet to a rolling terrace well drained by small streams; farther east, it rises another 200 feet to a terrace marked by small lakes and swamps. Farther east again, the Taconic Range rises to 2,700 feet. Distant ranges frame the scene: the Adirondacks to the northwest; the Shawangunks to the south.

The Mohawk meanders in great bends from Schenectady to Troy. The Hudson, in contrast, flows in a remarkably straight course for its entire length. The Hudson cuts its channel here through lakebeds deposited at the end of the Ice Age. The terminal moraine near New York City dammed waters from the melting glacier, forming Lake Albany between the city and Glens Falls. The lake was 30 miles wide at Schenectady. Albany and Schenectady sit on the deltas of tributaries entering the lake, now slightly higher than the surrounding lakebed. The Hudson eroded a deep channel into the lakebeds upstream as far as Troy. Farther north, rapids obstructed barge traffic until locks were built to circumvent them.

The Ice Age glacial lobe scoured a deep channel in soft sediments underlying the Hudson River valley. These rocks were deposited during 540 million to 470 million years ago on the margin of the Iapetus Ocean, which separated the core of North America from New England, easternmost Canada, and Europe. In one current interpretation, the Iapetus Ocean plate broke and began subducting eastward into the mantle, producing an island arc of volcanoes. The islands eventually collided with North America 450 million years ago, attaching or suturing to North America along the line now traced by the straight north-south Hudson River. This Taconic Orogeny, or mountain-building episode, created mountains from Newfoundland to Alabama. Today's Taconic Range is a tiny remnant of that ancient range, almost lost in the Appalachian system following two subsequent orogenies on much the same axis.

Finger Lakes, New York

LOOK FOR a wishbone-shaped lake in a series of otherwise linear lakes, all aligned roughly north-south.

❶ Pulteney   **❷** Bluff Point, 700 ft. higher than the lake   **❸** Keuka Lake   **❹** vineyards and wineries   **❺** Waneta Lake

Deep lakes in narrow valleys create the moderate local climates demanded by the vineyards ❹ you see on either side of Keuka ❸, Seneca, and Cayuga lakes. If you can't make out fine parallel lines crossing the clearings, don't worry: Most of the farmland in the belts immediately next to Keuka and the two bigger lakes is in vineyards. The deep water absorbs heat in summer and reradiates it slowly all winter; the valley holds the warmed air in place. Glacial till forms the terroir of the Finger Lakes Wine District.

During the Revolutionary War, Generals Sutton and Clinton destroyed Iroquois villages and crops around the Finger Lakes as retribution for Iroquois support of the British. At the end of the Revolution, the native lands were bestowed on veterans in lieu of payment for military service. Agriculture shifted from subsistence farming to commercial orchards and vineyards after the Erie Canal ended the region's isolation in 1825.

The Reverend William Boswick planted vines in 1829 at Hammondsport, at the south end of Lake Keuka. He gave away cuttings of his Catawba and Isabella grapes, which did well throughout the region. The Seneca Lake Winery opened in 1866 with an initial planting of 100 acres. You would be hard pressed to identify those acres today among the thousands now under viniculture. The wine industry flourished until Prohibition in 1919; the largest wineries converted to grape juice, and smaller ones died out. Though Prohibition was repealed in 1933, the industry did not revive until the 1970s, after Charles Fournier and Dr. Konstantin Frank demonstrated that New York could make good wines from the vinifera grape grafted onto rootstocks of American grape species. The first new winery in forty years opened in 1962.

The Finger Lakes highlight the pattern of valleys that glacial ice and meltwater carved into New York's portion of the Allegheny Plateau. The eleven Finger Lakes fill the deepest valleys, with their steep flanks and almost parallel alignment. In western New York, the glaciers advanced over terrain already dissected by rivers. Where the glacial flow aligned with a preexisting valley, erosion at the base of the glacier enlarged and deepened the river valley. Valleys perpendicular to the ice flow were not deepened. We see the result today as "hanging valleys" whose creeks drop as cascades or waterfalls where they enter the main valley. There are many of these along the sides of the Finger Lakes.

The glacial valleys fan out south of the lakes, then come to a halt at a long arc of valleys occupied by the Susquehanna River and two of its tributaries, the Cohocton and Chemung (also by Interstate 86). The rivers drain south to Chesapeake Bay, while the lakes drain north to Lake Ontario and the St. Lawrence. That would come as a surprise to anyone whose knowledge of the region came from seeing it from jetliners because some of the most obvious, conspicuous "river" valleys in the area connect the Finger Lakes to these south-draining rivers—but none of those valleys contains a stream going all the way between the lakes and the rivers. They were carved into their present form first by glaciers, and then by surging meltwater streams at a time when the ice had retreated somewhat but still blocked northward drainage. After the ice retreated beyond the St. Lawrence, the lakes were free to drain northward and hummocky (but otherwise inconspicuous) moraine deposits on the valley floors south of the lakes were enough to block their old courses southward.

The Ontario Lobe was this area's convexity on the southern edge of the Laurentide Ice Sheet. As the glaciers melted at the end of the last Ice Age, the Ontario Lobe's margin retreated northward—not steadily, but stalling several times. (The ice within the lobe kept flowing south, while the location of the melting edge retreated intermittently.) Glaciers continually deliver rock debris caught in the ice to their termini; especially big heaps of debris accumulate at these stall points. These remain after the ice is gone as long ridges called recessional moraines. These remain after the ice is gone as recessional moraines—often long, visible ridges, but in this case camouflaged by their positions on the valley floors.

Finger Lakes bedrock comprises sandstones and shales of the Devonian Catskill Delta. Collision between North America and Africa created a mountain range in eastern New York, extending southwest to Alabama. Voluminous sediments ran down the mountain slopes to form a delta on the east shore of a marine basin west of the range.

WESTBOUND: Go to pp. 20, 24

Ketchikan

Prince Rupert

Masset 326

Coast

Skidegate

HECATE STRAIT

Bella Coola

Bella Bella

CORRIDOR 13:
Anchorage–Seattle

Port Hardy

Tofin

Stunningly unlike the others, this corridor views terrain that's wilder, steeper, icier, and less marked by the human hand. On a clear day, this is our favorite air route in North America. Get a window seat on the east side of the plane.

Flights tend to stay within a relatively narrow corridor, offering similar views northbound and southbound. With precious little technology on view, three natural science topics come to the fore: forest ecology, glaciers, and plate tectonics.

The coastal rainforests from the Olympic Peninsula to Glacier Bay are a variant of the forest ecosystem southward to central California. (See page 245.) Being farther north diminishes two things— the number of species, and the growth rate of the trees—yet these forests do remarkably well, for their latitude. There is evidence that British Columbia may have grown the world's tallest tree; the candidates, Douglas-firs, were felled more than a century ago. Forests here are generally too wet to carry a fire, partly because the sun, being lower in the sky, can't dry things out as effectively, and partly because summer's share of rainfall increases northward. The very rainiest weather station in North America, with 256 inches a year, is on Vancouver Island's west coast. Gaugeless sites on mountain slopes farther north probably get more.

Most of the way, you'll see land masses incised by long, deep, watery gashes. These are fjords (if open to the sea), straits (if open at both ends), or fjord lakes (if fresh water). There are more fjords here than in Norway and New Zealand put together. Glaciers incised them during the Ice Ages. As you fly north, you will see that the Ice Ages are not quite out the door yet.

Landforms and forests you'll see north of the 49th parallel fall into five sections:

1. The length of Vancouver Island: on the mainland side, 13,000-foot Coast Mountains with massive icecaps and very long fjords; thick forests on both sides, now heavily logged.
2. Between Vancouver Island and Prince of Wales Island: 7,000-foot mountains, modest glaciers, thickly forested slopes

mostly unlogged and now slated to remain so; muskeg instead of forest on flat lowlands. Much of this is relatively far from flight paths.

3. Southeast Alaska: 10,000-foot mountains with massive glaciers on mainland (in the distance); forests, with heavily logged areas here and there, cover 3,000-foot to 5,500-foot mountains on the islands (usually in foreground from east windows).
4. St. Elias Mountains: mountains from 13,000 feet to 19,500 feet (usually at a distance from plane); vast glaciers, few fjords, few islands, few forests, no roads, no towns.
5. Chugach Mountains: 10,000-foot to 13,000-foot mountains (right beneath the plane, partway), fjords, long glaciers; forests present but too small for much logging.

Many of the inter-island straits run in parallel, aligned north-northwest to south-southeast. Glaciers carved the straits; the glaciers followed valleys; the valleys follow faults. North-northwest-slipping faults reflect the motion of the Pacific Plate relative to the North American Plate for tens of millions of years. It has been dragging fragments of continental crust north-northwest up the coast as it drags the part of California outboard of the San Andreas Fault.

Geologists analyze the entire West Coast from northern California to Alaska as an assemblage of pieces called terranes, areas of rocks unlike nearby rocks of the same age, separated from those different rocks by faults on which they have traveled to their present locations. As you read about terranes in this chapter, keep in mind that terrane analysis is a young science. Any block bounded by straightish lines where the rocks on the other side are different may get described as a terrane by some geologist. Over time, many of these terrane names may fall by the wayside, as geologic fieldwork shows some terranes to be parts of other terranes or of the continent.

Prince William Sound, Alaska

LOOK FOR a steep, mountainous coast of fjords with iceberg-calving glaciers and scattered islands, about 30 minutes out of Anchorage.

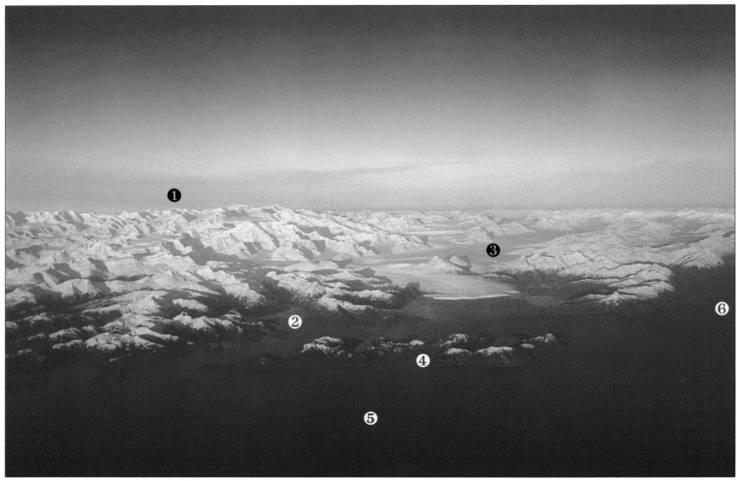

Facing north-northeast ❶ Chugach Mountains ❷ Long Bay ❸ Columbia Glacier ❹ Glacier Island ❺ Prince William Sound ❻ Valdez Arm; Bligh Reef, where the *Exxon Valdez* ran aground, is just out of frame to the right.

A row of long islands outlines Prince William Sound, a bay twice as large as Chesapeake Bay. Glaciers carved its valleys but now are in retreat, leaving long fjords. The Chugach Mountains ❶ rise thousands of feet directly from its shores, hinting at the intensity of plate tectonic activity.

The largest recorded earthquake in the Northern Hemisphere occurred here on Good Friday, March 27, 1964. The 9.2-magnitude event was located beneath the east shore of Unakwik Inlet, about 35 miles west of the Columbia Glacier ❸. Most of Prince William Sound south and east of the epicenter rose—as much as 30 feet at Montague Island—whereas the northwest Kenai Peninsula and adjoining Cook Inlet sank.

Evidence of the quake can be seen on the shores of Turnagain Arm, a long, slender limb of Cook Inlet followed by most flights in or out of Anchorage. Look for stands of dead trees along the shoreline; they contrast sharply in the summer with living brush but in the winter not so sharply. Subsidence during the quake caused saltwater to infiltrate the groundwater, killing many trees. The saltwater also preserved the trees, forming expanses of "ghost forest" around Turnagain Arm. (Other areas of dead trees away from the shores are more likely the work of an infestation of spruce bark beetles. The beetles have devastated large forest tracts on the Kenai Peninsula, but their impact is less severe in areas with high humidity, such as Turnagain Arm.) The earthquake also generated a tsunami, which virtually destroyed the town of Seward, southwest of the sound, and left damage from Kodiak Island to Crescent City, California.

A subsequent Good Friday disaster may loom larger in memory today but is less visible. On March 24, 1989, the oil tanker *Exxon Valdez* broke up on a reef a few miles east of the photo, spilling its contents into Prince William Sound. Virtually all of Alaska's North Slope oil production continues to be piped to Valdez and onto tankers for shipment to the lower 48 states.

Of the glaciers, the Columbia is the largest, the fastest, and likely the fastest melting. It maintained a constant length for 200 years, building a terminal moraine on the bottom of its inlet. Then in 1982, it retreated from its own end moraine, leaving its lower reach floating on the inlet. Without the moraine's support, the glacier calved many icebergs and retreated at least half a mile up the inlet each year. This process is likely to continue until the end of the glacier again rests on the sea floor about nine miles upstream from its 2005 position, leaving nine new miles of fjord.

During the Ice Ages, glacial ice covered the sound and the Kenai Peninsula, much of Cook Inlet, and all but the salient peaks of the Alaska Range. The sound's 150 present-day glaciers form in the mountains, where precipitation ranges from 60 to 170 inches each year, falling mostly as snow: Snowfall measurements have exceeded 900 inches in a year. Many glaciers have been retreating since they were first described by European explorers.

The rocks underlying the sound and the Chugach Mountains include basalts, granites, Mesozoic deep-water sediments, and fragments of an ocean crust. These rocks belong to the Chugach Terrane (see page 319); a smaller Prince William Terrane has also been described in the southern third of the sound. Both terranes formed as accretionary complexes along the Pacific Plate's subduction boundary. Sediments and igneous rocks on the sea floor rode on the moving plate a great distance to the subduction zone. Some of these rocks failed to follow the plate through the subduction zone into the upper mantle, piling up instead against the subduction zone's overriding plate. Over millions of years, these rocks formed a long, narrow belt of material that was accreted, or added, to the continent. The St. Elias Mountains are underlain by Chugach rocks that were buried more deeply than the ones here, resulting in high-grade metamorphism. All the buried rocks rose to the surface on thrust faults, including the major one, along the northwest side of the sound, which bounds the Chugach Terrane.

Malaspina Glacier and Mt. St. Elias, Alaska

LOOK FOR a vast, almost circular apron of glacial ice crossing a flat coastal plain at the foot of high, snowy mountains.

Facing north-northeast **❶** Mt. St. Elias, 18,008 ft. **❷** Mt. Logan, 19,550 ft. **❸** Malaspina Glacier **❹** Yakutat Bay **❺** Gulf of Alaska

The **Malaspina Glacier** is an enormous lobe of ice flowing across the Gulf of Alaska coastal plain. You may be able to trace the glacier into the St. Elias Mountains, where it forms from the merger of several large valley glaciers.

Mt. St. Elias ❶ (18,008 feet) is the tallest peak in the U.S. sector of the St. Elias Mountains, the highest coastal mountain range on Earth. Mt. Logan ❷ (19,550 feet), 27 miles inland from Mt. St. Elias, is Canada's highest peak.

Between 100 and 200 inches of precipitation fall annually on the St. Elias Mountains, primarily as snow. In the typical North Pacific winter weather pattern, a low-pressure system develops west of the Aleutian Islands. Winds circulate counterclockwise around the barometric low, blowing from the south across the Gulf of Alaska onto the coastal ranges. Moving over the warm Gulf, the air becomes saturated with water vapor, which then condenses as snow when the air rises over the mountains. The St. Elias Mountains rise in a series of "steps"; at 15,299 feet, Mt. Fairweather is not among the tallest peaks, but it is the wettest, estimated to annually receive 300 inches. These immense snows yield 5,000 square miles of glacial ice. Larger than Rhode Island, the Malaspina ❸ is North America's largest piedmont glacier, or one at the base of a range rather than in a mountain valley.

Alejandro Malaspina, a Spanish intellectual and navigator, explored here in 1791. Vitus Bering, a Danish seafarer exploring on behalf of Russia, had spotted this salient peak, his first view of the mainland, on July 16, 1741, the feast day of St. Elias. Later that year, Bering's party was stranded on the small, remote island that now bears his name (Bering Island, Russia), as well as the dust of his bones. Some of the party survived until spring and constructed a craft that carried them back to Kamchatka, Russia. They owed their survival partly to sea otters, utterly unafraid of humans and thus easy to approach and kill. Sea otter meat, they found, was something you would eat only if stranded on an arctic island in winter. Sea otter fur, on the other hand, was the warmest and softest ever. That discovery motivated further exploration of Alaska.

The Hubbard Glacier begins on the flanks of Mt. Logan and flows 75 miles into fjords at the north end of Yakutat Bay ❹. It is the largest of Alaska's glaciers that calve into the ocean. These glaciers are presently increasing in mass, in contrast to the shrinking valley glaciers in most of the world. The calving glaciers accumulate ice over large areas and then lose ice through melting over relatively small ablation areas. They all terminate within fjords, where they normally rest on submarine moraines. The Hubbard Glacier retreated during the Little Ice Age from 1350 to 1900, whereas most glaciers advanced. In recent years, the glacier has advanced and has repeatedly blocked Russell Fjord, forming a temporary lake in the fjord.

North of the St. Elias Mountains rise the volcanic Wrangell Mountains, including one active volcano, Mt. Wrangell. Composed primarily of andesite, this shield volcano is three times more massive than Mt. Rainier, with comparable height and relief. Despite their geologic differences and 160 intervening miles, Mt. Wrangell and Mt. St. Elias are combined in one national park, Wrangell–St. Elias National Park and Preserve (the nation's largest, needless to say). The Chugach Mountains rise west of the St. Elias, continuing almost to Anchorage, rising to 11,000 feet at their eastern end.

The mountain ranges record a remarkable geologic story, one that is not yet well understood because of the ice cover and remote location. The Chugach and St. Elias Mountains are part of the Chugach Terrane. The Wrangell Mountains, a giant volcanic pile, erupted over the past 26 million years onto the Wrangellia terrane. The Yakutat Terrane underlies the northern Gulf of Alaska and the coast. This fragment of continental crust is attached to the Pacific Plate, which is subducting beneath Alaska with some difficulty.

Wrangellia was an island arc on the margin of North America through most of the Mesozoic. The Chugach Terrane developed above a subduction zone where the Farallon Plate dove beneath North America. The pair of terranes were rectilinear until about 60 million years ago, when they folded into their present arc as western Alaska began to rotate counterclockwise. The Aleutian volcanoes began erupting 50 million years ago as the Pacific Plate subducted along the Aleutian trench. Thirty million years ago, the Yakutat Terrane was torn away from southeast Alaska to ride northwest on the edge of the Pacific Plate. Eventually, the Yakutat Terrane reached the subduction trench but was too buoyant to subduct, instead colliding and raising today's high-relief mountains.

Mt. Edgecumbe and Sitka, Alaska

LOOK FOR a small but obviously conical volcano on an outer island; very long, straight waterways between islands.

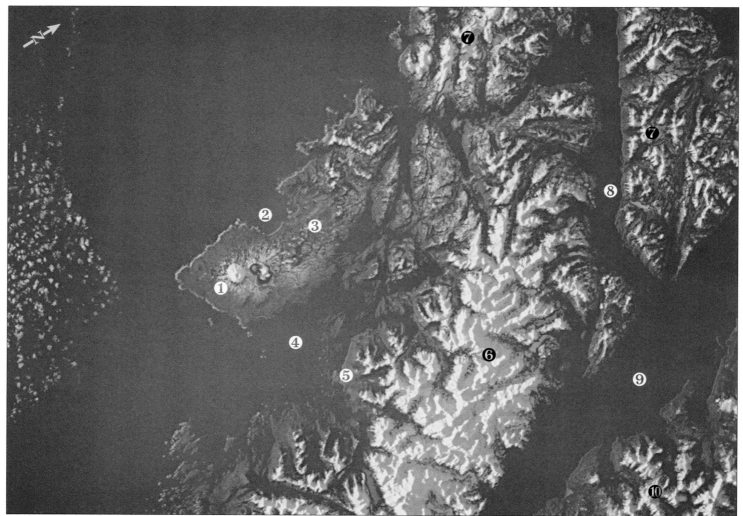

❶ Mt. Edgecumbe ❷ Shelikof Bay ❸ Kruzof Island ❹ Kruzof Sound ❺ Sitka ❻ Baranof Island ❼ Chichagof Island ❽ Peril Strait ❾ Chatham Strait and Chatham Strait Fault ❿ Admiralty Island. Broad astronaut view about 65 mi. across.

The flight path commonly takes you right over the Mt. Edgecumbe volcanic field on the southern half of Kruzof Island, across a sound from Sitka. Mt. Edgecumbe ❶ is a 3,201-foot composite cone built on the flank of an eroded caldera, visible just to its northeast. Look for several smaller cones nearby.

In other parts of the flight path, you may see much taller volcanoes in the distance: the active cones of the Alaska Peninsula and the Cascades, at opposite ends of the trip, and the older, eroded Wrangells. Those major volcanic groups lie inland from subduction zones. The Mt. Edgecumbe field does not; it's in the middle of a long gap in the Pacific Ring of Fire. The Pacific and North American plates slide past each other on a transform fault here (as they do in central and southern California) and there is no plate subducting under North America. Transform plate boundaries produce large earthquakes but relatively few and small volcanoes. The Queen Charlotte Fault lies offshore but divides into two branches as it continues northwest. One branch, the Fairweather Fault, comes onshore and augments its horizontal movement with vertical thrust movement, contributing to the lofty St. Elias Mountains.

Easier to see are fault traces bounding the far side of Baranof Island ❻. With help from Ice Age glaciers, they are dramatic saltwater straits. (The straits are straight and narrow, revealing their underlying faults.) Peril Strait ❸ trends northwest; the larger Chatham Strait trends just a few degrees off north. Chatham Strait ❾ runs 220 miles as saltwater to Haines. The fault bends there, joining the Denali Fault, which goes another 700 miles, past Mt. McKinley.

The straight valleys and straight straits that you see all over southeast Alaska mark additional faults, most of them oriented either north-south or northwest-southeast, like Peril and Chatham. Earthquakes are frequent. All these faults express the movement of the Pacific Plate past the North American Plate—and then at last under the North American Plate in a subduction zone that begins near the center of the Gulf of Alaska. The plate boundary is a messy affair. Fragments of continental crust were caught up by the Pacific Plate's edge at various times past but were too buoyant to sink with it on reaching the Aleutian subduction zone. Instead, they piled up along several parallel thrust faults to create the St. Elias, Chugach, and Alaska ranges.

Northwest of Kruzof Island, compression across the plate boundary produces those high mountains. But within this small area of one island, the plates are not under compression. Instead, quirky fault geometries create a local region of extension: A small area of the crust is pulled apart and thinned, reducing the pressure on the underlying mantle. Decompression is one way to lower the melting point of mantle rocks and to produce magma and seems to be the mechanism that led to a volcanic field here. The San Andreas Fault, analogous to the Queen Charlotte Fault, produces comparable volcanic fields in northern California. (See pages 204, 264.)

Sitka, Alaska, population 9,000, was Novoarkhangel'sk, the capital and chief port of Russian Alaska, from 1808 to 1867. Before that, it was Shee Atika, a Tlingit winter village.

Russia, Spain, and Britain competed to explore and claim coastal Alaska in the 18th century, drawn by the lucre of "soft gold"—sea otter pelts. Captain Bodega y Quadra named Sitka's volcano Montaña de San Jacinto in 1775; Captain James Cook gave it the name Edgecumbe in 1778. More significantly, he acquired from the Tlingit a few sea otter pelts, which his crew was able to sell in China a few months later at an unimaginable markup. The Russians had been selling otter pelts in China for 30 years but had kept it secret from the rest of Europe. Sea otters immediately became the *sine qua non* of Euro-American interest in Alaska. They were depleted by the time the trader Aleksandr Baranov took charge in Sitka; he tried to set limits that would preserve the population but was unable to enforce them among competing nationalities. Their interest waning, the Russians pulled up stakes in 1867, selling the whole shebang to the United States for less than a penny an acre. Sea otters were nearly extinct by the time trade in their furs was effectively banned in 1911, but they eventually rebounded to fairly healthy numbers on most of Alaska's southern coast.

Modest gold deposits were found near Sitka in 1870; the Klondike discovery and consequent Gold Rush followed in 1897. Miners sailed up Chatham Strait to Haines and trekked from there over icy mountain passes. With gold and soft gold gone, Southeast Alaska's economy rests on fishing, timber, and tourism.

Rose Point, Queen Charlotte Islands, British Columbia

LOOK FOR a large thorn-shaped sandy peninsula pointing northeast; a large island cluster that will typically be the only one on the west side of the flight path, near midroute between Seattle and Anchorage.

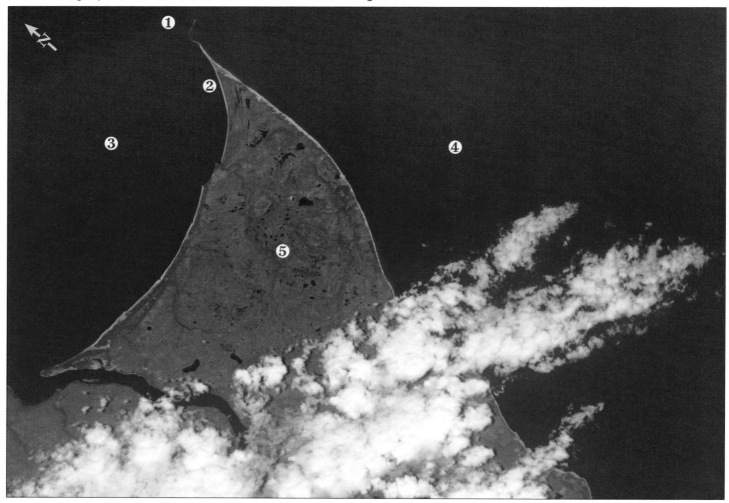

❶ Rose Point, Graham Island ❷ beach ridges ❸ Dixon Entrance ❹ Hecate Strait ❺ Argonaut Plain

The Queen Charlotte Islands lie north of Vancouver Island and south of southeast Alaska's islands, farther offshore than either. Typical flight paths just nick the thorn-shaped peninsula of Rose Point on the northeast corner of Graham Island; the rest of this archipelago would usually be seen only from west-side windows. Graham is its northern island and its largest.

Graham Island was covered by its own glacier during the Ice Ages. As the glaciers melted 10,000 years ago, streams carried glacial debris northeast, dumping it as an outwash plain that extended offshore. Northeast-draining meltwater channels are still visible crossing the Argonaut Plain ❺ in the direction of Rose Point ❶. This northeastern tip on the island is a young feature. Beach ridges ❷ form its northern half, and sand spits form its southern half. Strong currents swept Dixon Entrance and Hecate Strait during middle to late Holocene time, shaping the spits and ridges.

West of the plain rises the Skidegate (SKID-a-get) Plateau and then the Queen Charlotte Ranges, which are modest on Graham Island, taller southward on Moresby Island. Each upward step crosses a northwest-striking fault that slips both northwest and vertically. The ranges drop as steep cliffs on the far shore; from there, the sea floor descends 8,000 feet in less than 20 miles.

The islands are foggy, rainy, and very temperate in winter for their northerly latitude. This climate supports Northwest coastal rainforest vegetation. However, on the flat Argonaut terrain, peat mosses tend to hijack plant succession and hold giant conifers at bay by retaining and acidifying surface water. The result is a bog or, if it has a few stunted conifers, muskeg. The Skidegate Plateau grows rainforests that were heavily logged in recent decades. The northwestern slope of Graham Island is slated to be protected as rainforest forever, according to an agreement struck in 2006.

If your view is eastward, you may see many coastal islands blending visually as they rise to mainland mountains a little lower, with fewer glaciers, than those on either the Alaskan coast or the mainland coast behind Vancouver Island. The islands have a low, flat outer band about 25 miles wide, again producing muskeg or exposing bare granite bedrock. Farther inland, the rainforest here shows the least logging of any section of the Northwest coast.

The rainforest-preserving agreement of 2006 covers this entire section plus the Queen Charlottes—an area roughly equal to the five smallest U.S. states added together. One-third of it, in large parcels selected for unbroken mature forests and salmon streams, is supposed to remain unlogged forever; the other two-thirds is supposed to be logged in a new, ecosystem-preserving manner. Watch this space.

The islands are part of the Wrangellia Terrane. The Queen Charlotte Fault, off their western shore, controls their large-scale geometry. It is a plate boundary transform fault, analogous to California's San Andreas Fault. Both here and on the San Andreas, the Pacific Plate moves northwest past the North American Plate. In between them lie an ocean-spreading center and two small subducting plates, vestiges of the Farallon Plate, most of which subducted long ago into the mantle under North America's western edge. Like the San Andreas, the Queen Charlotte Fault also moves vertically in places—enough to raise the islands above the sea.

The islands' vertical movements that derive from the comings and goings of glacial ice are at least as interesting as those deriving from tectonics. The islands held a small ice cap. The mainland hosted an ice sheet with valley glaciers extending onto the continental shelf. The weight of ice depressed the crust; unglaciated areas to its west bulged upward, and at the same time global sea level was hundreds of feet lower owing to the volume of water tied up as ice on continents. Between the mainland and Queen Charlotte ice caps, a corridor of ice-free land and sea developed for a few millennia, perhaps offering a pathway for human migrants from Asia when inland routes were cut off by enormous continental glaciers. As glaciers melted late in the last Ice Age, the oceans rose, flooding the shelf between the Queen Charlotte Islands and the mainland. At the same time, an ice-free inland route opened from Asia to the Great Plains. Today, sea water drowns most of the formerly inhabitable shelf. If evidence of early coastal migration exists, finding it will take a long campaign of diving. Until that becomes a priority for scientific funding in either Canada or the United States, the coastal migration route will remain an intriguing hypothesis.

Vancouver Island, British Columbia

LOOK FOR fjords, alpine highlands, clear-cut logging, and fish pens.

Facing south ❶ Cowichan Lake, with the town of the same name at its east (left) tip

This mountainous island, the largest one so close to North America's coasts, exemplifies the rain shadow effect. Its winds almost always come from the ocean, laden with water vapor. Rising against the slopes, the winds cool, reducing the amount of vapor they can carry and forcing them to drop some of it as rain or snow. The same constant flow of marine air holds the sea-level temperatures between 32°F and 70°F almost all the time, so only the higher elevations get much snow. Descending the mountains' northeast slopes, the air warms again, gaining moisture. Points in the "rain shadow" along the eastern shore get less than 40 inches of rain a year, just 30 miles away from the western inlet that gets 256 inches.

Not too hot, not too cold, not too much rain or snow. Victoria, at the island's southeast tip, epitomizes the Goldilocks climate, even though it is too far south to be rain-shadowed by Vancouver Island's mountains. Washington's Olympic Mountains perform that service instead. Victoria's 34 inches of average precipitation include measurable amounts of snow on no more than 10 days. The average daily low in January is 33°F; the average daily high in July is 72°F. Victoria is the island's only sizable city and the provincial capital of British Columbia.

The climate excels at growing large trees, and timber has long been the top crop. You can't miss the clear-cuts. They run larger and leave less in the way of buffers along streams than do post-1980 clear-cuts in the United States. The forests cannot sustain the rate of cutting that you see. But if the result looks worse than in the United States, it is largely a matter of timing, as unrestrained logging did prevail in the Northwest states in earlier decades. Environmental regulation increased and logging declined in Oregon and Washington after 1990, mainly because the rate of cutting before that date was unsustainable. British Columbia filled the ensuing market void.

A newer island industry is salmon aquaculture, contained in floating pens mostly in coves on the eastern shore. Nets typically 30 to 100 feet across hang from either circular or square floats arranged in blocks of 6 to 20. Spotting them from 7 miles up would probably take binoculars.

Similar to the Olympic Mountains in height and ruggedness, the island's mountains also share a history of fluctuating alpine glaciers that left long U-shaped valleys. Both rose on numerous thrust faults in a subduction-zone setting complicated by the northwestward movement of blocks of continental crust.

Three long, straight valleys each cut all the way across Vancouver Island near its southern end. The southernmost, holding two small linear reservoirs, runs west from Victoria. The second holds no lakes but ends as a thumb-shaped bay at its western end. The third holds larger Cowichan Lake ❶ at its center and loses its western end in a confusion of islands and fjords. All three mark faults; the first two are terrane-bounding faults. The little strip between the first and the Strait of Juan de Fuca belongs geologically to the Olympic Peninsula, across the strait to the south. The Leech River Terrane reaches only from the first fault to the second.

From the second fault valley north, most of the island—but not the adjacent mainland—is part of the Wrangellia Terrane, whose other big parts underlie the Queen Charlotte Islands and Alaska's Wrangell Mountains. Wrangellia originated as a long-lived island arc, with active volcanoes 380 million years ago and again between 200 million and 170 million years ago.

A crooked set of connected fjords cuts most of the way across the island near its northern end. On one of them is an open-pit copper mine now filled with seawater. Briefly in the early 1990s, the bottom of the mine was dry land lower than Death Valley, lower than any dry land on Earth except the Dead Sea.

Three complexes of bays, islands, and fjords on the west coast are isolated and sparsely populated. In the late 18th century, they were the busiest ports on the Pacific Coast of North America; Spain and Britain went to the brink of war over them. Explorers in sailing ships found not only good harbors but also sophisticated native cultures eager for trade. They bartered metal tools, guns, clothing, and ornaments for sea otter pelts, greatly enriching both sides. Spurred by wealth, Northwest Coast art advanced to new heights, even as the populations were repeatedly decimated by the foreign cargo's tiny stowaways: germs.

SOUTHBOUND: Go to pp. 292, 246

Clouds and Winds,
Light,
Landforms,
Plate Tectonics

Clouds and Winds

Clouds may be the greatest single tribulation for those air passengers who always choose window seats. For the rest, turbulence ranks high among tribulations, and turbulence has much to do with clouds. Fortunately, the best cloudscapes are at least as spectacular as an average landscape. And you never know when clouds may part, offering a window beyond your window.

Jet travel offers a phenomenal viewpoint for clouds. Jetliners cruise above 28,000 feet, and most clouds are not that high. (Flying above weather and its turbulence is one of the main reasons jetliners cruise so high; the high, thin air also reduces frictional drag.) Meteorologists categorize clouds in terms of three broad layers, all of which we transect each time we move between a runway and cruising altitude. Low is below 6,500 feet, high is above 20,000 feet, and middle is everything in between. Any cloud close to your cruising altitude is in the high category.

Names of the main cloud types combine five Latin root words: stratus ("a layer"), nimbus ("rain"), cumulus ("heaped"), cirrus ("curl" or "sled-runner-shaped"), and altus (meaning "high," but applied to midlevel clouds). Each name assigns its cloud type an altitude level as well as a shape. The following kinds of clouds are commonly seen:

stratus: a low cloud forming a continuous layer
stratocumulus: a low heaped cloud
nimbostratus: a low rain cloud
altocumulus: a midlevel heaped cloud
altostratus: a midlevel cloud forming a layer
cirrus: a high sled-runner-shaped cloud made of ice crystals
cirrostratus: a high ice cloud in a sheetlike layer
undulatus: low clouds in rows or waves
cumulus: a low-through-high heaped cloud
cumulonimbus: a low-through-high storm cloud

Cooling moist air is the critical step in cloud formation. Clouds are made up of suspended tiny water droplets or ice crystals. Clouds form when the air cools and the water vapor in the air condenses to form droplets around very fine suspended particles, such as dust, smoke, salt, or sulfates produced by plants, volcanoes, or pollution. Further cooling may induce the cloud to dispense rain, snow, hail, or sleet (or one of those 20 other things some languages have words for). When the air warms again, the clouds vanish as the droplets revert to vapor.

undulatus or billow clouds over TN

low level cumulus clouds over eastern OR

effect of Lake Michigan on fog

Mountains and Clouds

When a mountain stands in the way of prevailing horizontal airflow, it forces the air to rise, cooling it and often causing invisible humidity to turn into visible clouds. A continuation of the same trend (if the air is humid enough to start with, or the mountains are high enough) produces rain or snow. The crests and west slopes of most U.S. mountain ranges are much wetter than surrounding areas because of this *orographic* ("mountain-written") *precipitation* within a zone of prevailing westerly air flow.

Anyone who has spent much time in window seats has noticed that clouds and mountains are unmistakably linked. Perhaps most striking are the small lenticular (lens-shaped) cloud caps that may sit enveloping a mountaintop, or sit well above the mountaintop, or stack up directly over the mountaintop, or multiply into a level series downwind from the mountaintop. See page 285 for more on orographic cloud effects.

Thunderstorms

Thunderhead clouds are vertically developed cumulonimbus clouds; they may tower well above our cruising plane, from a base far below it. They often stand on a stratus cloud base and wear an "anvil top" of cirrus clouds as a cap. Vertical development is a product of strong updrafts localized within the cloud, which we experience as turbulence when we fly into low-through-high clouds. For everyone's comfort and safety, pilots generally avoid these intense storm cells.

Air passengers can watch thunderstorms develop in lines parallel to a front (a moving boundary between warmer and cooler air masses). A *squall line* of thunderstorms up to 300 miles long may develop where a cold air mass advances into warm moist air. The largest thunderstorm cells, *supercells,* generate large hail and often tornadoes. Tornadoes are most frequent in summer and most common in Florida and in the central states.

The underlying cause of thunderstorms is *thermal convection,* which occurs on sunny days and produces storms most often in the afternoon or early evening. The sun heats the ground, which heats the air next to the ground, which then rises as "parcels" of air

top of a rapidly growing cumulonimbus cloud

through the surrounding cooler air. Rising parcels decompress and chill; if sufficiently moist they form a cumulus cloud when they reach an altitude at which the moisture condenses. The cumulus clouds from one afternoon will have flat bottoms at the same altitude and cauliflower-shaped tops that reveal the outlines of the rising parcels. Picture a column of rising air under each cumulus cloud, culminating at the cloud's top, and columns of cool air sinking in the spaces between the clouds.

Thunderstorms begin as cumulus clouds and grow through a series of stages. A towering cumulus cloud will rise to more than 20,000 feet tall and spread out to as much as 10 miles in diameter. If the air rises high enough, the water droplets freeze, releasing heat and exacerbating the complex of powerful updrafts and downdrafts. When the process reaches its mature stage, downdrafts carrying heavy rain or hail reach the ground; lightning and thunder commence; and the top of the now-cumulonimbus cloud spreads out to form an anvil shape. Abrupt rapid transitions (known as *wind shear*) between a headwind, downdraft, and tailwind associated with a storm are dangerous for planes close to the ground. Jetliners carry special instrumentation to anticipate wind shear.

Fog

Fog is simply clouds at ground level. Some fog is wispy or cottony; other fog makes a flat sheet, essentially a very low stratus cloud layer. The most interesting fog phenomena relate to oceans, lakes, and large rivers and can result either in fog or in clouds that look very low to us but would look distinctly aloft to a person on the ground. Often you see fog or low clouds hovering over oceans, lakes, or rivers. This occurs where warm, moist air blows across cold water and contact cooling causes the fog or clouds to form. At other times you will see the opposite: a stratus layer parted by a stripelike gap directly over a river, or a layer of low clouds over land but not water. (See photo on page 331.) This happens when a cool air mass has moved in and the water releases heat left over from previous days. The leftover heat rises and evaporates the clouds over the water.

Haze

While air passengers can look at clouds either as something blocking our view, or as a view in their own right—clouds' insipid cousin haze goes unredeemed. Haze begins by dimming the colors of the land we look at, then may go on to render it all but invisible.

Haze is anything in the air that scatters light. It can be any combination of humidity, particulates such as smoke, and aerosols such as sulfates. Eastern summers, when "it's not the heat, it's the humidity that gets you," are far hazier than any season in the West. Northern Utah, western Colorado, and southern Wyoming are least afflicted with haze. Arizona, where people go to breathe dry air, is good, but not as clear as Utah because Arizona is downwind of Los Angeles and it has massive coal-fired plants. The name Great Smoky Mountains long predates coal-fired power plants, yet the overwhelming majority of summer haze in the East is a partnership between humidity and air pollution from fossil fuel combustion. Before we had air pollution, the summer haze in the East was a fraction of what it was to become by 1970; from 1970 through 2000, increases were tempered with decreases, at least locally, as emissions from both power plants and automobiles were regulated. With more rigorous regulation, we can hope for modest improvements in visibility.

Fossil fuel power plants emit sulfur dioxide, an invisible gas. High humidity levels accelerate the conversion of these gas molecules to sulfate molecules which, though technically solids or liquids, are small enough to remain suspended in the air, serving as nuclei for water vapor to condense around. Cars, trucks, and jetliners contribute other pollutants with similar effects. The resulting wet aerosol particles quickly grow to a size that is most efficient at scattering light, or producing haze. On the other hand, they do not form raindrops as readily as vapor droplets with other kinds of nuclei, so they remain in the air a long time and have a net negative effect both on rainfall and on sunshine reaching the ground. When they do eventually fall as rain, it is acid rain.

Haze hangs heaviest on the East in polar air masses that sink and form a temperature inversion, a layer of relatively dense cool air that becomes grimly stable within the lower atmosphere. As your plane climbs, you often see a sharp haze horizon at around 7,000 feet. It may or may not look brown enough from above for you to recognize it as smog, but rest assured that air pollution is a major factor. Relief comes to the East Coast at least once most summers in the form of a surge of tropical air. Fresh off the ocean, this unstable air thins any haze materials by mixing vertically, as evidenced by fairly tall cumulus clouds.

Contrails

Jet condensation trails—"contrails" for short—mark the sky with long, linear traces. Since jets fly on more or less standardized routes, you often see several contrails (or several shadows of contrails on the ground) typically all parallel—and often parallel to the plane you are in.

Jet engines burn fuel at enormous rates, converting it to gaseous water, carbon dioxide, and other gases. Emerging from the engine, the water vapor condenses in the cold air as either water droplets or ice crystals. Contrails may appear abruptly when a plane enters a parcel of moist air, or disappear when it leaves one. They soon dissipate in dry air but linger and gradually spread out in moist air, becoming a major source of haze in some heavily flown urban regions.

Planes landing or taking off in very moist air sometimes create small, short-lived clouds around their wings. These condensation plumes require a relative humidity close to 100 percent. They form in the zone of reduced air pressure just above the wing, and may extend a short distance behind the wing. They often develop when flying through clouds but are hard to see there.

The Jet Stream

Pockets of clear air turbulence that pilots mention when advising you to refasten your seat belts for a few minutes are often associated with the jet stream. Jet streams are narrow globe-encircling belts of high-speed, high-altitude westerly winds. There are often two in the Northern Hemisphere and two more in the Southern, but here in the United States and Canada we are concerned only with the northern polar jet stream that streams along the top of the front between the polar air masses and the warmer air masses to the south. It is not a simple belt: It can "break," becoming discontinuous, and reappear elsewhere, and it often dips abruptly higher or lower or turns far to the north or south in big loops or branches. Typically 1 to 3 miles deep and a few hundred miles wide, it is found between 6 and 10 miles up. Wind speeds in the stronger spots are often more than 100 miles per hour and can exceed 300 miles per hour, especially in winter. If your pilot can catch a ride on a 120-mile-per-hour jet stream for two hours, you will reach your destination about half an hour earlier than you would have without the help. The airline is even more interested in the savings in fuel consumption. Since jet streams lie above fronts, we suspect that long westbound flights, which avoid jet streams, enjoy somewhat clearer views on average than long eastbound flights, which seek out jet streams. As they push good and bad weather around, jet streams have become a primary focus in weather forecasting.

Fronts

We've heard about warm fronts and cold fronts time and again on the evening news, and we may have a sense of what kind of weather typically follows each in our hometowns. In our jetliner, we can see them laid out as vast, sweeping divides between clear and cloudy skies.

The big lobes or loops in the jet stream mark the edges of lobes in the cold polar air mass that slowly and erratically work their way eastward. Where the cold mass advances upon warmer air, its leading edge is a cold front. Look for the classic manifestations: a thin line of cumulus clouds or a heavier squall line of cumulonimbus clouds, bearing thunderstorms. Where the warm air mass advances, it slides up over the top of a trailing wedge of the retreating cold air mass; the warm front's classic visible effect is a sheet of stratus clouds, perhaps accompanied higher up by sheets of altostratus and cirrostratus clouds. The trailing wedge of retreating cold air is shallow and broad, so that the sheets of clouds lie over the cold air, east of the warm front's surface expression. (If you're on the ground, that means the rain arrives before the warming.)

These eastward-crawling lobes are irregular in shape and uneven in speed, with cold fronts often moving faster than warm fronts. A cold front may overtake a warm front and meet up with the trailing wedge of the retreating cold air mass in front of the warm front. The warm air is *occluded*, or forced up above both cold masses. *Occluded fronts* are typically stormy but soon dissipate.

a glory on a low cloud layer

Light

Opposition effect

If you sit on the shady side of the plane, you will see the plane's shadow shrink and then disappear as the plane ascends. At the same time, the area immediately surrounding the shrinking shadow brightens. The bright spot persists after the shadow disappears, and it may hop onto cloud surfaces or hover in the middle of thin clouds. The bright spot and the shadow can trade places as the plane passes over clouds of differing elevations.

The bright spot has a surprisingly simple explanation. Suppose you are flying over a woodland of evenly spaced trees; in the area around your plane's shadow, the trees' shadows are all hiding directly behind the trees, so you see only sunlit surfaces. The farther the trees are from that spot (directly opposite the sun, from your point of view) the more shadow you see and the darker the woodland looks. Grains of sand or particles of soil exert this effect just as powerfully as trees. The particles on the moon's surface brighten considerably when you can't see their shadows: The full moon's brightness can only be accounted for by the opposition effect augmenting the full moon's greater visible area.

Glories

Sometimes a sort of circular rainbow called a "glory" surrounds the bright spot or the plane's shadow. It is rarely as bright as an earthbound rainbow, but like its terrestrial cousin, it can be double. Both glory and rainbow are prismatic effects of water droplets in the air. Small droplets form a large glory; large droplets form a small glory.

You need to be on the shady side of the plane to see glories and opposition bright spots. On the sunny side, you may see a colored "corona" when you look at the sun or moon through a thin cloud. Again, small droplets form a large corona, and vice versa. Ice halos occur around either the sun or moon when thin (cirrostratus) ice clouds intervene. Coronas and ice halos are similar, but coronas are blue on the inside and red on the outside, and halos are the reverse.

Fisher Pk. on Raton Mesa, overlooking Trinidad, CO, facing north

Plane Windows

A final category of mysterious color effects is less celestial; it originates not far from your eyeballs. If you wear polarizing sunglasses, the window may present a world with dazzling magenta to green color bands. If you take photographs through the window, you may find these unwanted colors stronger than your naked eye perceived them. Ultraviolet filters have little effect on them and polarizing filters aggravate them. Even PhotoShop cannot always overcome them, though it helped on many photos in this guide.

In part, the plastic window material is polarizing light. The effect may heighten as the plane rises and air pressure bows the plastic outward, straining its molecular structure.

The window is double, with a thin air space between two panes and a row of tiny holes perforating the inner pane. Water droplets often condense in the air space while the plane is on the ground, threatening your view. Fortunately, these evaporate as the plane climbs and fills with the exceedingly dry air produced by taking thin, cold, high-altitude air and warming and pressurizing it.

Landforms

Drainage Patterns

Flying across the country, we are the envy of those who founded geology, dazzled by sights that a century ago could only be imagined. Rivers and creeks pattern the landscape intricately, reflecting topography, bedrock material, and soil. The most common drainage pattern, called *dendritic* for its resemblance to tree limbs, typically forms on gently sloping land covered by fairly uniform soils or bedrock. On fine-grained soil such as clay or volcanic ash, most runoff remains on the surface and the streams are closely spaced. If the soil is sandy or coarse, most runoff drains down to underground aquifers, and surface streams are sparse. In limestone bedrock, an even higher proportion of runoff goes underground; the limestone literally dissolves to yield *karst* landscapes with sinkholes, disappearing streams, and valleys without visible streams, even in high-rainfall climates. (See page 137.)

Streams flowing on hard, resistant rock cut narrow valleys or canyons; those on softer rock cut wide valleys. Some valleys widen substantially where a stream crosses a contact between hard and soft rocks. Faults or fractures crush or crumble bedrock in linear zones that erode into valleys, dramatically interrupting the regional drainage pattern.

Streams run parallel down long steep slopes, or radially down conical or domal slopes, such as those of a volcano. Fan-shaped distributary stream patterns form in freshly deposited sediments in two contrasting settings: Where intermittent streams descend onto desert valley floors, they produce *alluvial fans*. Where rivers enter lakes or oceans, their sediments fan out as deltas—either *bay head deltas* within the confines of bays or *lobed deltas* that extend out into larger bodies of water. What those dry and wet settings have in common is a sharp drop in the stream's ability to move its sediment load. A long reach of stream too small to move its load of sand, gravel, and boulders except during floods becomes a *braided stream*, with innumerable channels anastomosing, or separating and reconnecting, around lozenge-shaped gravel bars.

In dendritic drainages, stream confluences (points where streams join together) are normally angled, forming a V that points downstream. Occasionally you see the reverse: a *barbed drainage*. This is where several tributaries enter a stream at angles that point upstream. The stretch of stream at a barbed drainage was likely flowing in the opposite direction when the tributaries originally joined it, and the confluence angles were formed, then pointing in the normal, downstream direction. The stream was later *captured* by a neighboring stream that was eroding its valley much faster. At some point, for the captured stream a direction that had been uphill before was now downhill. A stretch of the captured stream then reversed direction. Debate over the Grand Canyon's origin often touches on the barbed appearance of tributaries to the south-flowing stretch of the Colorado River just above the Grand Canyon and below Glen Canyon Dam.

drainage pattern accentuated by shrub growth on the shady sides of the draws; Southern California Coast Range

Floodplains

Where they cross gentle plains, rivers typically meander in S curves. On many such plains you will see countless arcs of former river channels. Abandonment of arcs occurs often because meandering rivers typically change course each time they flood. However, what you see now, in most cases, is not natural. The rivers you see are confined within levees. To shorten riverboat trips, engineers built levees to control the rivers, and left many rivers with far fewer meanders than they once had. Sometimes the engineers may have even made a perfectly straight channel from scratch (see page 34). Old abandoned meanders are often still visible, either dry or as oxbow lakes.

Look for two long, relatively straight parallel bluffs limiting the reach of the meanders on either side of a river. (See page 78.) The space between the bluffs is the *floodplain:* During floods, the entire floodplain is submerged, or at least it used to be in the days before flood-control projects. The lower Mississippi has meander-marked floodplains a hundred miles across (pages 170, 240).

Similar to these bluffs, but more subtle and sometimes multiple, are the river terraces that develop along some rivers, often revealed to airborne viewers by their differing vegetation. *Terraces* indicate levels of the valley floor in times past. Either the river's *base level*—the elevation of a lake or ocean into which it flows, placing a limit on its potential down-cutting—was higher than today, or this part of the river basin was uplifted by geologic forces. (Terraces have a different origin in a few cases close to northerly mountains, where past cycles of glacial advance and retreat built terraces through rapid deposition of glacial sediment.)

Vegetation

Geologists tend to look at plant cover the way window-seat flyers look at cloud cover: It's in the way of my view! But plant cover can also reveal geology: It can dramatically reflect bedrock chemistry, as in California's serpentine regions (pages 202, 264).

Much more commonly, geology affects plant growth by way of water drainage. In dry regions, green swaths are generally stream valleys where the water table is closer to the surface than it is on the more barren uplands. A line of vegetation crossing arid land with no water in sight may indicate bedrock faulting and fracturing, which allows water to collect below the surface. In wet regions such as the southeastern savannas, swamps, deltas, and Carolina bays, dramatically different plant communities grow in patches on the nearly flat terrain. They reflect contrasts between swampy land that is submerged for much of the year, sandy land that is thoroughly well drained, and clayey soils that remain soggy for months at a time but are rarely submerged.

It's worth noting that our maps assign shades of green and tan to different elevations above sea level; these colors can be quite misleading if you read them as plant cover. In some regions, such as Kansas and eastern Colorado, the choices of color do hint at the natural preagricultural vegetation, at least in spring: The lowest elevations, shown in dark green, often supported forest; slightly higher elevations, shown in paler green, tended to grow lush grasses; and the high plains, shown in tan, were mostly short-grass prairie, which is too sparse to look green from the air. However, the color correlations don't work that way in Arizona, where the lowest elevations are mostly desert, and forest grows only at high elevations.

Sandy Shores

Rivers deliver sand to the seashore. Most of it will eventually end up in the ocean depths but first it may be redistributed as beaches by a complex interplay of tides, waves, and ocean currents. Beaches advance, retreat, or remain in one place. Southward *longshore drift* of sand predominates along the Atlantic Coast.

Between Massachusetts and the southernmost tip of Texas, a high proportion of the coastline takes the form of long, narrow *barrier islands,* beach sands separated from the mainland by a *sound* or *lagoon.* Barrier islands tend to protect the mainland from storms but are themselves highly vulnerable to storm erosion. Efforts by engineers to maintain shipping channels through the inlets and to protect buildings and roads on barrier islands interrupt this flow of sand, leading to shrinkage of many beaches and islands, especially those just south of engineering projects. Tidal channels cut through the islands, flooding tidal flats twice daily and often forming small deltas. *Ebb-tide deltas,* extending out into the sea on either side of a pass, are conspicuous from the air even when shallowly submerged. They are especially prominent where tides are relatively strong but waves relatively weak—in Georgia, for example. *High-tide deltas,* developing as marshy flats between the barrier island and the mainland, are more active where waves are stronger and tides weaker, such as in Texas and North Carolina.

Faults and Folds

Looking down upon the land, we can see not only where water flows but also where the solid rock has flowed; it just takes a little more study and practice. It is easiest in regions of sedimentary rock because the rock is layered and the layers were all flat or very nearly flat when they were originally laid down as sediment. If they are not flat now, that indicates that during some past tectonic stress regime they *deformed* by faulting or folding or both. Both faults and folds can be spectacularly visible from jetliner windows.

Faulting is the process whereby rocks break and move along a resulting *fault plane,* usually during an earthquake. If a fault plane is vertical and the blocks move horizontally in opposite compass directions, it is a *strike-slip fault.* (The rocks slip in the direction of strike, which is the orientation of the fault line on a map.) *Thrust faults* result from squeezing (*compression*); in a cross-section diagram, a rising block would overhang a sinking block. *Normal faults* result from stretching (*extension*); a sinking block overhangs the lower portion of a rising block. If a fault plane dips (slopes at an angle) and the rocks move up on one side and down on the other the fault is either a thrust fault or a normal fault. Most faults have

long active lives with many earthquakes: Over a million years or longer, a rising block becomes a fault block mountain range and a sinking block becomes a valley. Often one or both blocks tilt as they move.

Differential Erosion

Folds with a concave side up, like troughs, are *synclines*. Folds with a concave side down, resembling arches, are *anticlines*. If the folds are young or still growing, the anticlines commonly form mountain ranges and the synclines form valleys. The reverse—valleys centered on anticlines and mountains centered on synclines—develops by differential erosion over a long period of time, as in the Appalachian Valley and Ridge Province. Each fold there may embrace several ridges and valleys. Each ridge is not an anticline but a cluster of relatively hard rock layers all tilted at roughly the same angle as they lie on one *limb* (slope) of a great encompassing anticline or syncline. Each valley is a cluster of softer rock layers, most likely similarly tilted.

Valleys of this type are called *strike valleys* because they are aligned with the strike direction of the sedimentary layers. (The terms "strike" and "dip" apply both to fault planes and, in analogous fashion, to tilted bedding planes or layers in sedimentary rocks. A horizontal line drawn along a tilted layer describes its *strike* direction.) On asymmetrical ridges such as cuestas (page 275), the gentle flank, the slope angle of which is roughly the same as that of the underlying rock layers, is the dip slope. The steeper flank cutting across the strata is the back slope.

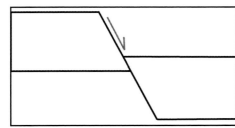

normal fault (side view)

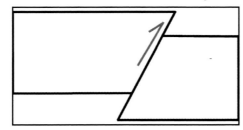

thrust fault (side view)

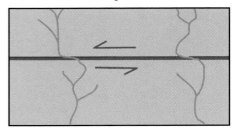

strike-slip fault (map view) showing displaced streams

Subsequent and Superimposed Streams

Strike streams in *strike valleys* are examples of subsequent streams, which inherit their alignment from the zones of fractured or soft rock that they eroded. These contrast with consequent streams, which develop their typically dendritic patterns in response to surface slope. A third type, once dubbed "antecedent" by J. W. Powell but now usually called superimposed, defies both the present-day topography and the bedrock structure and has provided geology with no end of avid controversy.

The provocation can be vividly clear from your window: a river that insists on flowing through a mountain, perhaps avoiding a nearby valley that would take it to the same destination. The Black Canyon of the Gunnison is a classic example.

Ice Sculpture

The area covered by Ice Age ice includes the Great Lakes (which were carved by the ice), the Dakotas and Minnesota, nearly all of Wisconsin, New York, and New England, and parts of Nebraska, Kansas, Iowa, Illinois, Indiana, Ohio, and Pennsylvania. We use the plural *"Ice Ages"* for the *Pleistocene glaciations* of the past 1.8 million years because glaciations were intermittent, separated by *interglacial stages* that were commonly longer than the 15,000 years of the postglacial Holocene epoch. (There were also prolonged ice ages hundreds of millions of years ago but clear evidence of them cannot be seen from aloft over this continent.)

Vast portions of the north central states are *till plains*. Till is glacial debris still lying where it was released from the melting ice, in contrast to *outwash,* which was moved by a river; the looser term *"glacial drift"* embraces till, outwash, moraines, and glacial lakebeds. Soils in drift often look strikingly mottled when seen from aloft because of patchy soil texture: Patches of sandy or gravelly soil drain quickly, becoming dry and pale, while adjacent silty patches retain moisture and stay dark.

Disordered drainage patterns characterize till from the most recent (Wisconsinian) Ice Age because it is too young to have developed dendritic drainages. Dendritic patterns can be seen on till plains of earlier (Kansan and Nebraskan) Pleistocene glaciations, where those are south of and hence undisturbed by the Wisconsinian Ice Sheet. South of all the ice sheet termini, rivers and streams draining the melting glaciers reworked glacial debris to form outwash plains. Areas of flatter, smoother plain are likely to comprise lakebed sediments. Temporary lakes lasting tens or hundreds of years commonly formed when the ice sheets were in retreat. By collecting fine sediment and then drying up completely, they became principal source areas for *loess* (windblown silt) deposits that provided many of the continent's deepest and richest soils. No doubt the dust storms that transported the loess were appalling.

The glaciers produced ridges and hills of several kinds. *Lateral moraines* piled up more or less parallel to the direction of ice flow, along the edges of ice sheets or of lobes or streams within an ice sheet. *Terminal* and *recessional moraines* piled up across the direction of ice flow, each in an arcuate line where there was a melting terminus, at least temporarily, of an ice sheet or lobe. Moraine ridges can be huge: Some on the Great Plains are hundreds of miles long and tens of miles wide, but generally moraine ridges are too subtle in their relief to be seen from the air. (Elongated wind farms might be your best marker for one of these great moraines in Iowa, Minnesota, or South Dakota.) Northeastern Iowa has *pahas*, small north-south ridges that tend to be wooded, making them more visible perhaps than the much larger moraines. *Eskers* are small-scale ridges, long and typically serpentine, often flanked by swamps or lakes; rivers deposited eskers within tunnels in the underside of an ice sheet. *Drumlins* are small hills in "swarms," all elongated in the direction of ice flow. Their origin is poorly understood (see page 276).

In the western mountains, the signature forms of alpine glaciation—U-shaped valleys, narrow sawtooth ridges, and sharp pyramidal peaks (horns)—are increasingly evident northward. These forms largely date from the Ice Ages. Colorado, Montana, Idaho, and California all have some active glaciers still; Washington, Oregon, Wyoming, and, of course, Canada and Alaska have active glaciers big enough for you to clearly recognize them as such.

Their Ice Age forebears were bigger alpine and valley glaciers, but ice extensive enough to be called an ice sheet or an ice cap entered the western states only in a few spots (pages 247, 287, 291).

Volcanic Regions

The western states display a wide variety of lava beds and volcanoes. Most numerous are *cinder cones;* these are relatively small, simple, conical, and young (because older ones are eroded rather easily, soon becoming unrecognizable). Cinder cones often have tongue-shaped, low-relief, basalt lava flows extending from their bases. *Shield volcanoes* range from medium to large but are not steep; those that are circular and isolated will likely suggest a volcano, but others come to look like nondescript mountainous areas. The tallest volcanoes are *composite volcanoes,* such as Rainier and Shasta, erupted from several vents over hundreds of thousands of years. Most are in the Pacific Coast states, though Arizona and New Mexico have a few fine specimens. Much larger still are the *calderas* left by *supervolcanoes*—volcanoes that produced eruptions many times larger than any in written history—but these are not recognizable as volcanoes; indeed, geologists did not recognize what they were until recent decades. Since the most famous one, Yellowstone, does not lie under a major flight corridor, we discuss large calderas in Colorado and New Mexico instead: Valles (page 94) is notably circular if you get all of it in your view at once, but La Garita (page 51) simply looks like a rugged mountainous region.

Basalt lavas are dark gray to black and very fluid, sometimes flowing hundreds of miles across plains. Erosion eventually dissects these lava plateaus, leaving flat-topped mesas and long ridges capped by the conspicuous flat layer of dark lava. Many mesas and lava-capped ridges are *inverted topography:* Lava flows filled valleys, the lowest topographic features when the volcanoes erupted, and the softer material that formed the adjacent higher slopes later eroded away, leaving the resistant lava as a high-standing ridge.

Certain mountains and monoliths originate not as erupting lava but as *magma* (molten rock) in the "plumbing" beneath volcanoes. Most magma has to rise from considerable depth—typically from the upper *mantle,* the zone beneath the earth's *crust*—before erupting. About 10 percent of the magma rising toward the surface eventually gets there and erupts, earning the name "lava." The remaining magma eventually solidifies within the crust, forming *intrusive* rocks such as granite. A body of intrusive rock may be a *batholith* (with a surface exposure larger than 36 square miles) or a *pluton* (smaller). Ship Rock, New Mexico, and the *dike swarm* around Colorado's Spanish Peaks are examples of relatively young, shallow magma plumbing already exposed by rapid regional erosion. In contrast, Stone Mountain, Georgia, shows how a magma intrusion can hold up as a mountain even 285 million years after magmatic activity ceased.

Rock Types

Volcanic rocks and intrusive rocks together make up igneous rocks, one of the three main groups of rock types. Earth processes continually recycle rocks, converting them from one type into another. Each of the three big groups is defined by the recycling process it derives from.

Igneous: solidification of magma produced by melting of the minerals in the mantle. (Examples: Basalt, granite, obsidian, pumice.)

Metamorphic: slow recrystallization under great heat and pressure, but without melting, deep in the Earth's crust. (Examples: Slate, gneiss, anthracite.)

Sedimentary: compaction into rock of sediment layers deposited by wind or water. The sediments may originate as living organisms or through fragmentation of rocks or through precipitation of minerals dissolved in water. (Examples: Limestone, shale, sandstone.) Not all sedimentary beds, even fairly old ones, are rock; geologists often skirt that issue, using the term "sediments" to embrace the continuum from hard sedimentary rocks to unconsolidated sediments.

Plate Tectonics

Geologic Time

This guide measures geologic time primarily in thousands or millions of years rather than in eras, periods, and epochs. We report the age of geologically brief events without the margin of error (for example, 25 million years ago rather than 24.7 ± 0.3 million years). When we report a time range (360 million to 300 million years ago) we are emphasizing the event's great duration—60 million years—as well as its antiquity.

A Brief History of the Continental United States

North America is the product of a long series of plate tectonic events. The earth's crust comprises several *plates,* which move slowly (a few inches per year) across the earth's surface, driven by convection of the underlying mantle. The convection results primarily from the heat of radioactive decay. Part of the upwelling mantle melts and the resulting magma rises toward the surface, where some of it erupts as sea-floor basalt along a *mid-ocean ridge,* also called a *sea-floor spreading center.* Oceanic crust is created at mid-ocean ridges and consumed, sinking back into the mantle, at *subduction zones.* ("Subduct" simply means "carry beneath.")

As oceanic crust ages and cools (far from the ridge that produced it) its density increases. Eventually it becomes so heavy that it subducts, or sinks, into the underlying mantle. As the subducting slab slips deeper into the mantle, it releases sea water. Remarkably, the addition of water causes some of the mantle above the slab to melt and rise toward the surface, where it typically erupts as a volcano. If this surface is on the ocean floor, the volcano may emerge as an island in a chain called an *island arc,* since subduction zones typically trace an arc on the earth's surface. If the slab is subducting under the edge of a continent, a volcanic mountain range, such as the Cascades in the Pacific Northwest, develops. These ranges are called *arcs* by analogy, even though continental ones are infrequently arcuate.

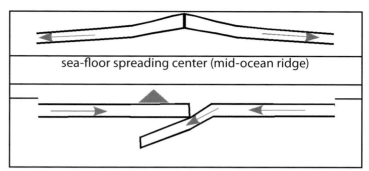

sea-floor spreading center (mid-ocean ridge)

subduction zone, with the red triangle representing volcanoes

At plate boundaries, plates move relative to each other in one of three ways: into each other at a subduction zone, away from each other at a sea-floor spreading center, or slipping past each other in opposite directions at a *transform fault.* Most of the world's transform faults are found under the oceans, but in North America one transform fault makes an appearance on land: California's San Andreas Fault.

North America's several core pieces were once parts of Rodinia, a *supercontinent* formed about 1.1 billion years ago. It rifted, or split, into smaller continents about 750 million years ago. Rifts opened the Iapetus Ocean to separate North America from Europe and Africa; these three continents were ancestral versions of their present selves, each comprising somewhat different combinations of pieces, in different configurations relative to one another, from what we see today.

The Iapetus Ocean plate broke into several fragments, forming subduction zones and mountainous, volcanically active island arcs both large and small, probably similar to those in the western Pacific today. Subduction zones and island arcs eventually collided with the eastern margin of North America in a series of three great *orogenies,* or mountain-building events:

Taconic Orogeny, 470 million to 460 million years ago;
Acadian Orogeny, 325 million to 300 million years ago;

and Allegheny Orogeny, 290 million to 240 million years ago.

The first two orogenies brought large island arcs, which *accreted*, or fused, onto North America. The third brought the whole show: Europe, Africa, and South America. The Iapetus Ocean was no more, and all the continents were joined together into the supercontinent Pangaea, meaning "all earth." These three orogenies created the Appalachian-Ouachita-Marathon mountain chain, reaching from Labrador to southwest Texas on this continent; major parts of the same ancient range are now found in northwest Africa and western Europe. The parts of this enormous chain separated when a new ocean, the Atlantic, began to open along a new rift roughly aligned with the old *suture*, 180 million years ago. As the Atlantic grew, its rift, the sea-floor spreading center now running down the ocean's center, became distant from North America, the eastern margin of which became tectonically passive, leaving the eastern half of the continent geologically quiet and the Appalachians subject mainly to the forces of erosion.

The continent's western margin had been similarly passive and quiet from the breakup of Rodinia until about 350 million years ago. Ever since that time it has been active, often with near-shore subduction zones and their associated chains of volcanoes. Far-traveled pieces of crust (terranes) sometimes accrete to North America, as they did in the East during the Taconic and Acadian orogenies. At other times, slices of the continent may have separated along transform faults and slid up or down its western margin, as the coastal side of southern California is doing today.

Around 130 million years ago, a single arc of volcanoes bounded the continent's margin, as the Andes bound South America today. This apparently simple subduction zone became complex about 75 million years ago as transform faults sliced the southwestern U.S. margin. The Laramide Orogeny began approximately then, creating many ranges we think of as the Rocky Mountains. By the end of the Laramide, 40 million years ago, much of the area from Idaho to Arizona was a high plateau, an "American Altiplano" by analogy to Bolivia. When the San Andreas Fault began transferring pieces of North America to the Pacific Plate about 20 million years ago, the plateau fractured along many faults and began lowering overall, creating the Basin and Range Province.

Index of Flights

This index suggests sequences of pages to read while flying flight segments other than those that appear in Corridor titles. The number of possible combinations gets very large quickly, so we limited this index to 35 of the busiest airports or airport clusters. We omitted city pairs that currently offer no nonstop flights, or offer nonstops only at night. We also omitted flight segments that do not cross any of our article locations (often because the cities are very close together). Some of those omitted city pairs do have an article on one or both cities.

The article on interstate highways (page 76) does not appear in this index because if it did it would appear in every entry. A few other featured subjects, such as forest fires, forest pests, wind farms, and center pivot irrigation, are also widespread; this index does suggest those on many flight segments likely to offer views of them, though we admit the selections are somewhat random.

This index refers you to several articles where you are unlikely to see the specific location named in the title or shown in the photo, but where you are likely to see the same type of feature that the articles discuss. For example, it sends you to Watts Bar Lake and Dam on all segments likely to cross a Tennessee Valley Authority lake; to

Spruce Knob on segments that cross the central Appalachian Valley and Ridge Province; to Short-Grass Prairie at Las Animas, Colorado, on segments that cross short-grass prairie; to Striped Crops near Windham, Montana, on segments that cross north-south strip cropping influenced by chinook winds; and so forth.

Note that this index may ask you to go through a range of pages backward, just as you leaf through corridors backward if you are flying west-to-east or south-to-north. Also note that if the Index of Flights refers you to a Corridor or part of a Corridor, you would do well to check not only the pages that fall within that chapter, but also the pages indicated on the blue "Go to" lines in the bottom corners.

Some segments to or from major Canadian airports are included here for the sake of subjects they present while in U.S. airspace. Long transcontinental segments to or from Canada are omitted, because on those that we have tracked, Air Canada pilots demonstrate impressive disregard for the NAVAID system, eschewing fidelity to any particular waypoints while tracing smooth arcs that vary widely in response to weather conditions. We would have to list so many pages that you're better off simply using the map.

ABQ Albuquerque

ABQ-ATL: 182, 64, 36, (Corridor 5: 176, 174, 172, 240, 170, 168, 142)
ABQ-CH: 182, 94, 82, 84, 36, 30, 28, 26, 24
ABQ-DC: 182, 84, 36, 82, 30, 28, 26, 24, 22, 74, 72, 234, 232, 110
ABQ-DEN: 182, 94, 92, 90, 88, 46, 44, 42
ABQ-DFW: 182, 36, 178, 176, 174, 172
ABQ-HO: 182, 36, 64, 306, 304, 302
ABQ-LA: (Corridor 5: 182, 184, 186, 188, 190, 192, 62, 64, 66)
ABQ-LAS: 182, 100, 102, 58, 60
ABQ-MCO: 182, 64, 174, 172, 300, 296, 298, 144, 146
ABQ-MEM: 182, 36, (Corridor 5: 178, 176, 174, 240)
ABQ-MI: 182, 64, 174, 172, 304, 302, 300, 298, 296, 144, 146, 148, 150, 134
ABQ-MSP: 182, 94, 86, 92, 90, 88, 84, 36, 38, 64

ABQ-MSY: 182, 64, 174, 172, 304, 302, 300
ABQ-PHX: 182, 100, 186
ABQ-SEA: 182, 98, 96, 50, 52, 214, 216, 218, 64, 290, 248, 246
ABQ-SF: 182, 100, 102, 58, 60, 266, 198, 64, 196
ABQ-SLC: 182, 98, 96, 50, 52, 214, 216, 218
ABQ-TPA: 182, 64, 174, 172, 304, 302, 300, 298, 296, 144, 146

ANC Anchorage

ANC-SEA: (Corridor 13: 319 to end)
ANC-YVR: (Corridor 13: 319, 320, 322, 324, 326, 328)

ATL Atlanta

ATL-ABQ: (Corridor 5: 142, 168, 170, 240, 172, 174, 176), 36, 64, 182
ATL-BOS: (Corridor 4: 164, 162, 160, 158, 156, 154, 153)

ATL-CH: (Corridor 3: 142, 140, 138, 74, 30, 26, 24)
ATL-CLE: 142, 140, 238, 236, 72
ATL-CVG: 142, 140
ATL-DC: 142, 164, 162, 118, 110
ATL-DEN: 142, 168, 240, 36, 82, 84, 44, 42
ATL-DFW: (Corridor 5: 142, 168, 170, 240, 172)
ATL-DTW: 142, 140, 138, 18
ATL-HO: 142, 168, 170, 302
ATL-LA: (Corridor 5: 141 to end)
ATL-LAS: 142, 168, 170, 240, 172, 174, 176, 178, 36, 182, 100, 102, 58, 60
ATL-MCO: 142, 128, 144, 132
ATL-MI: (Corridor 3: 142 to end)
ATL-MSP: 142, 140, 138, 74, 30, 24, 26, 276
ATL-MSY: 142, 168, 296, 300
ATL-NY: (Corridor 4: 142, 164, 162, 160, 114, 112, 110, 6); paths vary by arrival airport
ATL-PDX: 142, 240, 36, 82, 84, 44, 42, 46, 210, 216, 252
ATL-PHL: 142, 164, 162, 118, 110, 108, 69
ATL-PHX: (Corridor 5: 141, 142, 144, 146, 148, 150, 152, 154, 156, 158, 160, 162, 164, 166, 168, 170, 172, 174, 176, 178, 180, 182, 184, 186)
ATL-PIT: 142, 140, 238, 236, 72
ATL-SAN: (Corridor 5: 141, 142, 144, 146, 148, 150, 152, 154, 156, 158, 160, 162, 164, 166, 168, 170, 172, 174, 176, 178, 180, 182, 184, 190, 192)
ATL-SEA: 142, 240, 36, 82, 84, 42, 44, 46, 210, 216, 64, 290, 248, 246
ATL-SF: 142, 240, 36, 176, 82, 84, 86, 88, 90, 92, 94, 96, 98, 52, 54, 56, 220, 266, 198, 64, 196
ATL-SLC: 142, 240, 36, 82, 84, 44, 42, 46, 212, 214, 216
ATL-STL: 142, 140, 138
ATL-TPA: 142, 144, 146
ATL-YUL: 142, 140, 238, 236, 72, 14, 16, 316, 276, 64
ATL-YYZ: 142, 140, 238, 236, 72, 14, 16

BOS Boston

BOS-ATL: (Corridor 4)
BOS-CH: 154, 312, 64, 276, 20, 24
BOS-CLE: 154, 312, 314, 316, 16
BOS-CLT: (Corridor 4: 154, 158, 232, 69, 110, 118)
BOS-CVG: 154, 158, 10, 12, 14, 72
BOS-DC: 154, 156, 6, 106, 232, 108, 110
BOS-DEN: 154, 312, 276, 20, 24, 26, 28, 30, 32, 34, 36, 38, 40, 284, 42, 44
BOS-DFW: 154, 158, 69, (Corridor 8: 232 to end)
BOS-DTW: 154, 312, 276, 20
BOS-HO: 154, 158, 6, 69, 232, 110, 234, 236, 238, 138, 170, 302
BOS-LA: 154, 312, 276, (Corridor 1A: 20, 22, 24, 26, 28, 30, 32, 34, 36, 38, 40, 42, 44, 46, 48, 50, 52, 54, 56, 58, 60, 62, 64, 66)
BOS-LAS: 154, 312, 276, (Corridor 1A: 20, 22, 24, 26, 28, 30, 32, 34, 36, 38, 40, 42, 44, 46, 48, 50, 52, 54, 56, 58)
BOS-MCI: 154, 158, 10, 12, 14, 28, 30, 32, 80
BOS-MCO: 154, 156, 6, 232, 106, 108, 110, 112, 114, 116, 118, 120, 122, 124, 126, 128, 130, 132
BOS-MEM: 154, 158, 69, (Corridor 8: 232, 234, 236, 238)
BOS-MI: 154, 156, 6, (Corridor 2: 106, 108, 110, 112, 114, 116, 118, 120, 122, 124, 126, 128, 130, 132, 134)
BOS-MSP: 154, 312, 64, 276, 311, 20, 274
BOS-MSY: 154, (Corridor 4: 152, 154, 158, 160, 162, 164), 142, 168, 296
BOS-NY: 154, 156, 158, 6
BOS-PDX: 154, 312, 64, 276, 311, 20, (Corridor 10: 274, 276, 278, 280, 282, 284, 286, 288)
BOS-PHL: 154, 156, 158, 6, 106, 69
BOS-PHX: 154, 312, 276, 20, 24, 28, 30, 32, 34, 36, (Corridor 1B: 82, 84, 86, 88, 90, 92, 94, 96, 98, 100), 186
BOS-PIT: 154, 158, 12
BOS-SEA: 154, 312, 64, 276, 311, 20, (Corridor 10: 274, 276, 278, 280, 282, 284, 286, 288, 290, 292, 248, 246)
BOS-SF: 154, 312, 276, 20, 28, 30, 32, 34, 36, 38, 40, 284, (Corridor 7: 210 to end)

CLT-DFW: 118, 164, 140, 168, 170, 172
CLT-DTW: 118, 160, 236, 18
CLT-HO: 164, 142, 168, 300, 302
CLT-LA: 164, 140, 240, 242, 174, 176, 86, 94, 100, 102, 188, 60, 62, 64, 66
CLT-LAS: 164, 140, 240, 242, 174, 176, 86, 94, 100, 102, 58, 60
CLT-MCI: 164, 140, 138, 78, 80
CLT-MCO: 126, 128, 130, 132
CLT-MEM: 164, 140
CLT-MI: (Corridor 2: 126 to end)
CLT-MSP: 160, 238, 236, 74, 22, 24, 26, 276
CLT-MSY: 142, 296, 298, 300
CLT-NY: (Corridor 2: 118, 116, 114, 112, 110, 108, 106, 6)
CLT-PHL: 118, 116, 110, 108, 69
CLT-PIT: 118, 160, 236, 234, 72
CLT-SEA: 164, 140, 138, 28, 30, 32, 34, 36, (Corridor 10: 278 to end)
CLT-SF: 164, 140, 240, 36, 82, 84, 86, 88, 90, 92, 48, 50, 52, 54, (Corridor 7: 220 to end)
CLT-STL: 164, 140, 138
CLT-TPA: 126, 128, 130, 132, 144, 146
CLT-YYZ: 118, 160, 234, 14, 16

CVG Cincinnati

CVG-ATL: 140, 142
CVG-BOS: 72, 12, 314, 154
CVG-CH: 74, 30
CVG-CLT: 238, 160, 118
CVG-DC: 236, 234, 110
CVG-DEN: 30, 78, 80, 36, 84, 44, 42
CVG-DFW: 138, 240, 242, 172
CVG-DTW: 18
CVG-HO: 138, 170, 302
CVG-LA: 240, 36, 174, 176, 84, 86, 182, 100, 102, 188, 62, 64, 66
CVG-LAS: 240, 36, 174, 176, 84, 86, 182, 100, 102, 58, 60
CVG-MCI: 30, 78, 80
CVG-MCO: 138, 140, 128, 132
CVG-MEM: 138, 140

CVG-MI: 138, 140, 128, 132, 146, 148, 150, 134
CVG-MSP: 74, 24, 26, 30, 276
CVG-MSY: 138, 140, 168, 296, 298, 300
CVG-NY: 72, 14, 12, 8, 6
CVG-PDX: 74, 28, 30, 32, 34, 36, (Corridor 10: 278, 280, 282, 284, 286, 288), 252
CVG-PHL: 72
CVG-PHX: 240, 36, 174, 176, 82, 84, 86, 94, 182, 100, 186
CVG-PIT: 72
CVG-SAN: 138, 36, 176, 94, 182, 100, 184, 186, 188, 190, 192
CVG-SEA: 74, 28, 30, 32, 34, 36, (Corridor 10: 278 to end)
CVG-SF: 30, 32, 34, 36, 38, 40, 42, (Corridor 7: 209 to end)
CVG-SLC: 30, 32, 34, 36, 38, 40, 42, (Corridor 7: 209, 210, 212, 214, 216)
CVG-TPA: 138, 140, 142, 144, 146

DC Washington, DC/Baltimore metropolitan area (IAD, DCA, and BWI)

DC-ABQ: 110, 234, 236, 36, 82, 84, 86, 94, 182
DC-ATL: 110, 114, 116, (Corridor 4: 160 to end)
DC-BOS: 110, 108, 69, 6, 156, 154
DC-CH: 110, 234, 236
DC-CLT: 110, 118
DC-CVG: 110, 234, 236
DC-DEN: 110, 234, 236, 74, 78, 80, 82, 84, 36, 44, 42
DC-DFW: 110, (Corridor 8: 234 to end)
DC-HO: 110, 160, 140, 168, 170, 300, 302
DC-LA: 110, 234, 236, (Corridor 1A: 74 to end)
DC-LAS: 110, 234, 236, (Corridor 1A: 74, 76, 78, 80, 82, 84, 86, 88, 90, 92, 94, 96, 98, 100, 102), 58, 60
DC-MCI: 110, 234, 236, (Corridor 1A: 74, 76, 78, 80)
DC-MCO: (Corridor 2: 110, 112, 114, 116, 118, 120, 122, 124, 126, 128, 130, 132)
DC-MEM: 110, 234, 236, 138, 140
DC-MI: (Corridor 2: 110 to end)
DC-MSP: 110, 72, 18, 276
DC-MSY: 110, 160, 140, 168

DC-NY: (Corridor 2: 110, 108, 106, 105)

DC-PDX: 110, 234, 74, 28, 30, 32, 34, 36, 38, 40, (Corridor 10: 278, 280, 282, 284, 286, 288), 252

DC-PHX: 110, 234, 236, 36, 174, 176, 82, 84, 86, 94, 182, 100, 186

DC-SAN: 110, 234, 236, 36, 174, 176, 82, 84, 86, 94, 100, 188, 62, 190, 192

DC-SEA: 110, 234, 236, 24, 26, 28, 30, 32, 34, 36, (Corridor 10: 278 to end)

DC-SF: 110, 234, 74, 28, 30, 32, 34, 36, 38, 40, 42, 44, 46, 284, (Corridor 7: 210 to end)

DC-SLC: 110, 234, 236, 74, 28, 30, 32, 34, 36, 38, 40, 42, 284, 210, 212, 214, 216

DC-STL: 110, 234, 30

DC-TPA: (Corridor 2: 110, 112, 114, 116, 118, 120, 122, 124, 126, 128, 130, 132, 144, 146)

DC-YUL: 110, 108, 70, 6, 12, 314, 316, 64

DC-YVR: 110, 234, 236, 74, 28, 30, 32, 34, 36, (Corridor 10: 278 to end)

DC-YYZ: 110, 70, 12, 316

DCA, *see* DC (Washington, DC/Baltimore metropolitan area)

DEN Denver

DEN-ABQ: 42, 44, 36, 90, 92, 94, 182

DEN-ATL: 42, 44, 84, 82, 36, 240, 140, 142

DEN-BOS: (Corridor 1A: 44, 42, 40, 38, 36, 34, 32, 30, 28, 26, 24, 22, 20, 18), 16, 316, 314, 158, 154

DEN-CH: (Corridor 1A: 44, 42, 40, 38, 36, 34, 32, 30, 28, 26, 24, 64)

DEN-CLE: (Corridor 1A: 44, 42, 40, 38, 36, 34, 32, 30, 28, 26, 24, 64)

DEN-CLT: 42, 44, 84, 240, 138, 140, 160, 164

DEN-CVG: 42, 44, 38, 36, 80, 78

DEN-DC: 42, 44, 38, 36, 30, 28, 74, 72, 234, 110

DEN-DFW: 42, 44, 84, 36, 176, 174, 172

DEN-DTW: (Corridor 1A: 42, 40, 38, 36, 34, 32, 30, 28, 26, 24, 22, 20)

DEN-HO: 42, 44, 84, 36, 176, 174, 172, 304, 302

DEN-LA: (Corridor 1A: 42, 44, 46, 48, 50, 52, 54, 56, 58, 60, 62, 64, 66)

DEN-LAS: (Corridor 1A: 42, 44, 46, 48, 50, 52, 54, 56, 58, 60)

DEN-MCI: 42, 44, 84, 36, 80

DEN-MCO: 42, 44, 84, 36, 240, 168, 144, 128, 132

DEN-MEM: 42, 44, 84, 36, 240

DEN-MI: 42, 44, 84, 36, 240, 168, 144, 146, 148, 150, 134

DEN-MSP: 42, 284, 84, 36, 64

DEN-MSY: 42, 44, 84, 36, 176, 174, 172, 300

DEN-NY: (Corridor 1A: 44, 42, 40, 38, 36, 34, 32, 30, 28, 26, 24, 22, 20, 18, 16, 14, 12, 10, 8, 6)

DEN-PDX: 42, 284, 162, 288, 252

DEN-PHL: 44, 42, 84, 36, 28, 74, 72, 70, 69

DEN-PHX: 42, 44, 46, 48, 50, 88, 90, 92, 94, 100, 186

DEN-PIT: (Corridor 1A: 44, 42, 40, 38, 36, 34, 32, 30, 28, 26, 24, 22, 20, 18), 74, 14, 72

DEN-SAN: (Corridor 1A: 42, 44, 46, 48, 50, 52, 54, 56, 58, 60, 62), 188, 192

DEN-SEA: 42, 284, 162, 288, 252, 290, 248, 246

DEN-SF: 42, (Corridor 7: 210 to end)

DEN-SLC: 42, (Corridor 7: 210, 212, 214, 216)

DEN-STL: 42, 44, 36, 84, 82, 80, 78

DEN-TPA: 42, 44, 84, 36, 240, 168, 144, 146

DEN-YUL: (Corridor 1A: 44, 42, 40, 38, 36, 34, 32, 30, 28, 22, 18)

DEN-YVR: 42, 284, 162, 288, 252, 290, 248, 246, 292

DEN-YYZ: (Corridor 1A: 44, 42, 40, 38, 36, 34, 32, 30, 28, 26, 24, 22, 20, 18)

DFW Dallas–Fort Worth

DFW-ABQ: (Corridor 5: 172, 174, 176, 178, 180, 182)

DFW-ATL: (Corridor 5: 172, 170, 168, 142)

DFW-BOS: 172, 242, 240, 30, 16, 314, 316, 158, 154

DFW-CH: 172, 78, 28, 30, 26, 24

DFW-CLE: 172, 242, 240

DFW-CLT: 172, 170, 168, 142

DFW-CVG: 172, 242, 240

DFW-DC: (Corridor 8: 242, 240, 238, 236, 234, 110)

DFW-DEN: 172, 174, 36, 84, 44, 42

DFW-DTW: 172, 242, 240, 74, 18
DFW-HO: 172, 304, 302
DFW-LA: (Corridor 5: 172 to end)
DFW-LAS: (Corridor 5: 172, 174, 176, 178, 180, 182), 94, 100, 102, 58, 60
DFW-MCO: 172, 128, 144
DFW-MEM: 172, 242, 240
DFW-MI: 172, 300, 298, 150, 134
DFW-MSP: 172, 80, 32, 30
DFW-MSY: 172, 300
DFW-NY: 172, (Corridor 8: 242, 240, 238, 236, 234, 232, 231)
DFW-PDX: 172, 174, 176, 84, 86, 88, 90, 92, 48, 46, 212, 214, 216, 218, 288, 252
DFW-PHL: (Corridor 8: 242, 240, 238, 236, 234, 232), 69
DFW-PHX: (Corridor 5: 172, 174, 176, 178, 180, 182, 184, 186)
DFW-PIT: 172, 242, 240, 236, 72
DFW-SAN: (Corridor 5: 172 to end)
DFW-SEA: 172, 174, 176, 84, 86, 88, 90, 92, 48, 46, 212, 214, 216, 218, 288, 252, 250, 248, 246
DFW-SF: 172, 174, 94, 96, 98, 56, 54, 220, 226, 64, 198, 196
DFW-SLC: 172, 174, 176, 84, 86, 88, 90, 92, 48, 46, 212, 214, 216
DFW-TPA: 172, 300, 298
DFW-YUL: 172, 242, 240, 74, 18, 20
DFW-YVR: : 172, 174, 36, 84, 44, 42, 46, 162, 288, 290, 292, 246
DFW-YYC: 172, 174, 36, 84, 284, 36, 282
DFW-YYZ: 172, 242, 240, 74, 18, 20

DTW Detroit

DTW-ATL: 18, 138, 140, 142
DTW-BOS: 16, 316, 314, 158, 154
DTW-CLT: 18, 238, 234, 164
DTW-DC: 72, 234, 110
DTW-DEN: (Corridor 1A: 24, 26, 28, 30, 32, 34, 36, 38, 40, 42)
DTW-DFW: 18, 30, 172
DTW-HO: 18, 30, 240, 302
DTW-LA: (Corridor 1A: 24, 26, 28, 30, 32, 34, 36, 38, 40, 42, 44, 46, 48, 50, 52, 54, 56, 58, 60, 62, 64, 66)

DTW-LAS: (Corridor 1A: 24, 26, 28, 30, 32, 34, 36, 38, 40, 42, 44, 46, 48, 50, 52, 54, 56, 58, 60)
DTW-MCI: 24, 26, 28, 30, 80
DTW-MCO: 18, 140, 128, 144
DTW-MI: 18, 140, 128, 144, 146, 148, 150, 134
DTW-MSP: 20, 274
DTW-MSY: 138, 140, 300
DTW-NY: (Corridor 1A: 16, 12, 10, 8, 6)
DTW-PDX: (Corridor 10: 274, 276, 278, 280, 282, 284, 286, 288), 36, 162
DTW-PHX: 22, 24, 26, 28, 30, 32, 34, 36, (Corridor 1B: 74, 76, 78, 80, 82, 84, 86, 88, 90, 92, 94, 100), 186
DTW-SAN: 24, 26, 28, 30, 32, 80, (Corridor 1B: 82, 84, 86, 88, 90, 92, 94, 96, 98, 100, 102), 188, 190, 192
DTW-SEA: (Corridor 10: 274, 276, 278, 280, 282, 284, 286, 288, 290, 292, 248, 246), 36, 162
DTW-SF: (Corridor 7: 209 to end)
DTW-SLC: (Corridor 7: 209, 210, 212, 214, 216)
DTW-TPA: 18, 140, 128, 144, 146
DTW-YVR: (Corridor 10: 274 to end), 292

EWR, *see* NY (New York metropolitan area)
FLL, *see* MI (Miami area)

HO Houston (IAH and HOU)

HO-ABQ: (Corridor 11: 302, 304, 306, 308), 180, 182
HO-BOS: 302, (Corridor 8: 240, 238, 236, 234, 232, 231), 6, 156, 154
HO-CH: 302, 242, 240, 28, 26, 24
HO-CLE: 302, 140
HO-CLT: 302, 300, 168, 142
HO-CVG: 302, 140
HO-DC: 302, 240, 238, 236, 234; *or* 302, 300, 296, 142, 164, 118, 116, 110
HO-DEN: 302, 304, 172, 174, 176, 36, 84, 44, 42
HO-DFW: 302, 304, 172
HO-DTW: 302, 240, 74, 18
HO-LA: (Corridor 11: 302, 304, 306, 308), 180, 184, 186, 188, 190, 192, 62, 64, 66

LA-PDX: 66, 64, 206, (Corridor 9: 270, 268, 266, 264, 262, 260, 258, 256, 254, 252)

LA-PHL: 66, 64, 62, 60, 58, (Corridor 1B: 102, 100, 98, 96, 94, 92, 90, 88, 86, 84, 82, 80, 78, 76, 74, 72, 70, 69)

LA-PHX: 66, 64, 62, 192, 190

LA-PIT: 66, 64, 62, 60, 58, (Corridor 1B: 102, 100, 98, 96, 94, 92, 90, 88, 86, 84, 82, 80, 78, 76, 74, 72)

LA-SEA: 66, 64, 206, (Corridor 9: 270, 268, 266, 264, 262, 260, 258, 256, 254, 252, 250, 248, 246)

LA-SF: 66, (Corridor 9: 206, 204, 202, 200, 198, 196, 195)

LA-SLC: 66, 64, 62, 220, 214

LA-STL: (Corridor 1B: 66, 68, 70, 72, 74, 76, 78)

LA-TPA: 66, 64, 62, 186, 184, 182, 180, 178, (Corridor 11: 308, 306, 304, 302, 300, 298, 296, 295)

LA-YUL: (Corridor 1A: 66, 64, 62, 60, 58, 56, 54, 52, 50, 48, 46, 44, 42, 40, 38, 36, 34, 32, 30, 28, 26, 24, 22)

LA-YVR: 66, 64, 206, (Corridor 9: 270, 268, 266, 264, 262, 260, 258, 256, 254, 252, 250, 248, 246), 292

LA-YYC: 66, 64, 266, 224, 288, 162, 286, 284

LA-YYZ: (Corridor 1A: 66, 64, 62, 60, 58, 56, 54, 52, 50, 48, 46, 44, 42, 40, 38, 36, 34, 32, 30, 28, 26, 24, 22)

LAS Las Vegas

LAS-ABQ: 60, 58, 100, 182

LAS-ATL: 60, 58, 100, 182, (Corridor 5: 176, 174, 172, 170, 168), 142

LAS-BOS: (Corridor 1A: 60, 58, 56, 54, 52, 50, 48, 46, 44, 42, 40, 38, 36, 34, 32, 30, 28, 26, 24, 22, 20, 18, 16), 316, 314, 158, 154

LAS-CH: (Corridor 1A: 60, 58, 56, 54, 52, 50, 48, 46, 44, 42, 40, 38, 36, 34, 32, 30, 28, 26, 24)

LAS-CLE: (Corridor 1A: 60, 58, 56, 54, 52, 50, 48, 46, 44, 42, 40, 38, 36, 34, 32, 30, 28, 26, 24, 22)

LAS-CLT: 60, 58, (Corridor 5: 192, 190, 188, 186, 184, 182, 180, 178, 176, 174, 172), 242, 240, 140, 164

LAS-CVG: (Corridor 1A: 60, 58, 56, 54, 52, 50, 48, 46, 44, 42, 40, 38, 36, 34, 32, 30, 28, 26, 24, 22, 20, 18); *or* (Corridor 1B: 100, 98, 96, 94, 92, 90, 88, 86, 84, 82, 80, 78)

LAS-DC: (Corridor 1A: 60, 58, 56, 54, 52, 50, 48, 46, 44, 42, 40, 38, 36, 34, 32, 30, 28, 26, 24, 22, 20, 18), 236, 234, 110; *or* (Corridor

1B: 100, 98, 96, 94, 92, 90, 88, 86, 84, 82, 80, 78, 72), 236, 234, 110

LAS-DEN: (Corridor 1A: 60, 58, 56, 54, 52, 50, 48, 46, 44, 42)

LAS-DFW: 60, 58, 102, 100, (Corridor 5: 188, 186, 184, 182, 180, 178, 176, 174, 172)

LAS-DTW: (Corridor 1A: 60, 58, 56, 54, 52, 50, 48, 46, 44, 42, 40, 38, 36, 34, 32, 30, 28, 26, 24, 22)

LAS-HO: 60, 58, 102, 100, 182, 180, 64, 178, 306, 304, 302

LAS-LA: 60, 62, 64, 66

LAS-MCI: 60, 58, (Corridor 1B: 102, 100, 98, 96, 94, 92, 90, 88, 86, 84, 82, 80)

LAS-MCO: 60, 58, 102, 100, 182, 64, 178, 306, 304, 302, 300, 298, 296, 295, 144

LAS-MEM: 60, 58, 102, 100, 94, 86, 176, 174, 240

LAS-MI: 60, 58, 102, 100, 182, 64, 178, 306, 304, 302, 300, 298, 144, 146, 148, 150, 134

LAS-MSP: (Corridor 1A: 60, 58, 56, 54, 52, 50, 48, 46, 44, 42, 40, 38, 36), 30

LAS-MSY: 60, 58, 102, 100, 182, 64, 178, 306, 304, 302, 300, 298

LAS-NY: (Corridor 1A: 60, 58, 56, 54, 52, 50, 48, 46, 44, 42, 40, 38, 36, 34, 32, 30, 28, 26, 24, 22, 20, 18, 16, 14, 12, 10, 8, 6, 5)

LAS-PDX: 300, 262, 256, 252

LAS-PHL: 60, 58, (Corridor 1B: 102, 100, 98, 96, 94, 92, 90, 88, 86, 84, 82, 80, 78, 76, 74, 72, 70, 69)

LAS-PHX: 60, 58, 186

LAS-PIT: 60, 58, (Corridor 1B: 102, 100, 98, 96, 94, 92, 90, 88, 86, 84, 82, 80, 78, 76, 74, 72)

LAS-SAN: 62, 192

LAS-SEA: 300, 262, 256, 252, 250, 248, 246

LAS-SF: 266, 198, 64, 196

LAS-STL: 60, 58, 56, 54, 52, 50, 48, 288, 36, 92, 90, 88, 86, 84, 82, 80, 78

LAS-TPA: 60, 58, 102, 100, 182, 64, 178, 306, 304, 302, 300, 298

LAS-YUL: (Corridor 1A: 60, 58, 56, 54, 52, 50, 48, 46, 44, 42, 40, 38, 36, 34, 32, 30, 28, 26, 24, 22, 20, 18), 276

LAS-YVR: 300, 262, 256, 252, 250, 248, 246, 292

LAS-YYZ: (Corridor 1A: 60, 58, 56, 54, 52, 50, 48, 46, 44, 42, 40, 38, 36, 34, 32, 30, 28, 26, 24, 22, 20, 18), 276

LAX, *see* LA (Los Angeles metropolitan area)
LGA, *see* NY (New York metropolitan area)
LGB, *see* LA (Los Angeles metropolitan area)

MCI Kansas City

MCI-ABQ: (Corridor 1B: 80, 82, 84, 86, 94), 182
MCI-ATL: 80, 140, 142
MCI-BOS: 80, 78, 30, 28, 26, 24, 22, 20, 18, 16, 316, 314, 158, 154
MCI-CH: 80, 32, 30, 28, 26, 24
MCI-CLE: 80, 30, 28, 22, 18
MCI-CLT: 80, 138, 140, 234, 164
MCI-CVG: 80, 78, 30
MCI-DC: 80, 28, 30, 74, 236, 234, 110
MCI-DEN: 80, 36, 84, 44, 42
MCI-DTW: 80, 30, 28, 22
MCI-LA: (Corridor 1B: 80, 78, 76, 74, 72, 70, 68, 66)
MCI-LAS: (Corridor 1B: 80, 78, 76, 74, 72, 70, 68, 66, 64, 62, 60)
MCI-MCO: 80, 168, 128, 144
MCI-MI: 80, 168, 144, 146, 148, 150, 134
MCI-MSY: 80, 242, 300
MCI-NY: 80, 28, 30, 74, 16, 14, 12, 10, 8, 6
MCI-PDX: 80, 36, 38, 40, 284, 288, 162
MCI-PHL: 80, 28, 30, 74, 70, 69
MCI-PHX: 80, 82, 84, 36, 94, 182
MCI-PIT: 80, 28, 30, 74, 72
MCI-SAN: (Corridor 1B: 80, 82, 84, 86, 88, 90, 92, 94, 96, 98, 100, 102), 188, 62, 190, 192
MCI-SEA: 80, 30, 36, 38, 40, (Corridor 10: 284 to end)
MCI-SF: 80, 36, 84, 42, 44, 46, (Corridor 10: 212 to end)
MCI-SLC: 80, 36, 84, 42, 44, 46, 212, 214, 216
MCI-TPA: 80, 240, 168, 144
MCI-YYZ: 80, 30, 28, 22, 18

MCO Orlando

MCO-ABQ: 144, 296, 298, 300, 172, 174, 64, 182
MCO-ATL: 132, 128, 142
MCO-BOS: (Corridor 2: 132 to beginning), 156, 154

MCO-CH: 132, 128, (Corridor 3: 142 to beginning)
MCO-CLE: 132, 128, 142, 140, 238, 236, 72
MCO-CLT: 132, 126, 122, 128
MCO-CVG: 132, 128, 142, 140
MCO-DC: (Corridor 2: 132, 130, 128, 126, 124, 122, 120, 118, 116, 114, 112, 110)
MCO-DEN: 132, 128, 144, 168, 240, 36, 84, 44, 42,
MCO-DFW: 146, 296, 298, 300, 172
MCO-DTW: 132, 128, 142, 140, 18
MCO-HO: 146, 296, 298, 300, 302
MCO-LA: 144, (Corridor 5: 170 to end); *or* 146, 298, 300, 302, 304, 306, 308, 180, 182, 184, 186, 188, 62, 64, 66
MCO-LAS: 144, (Corridor 5: 170, 172, 174, 176, 178, 180, 182, 184); *or* 146, 298, 300, 302, 304, 306, 308, 180, 182, 184, 102, 58, 60
MCO-MCI: 132, 128, 168, 240, 80
MCO-MEM: 144, 168
MCO-MI: 148, 134
MCO-MSP: 144, 168, 140, 28, 30, 32
MCO-MSY: 146, 298
MCO-NY: (Corridor 2: 132 to beginning)
MCO-PHL: (Corridor 2: 132, 130, 128, 126, 124, 122, 120, 118, 116, 114, 112, 110, 108, 106, 104, 102, 100, 98, 96, 94, 92, 90, 88, 86, 84, 82, 80, 78, 76, 74, 72, 70, 69)
MCO-PHX: 144, (Corridor 5: 170, 172, 174, 176, 178, 180, 182, 184, 186); *or* 146, 298, 300, 302, 304, 306, 308, 180, 182, 184, 186
MCO-PIT: 132, 126, 160, 234, 236
MCO-SEA: 144, 168, 240, 30, 36, 38, 40, 280, 284, 288, 64, 290, 252, 248, 246
MCO-SF: 144, 298, 300, 172, 174, 176, 36, 84, 86, 88, 90, 92, 288, 48, 50, 52, 54, 56, 220, 226, 64, 196
MCO-SLC: 146, 298, 300, 172, 174, 176, 36, 84, 86, 88, 90, 92, 288, 50, 48, 214, 216
MCO-STL: 144, 168, 140
MCO-YUL: (Corridor 2: 132 to beginning), 314
MCO-YYZ: (Corridor 2: 132, 34, 126), 160, 234, 14, 16

MDW, *see* CH (Chicago)

MEM Memphis

MEM-BOS: 138, 14, 314, 154; *or* 140, 164, 118, 114, 112, 106, 6, 156, 154

MEM-CH: 240, 30, 26, 24

MEM-CLT: 140, 164

MEM-DC: 140, 238, 236, 234, 110

MEM-DEN: 240, 82, 36, 84, 44, 42

MEM-DFW: 240, 242, 172

MEM-DTW: 138, 30, 18

MEM-LA: 240, (Corridor 5: 172, 174, 176, 178, 180, 182, 184, 186, 188), 62, 64, 66

MEM-LAS: 240, (Corridor 5: 172, 174, 176, 178, 180, 182), 64, 100, 102, 58, 60

MEM-MCI: 240, 80

MEM-MCO: 168, 128, 132

MEM-MI: 168, 144, 146, 148, 150, 134

MEM-MSP: 240, 28, 30, 32

MEM-MSY: 170, 300

MEM-NY: 138, (Corridor 8: 238, 236, 234, 332, 231)

MEM-PHL: 138, (Corridor 8: 238, 236, 234), 110, 69

MEM-PHX: 240, (Corridor 5: 172, 174, 176, 178, 180, 182, 184, 186)

MEM-PIT: 140, 138, 72

MEM-SEA: 240, 30, 36, 38, 40, 284, 288, 64, 290, 252, 248, 246

MEM-SF: 240, 242, 82, 84, 86, 88, 90, 92, 94, 96, 98, 50, 52, 54, 56, 288, 220, 226, 64, 198, 196

MI Miami area (MIA, FLL, and PBI)

MI-ATL: 134, (Corridor 3: 150, 148, 146, 144, 142)

MI-BOS: (Corridor 2: 134 to beginning), 156, 154

MI-CH: 134, (Corridor 3: 150 to beginning)

MI-CLE: (Corridor 2: 134, 132, 130, 128, 126), 160, 236

MI-CLT: (Corridor 2: 134, 132, 130, 128, 126)

MI-CVG: 134, 150, 148, 146, 144, 142, 140, 138

MI-DC: (Corridor 2: 134, 132, 130, 128, 126, 124, 122, 120, 118, 116, 114, 112, 110)

MI-DEN: 134, 150, 148, 296, 298, 300, 36, 82, 84, 44, 42

MI-DFW: 134, 150, 148, 296, 298, 300, 172

MI-DTW: (Corridor 2: 134, 132, 130, 128, 126), 160, 236

MI-HO: 134, 150, 148, 298, 300

MI-LA: 134, 150, 146, 298, 300, 302, 304, 306, 308, 180, 182, 184, 186, 188, 62, 64, 66

MI-LAS: 134, 150, 146, 298, 300, 302, 304, 306, 308, 180, 182, 184, 102, 58, 60

MI-MCI: 134, 150, 148, 146, 144, 170, 240, 80

MI-MCO: 134, 148

MI-MEM: 134, 150, 148, 146, 144, 168

MI-MSP: 134, (Corridor 3: 150, 148, 146, 144, 142, 140, 138, 137), 24, 276

MI-MSY: 134, 150, 148, 298

MI-NY: (Corridor 2: 134 to beginning)

MI-PHL: (Corridor 2: 134, 132, 130, 128, 126, 124, 122, 120, 118, 116, 114, 112, 110, 108, 69)

MI-PHX: 134, 150, 146, 298, 300, 302, 304, 306, 308, 180, 182, 184, 186

MI-PIT: (Corridor 2: 134, 132, 130, 128, 126), 160, 236, 234

MI-SAN: 134, 150, 148, 146, 298, 300, 302, 304, 306, 308, 180, 182, 184, 186, 192, 190

MI-SEA: 144, 128, 168, 240, 30, 36, 38, 40, 280, 64, 290, 252, 248, 246, 284, 286, 288, 290, 292

MI-SF: 134, 150, 148, 146, 298, 300, 302, 304, 306

MI-SLC: 134, 150, 148, 146, 298, 300, 172, 174, 176, 36, 84, 86, 88, 90, 92, 288, 48, 50, 214, 216

MI-STL: 134, 150, 148, 146, 144, 168, 138

MI-TPA: 134, 150, 148, 146

MI-YUL: (Corridor 2: 134 to beginning), 314

MI-YYZ: (Corridor 2: 134, 132, 130, 128, 126, 118), 160, 236, 234, 14, 16

MIA, *see* MI (Miami area)

MSP Minneapolis–St. Paul

MSP-ABQ: 64, 30, 32, 34, 36, 82, 84, 86, 94, 182

MSP-ATL: 28, 30, 138, 140, 234, 142

MSP-CLT: 28, 30, 74, 138, 238, 140, 164

MSP-CVG: 30, 28, 26, 24, 74

MSP-DC: 18, 72, 234, 110

MSP-DEN: 64, 36, 40, 284, 42
MSP-DFW: 30, 32, 34, 174, 172
MSP-DTW: 274, 276, 20
MSP-HO: 64, 30, 32, 34, 80
MSP-LA: 64, (Corridor 1A: 36, 38, 40, 42, 44, 46, 48, 50, 52, 54, 56, 58, 60, 62, 64, 66)
MSP-LAS: 64, (Corridor 1A: 36, 38, 40, 42, 44, 46, 48, 50, 52, 54, 56, 58, 60)
MSP-MCI: 64, 30, 32, 34, 80
MSP-MCO: 32, 30, 28, 138, 140, 142, 128
MSP-MEM: 32, 30, 28
MSP-MI: 32, 30, 28, 138, 140, 144, 146, 148, 150, 134
MSP-MSY: 30, 32, 240, 170, 300
MSP-NY: 274, 272, (Corridor 1A: 20, 18, 16, 14, 12, 10, 8, 6)
MSP-PDX: 64, 36, (Corridor 10: 278, 280, 282, 284, 286, 288), 162
MSP-PHL: 172, 20, 18, 14, 70, 69
MSP-PHX: 64, 40, 38, 36, 44, 46, 48, 50, 88, 90, 92, 94, 96, 98, 100, 186
MSP-PIT: 172, 20, 18
MSP-SAN: 64, (Corridor 1A: 36, 38, 40, 42, 44, 46, 48, 50), 96, 98, 188, 192
MSP-SEA: 64, 36, (Corridor 10: 278 to end)
MSP-SF: 64, 278, 284, (Corridor 7: 210 to end)
MSP-SLC: 64, 278, 284, 288, 162, 210, 214, 216
MSP-STL: 32, 30, 28
MSP-TPA: 32, 30, 28, 140, 144

MSY New Orleans

MSY-BOS: 296, 142, (Corridor 4: 164, 162, 160, 158, 156, 154, 153)
MSY-CH: 170, 140, 138, 74, 24
MSY-CLE: 296, 168, 140, 138, 74
MSY-CLT: 296, 142
MSY-CVG: 296, 168, 140, 138
MSY-DC: 296, 142, (Corridor 4: 164, 162, 160), 110
MSY-DEN: 300, 172, 174, 36, 84, 44, 42
MSY-DFW: 300, 172
MSY-DTW: 170, 140, 138, 74

MSY-LA: (Corridor 11: 300 to end), (Corridor 5: 178 to end)
MSY-LAS: (Corridor 11: 300 to end), 178, 180, 182, 184, 102, 58, 60
MSY-MCI: 300, 170, 242, 240, 80
MSY-MCO: 298, 296, 144, 146
MSY-MI: 298, 296, 144, 146, 148, 150, 134
MSY-MSP: 170, 240, 28, 30
MSY-NY: 296, 142, 164, 162, 160, (Corridor 2: 118, 116, 114, 112, 110, 108, 106), 6
MSY-PHL: 296, 142, 164, 162, 160, 32, (Corridor 2: 118, 116, 114, 112, 110), 69
MSY-PIT: 296, 168, 140, 138, 74
MSY-SF: 300, 172, 174, 94, 96, 98, 56, 54, 220, 226, 64, 198, 196
MSY-STL: 170, 240
MSY-TPA: 298, 296, 144

NY New York metropolitan area (EWR, LGA, HPN, JFK, SWF, and ISP)

NY-ABQ: (Corridor 1B: 5, 6, 8, 10, 12, 14, 16, 18, 20, 22, 24, 26, 28, 30, 32, 34, 36, 38, 40, 42, 44, 46, 48, 50, 52, 54, 56, 58, 60, 62, 64, 66, 68, 70, 72, 74, 76, 78, 80, 82, 84, 86, 88, 90, 92, 94), 182
NY-ATL: 6, 232, 69, 110, (Corridor 4: 160 to end)
NY-BOS: 6, 156, 154
NY-CH: (Corridor 1A: 5, 6, 8, 10, 12, 14, 16, 18, 20, 22, 24)
NY-CLE: (Corridor 1A: 5, 6, 8, 10, 12, 14, 16)
NY-CLT: (Corridor 2: 105, 106, 108, 110, 112, 114, 116, 118, 32)
NY-CVG: 6, 232, (Corridor 1B: 69, 70, 72); or (Corridor 1A: 5, 6, 8, 10, 12, 14)
NY-DC: (Corridor 2: 105, 106, 108, 110)
NY-DEN: (Corridor 1A: 5, 6, 8, 10, 12, 14, 16, 18, 20, 22, 24, 26, 28, 30, 32, 34, 36, 38, 40, 42, 44)
NY-DFW: (Corridor 8: 231 to end)
NY-DTW: (Corridor 1A: 5, 6, 8, 10, 12, 14, 16)
NY-HO: (Corridor 8: 231, 232, 234, 236, 238, 240), 302
NY-LA: (Corridor 1A: 5 to end); or (Corridor 1B: 69 to end)
NY-LAS: (Corridor 1A: 5, 6, 8, 10, 12, 14, 16, 18, 20, 22, 24, 26, 28, 30, 32, 34, 36, 38, 40, 42, 44, 46, 48, 50, 52, 54, 56, 58, 60); or (Corridor 1B: 69, 70, 72, 74, 76, 78, 80, 82, 84, 86, 88, 90, 92, 94, 96, 98, 100, 102), 58, 60

NY-MCI: (Corridor 1B: 69, 70, 72, 74, 76, 78, 80)
NY-MCO: (Corridor 2: 105, 106, 108, 110, 112, 114, 116, 118, 120, 122, 124, 126, 128, 130, 132)
NY-MEM: (Corridor 8: 231, 232, 234, 236, 238, 240)
NY-MI: (Corridor 2: 105 to end)
NY-MSP: (Corridor 10: 273, 274, 276)
NY-MSY: 6, 232, 69, 110, (Corridor 4: 160 to end)
NY-PDX: (Corridor 10: 273, 274, 276, 278, 280, 282, 284, 286, 288), 252
NY-PHX: 6, (Corridor 1B: 69, 70, 72, 74, 76, 78, 80, 82, 84, 86, 88, 90, 92, 94, 96, 98, 100), 186
NY-PIT: (Corridor 1A: 6, 8, 10, 12)
NY-SAN: (Corridor 1A: 5, 6, 8, 10, 12, 14, 16, 18, 20, 22, 24, 26, 28, 30, 32, 34, 36, 38, 40, 42, 44, 46, 48, 50, 52, 54, 56, 58, 60, 62); *or* (Corridor 1B: 69, 70, 72, 74, 76, 78, 80, 82, 84, 86, 88, 90, 92, 94, 96, 98, 100, 102), 188, 190, 192
NY-SEA: (Corridor 10: 273 to end), 252
NY-SF: (Corridor 1A: 5, 6, 8, 10, 12, 14, 16, 18, 20, 22, 24), 74, (Corridor 7: 209 to end)
NY-SLC: (Corridor 1A: 5, 6, 8, 10, 12, 14, 16, 18, 20, 22, 24), 74, (Corridor 7: 209, 210, 212, 214, 216)
NY-STL: (Corridor 1B: 69, 70, 72, 74, 76)
NY-TPA: 6, 232, 69, 110, 118, 32, 126, 128, 144, 146
NY-YUL: 6, 314
NY-YVR: (Corridor 10: 273 to end), 252
NY-YYZ: 6, 10, 316

OAK, *see* SF (San Francisco Bay Area)
ONT, *see* LA (Los Angeles metropolitan area)
ORD, *see* CH (Chicago)
PBI, *see* MI (Miami area)

PDX Portland, Oregon

PDX-ABQ: 288, 214, 216, 218, 50, 52, 54, 98, 96, 94, 182
PDX-ATL: 64, 288, 284, 280, 40, 36, 34, 32, 30, 28, 138, 140, 142
PDX-BOS: 64, (Corridor 10: 288, 286, 284, 282, 280, 278, 276, 274, 312, 154)

PDX-CH: 64, 288, 284, 280, (Corridor 1A: 36, 34, 32, 30, 28, 26, 24)
PDX-CVG: 64, 288, 284, 280, (Corridor 1A: 36, 34, 32, 30, 28, 26, 24), 74
PDX-DC: 64, (Corridor 10: 288, 286, 284, 282, 280, 278, 276), 30, 24, 22, 72, 234, 110
PDX-DEN: 64, 288, 162, 42
PDX-DFW: 288, 216, 218, 48, 50, 46, 44, 42, 92, 90, 88, 86, 84, 176, 174, 172
PDX-DTW: 64, (Corridor 10: 288, 286, 284, 282, 280, 278, 276), 30, 20
PDX-HO: 288, 216, 218, 48, 50, 92, 90, 88, 86, 84, 176, 174, 304, 302
PDX-LA: (Corridor 9: 252 to end)
PDX-LAS: 252, 256, 262, 224
PDX-MSP: 64, (Corridor 10: 288, 286, 284, 282, 280, 278), 36
PDX-NY: 64, (Corridor 10: 288 to beginning)
PDX-PHL: 64, (Corridor 10: 288 to beginning), 69
PDX-PHX: 252, 224, 288, 58, 60, 186
PDX-SAN: 64, (Corridor 10: 288 to beginning)
PDX-SEA: (Corridor 9: 252, 250, 248, 246)
PDX-SF: (Corridor 9: 252, 254, 256, 258, 260, 262, 264), 228, 64, 196
PDX-YVR: 250, 248, 246, 252, 292

PHL Philadelphia

PHL-ATL: 69, 110, 160, 162, 164, 142
PHL-BOS: 69, 6, 156, 154
PHL-CH: 69, 70, 14, 72, 74, 22, 24
PHL-CLE: 69, 14
PHL-CLT: 69, 110, 118
PHL-CVG: 69, 70, 72
PHL-DEN: 69, 70, 72, 74, 76, 78, 80, 36, 84, 44, 42
PHL-DFW: 69, 70, (Corridor 7: 234 to end)
PHL-DTW: 69, 70, 72, 18
PHL-HO: 69, 70, (Corridor 7: 234, 236, 238, 240), 302
PHL-LA: (Corridor 1B: 69 to end)
PHL-LAS: (Corridor 1B: 69, 70, 72, 74, 76, 78, 80, 82, 84, 86, 88, 90, 92, 94, 96, 98, 100, 102), 58, 60

PHL-MCI: (Corridor 1B: 69, 70, 72, 74, 76, 78, 80)
PHL-MCO: (Corridor 2: 69, 110, 118, 32, 126, 128, 132)
PHL-MEM: 69, 70, 234, 236, 238, 138
PHL-MI: (Corridor 2: 69 to end)
PHL-MSP: 69, 14, 18, 276
PHL-MSY: 69, 110, 160, 140, 168
PHL-PDX: 69, (Corridor 10: 273, 274, 276, 278, 280, 282, 284, 286, 288), 252
PHL-PHX: (Corridor 1B: 69, 70, 72, 74, 76, 78, 80, 82, 84, 86, 88, 90, 92, 94, 96, 98, 100), 186
PHL-SAN: (Corridor 1B: 69, 70, 72, 74, 76, 78, 80, 82, 84, 86, 88, 90, 92, 94, 96, 98, 100, 102), 186, 188, 62, 192, 190
PHL-SEA: 69, (Corridor 10: 273 to end)
PHL-SF: (Corridor 1B: 69, 70, 72, 74, 76, 78, 80), 36, 84, 42, 44, 46, (Corridor 7: 212 to end)
PHL-STL: (Corridor 1B: 69, 70, 72, 74, 76), 30
PHL-TPA: (Corridor 2: 69, 110, 118, 126, 128, 144)
PHL-YUL: 69, 232, 6, 314
PHL-YYZ: 69, 232, 12

PHX Phoenix

PHX-ABQ: 186, 182
PHX-ATL: (Corridor 5: 186 to beginning)
PHX-BOS: 186, (Corridor 1B: 100, 94 to beginning), 16, 316, 158, 156, 154
PHX-CH: 186, (Corridor 1B: 100, 94, 92, 90, 88, 86, 84, 82), 36, 32, 30, 28, 26, 24
PHX-CLE: 186, (Corridor 1B: 100, 94, 92, 90, 88, 86, 84, 82), 36, 32, 30, 28, 26, 24, 22, 18
PHX-CLT: 186, 182, 36, 176, 174, 240, 140, 164
PHX-CVG: 186, 182, 36, 176, 80, 78, 30
PHX-DC: 186, 182, (Corridor 1B: 100, 98, 96, 94, 92, 90, 88, 86, 84, 82, 80, 78, 76, 74, 72, 70), 234, 110
PHX-DEN: 186, 50, 94, 92, 90, 46, 44, 42
PHX-DFW: (Corridor 5: 186, 184, 182, 180, 178, 176, 174, 172)
PHX-DTW: 186, (Corridor 1B: 100, 94, 92, 90, 88, 86, 84, 82, 80, 78), 36, 32, 30, 28, 26, 24, 22

PHX-HO: 186, 184, 182, 180, 178, 64, 308, 306, 304, 302
PHX-LA: 192, 64, 66
PHX-LAS: 186, 288, 58, 60
PHX-MCI: 186, (Corridor 1B: 100, 94, 92, 90, 88, 86, 84, 82, 80)
PHX-MCO: 186, 184, 182, 180, 178, 308, 306, 304, 302, 300, 298, 146
PHX-MEM: (Corridor 5: 186, 184, 182, 180, 178, 176, 174, 242, 240)
PHX-MI: 186, 184, 182, 180, 178, 308, 306, 304, 302, 300, 298, 148, 150, 134
PHX-MSP: 186, (Corridor 1B: 100, 94, 92, 90, 88, 86, 84, 82), 50, 46, 44, 42, 40, 38, 36, 34, 32, 30
PHX-MSY: 186, 184, 182, 180, 178, 308, 306, 304, 302, 300
PHX-NY: 186, (Corridor 1B: 100, 94 to beginning)
PHX-PDX: 60, 58, 288, 224, 252
PHX-PHL: 186, (Corridor 1B: 100, 94, 92, 90, 88, 86, 84, 82, 80, 78, 76, 74, 72, 70, 69)
PHX-PIT: 186, (Corridor 1B: 100, 94, 92, 90, 88, 86, 84, 82, 80, 78, 76, 74, 72)
PHX-SAN: 190, 192
PHX-SEA: 60, 58, 288, 224, 252, 250, 248, 246
PHX-SF: 60, 58, 266, 198, 64, 196; *or* 288, 64, 270, 206, 268, 202, 200, 198, 196
PHX-SLC: 186, 102, 58, 214, 216
PHX-STL: 186, (Corridor 1B: 100, 94, 92, 90, 88, 86, 84, 82, 80, 78)
PHX-TPA: 186, 184, 182, 180, 178, 308, 306, 304, 302, 300, 298

PIT Pittsburgh

PIT-ATL: 72, 236, 238, 140, 142
PIT-BOS: 14, 314, 156, 154
PIT-CLT: 234, 160, 118
PIT-DEN: (Corridor 1B: 72, 74, 76, 78, 80, 82, 84), 36, 44, 42
PIT-DFW: 72, 138, 140, 240, 242, 172
PIT-HO: 72, 138, 140, 170, 302
PIT-LA: (Corridor 1B: 72 to end)
PIT-LAS: (Corridor 1B: 72, 74, 76, 78, 80, 82, 84, 86, 88, 90, 92, 94, 96, 98, 100, 102, 58, 60)
PIT-MCI: 72, 74, 76, 30, 78, 80

PIT-MCO: 234, 160, 126, 130, 132, 134
PIT-MEM: 72, 138, 140
PIT-MI: 234, 160, 126, 130, 132, 134
PIT-MSP: 18, 276
PIT-NY: (Corridor 1A: 14, 12, 10, 8, 6); *or* 232, 6
PIT-PHX: (Corridor 1B: 72, 74, 76, 78, 80, 82, 84, 86, 88, 90, 92, 94, 96, 98, 100), 186
PIT-SF: (Corridor 1B: 72, 74, 76, 78, 80, 82, 84), 36, 42, 44, 46, (Corridor 7: 212 to end)
PIT-SLC: (Corridor 1B: 72, 74, 76, 78, 80, 82, 84), 36, 42, 44, 46, 288, 212, 214, 216
PIT-STL: 72, 74, 76, 30
PIT-TPA: 234, 160, 126, 128, 144
PIT-YYZ: 14, 16

SAN San Diego

SAN-ABQ: 192, 190, 186
SAN-ATL: (Corridor 5: 192 to beginning)
SAN-CH: 192, 190, 188, 186, 182, 288, 102, 100, 98, 96, 94, 92, 90, 88, 86, 84, 82, 80, 36, 30, 28, 26, 24
SAN-CVG: 192, 190, 188, 186, (Corridor 1B: 102, 100, 98, 96, 94, 92, 90, 88, 86, 84, 82, 80, 78, 76, 74, 72, 70)
SAN-DC: 192, 62, (Corridor 1B: 102, 100, 98, 96, 94, 92, 90, 88, 86, 84, 82, 80, 78, 76, 74, 72, 70), 234, 110
SAN-DEN: 192, 62, (Corridor 1B: 102, 100, 98, 96), 288, 36, 50, 48, 46, 44, 42
SAN-DFW: (Corridor 5: 192, 190, 188, 186, 184, 182, 180, 178, 176, 174, 172)
SAN-DTW: 192, (Corridor 1A: 62, 60, 58, 56, 54, 52, 50, 48, 46, 44, 42, 40, 38, 36, 34, 32, 30, 28, 26, 24, 22, 20)
SAN-HO: 192, 184, 180, 178, 64, 36, 308, 306, 304, 302
SAN-LAS: 192, 62, 60
SAN-MCI: 192, 62, (Corridor 1B: 102, 100, 98, 96, 94, 92, 90, 88, 86, 84, 82, 80)
SAN-MCO: 192, 184, 180, 178, 64, 36, 308, 306, 304, 302, 300, 298, 296, 144, 146

SAN-MI: 192, 184, 180, 178, 64, 36, 308, 306, 304, 302, 300, 298, 296, 146, 148, 150, 134
SAN-MSP: 192, 62, 60, 58, 56, 54, 52, 50, 48, 46, 44, 42, 40, 36, 64, 30
SAN-NY: 192, (Corridor 1A: 62, 60, 58, 56, 54, 52, 50, 48, 46, 44, 42, 40, 38, 36, 34, 32, 30, 28, 26, 24, 22, 20, 18, 16, 14, 12, 10, 8, 6); *or* 188, (Corridor 1B: 102, 100, 98, 96, 94, 92, 90, 88, 86, 84, 82, 80, 78, 76, 74, 72, 70, 69)
SAN-PDX: 66, 206, (Corridor 9: 270, 268, 266, 264, 262, 260, 258, 256, 254, 252)
SAN-PHL: 192, (Corridor 1A: 62, 60, 58, 56, 54, 52, 50, 48, 46, 44, 42, 40, 38, 36, 34, 32, 30, 28, 26, 24, 22, 20, 18, 16, 14, 12, 10, 8, 6); *or* 188, (Corridor 1B: 102, 100, 98, 96, 94, 92, 90, 88, 86, 84, 82, 80, 78, 76, 74, 72, 70, 69)
SAN-PHX: 190
SAN-SEA: 66, 206, (Corridor 9: 270 to beginning)
SAN-SF: 66, (Corridor 6: 206 to beginning)
SAN-SLC: 192, 62, 58, 288, 214, 216
SAN-STL: (Corridor 5: 192, 190, 188, 186, 184, 182), 94, 86, 84, 82, 80, 78
SAN-TPA: 192, 184, 180, 178, 64, 36, 308, 306, 304, 302, 300, 298, 296

SEA Seattle-Tacoma

SEA-ABQ: 246, 248, 290, 64, 216, 214, 52, 50, 96, 98, 182
SEA-ATL: 248, (Corridor 10: 292, 290, 288, 286, 284, 282, 280, 278), 36, 34, 32, 30, 28, 138, 140, 142
SEA-BOS: 248, (Corridor 10: 292, 290, 288, 286, 284, 282, 280, 278, 276, 274), 20, 16, 316, 314, 312, 154
SEA-CH: 248, (Corridor 10: 292, 290, 288, 286, 284, 282, 280, 278, 276, 24)
SEA-CLE: 248, (Corridor 10: 292, 290, 288, 286, 284, 282, 280, 278, 276, 274), 20
SEA-CVG: 248, (Corridor 10: 292, 290, 288, 286, 284, 282, 280, 278, 276, 24), 74
SEA-DC: 248, (Corridor 10: 292, 290, 288, 286, 284, 282, 280, 278, 276), 24, 22, 18, 72, 234, 110

SEA-DEN: 248, 292, 64, 252, 290, 288, 162, 42
SEA-DFW: 248, 292, 252, 216, 218, 48, 50, 46, 44, 42, 92, 90, 88, 86, 84, 176, 174, 172
SEA-DTW: 248, (Corridor 10: 292, 290, 288, 286, 284, 282, 280, 278, 276, 274), 20
SEA-HO: 248, 292, 252, 216, 218, 48, 50, 46, 44, 42, 92, 90, 88, 86, 84, 176, 174, 172, 304, 302
SEA-LA: (Corridor 9: 245 to end)
SEA-LAS: 248, 250, 288, 224
SEA-MCI: 248, (Corridor 10: 292, 290, 288, 286, 284, 282, 280), 40, 38, 36, 30, 80
SEA-MCO: 248, (Corridor 10: 292, 290, 288, 286, 284, 282, 280), 40, 38, 36, 30, 138, 140, 142, 128
SEA-MEM: 248, (Corridor 10: 292, 290, 288, 286, 284, 282, 280), 40, 38, 36, 30, 80, 78, 240
SEA-MSP: 248, (Corridor 10: 292, 290, 288, 286, 284, 282, 280, 278, 64)
SEA-NY: 248, (Corridor 10: 292 to beginning)
SEA-PDX: 246, 248, 250, 252
SEA-PHL: 248, (Corridor 10: 292, 290, 288, 286, 284, 282, 280, 278, 276, 274), 20, 18, 16, 14, 12, 232, 69
SEA-PHX: 248, 250, 288, 224, 60, 58, 186
SEA-SAN: (Corridor 9: 245 to end)
SEA-SF: (Corridor 9: 245, 246, 248, 250, 252, 254, 256, 258, 260, 264, 228, 64, 196)
SEA-SLC: 248, 290, 64, 288, 218, 216, 214
SEA-STL: 248, (Corridor 10: 292, 290, 288, 286, 284, 282, 280), 40, 38, 36, 34, 32, 30
SEA-YVR: 246, 292

SF San Francisco Bay Area (SFO, OAK, and SJC)

SF-ABQ: 196, 64, 198, 266, 220, 56, 54, 52, 50, 96, 98, 100
SF-ATL: 196, 64, 226, 220, 54, 52, 50, 92, 90, 88, 86, 84, 82, 36, 240, 140, 142
SF-BOS: 196, 64, (Corridor 7: 228, 226, 224, 222, 220, 218, 216, 214, 212, 210)
SF-CH: 196, 64, (Corridor 7: 228 to beginning)
SF-CLE: 196, 64, (Corridor 7: 228 to beginning) 22, 18
SF-CLT: 196, 64, (Corridor 7: 228, 226, 224, 222, 220, 218, 216, 214, 212), 46, 44, 42, 36, 240, 138, 140, 164
SF-CVG: 196, 64, (Corridor 7: 228, 226, 224, 222, 220, 218, 216, 214, 212, 210), 284, 40, 38, 36, 34, 32, 30, 28, 74
SF-DC: 196, 64, (Corridor 7: 228 to beginning), 22, 18
SF-DEN: 196, 64, (Corridor 7: 228, 226, 224, 222, 220, 218, 216, 214, 212, 210), 288, 42
SF-DFW: 196, 64, 226, 220, 54, 50, 98, 96, 94, 174, 172; *or* 196, 202, 268, 64, 62, 60, 102, 100, 182, 174, 172
SF-DTW: 196, 64, (Corridor 7: 228 to beginning), 22
SF-HO: 196, 64, 226, 220, 54, 50, 98, 96, 94, 174, 172, 304, 302; *or* 196, 202, 268, 64, 62, 60, 188, 186, 184, 182, 180, 178, 308, 306, 304, 302
SF-LA: (Corridor 6: 195 to end)
SF-LAS: 196, 198, 202, 266
SF-MCI: 196, 64, (Corridor 7: 228, 226, 224, 222, 220, 218, 216, 214, 212), 46, 44, 42, 84, 36, 80
SF-MCO: 196, 64, 226, 220, 54, 50, 98, 96, 94, 92, 90, 88, 86, 84, 82, 174, 172, 242, 240, 170, 300, 298, 296, 144
SF-MEM: 196, 64, 226, 220, 54, 50, 98, 96, 94, 92, 90, 88, 86, 84, 82, 240
SF-MI: 196, 64, 226, 220, 54, 50, 98, 96, 94, 92, 90, 88, 86, 84, 82, 174, 172, 242, 240, 170, 300, 298, 296, 144, 146, 148, 150, 134
SF-MSP: 196, 228, 224, 222, 288, 162, 36, 284, 282, 280, 278, 64
SF-NY: 196, 64, (Corridor 7: 228, 226, 224, 222, 220, 218, 216, 214, 212, 210), 284, (Corridor 1A: 46, 44, 42, 40, 38, 36, 34, 32, 30, 28, 26, 24, 22, 20, 18, 16, 14, 12, 10, 8, 6)
SF-PDX: 196, 64, (Corridor 9: 264, 262, 260, 258, 256, 254, 252)
SF-PHL: 196, 64, (Corridor 7: 228, 226, 224, 222, 220, 218, 216, 214, 212, 210), 284, (Corridor 1A: 46, 44, 42, 40, 38, 36, 34, 32, 30, 28, 26, 24, 22, 20, 18, 16, 14), 69
SF-PHX: 196, 64, 226, 266; *or* 196, 198, 202, 268, 270, 62, 188, 186
SF-PIT: 196, 64, (Corridor 7: 228, 226, 224, 222, 220, 218, 216, 214, 212, 210), 284, (Corridor 1A: 46, 44, 42, 40, 38, 36, 34, 32, 30, 28, 26, 24, 22, 18)
SF-SAN: (Corridor 6: 195 to end)

SF-SEA: 196, 64, (Corridor 9: 264 to beginning)
SF-SLC: 196, 64, (Corridor 7: 228, 226, 224, 222, 220, 218, 216, 214)
SF-STL: 196, 64, (Corridor 7: 228, 226, 224, 222, 220, 218, 216, 214, 212), 46, 44, 42, 84, 36, 80, 78
SF-TPA: 196, 64, 226, 220, 54, 50, 98, 96, 94, 92, 90, 88, 86, 84, 82, 174, 172, 242, 240, 170, 300, 298, 296, 144
SF-YUL: 196, 64, (Corridor 7: 228 to beginning), 274, 20
SF-YVR: 196, 64, (Corridor 9: 264 to beginning)
SF-YYZ: 196, 64, (Corridor 7: 228 to beginning), 274, 20

SFO, *see* SF (San Francisco Bay Area)
SJC, *see* SF (San Francisco Bay Area)

SLC Salt Lake City

SLC-ABQ: 214, 212, 52, 50, 96, 98, 182
SLC-ATL: 214, 212, 46, 44, 42, 36, 138, 140, 142
SLC-BOS: 216, 214, 212, 210, (Corridor 1A: 42, 40, 38, 36, 34, 32, 30, 28, 26, 24, 22, 20, 18, 16)
SLC-CH: 216, 214, 212, 210, (Corridor 1A: 42, 40, 38, 36, 34, 32, 30, 28, 26, 24)
SLC-CLE: 216, 214, 212, 210, (Corridor 1A: 42, 40, 38, 36, 34, 32, 30, 28, 26, 24, 22, 20, 18)
SLC-CLT: 214, 212, 46, 44, 42, 36, 138, 140, 164
SLC-CVG: 214, 212, (Corridor 1A: 46, 44, 42, 40, 38, 36), 80, 78, 28, 74
SLC-DC: 216, 214, 212, 210, (Corridor 1A: 42, 40, 38, 36, 34, 32, 30, 28), 74, 72, 234, 110
SLC-DEN: 214, 212, 288, 162, 46, 44, 42
SLC-DFW: 214, 216, 218, 48, 50, 46, 44, 42, 92, 90, 88, 86, 84, 176, 174, 172
SLC-DTW: 216, 214, 212, 210, (Corridor 1A: 42, 40, 38, 36, 34, 32, 30, 28, 26, 24, 22)
SLC-HO: 214, 216, 218, 48, 50, 46, 44, 42, 92, 90, 88, 86, 84, 176, 174, 172, 304, 302
SLC-LA: 214, 220, 60, 62, 64, 66
SLC-LAS: 214, 220
SLC-MCI: 214, 212, (Corridor 1A: 46, 44, 42, 40, 38, 36), 80

SLC-MCO: 214, 216, 50, 48, 288, 92, 90, 88, 86, 84, 36, 176, 174, 172, 300, 298, 296, 144, 146
SLC-MI: 214, 216, 50, 48, 288, 92, 90, 88, 86, 84, 36, 176, 174, 172, 300, 298, 146, 148, 150, 134
SLC-MSP: 216, 214, 212, 210, 36, 284, 282, 280, 278, 64, 30
SLC-MSY: 214, 216, 218, 48, 50, 46, 44, 42, 92, 90, 88, 86, 84, 176, 174, 172, 300
SLC-NY: 216, 214, 212, 210, (Corridor 1A: 42 to beginning)
SLC-PDX: 214, 216, 288, 252
SLC-PHL: 214, 212, (Corridor 1A: 46, 44, 42, 40, 38, 36, 34, 32, 30, 28, 22), 80, 78, 28, 74, 72, 70, 69
SLC-PHX: 214, 216, 58, 102, 186
SLC-PIT: 216, 214, 212, 210, (Corridor 1A: 42, 40, 38, 36, 34, 32, 30, 28, 26, 24, 22, 20, 18)
SLC-SAN: 214, 220, 60, 62, 192
SLC-SEA: 214, 216, 288, 252, 64, 290, 248, 246
SLC-SF: (Corridor 7: 214 to end)
SLC-STL: 214, 212, (Corridor 1A: 46, 44, 42, 40, 38, 36), 80, 78

SNA, *see* LA (Los Angeles metropolitan area)

STL St. Louis

STL-ATL: 138, 140, 142
STL-BOS: 30, (Corridor 1B: 74 to beginning), 156, 154
STL-CLT: 138, 140, 164
STL-DC: 30, 236, 234, 110
STL-DEN: 78, 80, 82, 84, 36, 44, 42
STL-HO: 242, 302
STL-LA: (Corridor 1B: 78 to end)
STL-LAS: (Corridor 1B: 78, 80, 82, 84, 86, 88, 90, 92, 94, 96, 98, 100, 102), 58, 60
STL-MCI: 78, 80
STL-MCO: 138, 140, 142, 128, 132
STL-MI: 138, 140, 144, 146, 148, 150, 134
STL-MSP: 28, 30, 32
STL-MSY: 240, 170, 300
STL-NY: 30, (Corridor 1B: 74 to beginning)

YVR-HO: 292, 252, 216, 218, 48, 50, 46, 44, 42, 92, 90, 88, 86, 84, 176, 174, 172, 304, 302
YVR-LA: 328, (Corridor 9: 245 to end)
YVR-LAS: 292, 246, 248, 64, 288, 262, 224
YVR-NY: (Corridor 10: 292 to beginning)
YVR-PDX: 292, 246, 248, 250, 252
YVR-SEA: 292, 246, 248
YVR-SF: 328, (Corridor 9: 245, 246, 248, 250, 252, 254, 256, 258, 260, 264, 228, 196)

YYC Calgary

YYC-CH: 284, 282, 280, 278, 36, 64, 278, 24
YYC-DEN: 282, 284, 288, 42
YYC-DFW: 284, 282, 42, 84, 82, 176, 174, 172
YYC-HO: 284, 282, 42, 84, 82, 176, 174, 172, 304, 302
YYC-LA: 284, 286, 288, 224, 266, 268, 270, 64, 66
YYC-LAS: 284, 286, 288, 214, 216, 218, 220, 222
YYC-SF: 284, 288, 290, 64, 258, 260, 262, 264, 196

YYZ Toronto

YYZ-ATL: 72, 236, 238, 234, 164, 142
YYZ-CH: 20, 24
YYZ-DC: 16, 70, 110
YYZ-DEN: (Corridor 1A: 20, 24, 26, 28, 30, 32, 34, 36, 38, 40, 42, 44)
YYZ-DFW: 18, 30, 172
YYZ-HO: 138, 240, 302
YYZ-MI: 72, 236, 234, 118, 126, 128, 130, 132, 134
YYZ-NY: 316

List of Articles

Corridor 12:
Boston—Chicago

Corridor 13:
Anchorage—Seattle

Bibliography

Alvarez, Walter, et al. "Synsedimentary Deformation in the Jurassic of Southeastern Utah—A Case of Impact Shaking?" *Geology* 26 (1998): 579–82.

Anderson, Wayne I. *Iowa's Geological Past: Three Billion Years of Earth History.* Iowa City: University of Iowa Press, 1998.

Arax, Mark, and Rick Wartzmann. *The King of California: J. G. Boswell and the Making of a Secret American Empire.* New York: Public Affairs, 2003. J. G. Boswell is quoted on the future of cotton farming in California on page 429.

Baars, Donald L. *A Traveler's Guide to the Geology of the Colorado Plateau.* Salt Lake City: University of Utah Press, 2002.

Bally, Albert W., and Allison R. Palmer, eds. *The Geology of North America: An Overview.* Boulder, CO: Geological Society of America, 1989.

Bates, Robert L. *Geology of the Industrial Rocks and Minerals.* New York: Dover Publishing, 1969.

Belsky, Ted. "The Role of the South Hadley Canal in Western New England's Development." www.bio.umass.edu/biology/conn.river/canal.html (accessed Feb. 3, 2005).

Beus, Stanley S., ed. *Centennial Field Guide. Vol. 2, Rocky Mountain Section of the Geological Society of America.* Boulder, CO: Geological Society of America, 1987.

Biggs, Donald L., ed. *Centennial Field Guide. Vol. 3, North-Central Section of the Geological Society of America.* Boulder, CO: Geological Society of America, 1987.

Brechin, Gray. *Imperial San Francisco: Urban Power, Earthly Ruin.* Berkeley: University of California Press, 1999.

Briner, Jason P. "Supporting Evidence from the New York Drumlin Field that Elongate Subglacial Bedforms Indicate Fast Ice Flow." *Boreas* 36 (2007): 143–47.

British Columbia Department of Mines and Petroleum Resources. *Geology of the Queen Charlotte Islands, British Columbia*, by A. Sutherland Brown. Bulletin 54. 1968.

Collom, Roy E., and Roy M. Barnes. "California Oil Production and Reserves." *AAPG Bulletin* 8 (1924): 212–40.

Colpron, Maurice, JoAnne L. Nelson, and Donald C. Murphy. "Northern Cordilleran Terranes and Their Interactions Through Time." *GSA Today* 17 (2007): 4–10.

Conzen, Michael P., ed. *The Making of the American Landscape.* New York: Routledge, 1994.

Easterbrook, Don J., ed. *Quaternary Geology of the United States.* INQUA 2003 Field Guide Volume. Reno, NV: Desert Research Institute, 2003.

Firestone, R. B., et al. "Evidence for a Massive Extraterrestrial Airburst over North America 12.9 ka Ago." *Eos Trans. AGU* 88, Jt. Assem. Suppl., Abstract PP41A-01.

Fogelson, Robert M. *The Fragmented Metropolis: Los Angeles 1850–1930.* Cambridge, MA: Harvard University Press, 1967.

Gabrielse, H., and C. J. Yorath, eds. *Geology of the Cordilleran Orogen in Canada.* Geology of Canada Series, no. 2. Ottawa: Geological Survey of Canada, 1991.

Galloway, William E., et al. "Cenozoic Depositional History of the Gulf of Mexico Basin." *AAPG Bulletin* 84 (2000): 1743–74.

Gilchrist, Ellen. "Delta of Three Rivers." *Millsaps Magazine*, Fall–Winter 2000. www.millsaps.edu/pubrel/magazine/fallwinter00/story3.html (accessed June 29, 2007).

Goddard, Stephen B. *Getting There: The Epic Struggle Between Road and Rail in the American Century.* New York: Basic Books, 1994.

Gradstein, Felix M., et al. "A New Geologic Time Scale, with Special Reference to Precambrian and Neogene." *Episodes* 27 (2004): 83–100.

Gresh, Ted, Jim Lichatowich, and Peter Schoonmaker. "An Estimation of Historic and Current Levels of Salmon Production in the Northeast Pacific Ecosystem." *Fisheries* 25 (1999): 15–21.

Harden, Deborah R. *California Geology*, 2nd ed. Upper Saddle River, NJ: Pearson/Prentice Hall, 2004.

Harding, T. P. "Tectonic Significance and Hydrocarbon Trapping Consequences of Sequential Folding Synchronous with San Andreas Faulting, San Joaquin Valley, California." *AAPG Bulletin* 60 (1976): 356–78.

Hatcher, Robert D., Jr., and Arthur J. Merschat, eds. *Blue Ridge Geology Geotraverse East of the Great Smoky Mountains National Park, Western North Carolina.* Carolina Geological Society Annual Field Trip Guidebook 2005. Durham, NC: Carolina Geological Society, 2005.

Hatcher, Robert D., Jr., William A. Thomas, and George W. Viele, eds. *The Appalachian-Ouachita Orogen in the United States.* Boulder, CO: Geological Society of America, 1989.

Hayward, O. T., ed. *Centennial Field Guide. Vol. 4, South-Central Section of the Geological Society of America.* Boulder, CO: Geological Society of America, 1988.

Hill, Mason L., ed. *Centennial Field Guide. Vol. 1, Cordilleran Section of the Geological Society of America.* Boulder, CO: Geological Society of America, 1987.

Hinshaw, John. *Steel and Steelworkers: Race and Class Struggle in Twentieth-Century Pittsburgh.* Albany: State University of New York Press, 2002.

Holmes, Richard Walker, and Marrianna B. Kennedy. *Mines and Minerals of the Great American Rift, Colorado–New Mexico.* New York: Van Nostrand Reinhold, 1983.

Howard, G. A., et al. "Evidence for an Extraterrestrial Impact Origin of the Carolina Bays on the Atlantic Coast of North America." *Eos Trans. AGU* 88, Jt. Assem. Suppl., Abstract PP42A-05.

Hudson, John C. *Across This Land: A Regional Geography of the United States and Canada.* Baltimore, MD: Johns Hopkins University Press, 2002.

Indianapolis Star. "History of the Indianapolis 500." Updated 5/29/2006. www2.indystar.com/library/factfiles/sports/autoracing/indy500.html (accessed May 9, 2007).

Ingersoll, Raymond V., and Peter E. Rumelhart. "Three-stage Evolution of the Los Angeles Basin, Southern California." *Geology* 27 (1999): 593–96.

Jackson, M.P.A., et al. "Structure and Evolution of Upheaval Dome: A Pinched-off Salt Diapir." *GSA Bulletin* 110 (1998): 1547–73.

Kanbur, Z., et al. "Seismic Reflection Study of Upheaval Dome, Canyonlands National Park, Utah." *Journal of Geophysical Research* 105 (2000): 9489–505.

Keck, E. B. "The Connecticut River Valley." The City Rocks! http://homepage.mac.com/ebandpck/cityrocks/connecticut.html (accessed Feb. 3, 2005).

Kennedy, Roger G. *Wildfire and Americans: How to Save Lives, Property, and Your Tax Dollars.* New York: Hill and Wang, 2006.

Lacey, Robert. *Ford: The Men and the Machine.* Boston: Little, Brown, 1986.

Larson, Lee W. "The Great USA Flood of 1993." NOAA/National Weather Service, www.nwrfc.noaa.gov/floods/papers/oh_2/great.htm.

Leonard, Eric M., et al. "High Plains to Rio Grande Rift: Late Cenozoic Evolution of Central Colorado." In *Science at the Highest Level,* 59–93. Geological Society of America Field Guide 3. Boulder, CO: Geological Society of America, 2002. www.gsajournals.org/perlserv/?request=get-fieldguide-toc&isbn=0-8137-0003-5 (accessed May 8, 2007).

Leonard, L., T. Clayton, and O. Pilkey. "An Analysis of Replenished Beach Design Parameters on U.S. East Coast Barrier Islands." *Journal of Coastal Research* 6 (1990): 15–36.

Lester, Peter F. *Aviation Weather.* Englewood, CO: Jeppesen Sanderson, 1997.

Leung, L. Ruby, and W. I. Gustafson Jr. "Potential Regional Climate Change and Implications to U.S. Air Quality." *Geophysical Research Letters* 32 (2005): L16711, doi:10.1029/2005GL022911.

Mangan, Jennifer M., et al. "Response of Nebraska Sand Hills Natural Vegetation to Drought, Fire, Grazing, and Plant Functional Type Change as Simulated by the Century Model." *Climatic Change* 63 (2004): 49–90.

Marchetti, D. W., J. C. Dohrenwend, and T. E. Cerling. "Geomorphology and Rates of Landscape Change in the Fremont River Drainage, Northwestern Colorado Plateau." In *Interior Western United States,* edited by Joel L. Pederson and Carol M. Dehler, 79–100. Geological Society of America Field Guide 6. Boulder, CO: Geological Society of America, 2005.

Martin, Glen. "A Tall Order: The Art and Science of Wetland Restoration." *Bay Nature*, Oct.–Dec. 2004. www.southbay restoration.org/pdf_files/BayNature%20Oct%202004.pdf.

McPhee, John. *The Control of Nature.* New York: Noonday Press, 1990.

Mitchell, Sara Gran, and David R. Montgomery. "Influence of a Glacial Buzzsaw on the Height and Morphology of the Cascade Range, in Central Washington State, USA." *Quaternary Research* 65 (2006): 96–107.

Morris, Peter S. "Whooping It Up in Chinook Country: Regional Ideas and the Montana-Alberta Borderlands." http://home page.smc.edu/morris_pete/papers/assets/apcg1998.pdf (accessed May 9, 2007).

Murphy, Carolyn Hanna. *Carolina Rocks!: The Geology of South Carolina.* Orangeburg, SC: Sandlapper Publishing Co., 1995.

National Oceanic and Atmospheric Administration. "Geologic Regimes of the Atlantic and Gulf Coasts." www3.csc.noaa.gov/ beachnourishment/html/geo/geo.htm (accessed Jan. 13, 2005).

———. "Historical Expenditures for Beach Nourishment Projects." www3.csc.noaa.gov/beachnourishment/html/human/ socio/geodist.htm (accessed Jan. 13, 2005).

Neathery, Thornton L., ed. *Centennial Field Guide. Vol. 6, Southeastern Section of the Geological Society of America.* Boulder, CO: Geological Society of America, 1986.

Opie, John. *Ogallala: Water for a Dry Land.* Lincoln: University of Nebraska Press, 2000.

Pazzaglia, F. J., and J. W. Hawley. "Neogene (Rift Flank) and Quaternary Geology and Geomorphology." In *The Geology of New Mexico,* special publication 11, edited by G. H. Mack and K. A. Giles. Socorro, NM: New Mexico Geological Society, 2004.

Pierce, F. W., and J. G. Bolm, eds. *Porphyry Copper Deposits of the American Cordillera.* Arizona Geological Society Digest 20. Tucson: Arizona Geological Society, 1995.

Plafker, George, and Henry C. Berg, eds. *The Geology of Alaska.* Boulder, CO: Geological Society of America, 1994.

Poag, C. W. "Synimpact-postimpact Transition Inside Chesapeake Bay Crater." *Geology* 30 (2002): 995–98.

Pollan, Michael. *The Omnivore's Dilemma: A Natural History of Four Meals.* New York: Penguin, 2006.

Portlandct.org. "The Connecticut River, Our Living Heritage." www.portlandct.org/Portland/history/river.htm (accessed Feb. 3, 2005).

Reiners, Peter W., et al. "Coupled Spatial Variations in Precipitation and Long-Term Erosion Rates Across the Washington Cascades." *Nature* 426 (2003): 645–47.

Reisner, Marc. *Cadillac Desert: The American West and Its Disappearing Water.* Rev. ed. New York: Penguin, 1993.

Rhoads, Ann Fowler, and Timothy A. Block. *Trees of Pennsylvania: A Complete Reference Guide.* Philadelphia: University of Pennsylvania Press, 2005.

Rich, F. J., and G. A. Bishop. *Geology and Natural History of the Okefenokee Swamp and Trail Ridge, Southeastern Georgia and Northern Florida.* Georgia Geological Society Guidebooks, vol. 18. 1998.

Roy, David C., ed. *Centennial Field Guide. Vol. 5, Northeastern Section of the Geological Society of America.* Boulder, CO: Geological Society of America, 1987.

Schneiders, Robert Kelley. *Unruly River: Two Centuries of Change Along the Missouri.* Lawrence: University Press of Kansas, 1999.

Sheridan, Robert E., and John A. Grow, eds. *The Atlantic Continental Margin: U.S.* Boulder, CO: Geological Society of America, 1988.

Short, Nicholas M., and Robert W. Blair, eds. *Geomorphology from Space: A Global Overview of Regional Landforms.* Washington, D.C.: Science and Technical Branch, NASA, 1986.

Sloss, L. L., ed. *Sedimentary Cover, North American Craton, U.S.* Boulder, CO: Geological Society of America, 1988.

Smith, W. Everett. *Geomorphology of the Mobile Delta.* Geological Survey of Alabama Bulletin 132 (1988).

Steltenpohl, Mark G., et al. *Geology of the Southern Inner Piedmont, Alabama and Southwest Georgia.* Guidebook for field trip 7, 39th Annual Meeting, Southeastern Section, Geological Society of America. Tuscaloosa: Geological Survey of Alabama, 1990.

Stoffer, P., and P. Messina. Geology and Geography of New York Bight. www.geo.hunter.cuny.edu/bight/highland.html (accessed Jan. 13, 2005).

Texas State Historical Association. *The Handbook of Texas Online.* www.tsha.utexas.edu/index.html (accessed May 1, 2007).

Thieler, E. Robert. "Shoreface Processes in Onslow Bay." In Carolina Geological Society 1996 Annual Meeting, edited by W. J. Cleary. Cape Lookout, NC: Carolina Geological Society, 1996.

Thom, Bruce G. "Carolina Bays in Horry and Marion Counties, South Carolina." *GSA Bulletin* 81 (1970): 783–813.

Thomas, William A. "Tectonic Inheritance at a Continental Margin." *GSA Today* 16 (2005): 4–11.

Thornbury, William D. *Regional Geomorphology of the United States.* New York: John Wiley, 1965.

Turner, Paul Venable. *Campus: An American Planning Tradition.* Cambridge, MA: MIT Press, 1984.

U.S. Department of Energy. "About Fermilab." www.fnal.gov/pub/about/index.html (accessed May 8, 2007).

U.S. Department of the Interior. *Deformation of Host Rocks and Flow of Magma During Growth of Minette Dikes and Breccia-bearing Intrusions Near Ship Rock, New Mexico,* by Paul T. Delaney and David D. Pollard. U.S. Geological Survey professional paper 1202. 1981.

———. *A Geologic Guide to Wrangell-Saint Elias National Park and Preserve, Alaska: A Tectonic Collage of Northbound Terranes,* by Gary R. Winkler. U.S. Geological Survey professional paper 1616. 2000.

———. *The Geologic Story of Gunnison Gorge National Conservation Area, Colorado,* by Karl S. Kellogg. U.S. Geological Survey professional paper 1699. 2004.

———. *U.S. Geological Survey Karst Interest Group Proceedings, Rapid City, South Dakota, September 12–15, 2005,* edited by Eve L. Kuniansky. U.S. Geological Survey scientific investigations report 2005-5160. 2005.

———. *Volcano Hazards from Mount Rainier, Washington,* by R. P. Hoblitt et al. U.S. Geological Survey open-file report 98-428. 1998.

U.S. Department of the Interior in cooperation with the U.S. Fish and Wildlife Service. *Science to Support Adaptive Habitat Management: Overton Bottoms North Unit, Big Muddy National Fish and Wildlife Refuge, Missouri,* edited by Robert B. Jacobson. U.S. Geological Survey scientific investigations report 2006-5086. 2006.

Utah Division of Water Resources. *Utah State Water Plan: West Desert Basin.* Salt Lake City: Utah Board of Water Resources, 2001.

Van Arsdale, Roy B., et al. "Origin of Crowley's Ridge, Northeastern Arkansas: Erosional Remnant or Tectonic Uplift?" *Bulletin of the Seismological Society of America* 85 (1995): 963–85.

Von Bandat, Horst F. *Aerogeology.* Houston, TX: Gulf Publishing Co., 1962.

Wakabayashi, John, and Thomas L. Sawyer. "Stream Incision, Tectonics, Uplift, and Evolution of Topography of the Sierra Nevada, California." *Journal of Geology* 109 (2001): 539–62.

Walker, I. J., and J. V. Barrie. "Geomorphology and Sea-Level Rise on One of Canada's Most 'Sensitive' Coasts: Northeast Graham Island, British Columbia." *Journal of Coastal Research* special issue 39 (2004).

Wesnousky, Steven G. "Active Faulting in the Walker Lane." *Tectonics* 24 (2005): doi:10.1029/2004TC001645.

Wetmaap. "Cape Hatteras, North Carolina." www.wetmaap.org/Cape_Hatteras/Supplement/ch_backgroundessay.html#Cape%20Hatteras%20and%20Cape%20Lookout%20Outer%20Banks (accessed Jan. 13, 2005).

Williams, R. S. "Glaciers and Glacial Landforms." In Short and Blair, *Geomorphology from Space.*

Worley, William S. *J. C. Nichols and the Shaping of Kansas City: Innovation in Planned Residential Communities.* Columbia: University of Missouri Press, 1990.

Wyatt, D. E., and M. K. Harris, eds. *Savannah River Site Environmental Remediation Systems in Unconsolidated Upper Coastal Plain Sediments—Stratigraphic and Structural Considerations.* Carolina Geological Society 2000 Field Trip Guidebook. Durham, NC: Carolina Geological Society, 2000.

Illustration Credits

Robert L. Anderson, U.S. Department of Agriculture, Forest Service, www.bugwood.org: 164 (inset)

Appalachian Voices, www.ilovemountains.org: 236 (map)

John Brew: 262, 292 (main)

Paul Corbit Brown: 236 (photo)

California Spatial Information Library, a NAIP partner: 62, 226, 228, 266

Ed Carr: 142

Climax Molybdenum Co., Phelps Dodge Corp.: 47 (inset)

Florida Department of Environmental Protection, a NAIP partner, http://data.labins.org/2003/: 131, 133, 134, 144, 147, 151

William F. Holmes: 42, 44, 98, 99, 189

Indiana Spatial Data Service, a NAIP partner, www.indiana.edu/~gisdata/naip.html: 22, 74

Iowa State University GIS and Massachusetts Institute of Technology, NAIP partners, http://cairo.gis.iastate.edu/: 30, 32 (left), 34

James S. Jackson: 12, 48, 58, 60, 84, 157, 178, 184, 215, 216 (right), 218, 223, 225, 232, 246, 270, 298 (inset), 308, 320, 322, 331 (center), 338, 341

Kansas Data Access and Support Center, a NAIP partner: 82

Kentucky Division of Geographic Information, a NAIP partner: 138, 238

Louis J. Maher: 139, 274, 280 (inset)

Massachusetts Water Resources Authority/Kerwin: 154

Daniel Mathews: 2, 26, 28 (left), 50, 51, 54, 69, 86, 87, 88, 90, 92, 175, 196, 198, 202, 205, 206 (left), 212 (inset), 221, 240, 254, 256, 258, 259, 264, 268, 331 (left and right), 332, 335, 336

Mississippi Automated Resource Information System, a NAIP partner, www.maris.state.ms.us/home.htm: 170

Missouri Spatial Data Information Service, a NAIP partner, www.msdis.missouri.edu/index.htm: 28 (right), 78

Montana Natural Resource Information System, a NAIP partner, http://nris.mt.gov/default.asp: 284, 286

National Aeronautics and Space Administration, Johnson Space Center, Image Science & Analysis Laboratory, http://eol.jsc.nasa.gov: 6, 25, 47 (main), 52, 66, 68, 80, 94, 100, 102, 107, 111, 113, 114, 117, 119, 120 (main), 120 (inset) 124, 148, 159, 161, 164 (main), 169, 172, 176, 179, 181, 182, 186, 190, 192, 200, 210, 212 (main), 216 (left), 260, 278, 288, 290, 296, 298 (main), 302, 306, 316, 324, 326, 328

Nebraska Department of Natural Resources, a NAIP partner: 36, 38

New Hampshire GRANIT, a NAIP partner, www.granit.sr.unh.edu: 312

New York State GIS Clearinghouse, a NAIP partner (with permission of the NYS Office of CSCIC): 17, 314

North Dakota GIS, a NAIP partner, www.nd.gov/gis/: 282

Matthew Ottosen: 248

Frank M. Riley, Jr., Georgia Forestry Commission, www.bugwood.org: 162 (left)

John Scurlock: 292 (inset)

Storm Bear: 56

Tennessee Valley Authority: 140

Charles Tilford: 334

U.S. Army Corps of Engineers: 311

U.S. Department of Agriculture, Farm Services Administration, Aerial Photography Field Office, National Agriculture Imagery Program (NAIP): 10, 15, 19, 20, 32 (right), 40, 66 (both), 76, 108, 122, 127, 128, 243, 252, 280 (main), 301, 304

U.S. Department of Agriculture, Forest Service, Ogden Archives, www.bugwood.org: 162 (right)

U.S. Department of the Interior, National Park Service: 8, 96

U.S. Department of the Interior, U.S. Geological Survey: 207 (right)

U.S. Department of the Interior, U.S. Geological Survey, Cascades Volcano Observatory, John Pallister: cover photo, 250, 251

U.S. Department of the Interior, U.S. Geological Survey, National Atlas of the United States, adapted by James S. Jackson and Daniel Mathews: maps prior to page 1 and on 68, 104, 136, 152, 166, 194, 208, 230, 244, 272, 294, 310, 318, 330

U.S. Department of the Interior, U.S. Geological Survey, National Atlas of the United States, W.E. Davies et al.: 137

University of Wisconsin Environmental Remote Sensing Center, a NAIP partner: 275

West Virginia GIS Technical Center, a NAIP partner, http://wvgis.wvu.edu/index.php: 72, 234

Index

**Password to access CD-ROM:
AftA07**

**For Customer Service, e-mail:
trade_webmaster@hmco.com**